A Call of Urgency
Messages to the World

1997 – 2006

"My Dear Children,

Prepare your hearts for a great time of change soon comes. I urge you to read my messages and discern that which has been revealed to you. Your time for decision seeps swiftly through the hour glass of life's unending challenges." Message 12-01-97

Our Lady of the Sierras Shrine

Published by Our Lady of the Sierras Foundation.
P.O. Box 269
Hereford, AZ 85615

Email - [www.ourladysierras@theriver.com]

Web site [www.ourladyofthesierras.org]

Or search on the web. "Our lady of the Sierras".

Original publication 1997 – 2004, Our Lady of the Sierras

"A CALL OF URGENCY"

ISBN 1-893757-46-3

Second printing and revision May 2005

Third printing and revision March 2007

Spanish Edition published July 2007

Printed in the United States of America

Cover design by Lou Morales - Arizona Sunrise Over Shrine.

Dedication

We dedicate this book to Our Lord and His Mother in response to all that has been given to our small community of Our Lady of the Sierras here in Southeast Arizona.

These messages are simply repeated "as is" from previously published archives with the hope our Christian community also feels the depth of love interlaced with responsibility in their contents.

.. ..

Notes, History, Commentary and General Editing by

The Founders

of Our Lady of the Sierras Foundation

Declaration

We reference the abolition of Canon 1399 and 2318 of the former Canonical Code by Pope Paul VI ASS 58 (1966) 1186. Publications about appearances, revelations, prophecies, miracles, locutions, etc. have been allowed to be distributed and read by the faithful without expressed permission by the Church, providing they contain nothing contrary to faith and morals. The author and publisher recognize and accept the final authority regarding private revelation rests with our Roman Catholic Church.

CONTENTS

Pat's Personal Notes

The following text is given from Pat's personal notes relating to Private Revelations, perceived coming from Our Lord Jesus and His Blessed Mother from 6-01-97 to the present time

"It is most difficult when one feels so inadequately prepared and spiritually immature to put into words the intense beauty and wisdom Our Lord and His Blessed Mother have shared with us during this, our spiritual journey, our personal road to Emmaus. Perhaps if you are like me, you ask yourself again and again. "Lord are you certain you have the right person?" It is a real attention getter when you clearly hear; "Yes, the choice has been made." Well then, that leaves us aside from perspiring profusely and with a huge lump in our throat barely getting out what we hope resembles "Thy will be done."

Praise God! Nothing remains the same once we truly commit ourselves to the Will of the Father. We slowly begin to learn through peace, prayer, penance, fasting, reconciliation, sacrifice and most importantly love, that the true beauty of life has remained hidden behind the doors of our own selfish pride, envy and jealousy. Those worldly entrapments which have slowed our even most meager attempt of conversion. As our dear Mother often reminds us, we seek the security of having one foot firmly planted in a spiritual life and unfortunately the other foot undecided. Perhaps this could be compared to sports enthusiasts who hurl themselves down steep mountains or crevices knowing their "life line" is securely attached in case they should lose their footing. Fortunately for us, my brothers and sisters in Christ, He is our life line. We need hold on to no one but Him. It's time to jump with both feet. It's called commitment time. It's a leap of faith securely bound with trust in the mercy of Jesus.

When I was asked to go through the various messages and select a few special ones we have received through the years, I experienced a rather peculiar sensation that God had something more to say about this. In the spring of 2004 this became clear.

As the first messages began to come in early June of 1997, they were quite simple in nature. Nothing to overpower us or cause undue concern with what we were being told. They were very simple and in a way, childlike. That was about all I could handle at the time. I needed simple words because I am simple a simple child of God . I require a great deal of prayer and discernment and an abundance of Spiritual Direction to help me remain truly focused on what is God's Will for my life. We have been blessed with many beautiful priests who have patiently listened and observed what is taking place here at Our Lady of the Sierras. Their discernment has proved most beneficial at this point.

The messages we have been receiving within the later years have taken on a little different direction in that on many occasions we are allowed to accompany our Blessed Mother and sometimes our Lord, in what we appear to "visually" see what they are expressing in words. Perhaps it would be appropriate to say we are being told a story which materializes to such a point that we find ourselves <u>actually smelling the flowers, hearing the birds (which can be heard on audio tape) and feeling the grass beneath our feet as we walk along with them listening and learning as they teach us how to live a more Christ like life.</u> There is such a peace which envelops each of us as we are allowed to come into their presence.

"A Call of Urgency" certainly awakens us to prepare for what we believe scripture reveals to each of us. The real awakening however has been that daily call to preparation to have our souls ready to meet Our Lord at any given moment. Are we setting Christ-like examples in our daily lives? Have we discovered that hidden grace that allows each of us to see our Lord in the smallest, the weakest, the lost and forgotten souls of this world? That, my dear friends is the real "Call of Urgency". It is the call of love. Perhaps, with the guidance of the Holy Spirit, you will be able to experience the indescribable joy we have experienced in this our personal journey to the Cross."

Pat

History - Our Lady of the Sierras Shrine

The seeds of the building of the Shrine of Our Lady of the Sierras may trace back to the forming of the Huachuca Mountains that were formed eons ago by our Creator in Southeast Arizona. In early times when the Native Americans occupied the area, legend confirms the mountains already had spiritual meaning to them.

In the early 1600's the shrine area was first explored by the Spanish and later became part of Mexico. Upon the signing of the Gadsen Purchase in 1853 the area became a territory of the United States. By the 1870's well before Arizona became a state the area became known for mining, lumbering and raising cattle. The Indian chief Cochise and Geronimo were some of the last holdouts in what is now Cochise County Arizona. Nearby Fort Huachuca was opened in 1877 to deal with the Indian problem and was the early home of the Buffalo Soldiers. This fort is now the "Intel Center" of the US military and is located 12 miles North of the shrine next to the city of Sierra Vista, Arizona. To the East are the old west towns of Bisbee and Tombstone.

Although the state and federal governments own the majority of land in Arizona some land became available for private use due to land grants, mining claims under "patent laws" and purchases through normal channels. In 1987 a couple from northern Illinois [Gerald and Patricia Chouinard] came down to the area to visit a family member and while hiking stumbled across a "for sale" sign in the weeds indicating a parcel of land was available in Ash Canyon on the lower mountain slope. This parcel allowed an unlimited panoramic view to the East of the high desert San Pedro valley 400 ft below and opposite to the West the winter snowcapped Huachuca Mountains. Upon investigation the couple purchased eight acres of land in 1988 for their future retirement home and consigned an architect to draw up plans for a unique hillside residential home.

In 1990 just prior to commencing construction the couple felt called after reading an article about a religious event happening in a place called Medjugorje, Yugoslavia. In November 1990 as with many thousands of others they went on the Medjugorje pilgrimage with a small group flying out of Chicago. With the usual unforeseen hardships the couple found an area that radiated "much spirituality", especially impacting the convert wife's Catholic faith. It was one of the few times individuals were seen pushing to get into a church. However the couple did not experience very much exceptional visual phenomena as many others did. Most visually impressive was the mountain view of the valley below while standing by the large stone cross located on Mt. Kriscivac. It had some similarities to the land they had purchased for their new home above the 5,000 foot high Arizona Sonoran desert.

Upon returning in November 1990 the couple commissioned the construction of their Arizona home which was completed in late 1991. Near the end of the construction as the husband was standing with the contractor looking down into the San Pedro Valley below, He [the husband] said it would be charming to erect a twenty foot cross that faces the valley below. This was the moment destiny began its further course. Thinking of the cross in Medjugorje, the size and composition of the proposed cross grew.

As a result of an atrium being constructed in the couples home they became familiar with a company in Tucson that was capable of fabricating large remarkable creations formed out of fiberglass, steel and concrete composition. Upon consultation it was determined that if a larger cross was desired one could be built over 70 feet high. The wife expressed a strong desire that a statue of The Blessed Virgin Mary belonged next to the cross. It was discerned that the statue of Mary should have an outstretched arm pointing to the cross; not only to the cross but also to Mexico which is five miles due South. Structural plans were then drawn up for the proposed project and then the Cochise County Planning Department was consulted for preliminary approval.

Initially they, [now called the founders] were told what they had in mind probably could not be done in Cochise County. Regulations did not normally allow structures, religious or not over thirty feet high. However there were a few exceptions; one being that monuments were exempt. They were also told no permit could be issued on the two proposed structures alone. It was then determined that a small chapel would be acceptable to comply with the Cochise County regulation and the cross could legally be considered a monument. Again destiny dictated a small unplanned chapel would join the Cross and Madonna statue. Many other situations and regulations almost stopped the project.

Based on tentative county permit approval the Cross and Madonna fabrication projects were commissioned in the fall of 1993. The couple sharing their enthusiasm with a neighbor became a mistake. Immediately a group of opponents organized and on the basis of the project being permitted or not, it was not going to be built in their Canyon. Opponent's organized and funds were collected as far away as California to file any kind of action necessary to stop which one called "Visual Pollution". At first the local paper picked up the controversy, then the Tucson TV stations and finally the newspapers as far away as The Los Angeles Times. The founders could not believe the intensity of the opponent's opposition. However this intense opposition by the opponents also sent out signals of increasing support for the project from many other observers.

As a result, this also became a political issue and more county hindrances mysteriously appeared. Before a permit was issued the opponents filed a complaint with The Board of Adjustment for a hearing to rescind the original pending permit. The opponents lost and the county issued a permit, which opened the door for a second Board of Adjustment. At the second hearing, even with the support of Pastor Fr. Bryerton and a large supporting group, it was apparent the founders were going to lose. However based on a voting technicality the county issued permit was still allowed. The opponents immediately filed an appeal in Superior Court in Bisbee Arizona to stop the project.

The founders began to prepare to commence work on the project, as the lawsuit had no direct effect on the upcoming construction. Three months after the permit was issued, the county mysteriously came up with a directive that stayed the permit based on an approach road technicality. Complying with the necessary approach road changes triggered another county directive that dictated another permit application would be necessary. In the fall of 1994 after complying with the new impediments a second county permit was issued. This opened the door for a third Board of Adjustment and this time it was an apparent done deal in favor of the opponents. The permit was legally overruled and the project was stopped cold. Filing their [the founders] own lawsuit in Superior Court would take at least 18 months to be heard.

The founders then had to either quit or carry on with their own lawsuit in Superior Court to reinstate their permit. Of interest The County Planning Department director stated on Tucson television that all requests by all their department had been complied with. Three Board of Adjustment appointees consisting of two neighbors living in the canyon and another from outside had the power to stop all the efforts of three years of hard work. In 1995 the founders decided to file their own lawsuit in Superior Court for a reinstatement of their permit. In the fall of 1996 after spending approximately fifty thousand dollars in costs and legal fees, the presiding judge in Superior Court reinstated the permit. In essence confirming all conditions requested by the county had been met and the Board of Adjustment was in error. Although the suit was always a strong property rights issue, it never became a strong religious issue. Project construction started in March of 1997.

The chapel originally was basically a simple layout to comply with the county requirement. Then as construction started small events started to happen. The outside of the chapel was slated to be stucco. However in a local parcel, a wash was located that appeared to contain many river rocks that had washed down from the Huachuca Mountains for centuries. It was decided to try and do one chapel elevation in this river rock. Un-believably upon surface mining this rock it continued to yield river rocks similar to the scripture account of the multiplication of the loaves and fishes.

Viewing the chapel, surrounded by live oak trees it rises out of the mountainside in a majestic manner complementing this rock. A wood craftsman in nearby Benson, Arizona had a treasure of original hand hewed oak beams that he had brought down from a dismantled Dutch barn located in central Michigan. From this authentic wood, overhead beams were created and also exceptional doors and cabinetry. The inside ceiling consists of unpeeled Northern Arizona Aspen. The Chapel was completed in March 1998.

After completion, inside the chapel a magnificent mural of the risen Jesus awaits, standing with outstretched arms greets incoming visitors. Beneath this mural is an antique painted wood Spanish Crucifix that suggests in depth spiritual feelings of sorrow. In front of the mural is a quaint altar of which three Bishops and over seventy priests have celebrated Mass. In the fall of 1998 the Bishop of Tucson allowed The Blessed Sacrament to be housed in a tabernacle donated from the founders original home parish in Saint Charles, Illinois.

The 75' Celtic Cross follows a Benedictine design with a man made created sculptured effect of hand hewed oak rising out of a huge tree. A waterfall is to the left of the cross with a stairway leading further up the mountain leading to a small grotto and the 14th Station of the Cross. The top center of the Celtic cross has the Crown of Thorns encapsulating the cup and host relief. Large circular letters "V I T A" which means "life" complete the large circular Cross design.

A 31' high statue of The Blessed Virgin Mary stands on a pedestal to the right of the large cross. She stands with her right hand pointing to the Celtic cross. Above her head is a crown of twelve Stars. Upon occasion spiritual phoneme has been associated with much that surrounds her likeness.

In 2002 the completion of fourteen outdoor Stations of the Cross were concluded, allowing visitors to make the 600 foot spiritual journey up the mountain side trail from the lower parking lot. These stations were exclusively constructed by two Hispanics (Jose and Jesus) and the shrine's local volunteer crew. Cast bronze plaques donated by various individuals also contributed to this magnificent undertaking.

Summer 2004 marked the installation of a ten foot high "Angel of Revelation" poised to the right of the large cross and statue of Mary. A second angel stands above the consecrated ground of station twelve. Fall 2004 marked the completion of the small "Our Lady of Guadalupe "grotto. In 2005 a third white marble angel "Guardian of the Children" was placed near the North chapel entrance.

In 2006 a small prayer area was constructed just under the marble angel, "Guardian of the Children". A bronze plaque marks the area explaining it's purpose concerning " final closure" of one being involved in an abortion. There is a small quartz box into which one may place the name of the aborted child. The child now has an identity which aids in the process of healing!

Directly diagonal from the shrine front entrance on a scenic hill is another building [prayer house] named "Mary's Knoll". This is open to the public and has become a place of serenity and prayer for interested visitors. Inside in the prayer room is a mural painting of Jesus sitting on a wall as if he is speaking to us. To His left is a full size statue of Mary reaching out her hands to us. Much phenomenon has been associated with this scene. Every Friday at 7:30 pm at Mary's Knoll a public family Rosary invites all to share in the warmth of Our Lady.

QUESTIONS FREQUENTLY ASKED OF OUR STAFF

Q: *Are there miracles happening on this hill?*

A: There have been written and verbal documentation of which many have confirmed as an "unexplained healings" of either the body or heart.

Q: *Has the Catholic Church investigated any acclaimed miracles?*

A: No, nor presently do we intend to ask for church investigation.

Q: *Has any unexplained phenomena occurred on this hill either visually or photographically?*

A: Yes. We have many testimonies and pictures on file.

Q. *Are there messages from a supernatural being given to a locutionist [s] in the Shrine area.*

A: Yes, in our opinion.

Q: *Who gets them and what is the documentation?*

A: Primarily by a person who is called "Pat" or in broader terms [the recipient of the messages]. There is no absolute documentation except what ones feels after hearing or reading the messages.

Q: *Is the recipient a visionary?*

A: We prefer to call her a locutionist. A visionary is a broad term that applies to a lot of situations that can be misinterpreted.

Q: *Explain how the recipient gets these messages and does she see anything?*

A: In the early years they were inner locutions. In the later years most are audibly and sometimes visually given while she is in a spiritual state sometimes called "ecstasy".

Q: *Does she claim to see spiritual beings or "Phoneme of a supernatural nature"?*

A: Upon occasion she has stated what she sees can be vivid, especially if it is a vision of something she is told to relate back to the community. In most cases she sees a being in a translucent body form, sometimes accompanied with beautiful colors or lights.

Q: *What do these messages consist of?*

A: These messages concern these times and focus around love, forgiveness, the Mercy of Our Lord and teachings of how we should live our lives and relate to God. They do not focus on fear.

Q: *Who gives these messages and why:*

A: It is our discernment that they are permitted by Our Lord Jesus Christ and come from Him, His Mother and upon occasion other permitted heavenly beings.

Q: *By what authority are these messages published?*

A: They are allowed to be published under "Private Revelation" and also by the recipients two previous and current Spiritual Advisors who are priests.

Q: *What approach does the local Diocese take concerning these messages?*

A: Since we did not ask the church for any formal recognition, they have issued a letter confirming their position as "It is a Private Matter".

Q: *Has the clergy visited and said Mass at the shrine?*

A: Yes. One Arch-Bishop, two Bishops and over 80 priests have said Mass here.

Q: *How long has she been getting messages and or visions?*

A: Formally since June 1st, 1997

Q: *Do you expect the messages to continue?*

A: It has been stated that they will slow down, as so much has been said. Our Mother has repeatedly said, "go back and read the messages". In April 2004 we were informed that the last of the seven year series of messages would conclude on the hill site of the first original message. This occurred on June 1st, 2004.

Q *Will there be more messages?*

A. Jesus periodically speaks. Our Mother has stated She will respond if Her Son sees a need for additional response such as the December Christmas messages.

Q. *Have all the given messages been published?*

A. No. Some were never recorded, many are private and a few were discerned not to be published.

Q: *Is recipient or are any of the prayer teams "healers"?*

A: Jesus is the "healer". We are nothing but intercessors praying to God to intervene for the benefit of a requested person or situation.

Q: *If one is being prayed over what should he or she do?*

A: Focus on the love and power of Our Lord and ask that your request be granted.

Q: *Are most prayer requests answered?*

A: Yes! God always answers prayer; but it is always in His time and in His way. Read the last part of paragraph three of the message of July 11th, 2003 on page 311.

Q: *How would one summarize the reason for coming here?*

A: It has been confirmed in the messages. This is a "Mountain of Mercy". Give thanks and pray for God's mercy and blessings. If you are open He will do the rest.

Q. Are all faiths welcome?

A. Yes.

Q. Do you have a resident priest or scheduled Masses?

A. Check our interior posted information or our website for information.

Q. *What is your website?*

A. [www.ourladyofthesierras.org]

Prayer for Our Lady of the Sierras Foundation

Dear Jesus and
Blessed Mother Mary,

We implore Your blessing and
guidance upon the Foundation,
all visitors and their intentions
and on those who serve You.
Hold us in Your merciful hands
close to Your heart burning with
light and love, so that protected
and defended by You we may be
fit and faithful instruments,
bringing others closer to You and
bringing You to others. Fulfill in
us Your Divine Will which You
have destined from all eternity.
Grant us the vision that in
whatever we do: we may
See You in All
Serve You in All
and Love You in All.

Dawn Dugie

Introduction – Messages June 1, 1997 – December 2000

The following text is private revelation given to "Pat" who now resides in Southern Arizona. Her Address, last name, has been mostly screened from this revised publication at the request of her current Spiritual Advisor and Pastor of her Arizona Parish. The following original statement had been made by Pat's long term, now deceased spiritual advisor, Fr. Louis Hasenfuss O.S.B., Prior of Holy Trinity Monastery, Saint David, Arizona regarding these revelations.

In 1997 Fr. Louis stated the following:

"You have my permission to publish these messages as private revelation, but I cannot give you the imprimatur of the Catholic Church". He also stated in his opinion, there is nothing in the messages contrary to Catholic morals or teachings. These are prophecies which uphold Catholic teaching and uplift the people."

Father Louis graciously said should you desire to publish, you have my permission to use my name! These messages must only be repeated in their entirety and not taken out of context.

* * *

NOTE: Many people who are familiar with the gifts that God grants us through the power of the Holy Spirit are familiar with prophecy. Prophecy has many different vehicles, dreams, speaking in tongues, locution, etc...

The early messages were given to Pat in English, in an audible manner, that was usually in a form of dictation. As she heard she wrote in shorthand or script, paused for additional input and continued until the message was complete. The original script copies are on file. The authors of these messages have their own distinct personalities.

We caution that even though we have been requested to publish these messages, not all of these are for everyone. Please carefully discern what should apply to a given individual or group. The final 12-1-97 message of this series confirms this request. Any translations to other languages could alter the meaning.

* * *

Readers note. As these message progress and more personal dialogue exchange appears in this book, more italics and dashes for clarification will appear in the text.

Messages from Jesus and Mary

June 1, 1997- December 1, 1997

June 1, 1997 (Jesus)

My children; Build it; they will come.

June 5, 1997 (Jesus)

My daughter; Prepare thyself!

June 6, 1997

(Friday night canyon rosary) (Mary)

Thank you, my children, for having gathered here together to praise and honor My Son. Let me lead you to My Son through prayer. It is through your prayer that you will find true peace.

June 9, 1997

(Gail and Pat on hill) (Message for Gail) (Jesus)

Place your hand in mine and I will give you strength.

June 16, 1997

(Rosary on Monday night at St. Peter's in Geneva, IL) (Jesus)

Surrender yourself unto my peace. Joy will fill your soul. Your burden will be light and your sadness will be turned into joy.

June 19, 1997

(3:00 am. Pat's original Illinois Residence) (Mary)

My Dear children:

When you pray, open your hearts and minds to the gifts of the Holy Spirit. Be as little children eagerly awaiting a special gift. Be not afraid but accept what is given to you in faith. Let it be as a little seed which is planted, nurtured, and grows into a beautiful creation reflecting the light of Jesus.

June 23, 1997

(7:30 pm. St. Peter Church, Geneva, Illinois - Rosary meeting) (Mary)

My dear little ones,

Tonight I gather each of you under my mantle of love and protection. Continue to persevere in your prayer life and I will help lead you onto the path of holiness. Thank you my little ones. Thank you for responding to my call.

June 28, 1997 (Jesus)

My children;

Persevere, persevere in your prayers. Run the race which I have placed before you. The enemy is strong and great will be your trials, but I have overcome the enemy. I am the light which brightens your path. Focus on me. The race will soon be over.

June 30, 1997

(7:30 pm. St. Peter Church - Rosary meeting) (Mary)

My Dear little children,

You are called to holiness. You are vessels created to carry the light of Jesus into this dark and hurting world. Pray, pray from your heart and I will intercede for you. Do not seek to avoid suffering but unite your suffering to that of Jesus on the Cross. Your sufferings then become as fragrant flowers which I place before the Father. Peace my little ones, peace.

(The following message was found the first week of July 1997 in Pat's book.)

My children; The alarm has been sounded. Rouse my people to conversion for time, as you know it, runs short. Many will be lost without great sacrifices.

July 3, 1997

(8:00 pm. Pat's then, Illinois residence - Chaplet with Pat & John Kuplin of Angel Kisses) (Mary)

My dear little ones,

Thank you for gathering here to pray. I love you and want you to receive the graces which I have prepared for you. Open your hearts, believe; others will come.

"For Jerry" - Open your heart - Many graces will come

July 4, 1997

(7:00 pm. I-44 Missouri. Mile post 120 en route to AZ) (Mary)

My dear little ones;

Today you celebrate the independence of your country. Today I, your mother, ask you out of love to celebrate your dependence on God. Know that you are loved beyond measure. You are called my dear ones to pray much. Make sacrifices as often as you can, and yes, also to suffer with complete acceptance.

You do not realize the great trials before you. Much will be required. Ask for the Holy Spirit to fill you with His presence so that you will be able to withstand that which comes your way. Rejoice; know that you are loved.

July 9, 1997 (Mary)

My dear children;

I need your prayers. They are the weapons which I hurl against the enemy. Be vigilant in your commitment to God. He loves you and wants what is best for you. Strengthen yourself with Holy Scripture to dispel the subtle attacks of Satan. Let not doubt take root in your hearts. I, your Mother, am here to help strengthen and protect you. Do not fear. I will never abandon my children. Peace my little ones.

July 10, 1997

(During the Rosary at Our Lady of the Mountains Church) (Mary)

My dear little ones;

My peace I give you. Do not let your hearts be troubled by the trials of this world. Your trials are like the weeds in the field which, try as you may, you cannot discharge them. You my little ones are the wild flowers which have taken root among the weeds. I gather each of you into a bouquet which I take to my Son. Peace my little ones.

July 11, 1997

(Early morning) Personal message - visual (Jesus)

My daughter,

(I was struggling to get up to write - pain was intense)

Do not write, but come to me and lay your head upon my knee. Know this suffering was by your choice, offered for the poor souls who do not as yet know me and those already in Purgatory awaiting the light of My presence. Let the joy they experience as they enter into My Kingdom, be the balm which soothes your pain. REST MY CHILD!!

July 11, 1997

(During the Rosary at the "Farm", Ash Canyon) (Mary)

My precious little ones,

Thank you for joining your hearts in prayer this night. Know that my Son stands in your midst gently tugging on the strings of your hearts.

How my little ones can we express our love to you? I, the Mother who lovingly held the new born baby in my arms so full of joy that my heart could not contain itself. I am also the Mother who lovingly outstretched her arms to receive her lifeless Son.

Do you not understand you are not given more than you can bear? You are never alone - let faith take charge of your life. Your time grows more and more precious. Use it wisely my children. Peace my little ones.

July 12, 1997

(AT 6:00 p.m., little hill) This message is from later recollection, not a 100% quote.

(Mary) My precious little ones;

Thank you for praising my Son. Know that we are with you. Look at the Cross and see the Crown of Thorns. Today my Son gives each of you a Crown of Thorns. It is not heavy - do not fear the pain. Each will be able to carry that which is given to them. Peace my little ones

July 14, 1997 (5:00 am.) (Jesus)

My dear children;

You, my children in your humanness struggle not to struggle. Your wills are losing the battle of the desires of the flesh. Remember your bodies are the dwelling place of the Holy Spirit.

Depriving oneself of earthly pleasures, fasting and sacrifices have become just words clouded by unwillingness to surrender. Yes, surrender. Give Me your wills that I might give you Mine. Until you completely convert, you cannot overcome this world's temptations. My Heart is on fire for love of you - Let me help you my children. Desire Me with all your heart and I will give you peace.

July 15, 1997

(While in prayer - Chaplet of St. Michael) (Jesus)

My daughter;

I draw you close unto My Heart. Do not be troubled by those seeking answers for in time all hearts will be one with Mine and there will be no more questions. Trust Me, my child. Let all who have ears hear my call.

July 16, 1997 (Mary)

My precious ones;

Praise be Jesus. Thank you my little ones for steadfastly following the rocky path placed before you. You have been given a great responsibility. Do not slacken in your zeal. Much good lies ahead. Take comfort, my little ones, for your strength lies in Jesus. I, your Mother, will be your comfort and guide in leading you to Jesus. Rest in the assurance of your faith - you will be able to overcome the hurdles placed before you.

Peace, my little ones, peace.

July 17, 1997 (8:15 a.m.) (Mary)

My dear little ones,

I bring you Our love and peace. Oh, my precious ones, let this gift you are being given find a resting place in your souls. You are being prepared as the jewels of a crown. Know that all jewels in order to reach a perfection of beauty must also be purified. So must you, the jewels of my Son. Let me, your Mother, polish your stones of love and devotion to my Son. Peace and joy my children.

July 18, 1997

(4:20 p.m.) (Mary)

My daughter,

Peace, my child. Be filled with the confidence of the Holy Spirit. I ask of you to invoke the presence of my spouse before your prayers so that His mighty work will be accomplished in all who call upon him. Tell them my daughter - each prayer helps wipe away the tears of your Mother being shed for all humanity.

Light your Holy candles. As the candle burns rays of light will fill all hearts with the love of Jesus - THE LIGHT OF THE WORLD! Carry His light until there is no more darkness. Know that I need your prayers. Peace to all who hear and heed my message.

(Personal note: After the message, Pat went back upstairs to finish working on a rosary she was making. Her physical state was so drained she said mentally - "I don't think I will make the Rosary tonight - I'm not going". She immediately heard - "Yes you are dear - Yes you are dear". Then I (Jerry) came in from the cross site and called for Pat. Pat came down and related what had happened at the kitchen table. While we were sitting there, I saw two light brown desert doves with white highlights under their wings on the stucco wall 20' from where we were sitting. This pair of doves just sat there for awhile and just looked at us. When Pat and I went outside on the path to the cross site, the two doves flew right over our head. The situation was enchanting

July 18, 1997

(6:30 p.m.) (Jesus) ---Suggested reading: Rev. 14:14

My children,

You are the grains of wheat planted in the fertile fields. Grow where you are planted and produce much fruit. HARVEST TIME GROWS NEAR!

July 18, 1997 (Canyon Rosary) (Jesus)

My daughter,

Why do you fear those who would hear my message. Is it more important to you what people think of you - pride, my daughter - I detest pride. Step out in faith. Have I not said you are my messenger. Repeat my message if you love me! I do not demand, but ask out of love. My people MUST hear!

July 19, 1997 (Saturday, 12:00 noon) (Mary)

My precious ones,

Do not let your hearts be troubled when it seems as though you are being scolded as a disobedient child. Know my precious ones the path you have chosen is that of holiness and requires much obedience and sacrifices. Find comfort my little ones in knowing we stand beside you gently guiding your path. Love such as you have never known is your shield of protection. Peace my little ones - rest in Our peace.

July 20, 1997 (12:00 p.m.) (Mary)

My little ones,

I find joy in the hearts that have been given to me. I love you and desire your happiness. My little ones, know true happiness is to be found in Jesus.

Be the glow emitting from the candle which burns ever so brightly. So must your love for Jesus burn within your hearts. Watch as the gentle breeze tosses

the candle light to and fro, yet the light still burns. The breeze is your time of trouble, yet because you trust Jesus, your light still burns. Be patient , my little ones, do not let your light go out. Peace to you, my candles of love.

July 20, 1997

(Arizona residence: Paul, Lucy, Jerry and Pat) (Mary)

My precious little ones,

Know that I your Mother am here in your midst joining my prayers with yours. Delight my precious one in the joy of the souls who have this moment joined the Saints in heaven. My love surrounds and protects you. I thank you, my little ones----rejoice! *(Lucy could smell the fragrance of roses about the fourth decade of the rosary --- A gift from our Mother)*

22

July 21, 1997

(Monday night rosary at St. Andrew's) - (7:30 p.m.) (Mary)

My dear little one,

Thank you for coming out of love to adore my Son. He stands within your midst with His Most Sacred Heart filled with love and mercy.

Oh, my little ones, if you could only imagine even the smallest degree of His mercy, you would run to Him with a fire in your heart burning with such intensity you would expire from sheer joy.

Trust my children and press on - the time of mercy grown short as the clock runs down. Go in peace.

July 21, 8:00 p.m.

(the same night) (Personal message) (Mary)

My daughter,

Because of your love of neighbor, your prayers have stormed the gates of Heaven and I your Mother will intercede for you and all those, who out of love, have denied self and sought the life of another.

July 22, 1997 (Mary)

My dear ones,

Many gifts have been given to you through the Holy Spirit. Your eyes, ears and hearts are already being prepared to accept the signs I have given and will give. Look my little ones at the night time sky filled with the sparkle of diamonds, the handwork of God.
You my dear ones must shine as the stars for you too are His handwork. Show your love for Him who loves you so intensely by being His vessel of light and purity.
Peace My little ones.

July 23, 1997 (Personal message)

My daughter,

The uncertainties of this world are as numerous as the leaves on the trees. Leaves fall, and in season, are reborn nourished by the goodness of God. So must you, my child, fall, be nourished and reborn.

Much will come your way making the path difficult, but you have been strengthened to withstand the arrows aimed at your faith. Continue to praise Jesus as He will carry you when your burdens seem insurmountable.

I your Mother take you into my arms. Rest easy, my child. You have received the grace of knowing Our love. This, my daughter, will sustain you!

July 24, 1997

(3:15 a.m. while praying the Chaplet of Divine Mercy) (Mary)

My dear little ones,

You my children are my cohorts in this battle between good and evil. This is the time for decision. You to whom the grace of suffering has already been given will need the physical presence of my Son more and more. He, the One who is in you, is far greater than the one who darkens the world with the heavy clouds of despair and hopelessness

Call upon Him, your strength, and We will come arming you with the weapons of assurance, faith, hope and love.

You are not called to embark upon an easy journey, but one of much suffering. For great within you now is the love for others and your hearts are now filled with the pain of your Mother whose heart bleeds for her wayward children. Unite your sufferings and sacrifices to the Passion of Jesus so that goodness will prevail. Many things you do not understand, but the greatness of God's love will enlighten your understanding as your journeys here draw to an end.

Trust my precious one - let all who believe trust! For great is the mercy of God!

July 24, 1997 (Canyon Rosary) (Jesus)

My children,

You come seeking peace - My peace I freely give. You, my sheep, whom I have called by name, have found your pasture in My heart.

I, your Jesus of Mercy, call you while there is yet time to do the will of My Father. You are being prepared for a great task ahead. Know My Sacred Heart and the Immaculate Heart of My Mother are your only true refuge ---your "pasture of peace".

My love is being poured out this night. Receive what is given with a grateful heart; it is only by the intercession of My Mother that time has been extended.

July 24, 1997

(Approx. 2:00 p.m. in the afternoon during Rosary with Paul, and three beautifully humble monks from Patagonia) (Mary)

My dearly beloved sons,

You desire a message - then let your hearts be opened to the graces I, your Mother, have bestowed upon you. I embrace you, my sons, and give you my Motherly blessing. Your years of sacrifice have not gone unnoticed. Persevere, my dear ones, your crowns await you.

July 25, 1997

(3:30 a.m. during Chaplet of Divine Mercy) (Mary)

My dear children, I have made many appearances and let my messages be known throughout the world now more than ever before. You, my little ones to whom I have entrusted much, must prepare your hearts, minds and especially your very souls to that which lies ahead. NEVER FEAR for that is not of God. He wishes you to be prepared, my little ones. Do as I have instructed you. Only through your total conversions will you be ready to accept and endure the trials ahead.

Let love be your guide -- do what We require of you; prayer, fasting, penance, sacrifice, and as often as possible, reconciliation. These are not just words, my little ones, but powerful weapons of protection. HEED MY WORDS! Peace, my little evangelists.

July 26, 1997 (Approx. 4:00 a.m.) (Mary)

My dear little ones,

Praise be Jesus! In His infinite mercy, He has sent His angels to guard and protect you. Your hearts are to be filled with the joy of the sunrise giving light to a new day of life.

Let the rays of light which penetrate the hearts of His chosen ones draw souls close to the FOUNTAIN OF MERCY There THEIR THIRST FOR SOULS will find refreshment.

In your journey to holiness, YOUR THIRST will become greater as My Son's presence will be ever more apparent in your lives. Continue onward, my little ones. Do not look back, but focus always on Jesus who stands before you. Peace my precious ones.

July 27, 1997 (Mary)

My dear children,

So much of your time is wasted in your efforts to try and control the events of your life.

I, your Mother, ask each of you to empty yourselves of all that which conflicts with the will of the Holy Spirit. Let Him fill you with His presence so that your life then becomes a beautiful melody which sweetly reaches the throne of God.

Pray much, My little ones --- with each of the trials that comes your way so too will the grace required to accept them be poured out upon you.

Praise be Jesus whose love continually surrounds you. Peace, My children!

July 28, 1997 (Mary)

My dear ones,

Know I am with you as you journey to perfect the love and obedience asked of you by God. Each day will be as a stone when placed one upon the other takes unto itself shape and character. The stronger the mortar which joins the stones, the stronger the structure becomes. My dear ones, let me help you become that which God desires. Your strength is in Jesus. If you allow me, My children, I will be the mortar which binds you to Jesus, My Son. Call upon us and We will hear and answer you.

Peace---perfect your trust in Jesus and you will have perfect peace.

July 28, 1997 (St. Andrews family prayer night) (Mary)

My precious ones,

Look with love and adoration upon Him who stands before you. Let the brilliance of His Divinity light your path to holiness.

July 29, 1997 (Mary)

My daughter,

Do not let the spirit of anxiety overwhelm you. The gifts you have been given will require many sacrifices, but I have told you with the power of the Holy Spirit all things will be possible.

Immerse yourself in daily prayer. Seek Jesus in all that you do so that the souls for which He thirst will be refreshed in the fountain of His mercy. Peace and joy, our messenger of love.

July 30, 1997 (Mary)

My dear children,

I come this day surrounding you with My Motherly love. I wish to instill in you perfect peace which comes from knowing Jesus. My children, do not be misled by the prosperity of worldly goods and find your spiritual self in a state of poverty.

I, your Mother, weep for you. As a mother feels the pains of her child and would offer herself to alleviate that pain, so I offer Myself to you. Seek refuge in My Immaculate Heart while there is still time. Come under My mantle of love and together we will walk to Jesus!

I caution you, My children, DO NOT BE MISLED. HEAR THE URGENCY IN MY CALL --- prepare yourself for that which is soon to come. Pray, little ones, pray.

July 31, 1997 (Jesus)

My daughter,

You have been given strength and made well. I now ask you to make more preparations for that which is soon to come. You have been given the means by which to accomplish My purpose in helping others.

The heart of your husband has been prepared---he now hears my words through you.

(I then saw many people gathering around with a look of despair. Saw a food storage area with many supplies including gardening equipment. The message was repeated several times along with the visual effects). (I tested the message as we are asked to do. The voice was strong yet soothing -- I felt no fear or anxiety, only peace).

August 1, 1997 (Mary)

My daughter,

Our hearts are filled with joy over that which you have undertaken. There is so little joy now, my child, because of the weight of the world's sins.

We seek those souls who willingly abandon their will to those of My Son. He is the Pure Joy brought to those hearts who will allow Him to enter.

Continue to persevere in prayer and We will guide you and protect that which is of immeasurable value---your very souls. Peace.

August 2, 1997 (Mary)

My dear ones,

You, my children, are living in the age of decision. Many have already heard my call for conversion and have responded by surrendering their wills to Jesus. Only by living in His Divine Will can peace be obtained in your world as you will only seek that which pleases My Son---to love Him and your neighbor. Seek to be humble and in your humility, We will shower you with graces.

Peace my dear ones.

August 3, 1997 (Mary)

My little ones,

Peace my little ones --- We bring you Our peace. Know, my children, we will meet all your needs and give you the grace to sustain you as the trials begin. The only hope for your world is Jesus and many have turned away from Him seeking only what brings them comfort and pleasures. You are given our messages as a means to bring hope to the souls whose faith has faded or grown lukewarm. They would like to believe, but because they do not see, they do not believe. Blessed are they who believe and have not seen.
Use the graces you have been given to bring souls to the fountain of My son's love where they will be refreshed.

Let His light shine brightly so that all may see Him in you. You are the soldiers I am sending into battle armed with My rosary and scapular. With these weapons, many souls will be saved from eternal fire and damnation.

My precious ones, if you could see what lies ahead, you would waste no more time. Live the Gospels. HEAR THE URGENCY OF MY CALL. Peace.

August 4, 1997

(Ref. Revelation-HARVEST] (Jesus)

My children,

See the fields of wheat moved by the wind like the waves of the seas. You, my children, are My fields of wheat preparing for Harvest. You have met the wind, the obstacles of life, armed with My love. Where there is true love, there is peace - My peace. Come, My children ---- I, the Harvest Master, call you by name. The Harvest begins.

August 5, 1997 (Mary)

My dear little ones,

I bring you peace and My blessing of Motherly love. My children, do not slacken in your zeal to love and serve My Son. He stands in your midst commanding His angels to guard and protect you during these difficult times and the more difficult times to come.

NOW IS THE TIME OF MERCY! Do not be idle, My little ones. So many souls are in danger of being lost. Your prayers must continually rise to Heaven seeking the mercy of Jesus. Prepare --- prepare your souls as you have been instructed. It grows late My children. See our two hearts joined as one where you will find refuge.

August 6, 1997 (Mary)

My dear children,

Know that many graces continue to be poured out upon you at this time --- now more than ever before.

I the Mediatrix of all graces have come to gather My children under My mantle of love to guide each of you to My Son. He patiently awaits the door of your hearts to be opened to Him. I ask you to reaffirm your faith by letting Jesus be the focal point of your life.

You must not be weak, My children. Rely on the Mass and the sacraments for your strength. Seek My Son with your whole heart and truly you will find Him.

Encourage each other continually as the path you are traveling draws narrower each day. Peace and love My children.

My daughter,

I come this day to encourage you in your service to My Son. You say you are weak --- yes, My child, but we have taken your weakness and turned it into a vessel of strength which carries the Light of Love, Jesus.

Continuously feed your soul with prayer and holy scripture. You will need this strength to be fortified against that which hastens your way. The trials have only begun, My daughter. Know that we are always with you especially in those times of purification. Be filled with joy and take My hand as I will be your guide on this journey to holiness. Peace and love, My child.

August 8, 1997 (Personal message) (Mary)

My daughter,

I bring you My motherly love and comfort in this your time of trial. We are the strength you need to face all that will come your way. Do not be saddened, My little one, by those who unknowingly are instruments of the spirit of disbelief.

Be filled with Our peace. Embrace the suffering which comes your way as your purification continues. You are the clay the potter is molding into His image. Rejoice always for you have been greatly blessed.

August 8, 1997 (Evening message) (Mary)

My children,

Come My dear ones as I, your Mother, take your hand and gather you under My mantle.

I ask you this day to seek the will of Jesus in all that you do. As you continuously seek Him Who is Holy, you too become one with Him and share the joy of true love.

My precious ones, as you gaze into the mirror know that the image which reflects back is the dwelling place of the Holy Spirit. Let the purity of heart and the Light of Love meet your every gaze. You are the beacons of My Son's light and love. Live each moment with confidence in Him whose love has no bounds. Peace and joy my children.

August 9, 1997

(4:00 a.m. after Chaplet of Divine Mercy) (Jesus)

My children,

Arise from your (spiritual) slumber. This is the dawn of a new day in which I commission each of you to be my Apostles. Spread My word of hope where there is despair! --- be My carriers of light in your world darkened by the clouds of sin. The battle rages --- moments are precious, My children. Prepare now --- THE CLOCK WINDS DOWN!

August 10, 1997 (Mary)

My children,

Praise be Jesus Who in His infinite mercy has allowed Me to be with you. My little ones, always seek the Will of My Son as your time here on earth draws to an end. Your life is a precious gift from Jesus. You are charged with the task of caring for this gift first spiritually then physically.

Form good spiritual habits, My children. Pray --- pray much for therein lies much power to defeat the evil which encircles around you. We love you, little children, and desire only that which is best for you. Do not become discouraged when your trials increase, but trust. Call on us and We will hear and answer you. Peace and love My children.

August 11, 1997 (Mary)

My children,

I come this day to encourage you in your journey to holiness. Draw strength, My children, through communion with God in prayer. Pray little ones -- make a greater effort to increase your prayer life that you may experience the true joy of peace in your hearts --- the peace of a personal relationship with Jesus.

I, your Mother, know of your sufferings and doubts. I desire a complete abandonment of your will to that of Jesus. Immerse yourself in Him Who is all goodness and love and you will receive the graces to sustain you through this life.

Much awaits you, My precious ones. Each day is a glorious gift from God. Soon you must give an accounting for that which has been given to you. Be bold, my little ones. Peace and love!

August 11, 1997 (Monday night prayer service at St. Andrew's) (Mary)

My children,

We will rain showers of blessing upon all those who come to the mountain seeking the mercy of My Son. Your efforts, My children, will not go un-rewarded.

Peace and love.

August 12, 1997

(During erection of Cross and statue of Mary on the mountain there was unsettled weather all around us .However we did have a circle of blue sky all around us for several hours---it never did storm)

(Mary) My dear children,

Thank you, My little ones, for that which you have accepted on faith as a call from us. Look about the mountain and see with your hearts the multitude of angels whose joyful praises are rising to the throne of Jesus. Know, My precious ones, Jesus in His mercy has allowed this journey to perfect the hearts of those who have heard and answered His call.
We draw you close to Our hearts to gently caress the wounds caused by the poor misguided souls whom you did not abandon but lifted up to My Son for mercy and forgiveness.

Rejoice, My precious children, for heaven rejoices with you.

August 13, 1997 (Mary)

My dear children. You My children, are witnessing but a small portion of a grand plan predestined long ago. This is a link in the chain I am forming to gather My children.

I desire, My precious ones, that the love of My Son shine more brightly in you as these days progress. Many souls are searching but do not know Him Whom they seek.

This is a beacon of My Son's love for all mankind to see. Know, My children, they will come as hunger for Him increases. Open wide your hearts, oh little lambs, for this will become a pasture of My Son's goodness and mercy!

Much as been entrusted to you. Pray for the strength to persevere.

August 14, 1997 *(While making a rosary) (Mary)*

My daughter,

We offer you the peace and joy in Our hearts intertwined in Divine Love. As you draw closer to us each day in prayer, you will feel the warmth of our hearts beating for all humanity.

The messages with which you have been gifted are to be a source of hope and preparation for God's people. My daughter, there is much to come requiring obedience and self sacrifice. As you have asked so shall you receive ---- now is the time to make known that to which you have been instructed. The pieces of this life's puzzle are now fitting into place. I am calling the faithful ---- be vigilant and prepare. Oh little messenger of love, dispense our messages

August 15, 1997

(During Chaplet of Divine Mercy) (Mary)

My dear children,

You, My children, are My faithful remnant called into the service of My Son. Arm yourselves well with prayer. The Holy Spirit stands ready to assist you ---- He but awaits your call. Legions of angels are preparing for battle ---- the final battle draws near.

I desire you to offer your daily tasks as required by this life as prayerful flowers gathered to adorn the throne of Jesus. Each of you is uniquely precious ---- each one handcrafted by God and created to take your place in His master plan. Nothing happens by chance ---- accept His Divine Will ---- a precious gift presented to all wrapped in His love and compassion.

I thank you, My little ones, for honoring Me this day. Draw unto My heart and receive My Motherly blessing.

Peace dear ones - peace!

August 15, 1997

(During Friday night canyon rosary) (Mary)

My dear precious children,

My heart is filled with joy over all who have come on this My feast day. Know,

My children, where I am there also is My Son. Look with your hearts, Oh precious ones, and see His nail scarred hands which He stretches out before you. Rejoice, for this night it is My Son who blesses you. We have heard the petitions of your hearts and draw each of you into our fountain of love and mercy!

August 16, 1997 *(While praying rosary) (Mary)*

My children,

You whose hearts have been made ready to receive Our messages are embarking upon a great journey requiring total trust and conversion. We require much faith for the fruits of your calling are progressing towards fulfillment.

No longer can My Son watch the creation of His hands be discolored through the disobedience of His children. He loves you little ones and because of His pure love, He must correct the errors of this world.

My precious ones, do not fear what comes but embrace the chastisement as a sign of His love for soon all eyes will see and all hearts will know the glory of His presence.
You are the house built upon the rock against which the gates of hell shall not prevail. Courage, My little ones, we surround you with our angels to strengthen and protect you. Call upon them as they await your commands. Peace My dear ones!

August 17, 1997 (Mary)

My dear children,

Praise be Jesus. Our hearts rejoice in those who come seeking His presence in this holy place. Know, My children, we are here and await those who come seeking the peace and love of Jesus.

You, My dear ones, must prepare your hearts to embrace those who come filled with desire to know Him as you do. You in your small but significant way possess much power as you unite yourselves to My Son.

Know, My children, the heart of your Mother is consumed with love for each of you. My time here grows short as the cup of My Son's wrath now boils beyond that which My hand can save.

You, My children, have received My messages of love and hope. Know that through the intense sufferings ahead graces will flood your souls bringing peace to endure the darkness. The clouds gather, My children. Peace!

August 18, 1997 (Mary)

My children,

I ask you this day to pray more earnestly for the many souls who live in darkness. Many read My messages to pray, but their hearts do not respond as I desire ---- true prayer from the heart, My children, requires patience and an overwhelming love for those for whom you pray. Such love, My little ones, is instilled in you by Him Who is pure love.

Seek My Son ---- make Him the focal point of your life. It is only by completely abandoning yourself from this material world will you be able to accomplish the great task ahead.

Do not tarry ---- do as I have asked. Make preparations as your station in life allows. There is little time, My children ---- you have received My messages ---- act accordingly.

You are dearly loved and will be guided during this journey to perfection. Go in peace knowing you are never alone. Feel Our love as it fills your soul.

August 19, 1997 (Jesus)

My daughter,

I come seeking open hearts in which to plant My seeds of faith and obedience. Be the fertile ground into which these seeds are planted and My graces will rain upon you producing much fruit.

I wish, My daughter, that you go quickly about the tasks I have given you. I have said many will come ---- are you, My child, prepared? They will seek Me ---- My love and protection. You have been asked to prepare spiritually and physically. Those few to whom My messages have reached have not reacted.

The time approaches, My child, when choices will no longer be yours to make. Gather supplies and make provisions for many will require assistance. What do you wish Me to multiply when the wine cellar remains empty?

My, little messenger, I know of the times in which you live and the caution which My church has fallen into ---- hearts must be opened to My call or many will needlessly perish. Do what you can, My child, and I will do the rest. Ask those in whom you seek guidance to seek My discernment for they, as you, can surely see the signs of the times.

Peace, my daughter ---- rest now for a new day of hope soon dawns!

My dear children,

I bring you peace and love and the gentleness of my heart filled with compassion for you whom we have called. You have been told this journey is not an easy one but which is filled with many obstacles which will greatly test your obedience and devotion to My Son.

Our messages are clear to our faithful remnant. You recognize the signs of that which is soon to come but feel inadequate and frustrated because your hands have been tied with cords of bureaucracy. This, my children, is as it has been through all of history. Only those whose strength has been increased by the Holy Eucharist and a pure conscience will be able to persevere in the great purification to come. Do make haste, my precious ones, but in all your agendas, Christ must come first or there will be no peace to pursue your obligations.

I desire the will of My Son that you prepare for those whose souls will soon be stirred by a great sign ---- a final grace of My Son for conversion. This, in deed, will be a great grace for all hearts. Those who recognize it as such will repent and totally convert. There will also be the unfortunate souls who will temporarily fall into shock, but it will not have a lasting impression.

My children have been marked by my angels ---- you will recognize those whom you can trust. The Holy Spirit will guide and protect you. Let all hearts hear His words.

We desire you to store provisions* ---- at least enough for a period of one year. The coming times are very difficult ---- doctors, nurses and medical supplies will be scarce to non existent. We will send those your way whose hearts burn with compassion and love of Jesus. *(Discernment: For those with means and with the intention of sharing with the community). Enough, my child, ---- prepare for there is much to come. I extend my motherly blessing on my faithful ones. Peace, my children.

August 21, 1997 (Mary)

My daughter,

Let our peace fill you with the assurance you require to confidently continue the task we have given you. Do not despair as some messages seem too intense for you to comprehend.

Be patiently persistent in your prayers always seeking our guidance We are here, little one. Our hearts are filled with love and compassion. We seek not to alarm our children but to prepare them. You have not chosen an easy path, my daughter, but the one which leads to eternal life.

All those who are seeking answers will soon find that which will leave no more doubt in their minds and hearts. Pray much for many souls waiver on the fence of decision. They must decide ---- for only one side brings peace.

Trust in My Son's merciful heart!

August 22, 1997 (Mary)

My children,

I draw each of you unto my motherly heart filled with compassion as each of you in your own way has embarked on the journey to holiness.

I come with the reassurance of our presence ---- here and now. Look upon my mountain and see us as we stand before you guiding you in your daily struggles. Our hearts are so full of love for you, oh lambs of My Son.

You are the gift which He has entrusted to me. Let all hearts be opened to experience the power of God. Do not, in your human ways, set limitations upon Him, The Master Planner! There is NO LIMIT, my children, on Him who is above all things ---- the only limitation is that which you have set in your own minds. Trust in Him who will never fail you. If you trust, you will surely believe and willingly with grateful hearts do that for which we have called you. Prepare, my little ones ---- We surround you with our peace!

August 23, 1997 (Mary)

My dear children,

We take great delight in that which you have so willingly undertaken. Our hearts fill with joy as our children gather ---- responding to our call for preparation. We bless you, little ones, for your hearts are open and receptive to our will.

Rejoice, dear children, for the sorrow of our hearts has been turned into hope for many do hear and with your faithful prayers of devotion, we will turn hope into victory.

Thank you, my children. Let the joy of My Son's heart be your reward.

Peace and Love.

August 24, 1997 (Mary)

My dear little ones,

Praise be Jesus my most merciful Son. Thank you, little ones, for allowing us to work through you spreading our messages of hope and love. Never hesitate to allow the Holy Spirit to minister to those seeking the peace and comfort of My Son ---- be open, my children, to His direction as He will lead you if you remain the open vessels of Our hearts overflowing with love ---- the love of Jesus!

I desire you, my dear ones, to heed our messages. Have no fear, my children in these times which approach, but diligently seek obedience to the Divine Will. Hear Us, my children, and help others to hear! Pray much and prepare. I have said the clock is running down ---- and so, my precious ones, it is!

August 25, 1997 (Jesus)

My children,

Thank you for seeking My heart first in all that you do. Yes, I know you often stumble, my children, for the burden of sin is great in your world. Know it is My arms into which you fall ---- My hands which caress your wounds ---- and My heart which feels each pain as you faithfully resolve to finish this race I have placed before you.

I am filled with joy as I watch each stone that is carefully placed in this holy place. Let there be no doubt, My children, We are watching. Let your hearts be opened to feel our presence. Rejoice with us ---- you have not labored in vain. My hands are outstretched this day as I bless you with My love and peace.

August 25, 1997

(Family prayer night at St. Andrews) (Ref. Revelation-ABYSS] (Jesus)

My daughter,

The hour of decision has come. Your world now teeters on the brink of the abyss. All that has been foretold to you is about to be unleashed. Fear not, my little one ---- let all come to My Son Who is the love and purity of life. Let those come who love Him, but do not hinder those who come from fear, for He accepts all who approach Him with pure repentance. Seek holiness, my daughter. All who hear my call must respond.

August 26, 1997 (Mary)

My dear children,

Peace, my precious ones ---- your days are filled with activities ---- your coming and going tending to your daily tasks. Do not, dear children, in these endeavors fail to give My Son His time in your life. There is no greater importance in your life than the quiet moments you share with Jesus!
Oh, little ones, hear Me! How many messages must We give before you realize the urgency of Our requests? Make your peace NOW! TOTAL CONVERSION IS NOT AN OPTION ---- ---- IT IS ESSENTIAL! Be alert and read these signs of the times.

August 27, 1997

This was a verbal message given in front of "The Good Shepherd" mural while praying the Divine Chaplet with Joe and Emily Camaioni.

This personal message pertained to a confirmation Emily desired.

August 28, 1997 (Mary)

My precious children,

Come, my little ones, as I gather the Harvest of My Son's fields. Seek the refuge of Our hearts while there is yet time.

Prepare as you have been asked, but do not lose sight of the most important preparation ---- that of surrendering your will unto His! Your strength to endure lies in Jesus ---- not in the earthly things upon which you have come to rely.

My dear ones, your understanding of coming events has many limitations. You must completely rely on trust and the faith which has taken root in your hearts. Do make ready little lambs for soon you will be called into a greater service of My Son ---- the battle of good and evil. Draw strength upon Him who is the source of all strength. Come and adore Him while He may yet be found. Seek the cleansing of your souls that you in turn will find a greater degree of holiness.

Many will not endure that which approaches ---- a great and final act of love and mercy from Jesus. His mercy is now like the hour glass ---- slowly sifting into the final countdown.

Pray and prepare, oh precious ones, for life as you now know it reaches its final climax. Trust, little ones, with the childlike trust Jesus desires.

He holds you in the palm of His holy and mighty hands ---- Go about your life with the reassurance of Our love and protection. Peace, my children.

August 29, 1997 (Mary)

My dear children,

Praise be Jesus who in His love and mercy has endowed each of you with His weapons of defense against the arrows of the enemy. My dear littler ones, Jesus awaits you in the Blessed Sacrament ---- He is the living miracle for all to see and adore each day ---- draw from Him, The River of Strength, that portion of which you require to sustain you each day. As His river of life flows into you, so must you become fountains of Him who has created you.

I desire, My precious ones, you allow Me to help mold you into these fountains that all may see the living Jesus in you.

Let these messages be a wake up call to all who will hear. So many are indifferent, my children. They have become hardened by this world's material offerings, choosing only to select the wide pathway of destruction ---- -eternal destruction!

Carry the light of Jesus that you may boldly follow Him along the very narrow path to holiness. For you, oh little ones, the call to holiness must penetrate every inch of your being ---- as the sponge quickly absorbs the water ---- so must you absorb all that is goodness and light ---- My Son who is the source of all goodness.

Peace, my children ---- know that you are called by name. Listen as you are summoned into duty ---- It is the gentle whisper of Jesus who calls. Open wide the doors of your hearts for He enters!

August 30, 1997

(Ref. Revelation-THE FOUR HORSEMEN) (Mary)

My daughter,

We enter into your open heart bringing Our peace and strength to prepare you for those who come seeking the realization that God exists. My sons *(priests)* must hear Our call ---- the battle for souls grows more intense as each must now decide to follow My Son or the persuasions of your world's New World Order.

My child, darkness must come before the new day dawns. This is not a time for the faint of heart! Take courage, oh little messenger ---- you will need to endure much. Prepare for My little remnant ---- My faithful ones. Draw strength from one another as We draw each of you unto our hearts.

Our angels have been dispatched to take charge over you. Know, my little ones, it is Jesus who controls your final destiny ---- keep focused on Him ---- He is the shield which guards your souls. Rally behind Him who goes before you . The Mighty One whose victory approaches. Trust, my child. seek always a state of grace ---- grace which leads to holiness. Soon you will rejoice with Him whose mercy has allowed the gates of heaven to open to receive those who have been called.

The four horsemen gather. Pray much, oh little ones. Evil cannot exist where prayer prevails!

August 31, 1997

(Message given at small shrine on hill for visiting guests including Frank and Gloria Costello , families and friends) (Mary)

My precious children,

As you have sought me this day so I your Mother come. Receive my motherly blessing. Feel my presence in the gentle breeze as I caress you my faithful ones. I gather each of you unto my heart and present your prayers and petitions to My Son.

Peace and Love, my little ones.

September 1, 1997 (Mary)

My dear children,

I desire this day you, my little doves of peace, prepare for the great harvest ahead. Pray much especially for the gifts of the Holy Spirit which you will need to sustain you in the difficult times which rapidly approach. Draw close to My Son seeking His mercy. Desire Him with your whole heart and let His love fill every fiber of your being.

My dear ones, love such as His must truly be the desire of your heart for such a love will require much sacrifice. Without this love, you cannot exist for God is Love. You are created in the image of Divine Love and must, in accordance, reflect this love for your Creator.

Let all fear and doubt flee from your hearts as we are always here to assist you. Continue to trust as your faith will deepen each day.

September 1, 1997 *(Family prayer night at St. Andrews) (Jesus)*

My children,

Do not let fear keep you from the embrace of My Most Sacred and Merciful Heart. I am He who comforts you ---- seek Me while there is yet time. I tell you, you are loved, my children. My heart pours forth mercy on all those who will come. Trust in your Jesus of Mercy!

September 2, 1997 (Mary)

My children,

Today I solemnly ask each of you to seek the virtue of humility for in becoming humble, my little ones, you possess much strength. In the littleness of your humility, you will see the beauty of life as God intended it to be. Again, I ask you to abandon your will to that of My Divine Son's. Complete abandonment ---- - complete conversion ---- through which many graces will fill the soul and peace as it was intended will at last be yours. Persevere, my precious ones. All must hear and obey my call to return to God while there is yet time. Do not fear, but allow the expectation of that which comes to bring a holy desire of love and devotion to Jesus. I bless you as I gather you under my mantle!

September 3, 1997 (Mary)

My dear children,

Soon the sun will rise upon a new day ---- a new day to praise and glorify God. Take time, my little ones, to thank Him for each new day He allows you to see. Thank Him for this precious gift of life before arising thereby giving Him the first thoughts of your day.

My children, He must come first. You are here to glorify Him above all else. Let all you do ---- let all you say be a hymn of praise to the One Who is above all else. Prepare yourselves each day by examining your conscience. Truly, I say unto you ---- many out of indifference or ignorance do not know How to properly and effectively do this. Learn ---- seek those whose hearts belong to My Son and they will teach you.

You must prepare your souls by being reconciled to your God. Realize, my little ones, this is a great gift which will cultivate the seeds of humility which are so necessary if you are to attain eternal life.

Do not let what time you have left slip by ---- - you are my remnant and must, as such, offer examples to the lost and searching souls. Prepare ---- prepare as never before ---- go quickly gathering the sheaves.

Call upon the angels ---- THEY ARE REAL and watch and guard you daily. They have been assigned to watch and protect you. DO NOT OFFEND THEM WHOM GOD HAS SENT ---- they are a source of powerful protection. Awaken your senses that you may feel their powerful protection. Pray, my Little ones ---- pray and prepare!

September 4, 1997 (Mary)

My dear children ,

I come this day to tell you of my motherly love. My children do not hear the urgency of my call. My messages are not taken to heart, but I out of love will continue to repeat them until they have reached fertile hearts!

Parents in their efforts to correct their children often must repeat their warnings of instructions ---- not out of anger but out of deep love. They wish to spare their children from the unpleasant repercussions of their course of actions which they know will follow as the results of not adhering to the lovingly given warnings. So, I your mother, have repeatedly given you my instructions to prepare. Hear me, my little ones. Some of those who love me have, out of love and faith, received my words and have let them fall upon the fertile grounds of their hearts producing the fruit of which I have asked.

All must hear and respond! THE REPERCUSSIONS OF INDIFFERENCE WILL NOT BE PLEASANT! Act now, my precious ones ---- take that leap of faith and come to me, your mother, whose love is gentle and kind. I will gather each of you, if you so allow, and present you to My Son whose love endures forever. Peace, my precious ones. Accept our gift of peace as its strength will provide graces beyond measure.

September 5, 1997 (Mary)

My children,

We gather each of you unto our hearts which beat for love of you. Know precious ones of the many graces you have received which have allowed the scales to fall from your eyes permitting sight ---- sight to see the beauty of God and that which has been tarnished through neglect and disobedience. That which is of this world will soon fade, but you My faithful ones must not allow your souls to wither and die. Learn to nourish them daily ---- become conscious of that which pleases God ....to obey and do HIS HOLY WILL.

As each day passes you must become more and more prepared ---- learning to solely depend on God. There is nothing you can do my children without surrendering your wills to His. There can be no true peace or love unless you choose to walk in the footsteps of My Son. If you so choose this journey we will walk with you supporting you from either side. Believe my precious ones, for your cross must be carried ---- your walk to Calvary cannot be avoided. If you truly love My Son hear His words ---- pick up your cross and follow Him. Do not waste time ---- there is little left my children. Please be filled with peace knowing you journey home from whence you came.

September 6, 1997 (Mary)

My precious remnant,

You my little ones are the threads being woven into the canvass of life. Though you do not know the pattern your life has chosen, you faithfully allow yourselves to be the weaver's thread. Blessed are you whose trust is unshakeable. Your reliance on My Son has allowed Him in His Divinity to weave your child like faith into a beautiful garment of love and protection which He uses to gather his children.

The mercy of My Beloved Son has provided many graces which He has allowed, Me, your Mother, to dispense. Praise Him ---- love Him ---- and obey His commandments.

My children, the time of many trials and persecutions comes more quickly than you are able to comprehend! Seek the gifts of My Son's graces. This is the food --- the nourishment of your eternal survival. Live the messages as We bring you hope , not despair! Peace my precious ones.

September 7, 1997 (Mary)

My dear children,

Precious be The Name of Jesus! Joy fills my heart as you prepare to honor Me in such a special lovely way. Thank you my precious ones for your continual devotion to My Son and myself. Receive the gifts we have bestowed upon you with grateful hearts.

You my dear ones, know of the great trials ahead; yet out of true faith you continue on this beautiful journey of life. Thank you, oh precious ones, for the trust, love and devotion you have shown us as you have not shirked from your great responsibility, but have out of faith embraced the trials ahead. You do not have long to wait for soon you will be tested. Prepare oh lambs, trust in God as He awaits your call for mercy. Do not fear ---- He is the father who eagerly awaits the return of the prodigal son. There is no condemnation, only love and forgiveness.

44

He loves you unconditionally ---- still there is much to endure. Be strong and accept with a grateful heart all which comes your way. Prepare ---- prepare my children while time as you now it, permits. We bring you peace and the self assurance that holiness is possible. Fear not but persevere to the journey's end. Be consoled as you are chosen ---- great is the trust we have placed in you, for you are greatly blessed. Peace and love!

September 8, 1997 (Mary)

My dear children,

I bring you the joy of a mother's heart filled with love and compassion for her children. My precious ones, continue to seek My Son's will in all that you do. Keep your thoughts focused on the things of heaven thereby detaching yourselves of worldly desires. Such actions when practiced frequently will become habits ---- good spiritual habits of holiness. You must form good spiritual habits now ---- teach them to others by your example. Especially help the children whose lives are daily torn by the pressures of evil. They unknowingly become pawns in the battle which rages more and more intensely each day. Reach out to them with Christ like love for you belong to My Son and must be His vessels of love and compassion.

My daughter, in all your preparations do not forget the children. The approaching trials will be difficult enough for you --- so much more so for those who are so young. You are My Son's caretakers, the responsibility is great! Pray much that you may prove yourself worthy for the day of justice soon comes. I bless you this day in a special way. Thank you my dear precious children

September 9, 1997 (Mary)

My dear children,

Praise be Jesus. Know my dear ones it is only through the merciful heart of My Son ---- filled with love and compassion for His children --- that enables Me Your Mother ---- to be with you ---- bringing hope to hearts consecrated to His Most Sacred Heart and My Immaculate Heart.

Let all fear and despair be turned into joy for the power of righteousness stands guard over those who trust in the fountain of mercy. Come little lambs and refresh yourselves while time permits. Seek our sons whom we have sent for the time of preparation draws ever so close. Be cleansed of all impurities through the beautiful gift of reconciliation. Rid yourselves of the burdens of sin ---- the disease of your souls which proves fatal if left unattended.

Act now, my children, as your world is changing more rapidly than you can possibly imagine. I continuously ask you to prepare ---- first and foremost spiritually. Ask My Son for a precious drop of His Holy Blood to cover you each

45

day that the fruits of your labor will produce a great harvest of souls for Jesus.

Thank you for heeding my calls for preparation. Plant that little mustard seed of faith ---- nurture it and it will grow. Many will come ---- embrace them with the love of Jesus --- for you, as you have so chosen, are the vessels which carry the pure light and love of Jesus! Do not look back ---- but in your desire for holiness accept with grateful hearts the trials and sufferings of this world. Their fragrance rises before the throne of Jesus touching His heart with mercy for His beloved children.

We bless you, oh little ones, with our love and peace!

September 10, 1997 (Mary)

My daughter,

Take my hand which I have extended to you for the journey ahead is long and difficult and you, my child, have much to learn. Many will come to support your efforts. Be patient, my gentle daughter, ---- let your love continue to flourish and you will become stronger. Others now will draw from that strength which we have given you. Be filled with our love as we will make our presence felt in this holy place. Prepare little one ---- pray and prepare. Draw those close to you whom we have entrusted in your care that they too will see and feel the presence of His love and peace. Do not delay, my daughter. Continue to obey our call ---- make ready as you have been instructed.

Peace, my child!

September 11, 1997 (Mary)

My dear children,

You, my children, are living in the final days of decision. My presence here has been allowed as a precious gift which one may accept or reject. I ask that you discern this time of grace ---- recognize it for what it is ---- a great gift of love and mercy from My Son.

We desire, my children, your total conversion that you may experience Our peace deep within your souls. Others must truly see this great grace to change their hardened hearts of stone into the potter's clay. Allow Jesus to give you new hearts which He will mold into earthen vessels filled with His love. We desire your happiness ---- true happiness. Accept the gifts we offer out of gratitude for great is the love and mercy of Jesus.

Do not waiver from your desire for holiness as you, my children, know a great purification must come. Embrace your trials and sufferings as each will be a grace raising you to a greater degree of holiness. Let love always be your guide. True love ---- true peace through Jesus. I am here to present you to My Son. Fear not, oh little ones, as this chapter of life draws to an end.

Pray and prepare.

September 12, 1997 (Mary)

My dear children,

I call you to the refuge of My Immaculate Heart where you will find peace and repose for your soul.

Many of my children needlessly suffer because the world of materialism has engulfed their hearts and blurred their vision. They no longer see the beauty in the simplicity of life which God created. I desire, my little ones, your hearts ---- those pure hearts which yearn for My Son.

There is much sickness in your world for people seldom seek The great physician, Jesus, who is the healer of all life's afflictions. Allow Him, my dear ones, to make you well. He eagerly awaits the unburdening of your souls that He might refresh you with living water.

Come quickly, little ones, refresh yourselves ---- prepare! Hear the urgency of our messages and do not become complacent, but tirelessly seek to bring souls to Jesus. Our hearts are filled with pain for many of our children are falling into the pit of destruction. Ease our pain, oh faithful ones; apply the ointment of your love to our hearts ---- pray ---- for the great day of justice comes. How many will My Son find ready?

September 13, 1997 (Mary)

My dear children,

There are so many souls who can be turned by a simple prayer from your heart for prayer from the heart has much power. See how the Holy Spirit works when you allow Him access into your hearts. Be open to Him. You live in a time of miracles ---- a great movement of the Holy Spirit. Allow yourselves to become vessels into which His many gifts may be poured for you are our instruments of peace ---- Our prayer warriors being sent into battle. It is my rosary, when prayed with great love that has the power to defeat the enemy.

Continue to gather in prayer while you yet can as these times may soon be but precious memories to you. Strengthen yourself for soon you must rely only upon the spiritual food you have been feed. Pray, my children, as never before ---- your world has reached its crisis. Always seek My Son ---- His love ---- His mercy. Do not fear, my precious ones, we are always with you. Call upon us with pure hearts and we will make ourselves known to you. Peace, my children. I bless you with my love and peace!

September 14, 1997 (Mary)

My dear children,

You have but to look about you and see the change and moral decay of your world. My precious ones, Jesus is your only hope ---- the only hope to save a world so bent on self destruction. Look into the faces of those whom you meet. Do you see peace ---- My son's peace? I think not, my dear ones.

There is such an intensity to get through life that it is over before my children realize what has happened. Take time each day to spend with My Son. He always has time for you ---- it is you who do not ---- will not ---- fit Him into your schedule of life.

Know my little ones, from Him whom life came so to Him will all life return. Prepare, dear children ---- make the peace of Jesus of the utmost importance in your life. You must strive for holiness. Take the lives of the Saints who through their human sufferings found peace ---- the treasure of life which they presented to My Son with hearts full of love and gratitude. I desire, my precious ones, you take this precious gift of life with all its stains and imperfections and offer it unconditionally to My Son who will weave it into the tapestry of eternal life.

My children, my stay here grows short. I have come as the loving mother to encourage you that you may in turn encourage others. The darkness soon comes and you, lambs of My Son's, must be prepared. Increase your prayers with great intensity. So many souls have become smothered by the weeds of the fields ---- you are the gardeners who must lovingly pick the delicate souls from the fields which I your mother, will gather and present to My Son. Hurry, children. Please hurry. Peace!

September 15, 1997 (Mary)

My children,

Praise be Jesus the Lord and giver of life. My dear ones, I desire the complete conversion of your hearts to that of My Divine Son so that true peace will engulf you as you journey through the obstacles of this world.

Pray, my children! You must fortify yourself with prayer to endure all that now approaches. Many out of ignorance foolishly say they will amend their lives when

48

they see the approaching danger. I solemnly tell you the danger is real and present. You have but to open your eyes to the evils of your society ---- We cannot condone such behavior. The justice of My Son soon will cleanse the world of its decay, and all hearts will know of His love and mercy.

Persevere, my precious ones, for yet awhile longer. Continue to make preparations as you have been instructed. Every moment counts for there is still much work to do and so little time.

 Peace, my children!

September 16, 1997 (Mary)

My dear children,

I bless you this day with My Motherly Blessing of peace and love. I am the Mother of Mercy ---- the Mother of your Jesus of Mercy. Hear me, my precious ones, as my words are true and are filled with hope for all who trust and do the will of My Son.

We do not come, oh little ones, to condemn, but to heal ---- to bring strength to the weary and hope to the hopeless. Rejoice, dear children, for we are with you constantly and our strength will provide the power by which you will become vessels of living waters. Heed our words, dear little ones, with your ears, but most importantly with your hearts for it is by the door of your heart that My Son will enter.

Make ready, my children, for soon ---- very soon ---- all which has been prophesied will be fulfilled. The Lord Our God has heard the cries of His martyred children and He, the Just Judge, will avenge the desecration of life. Pray ---- pray from your hearts as you do not comprehend the immensity of that which soon befalls you. Always remember you are loved beyond measure. Let peace fill your hearts.

September 17, 1997 (Mary)

My daughter,

I come to draw you close to our hearts to strengthen your endurance as the trials and afflictions increase. Know the pleasure you have given My Son by offering to Him your afflictions mixed with the love and gratitude of your heart. Make known, my daughter, the great value of the precious suffering souls. As the radiance of the sun breaks through the darkened clouds, so too the radiance of the suffering soul breaks through the darkness of sin. Rest now, my daughter.

 Peace and love!

September 18, 1997 (Mary)

My dear children,

You, my children, have been greatly blessed with an abundance of graces to fortify your souls in this the battle for souls. You have heard our messages ---- Our calls for preparation. You in whom our messages have been implanted must in turn be messengers too. Spread the Good News of Jesus' s love and mercy in a world which has turned its back upon Him who is all goodness and love.

My children ---- seek to live in the Divine Will of My Son. Only by placing Jesus first in your thoughts, words and deeds will you come to the realization of peace and harmony as it was meant to be. I, your mother, weep for those souls who no longer seek to be reconciled with My Son and thus have embarked on the despairingly painful journey into spiritual darkness. You, my precious ones, must be in constant prayer for all the lost sheep of My Son's flock. Gently gather them, encourage them and help lead them to Jesus. I, your mother, will provide all the graces necessary to complete your task. Be diligent in your efforts. There is much work to do and so little time.

Peace and love!

September 19, 1997 (Mary)

My precious children,

Come, my little fragrant flowers, as it is time for you to take your position as the faithful remnant of the church. My Divine Son has placed you in my care so I now gather you under my mantle of love where you will find a safe refuge as the evils of this world ensue around you.

Take courage and rejoice as you have been chosen to be beacons of the Light of Love. I urge you, my precious ones, to seek all the peace and strength which is offered to you through the Mass and Holy Sacraments as these gifts will soon be only a shadow of what they were intended to be. Prepare now ---- you must out of love for Jesus reach out to all His children.

Pray for the gift of humility whereby your life in itself will reflect a desire for true holiness. Allow Me, my children, to walk this path of holiness with you. I am your guide to Jesus where your souls will find eternal peace. You must decide now ---- there is no place for the lukewarm ---- the faint of heart. YOU MUST MAKE YOUR DECISION NOW. I can only guide you and urge you, my precious ones, for by your own free will --- the choice must be yours. Choose wisely,

My children. Know how dearly you are loved ---- Peace.

September 20, 1997 (Mary)

My dear children,

Today I come as the loving mother whose arms are outstretched to embrace you with my message of hope. Draw close to my heart ---- listen as each beat gently fills your soul with peace. Do not let fear of the unknown steal your peace but trust, little lambs, in the mercy of My Son.

I desire, dear children, that you offer each remaining day of life as a precious gift to Jesus which you will wrap in your desire for holiness and tie with the cord of self denial. Seek to ease the sorrow of Him who loves you above all else by turning from the darkness of sin into the light of holy obedience in truth.

His footsteps have long ago been imprinted in the hearts of those who love Him. Accept the cross in life which has been precisely measured for you and follow in His steps upon the path of righteousness. Praise Him as you journey onward and your burden will become light. Praise be Jesus, the Giver of Life!

September 21, 1997 (Mary)

My children,

Know, oh precious children, we are here to lead you through this maze of life's subtle deceptions. Take caution, little ones, lest you be lost for each turn taken away from Jesus draws you closer to the painful separation from Him whose healing love has been poured out upon your hearts to awaken the human desire for holiness.

Dear children, we have continuously called you to prepare both spiritually and physically, for you must sense in your hearts the urgent necessity to comply or be lost. What words must I use to impress upon you the severity of times rapidly approaching? You, as children of God, have accepted the obligations and responsibilities which have been delegated to you. We bless you for accepting with blind trust the obedience we have placed in your heart. Oh faithful prayer warriors --- trust completely and never falter as soon you will be put to the test. There is only a pass or fail grade, my children ---- choose one or the other. Again, this is your choice. We love you, dear ones, and desire no one to be lost. Take courage and draw your strength from Us.

Rejoice, for soon your reward will be that which is implanted in many hearts. Peace, my children!

My children,

You have witnessed the powerful intercession of My Mother who has come to restore peace and confidence in the power of God and His mercy. My children must learn to trust in His timing ---- not in human timing ---- but in Divine Intervention which is always perfect!

Discern and pray, my children, for soon you must choose the direction your life will take. Prepare ---- be filled with eternal grace ---- grace which will strengthen and sustain you in the great trials ahead.

Everything now begins ---- take courage. Seek preparation (spiritual and physical) and strength for that in which you believe will be greatly tested. Trust us, little ones, for stumble though you may, We will catch you and once again set you upright to continue this beautiful but difficult journey.

I bless you for your trust in Me ---- I am your comfort ---- seek Me and you shall find me. Rest in my peace for soon the trumpet will sound ---- listen closely as your name is called. Fear not, my children, for I have gone before you to prepare the way! Come follow Me. I bless you this special day. Rejoice with me whose heart has been filled with joy. My faithful ones, there is much to do and time as known to you, is not on your side.

Peace, my faithful ones.

September 23, 1997 (Mary)

My little ones,

I desire this day to further instruct my children in their prayer life. Many children do not realize the power in prayer and devote very little of this precious time on earth in developing good spiritual habits. My children, you can only become strong by joining yourselves to God through prayer. Pray from your hearts ---- share your inner most thoughts with Him and you will feel the warmth of the Father's love.

Peace ---- your world longs for peace but it has become elusive to many for though they cry for peace their hearts are hard and void of feeling. Allow our love to enter your hearts to soften them and make them beds of warm repose for weary souls.

Oh faithful prayer warriors, pray as never before ---- I need your prayers! I have told you of the difficult times ahead and that they will be unavoidable; yet, still many do not hear the urgency of our calls. Trust, my children, and do as we instruct you. Prepare ---- prepare now!

My messages are falling upon deaf ears and sorrow fills the heart of your mother. I am reaching out to all of my children, but only a few are accepting my invitation to holiness. My faithful ones, help your Mother ---- -too many souls are losing this terrible battle. Remember, life without Jesus is not life, but eternal darkness and suffering. Do not be afraid to reach out to others, but boldly ---- out of love ---- seek to bring others to My Son.

Peace, my children.

September 24, 1997 (Mary)

My daughter,

We bring you our peace that you will grow in faith and obedience. Place your total trust in us as the floodgates are now open and you will be greatly tested. Come, my daughter, let us join your heart to ours that you will feel the intensity of our love for mankind.

Be filled with joy for in your suffering many souls will obtain graces to strengthen them in this their journey through life. Pray much for many will come and you must be strong. Receive our blessing which we bestow upon this special place and upon those who come seeking peace.

September 25, 1997 (Mary)

My dear little ones,

You are called to patiently persist in your efforts of preparation. Wait upon Him in whom you have placed your trust as the angels of the Lord have been dispatched and have taken their positions for this great battle.

My children, you have a great ally in these My Son's defenders of truth. I desire that you use every means of protection We have made available to you ---- call upon the angels, especially your guardian angel, as they will help guide you through the perils of your world. Listen, my children, with childlike faith to our messages. Feel our love and let the light of Jesus shine brightly within you. Make the extra effort, little lambs, to have a ready smile, an open ear and an understanding heart. Many are so in need of compassion. Your world has become self-centered, self-serving and, thus, self-destructive.

Hear my words children. The Harvest has never been more ready. You have been commissioned and sent into the field ---- accept or reject your responsibility as you so choose, dear ones, but know the hour of accountability approaches. Fear not and love much as by your actions you shall draw others to Jesus.

Pray, my children, and I, your Mother, will intercede for you. I bless you in the name of the Father, Son, and Holy Spirit!

September 26, 1997 (Jesus)

My children,

It is in these times of worldly despair that you must seek My Divine Will and desire within your hearts to live a life of charity and love for thy neighbors. This is a time of purification which you have been given as My Mother continuously and lovingly intercedes for you, my wayward children.

Embrace the trials and sufferings of my love, for in these difficult times, which you perceive as physical weaknesses, you are being strengthened ---- strengthened my children and molded into vessels of perfection.

Seek Me in all that you do. You are never alone, but you often fail to rely upon Me and Me alone! Until you freely surrender your human wills to that of divinity, you cannot find peace ---- My peace which I freely give. Take time while there is yet time to draw close to Me. You must realize the appearances of My Mother throughout your world are a great and final grace which I am allowing. Heed her words ---- She remains with you but a short while.

I bless you, my children, as you are the sheep of my pasture ---- no matter how far you stray, I will always seek to draw you back to Me, your Merciful Savior.

September 27, 1997 (Mary)

My dear children,

Let your hearts be filled with peace that you may hear my words as I seek to bring you into the Light of Love, Peace, and Joy of Jesus. Receive all that is good and pure now, my children, for soon oppression will search your world to stifle the flame of hope from your hearts. Join your hearts to ours, dear ones, while that opportunity is still available.

Darkness must come, but it cannot extinguish that light which has been deeply rooted in truth. Grasp that light for by your faith the brightness will shine forth as a beacon of hope to all who seek the reassurance of God's love.

Never doubt nor fear but by sheer steadfastness press forward ---- although you cannot see you must believe. Blessed are you, my precious ones, who though at times misunderstood, will persevere until the end. Make ready ---- the bridal feast approaches. The invitations have been sent. Contemplate with open hearts that which has been revealed to you. Prepare and rejoice, oh chosen ones.

September 28, 1997 (Mary)

My little ones,

Know, my children, of the great grace you are receiving from My Son who in His Divine Love for you has sent Me, His Mother and your mother, to bring His message of hope. Look beyond that which lies on the surface, a false sense of peace, for soon the great deception will be unleashed and many will fall prey to fear and chaos.

We do not bring fear but a loving warning of that which is soon to befall even your country. Only by your prayers can you mitigate the severity of My Son's justice ---- but justice must and will come.

Pray the rosary daily and come under my mantle of love and protection. Bond together in the common unity of prayer for therein lies much power. The power to prevail over all I have predicted! Do not be over zealous, my children, in your anticipation of future events ---- but wisely and without fear or anxiety prepare. By your example of calm perseverance others will respond to My Call. I bless you, my dear ones, ---- pray and prepare.

September 29, 1997 (Mary)

My dear children,

You have been made aware of the great deception which fills the air around you. I call you, my little ones, to filter the truth from deception ---- the good from the evil. Believe in that which has been foretold to you, as you must gather your spiritual strength and prepare for the unveiling of the great apostasy. The curtain opens, little ones, upon the stage of life in which each of you must play a role predestined from the beginning of time.

Hear, my children ---- the music begins ---- each has been assigned their role. The curtain of life goes up. All is in order. Pray and prepare. Remember always ---- you are greatly loved! Walk in this confident assurance of love with pure faith and trust whereby will come Our peace to comfort you as you continue your journey but a short while longer.

Peace and love.

55

September 30, 1997 (Mary)

My dear little ones,

Peace, my children. We desire that all hearts be filled with our peace. Focus on the beauty of My Son's love and mercy.

Do not become distracted by the fleeting moments of worldly pleasures, but seek always the source of true happiness, Jesus!

By His redemptive powers you have been set free ---- free to become holy people of God. The gift of life, my children, must be highly cherished and protected.

Pray from your hearts for the many souls whose lives have been extinguished ---- those whose contribution to life will never be known. I weep, my children, for those who take life so lightly ---- this precious gift from my Son. Know, my children, He is greatly saddened by this grievous offense to life. Pray intensely for an end to this sin of abortion for the consequences of this injustice have greatly stirred the Justice of My Son. He will avenge His Little Ones. Pray ---- the time of justice draws near. Peace, dear children!

October 1, 1997 (Mary)

My dear children,

We bring you our gifts of love and peace to lighten your burdens as your journey through life. Understand, my children, the beauty and importance in accepting the trials and sufferings which come your way as a means to bring souls to the fountain of My Son's Mercy. He is the loving Shepherd who protects His flock from danger sending His angels to guard your every step in your journey through life.

We call you to trust, dear children ---- trust in the God of Mercy and Love. Seek to be obedient in your service to the Lord. You must become strong and deeply rooted in your faith for soon that faith will be put to the test. Your time here is precious. Each day of life presents an opportunity for conversion ---- for spiritual growth. Prepare now and prepare well, for many will come seeking the love and compassion of Jesus. You are His earthen vessels of love ---- reach out and embrace those who are lost and gently lead them to Jesus.

Prepare, my children, as the time of change comes. Persevere ---- do not be anxious, but take each day as it comes ---- one at a time.

Peace, My children!

October 2, 1997 (Mary)

My children,

I encourage each of you to begin your day with prayer thus by feeding your spirit, you will be strengthened to resist the temptations of this world. Arm yourselves well with my rosary as evil plots against you, My faithful ones, seeking to devour your hearts, minds and souls. Remain firm in your resolve to do My Son's Will as I continuously intercede for you. I hear the intentions of the pure hearts ---- those which burn out of love for the misguided souls who have taken the wrong path in the crossroad of life.

Be patient, my children, and endure your trials of purification. The battle intensifies as the evil one's time grows short. Pray as if this were your last day on earth for truly you do not know how quickly the hour approaches.

I gather you under my mantle where you will find shelter in My Immaculate Heart. You are loved, little ones, well beyond your understanding. Peace and Love.

October 3, 1997 (Jesus)

My daughter,

You, as well as others, have received many graces in this special place. I tell you this will be a place of conversion as many who come will receive spiritual and physical healings.

You will find it difficult at first, my daughter, but continue in your trust of Me as you will be strengthened to continue your mission. Be faithful to Me as I search all hearts and know your inner most thoughts. Be filled with My love ---- My peace as I will flood your very soul with graces. I tell you, my child, My presence here will be felt by others and this , in itself, will draw the parched souls to the fountain of My Mercy.

Your responsibility is great. Do not fear, but trust as I will turn your weakness into strength. Pray for all souls as My Heart still bleeds for my children, my lost sheep. Tell them I will never give up; I give them until the final moment of their life to turn to me.

Soon I will call my children. I have extended every mercy to them. I have given My life for them and I have sent My Mother as a final grace to gather My lost lambs. Hear her as she lovingly draws you under her mantle guiding all to My Sacred Heart. Time is of the essence ---- listen well. Come while the door of My Mercy is still open.

October 4, 1997 (Mary)

My dear children,

Many hear my words but they have become words without meaning. My messages echo throughout your world and seldom are they heeded.

I have called you to pray and fast ---- to make sacrifices and to be reconciled that you may learn from me, but still, my children, peace eludes you. What do you wish of Me, your Mother ---- that I would manifest myself before you? What then, my wayward ones. You would gradually become indifferent and slip back into old habits ignoring your mother's warning and her love.

Through my tears, I gaze into your human hearts - those with whom to intimately share My Son's love. There are so few hearts willing to abandon themselves to self and thus my search continues.

I urge you, my children, to allow your hearts to become fertile ---- the fertile ground into which My Son's words fall and grow. You are vital links in this chain of life. As each link is joined, its strength increases.

My faithful ones, let the love of Jesus be the solder which when applied to the links increases the strength of the chain. Praise Him, honor Him and love Him who is all you will need to safely reach your journeys end.

Trust Him, Oh dear children, as His love surpasses all understanding. Rest in our peace!

October 5, 1997 (Mary)

My dear children,

I come as your loving mother bringing peace and the reassurance of God's love. My heart is heavy, little ones, and my eyes are still filled with tears for the hardened souls whose eternal destiny hangs in the balance.

Let all who seek the guidance of My Son's Divine Will and those into whose hearts our messages have rooted become disciples of our peace and love. You are chosen ---- the hour of decision is here and now. You are called into this final battle for souls. Prepare and find comfort in the mercy of Jesus who has provided for your heavenly protection.

I tell you this day ---- those who seek with a pure childlike heart shall find and those whose ears are open to the gentle whispers of hope shall hear.

Keep blessed candles and holy water close at hand ---- continue to wear blessed medals ---- your crucifixes and scapulars for these are powerful weapons which repel the enemy. Pray, My children, pray and sacrifice for many face an eternity of darkness. I need your prayers. Hear me ---- hear and understand, my call is urgent! Peace and love, dear ones.

October 6, 1997 (Jesus)

My children,

Listen well, my people, and comprehend the seriousness of your sins. Your world is corrupt and without conscience. My peace and love which I have freely given as a source of healing have been greatly neglected and ignored.

What then, my people, must I do to draw you back to repentance. If I bring darkness ---- will you see the light! If I remove the air ---- from where will the breath of life appear. You do not challenge me, my children, but impose undo burdens upon yourselves.

I am He who comforts you. I will wipe away all tears and give your souls peaceful tranquility. It is but a matter of choice ---- your choice.

The signs of the times grow more and more vivid, but many are blinded by self worth and indulgence of pride. Rid yourself of pride and seek humility. I came into your world as Savior, Yet humble God/Man, so you, my sheep, must choose to leave this world as humble men and women who seek only the perfection of My Divinity within your souls.

I give you but awhile longer to choose. Hear Me as I call your name ---- as, I your Jesus, will hear you in your final hour for mercy. You are my people whom I love.

Receive my blessing this day ---- reach out to Me and I will lift you from the depths of despair.

October 7, 1997 (Mary)

My daughter,

Be at peace, my child, for in surrendering your will to Jesus you have become one with Him and His desires are now the desires of your heart. Continue to live in the light of My Son as others will see the purity of your intentions and be drawn to Him through the gifts you have been given.

Your life is now an open book. Be prepared as many will read its contents searching for answers while others will scrutinize looking for error and deception. Be strong and endure that which has been permitted to come your way.

We are here to comfort and guide you. In your imperfections you will falter, but rest assured you will be given the graces necessary to continue. Words do not come easy for you, my daughter, but know that by your example, others will seek Him who dwells with in you, Jesus. Let His light shine brightly as darkness comes and many are unprepared.

October 8, 1997 (Mary)

My dear children,

I desire, my precious ones, that each of you come to the realization that prayer is true communion with God. Prayer is warmth of love and understanding ---- an abode where the heart finds peace. In finding peace you find strength and in strength - courage to persevere in your quest for truth.

As you earnestly strive to become pure of heart, you will leave the desires of this world and thus enter into the realm of holiness.

We stand close to you, dear children, ready to assist in all your needs. You have but to make the effort ---- desire with your heart ---- and graces will flow to sustain and encourage you. Trust, little ones and allow your faith to grow as I, your Mother, intercede for you carrying your heart felt petitions before the Lord. Pray and encourage each other always.

Peace, My children!

October 9, 1997 (Mary)

My daughter,

I desire this be a place of comfort and compassion for all my children who will come seeking peace of mind, heart and soul. Those of great faith will come as well as my little ones whose physical need to see has out weighed their spiritual sense to feel (Our presence).

The Harvest has begun, my daughter ---- pray for the grace to help gather these lost souls for whom I weep. Each is a priceless gift which I wish to bring to the throne of My Son. Pray as you are sent into the fields bathed in Christ's love and clothed with humility. You are our little beacon of light. Shine brightly as many who are in darkness will witness the light of God's love through His faithful ones. Take courage for the angels too, are here to do our bidding. Always seek their assistance as they await your instructions. Do not be afraid, but take that leap of faith for by the power of My Son, you will accomplish much. Do not be anxious, but rest in the calm assurance of our love as we will never leave you nor forsake you. Peace, My daughter ---- you are never alone!

October 10, 1997 (Mary)

My dear children,

I invite you this day to become apostles of joy. As the angels announced the Joy that was brought into your world many years ago, so I now entreat you to become My Son's joy-filled ambassadors of hope and love.

I have asked many times for you to hear the <u>urgency in My call</u> ---- to prepare spiritually and physically ---- yet, my little ones, I do not wish you to ignore the gentle melody of hope which I continuously weave into my messages. Listen with hearts of joy and anticipation for beyond the trials a new day dawns ---- a new song to be sung!

Praise Jesus, my children, for great is His love and mercy. As the angels sing their songs of praise to Jesus, I ask you to live your life as a song that one day you will sing before the Lord. I bless and intercede for you this day that your song will fall sweetly upon His ears.

Peace, little ones.

October 11, 1997 (Mary)

My dear children,

Through the infinite mercy of My Son, I have been allowed to guide you onto the path of humility which leads to a greater understanding of the Divine Will. This, my children, is essential as you strive for a greater degree of holiness in your lives. As you draw closer to purity of heart and mind know you are truly becoming one with your Creator and thus this world will hold no attachments for you. This is spiritual joy and fulfillment which the soul seeks in its efforts to return to Him, the Lord and Giver of Life.

Your journey will become increasingly difficult as the underlying deceptions are now filtering into the Church. Know your true faith ---- read and learn ---- teach one another and align yourselves with the true Magisterium of the Church. Prepare ---- ---- pray and prepare. There is so much to do, dear ones. Many battles lie ahead and you, My faithful remnant have much responsibility.

Peace and love.

October 12, 1997 (Marry)

My dear children,

You into whose hearts my words have found rest are urged to be tireless warriors in the now intense battle for souls.

As you draw closer to God's pure love, you will gradually comprehend that without this love nothing can exist ---- for out of love you were created and out of love, Divine Love, you are called in turn to love. Only by loving with pure hearts can the evils which have taken control of so many souls be thwarted.

You are given the graces to take charge of your own lives, but you must choose to do so. You must willingly seek humility for in your humility you will draw closer to God. He deeply loves the humble souls who allow Him to be first in their lives. Place God first always, my little ones, and your journey will lead to holiness.

Love and peace, my children!

October 13, 1997 (Mary)

My dear children,

Peace and love I extend to you this day as I gather you under My Mantel . You, my little remnant of prayer warriors, do not fully comprehend the great responsibility that comes as you choose to be obedient to My Son's will. This obedience must be in your actions as well as in your prayer life. The time of accountability rapidly approaches ---- you, my little ones, must account not only for what you have done ---- but also for what was left undone.

Those hearts which have willingly received and nurtured my messages are themselves now messengers. I solemnly tell you ---- greater is the responsibility of one who has heard then one who has not heard. My messages which have fallen upon the rocky soil of unreceptive hearts will bear no fruit ---- but your hearts, my precious ones, have been prepared as the fertile fields of evangelization and thus must bear much fruit.

My children, so little time remains. Seek mercy while mercy is still offered. The time soon comes when this great gift will elude you. Pray with sincere hearts and I will intercede for you.

Peace and love, my little ones.

October 14, 1997 (Jesus)

My children,

You are well advised to take caution in discerning the events of your time. Be prayerful people as many false prophets will come trying to deceive you ---- to steal your peace. Do not be misled, but be well rooted in My Word. I have not changed nor has My Word which was given to you many centuries ago. Diligently search My Holy Scriptures for therein lies the answers you seek ---- the great mystery of life is unveiled . Many do not seek and thus remain blinded ---- My intended tranquility of life has been replaced by chaos and anxiety.

My Mother is the tireless crusader of lost souls. She lovingly pleads for you, my lost sheep, as she gently gathers each of you under Her mantle of love guarding and guiding you to the peace of My Heart. Listen well to Her call ---- prepare your hearts ---- do not persist in your unbelief, but faithfully test that which is revealed to you and believe!

I caution you, my children, be prepared. The hour soon comes when all will know of My existence. Will I find you eagerly awaiting your loving Savior? The entrapments of worldly desires have blocked your vision and thus you must diligently pray for the scales to fall from your eyes ---- open your hearts as I pour forth My love and mercy upon all who will receive Me.

You are my beloved children ---- come as my arms are outstretched to draw you close to My Heart. I bless you with My peace as I ask you to walk in the confident assurance of My Love.

October 15, 1997 (Mary)

My dear children,

You are called to a simple way of life ---- one not cluttered by worldly desires or ambition. Jesus must be first and foremost in your lives, but in your human weakness your priorities have become out of order. You struggle to fit so many needless things into your daily life and thus anxiety fills your soul robbing you of your peace.

Jesus is your life, little ones. Do not deepen His sorrow by offering Him only those few left over moments ---- the crumbs of your day. Be vibrant in your faith diligently seeking to grow wiser and stronger each day. You must prepare now ---- too many are still lukewarm ---- lacking total commitment to My Son. Time is too precious to waste ---- hear the urgency of your Mother's call for soon My voice will be silent. Peace, my dear children.

My dear children,

Let your hearts be filled with praise and your voices echo the songs of the angels as you comprehend the true existence of God. As I spoke my words to the children of Medjugorje , "I came to tell you that God exists", so I tell you, my little ones, God is present within each heart that has prepared Him room.

So many of my children's hearts are heavily burdened ---- buried under layers of doubt and distrust. I am here to lift your burdens and restore your peace. I bring you the comfort of our love and the reassurance that you are greatly blessed.

I ask you, my dear ones, to outstretch your arms and embrace the trials and sufferings which you have been given. Your sorrows will be turned into joy when you realize the great value of these gifts of purification which you are asked to bear in silent gratitude.

This life's journey soon draws to a close. Let my tears wipe away your fears and take hold of My hand as Jesus awaits your return home. Peace and love.

October 17, 1997 (Mary)

My dear children,

I call you my children as indeed you are the precious gifts placed into my loving hands by My Divine Son. Come to me, little ones ---- speak to me ---- I am here and desire that intimate relationship a mother has with her children. Tell me of your joys that I may smile with you as together we will share in the beauty of God's goodness. Come to me with your problems and heartaches and together we will find solutions to problems and my gentle spirit will soothe your heartache.

Learn my children, to let go of that over which you have no control. Listen closely to the whisper of love and hope which we instill in your soul as it cries out in times of despair. We are not worlds apart, little ones, but only a touch away . Trust and believe, my children, as graces are being poured out as never before ---- open your hearts and receive your allotted share. No one is turned away in this time of great mercy.

I urge you to realize the greatness of this time of mercy. Pray, pray, pray. The great time of darkness is eminent, but the light of faith and hope will not be diminished from the hearts of my faithful remnant.

Peace and love, my children.

October 18, 1997 (Mary)

My dear children,

I invite you this day to live my messages. You have been called into the service of My Son's army of prayerful warriors of love. My children, draw close to me and follow my example always seeking to bring others to Jesus. You must be patiently persistent in your desire for holiness as each day presents its own page of life written with joy and disappointments. Pray, my children, to love others as Jesus loves you.

The more Christ- like you become on this your journey through life, the more you will love. It is in this love you will learn to detest sin in all its horror and disfigurement. Turn away from your old evil nature as now you are new creatures in Christ Jesus. Others will see the light of My Son shining forth from you and will be drawn onto the path of righteousness by the example of your love. Live your faith ---- you must not be hearers only, but also doers.

Pray for a deeper understanding of this gift of true love. Love, my children, can change many hearts and alter the course of their final destiny. Be the simple soul who seeks only to do the will of God as great will be your reward in heaven. Rest in Our love and peace, my children.

October 19, 1997 (Mary)

My dear children,

As My Son has offered His unconditional love to you, I ask you in return to love one another. Where there is un-forgiveness there cannot be true love. Love is not self centered or envious, My little ones, but is pure and total abandonment to self. As you learn to seek humility, your soul is freed from self wants and desires seeking only to uplift and serve others.

I urge you, my precious ones, not to become preoccupied with the cares of this world but focus on the great treasures of Heaven. The obtainment of these treasures is exemplified by the lives of the Saints ---- ordinary souls who chose simplicity of life and won favor with God.

My children, there are many forks in the road of life. You must be well prepared for by your choices, you determine the direction your soul will take. Only one way leads to eternal life. Pray much that you will not be deceived for subtle deception lurks around each corner.

Pray, dear ones, and we will come to your assistance lighting your path to holiness. Rejoice for your journey nears completion. Peace and love.

October 20, 1997 (Mary)

My daughter,

You gaze rests upon the Cross and your heart feels the magnitude of its greatness. Know, my child, as you give thanks for this accomplishment, your work has just begun. Now you must gather your strength which My Son has given you and prepare for the great battle ahead.

I am sending My Priest Sons ---- my special sons ---- to this place where they will be blessed and in turn will bless those who come. Ask my sons for their blessings upon this mountain for this is a holy place ---- a place of healing.

I desire, My child, a chaplet of My Son's Divine Mercy be said here each Sunday at 3:00 p.m. This is in preparation for that which soon comes. Join your hearts and voices in prayer and beseech the Mercy of Jesus ---- time passes more swiftly than you think. Much needs to be accomplished ---- many, many souls hunger for My Son. Be an instrument of His love and peace as I gather His beloved souls ---- those who come seeking mercy.

Rest now, my daughter. Peace.

October 21, 1997 (Mary)

My dear children,

All praise and glory to Jesus for He is infinitely kind and merciful. In His mercy there is love and there is justice. Justice comes, my children, as the great time of purification rapidly approaches. Your world has turned its back on the light of My Son's love thus the dark entangling web of sin must run its course.

Pray ---- read and reread my messages for those who seek mercy shall find mercy. You, My children, carry a great responsibility for your hearts are now filled with compassion. I urge you to make sacrifices for those souls who have chosen unwisely and thus face eternal damnation.

We love you, dear children, and bring you comfort for all will be tested. Draw strength from our peace ---- be filled with joy for those who belong to Jesus will be triumphant.

Peace, Our precious ones!

October 22, 1997 (Jesus)

My children,

Know, My children, I am with you always ---- I come to bring you My peace and encouragement for the times ahead are difficult and filled with uncertainties. Rely solely upon Me and I will see to your needs and those pure desires of your heart. I hear your every thought ---- nothing is hidden.

I am sending special priests, My sons whose hearts are quickened with the desire to serve Me. Seek them as you will find a peaceful refuge in these troubled times. The false teachings of this world will cause doubt and will lead many astray. You are forewarned but know My mercy is great and My forgiveness unlimited.

Call upon Me ---- seek Me and search with all your hearts for I am your loving Savior here to draw you to My fountain of mercy while you may yet be refreshed. Let Me fill you with peace and assurance that my love endures forever. Never doubt but trust always. I love you, my children and desire your true happiness. Come to Me while there is yet time. Pray and I will hear and answer you. I bless you this day in my joy and peace.

October 23, 1997 (Mary)

My children,

Let my words take root deep within your hearts ---- nurture them and believe them. The condition of your world brings sadness to my heart and tears to my eyes. I have warned you, my little ones, and urged you to have a complete conversion of heart. Do not delay but react with a positive attitude of love and obedience. Be reconciled to My Son while there is yet time.

Hear me as my message is urgent ---- prepare ---- prepare your hearts. The events which I have predicted are close at hand. Those who have not responded to my words risk languishing in the pit of agony.

Pray for your brothers and sisters who deny the true presence of Jesus. He is your healing Lord who comes to bring peace and love into a world bent on destruction and hate. Make room for Him, little ones, salvation is the precious gift freely offered by My Son. Rejection of this divine gift brings only eternal heartache.

You do not have long to wait, my children, the angel of the Lord is separating the sheep from the goats. Pray as I will pray and intercede for you. Urgency pounds on the door of your hearts.

Peace and Love.

My children,

I have woven the threads of My promises into the hearts of My people. In their weakness, I have instilled strength to combat the evils of this world. Blessed are my children who hear My word and practice humility with justice for their lives are pleasing to Me. They bear their own cross yet stoop to help carry the cross of their neighbors. This is love as it was meant to be ---- unselfish and enduring.

Hear the words of My mother who is Queen yet loving and obedient. She is the precious gift given to you in these difficult times. Do not offend her! She weeps for those who will not heed her words and implores my mercy upon all my children. Listen closely to her words ---- learn from her ---- for the path upon which she leads you is narrow and the journey difficult, but her presence will reassure you of the great reward ahead. Do not lose hope, my people. I await your return.

October 25, 1997 (Mary)

My dear children,

I repeat and repeat my words of warning to you and so I shall until the reality of their meaning has awakened your soul. My children, do not take each day for granted ---- for though you live and breathe busily tending to each day's tasks know this in itself is a gift from God. Cherish each moment ---- all too soon changes will occur affecting your lives to a major degree. Embrace this great time of grace for My Son pours forth His mercy upon you. You must prepare as you, in turn, are being prepared. There is still much required of you. Bond together in the common unity of prayer as you are to become fortresses of love and hope. Despair will fill your air, fear and anxiety will abound, but those who trust in Jesus will rest in the tranquility of Our hearts.

Draw close to Jesus ---- prepare and be reconciled. Seek always to be in a state of grace. Guard your thoughts and your tongues for both lash out against your neighbor ---- one silently, the other with the viciousness of wild animals. Pray for your guardian angels to guard your thoughts and words. Let only purity and love dwell within you. Pray ---- pray from your hearts. We are here, my children . Hold tightly to your faith as the storm clouds gather.

Know you are loved. Peace, little ones.

October 26, 1997 (Mary)

My dear children,

68

Know each day in this beautiful journey of life you draw closer to the beauty of eternal joy and peace. As you rely more and more upon Jesus, life's burdens will become lighter and your spirit will soar higher and higher until you at last have reached the final plateau of holiness.

Do not look back, my children ---- the past will take care of itself, but focus always ahead on Jesus. Look to Him who holds the future ---- the great Architect of life. You are the designs of His Divine Hands ---- His people whom He calls. Listen, my little ones, for all is in order in this great drama of life.

Rarely has an age where sin abounds been given such a time of mercy. Pray for His Divine Mercy upon your families and upon the world for most do not see nor comprehend the magnitude of the judgment which lies ahead. Receive my motherly blessing this day. Peace and love!

October 27, 1997 (Mary)

My dear children,

Praise be Jesus. Thank you, my children, for honoring my request in beseeching the mercy of Jesus. Know your prayers were carried by the angels and laid before the throne of God. These prayers, my children, are most important for as they rise toward heaven. My Son's mercy falls upon the earth as the rain from the clouds. As the rain refreshes the earth so His mercy refreshes the parched soul.

Prepare yourselves, my little ones, as many hearts are now hearing the <u>Urgency of My Call</u>. They will come with a great hunger and thirst for Jesus. I am opening hearts and sending my faithful ones to encourage and assist you. Pray and discern for much will be required of you. The hour is late, my children, and the Harvest is ready. Be filled with joy as you go forth to love and serve My Son........ Peace.

October 28, 1997 (Mary)

My children,

Be at peace, my little ones, as I draw you close to my heart. Let my love calm all fear and fill you with the confident assurance of our love. My children, you cannot imagine the infinite love and power of God who is pouring out His mercy upon his people. He calls you to open your hearts and receive the many gifts He wishes to bestow upon you. It is you, my children, who impose restrictions upon God---- thus limiting your ability to receive grace ---- the amazing grace of which you sing ---- the grace which saves!

Confusion and fear have caused your hearts unnecessary burdens. Trust, dear children , as God is pure love and wishes only that which is best for you. He does

69

not deny your happiness ---- but know, dear ones, true happiness comes in your service to others. Become the humble servants of Jesus as in your humility you will become one with Him who loves you. Peace and love.

October 30, 1997 (Mary)

My dear children,

You, the precious ones who hear and heed my words, are being prepared with heavenly strength and love. That which is revealed to you is given as a sign of hope, not despair. Do not dwell upon the negative for that is time wasted ---- precious time, my children, that is gone forever.

You are called to the awareness of events to come. My messengers throughout the world are proclaiming my words of caution lovingly mixed with encouragement. We bring you Our peace ---- the peace of eternal love and joy. Learn , dear ones, by putting your faith into practice. Embrace your trials and sufferings, knowing the Father has out of great love for you, allowed each one to carry his cross of purification. Find joy, my children, in all that comes your way, for truly these are treasures which you will cherish and one day lay before the throne of God. Rejoice, My dear ones. Peace!

November 1, 1997 (Mary)

My dear children,

We are with you to instill peace in your hearts and minds. Without our peace, you will become lost and easily be misled as time swiftly reaches the final hour of decision.

My children, do not allow the concerns of this world to infiltrate the peace and tranquility of the futile fields of your soul. Realize, My dear ones, our messages must be heard even if it is in the silence of your hearts. Be warned and cautious yet faithfully resolve to persevere until the end. All that is revealed must and will take place. It is you, my precious children, who will choose how to disseminate the information given. Pray much and ask for the Holy Spirit to fill your hearts with wisdom whereby knowledge and peace will fill your hearts. Cast away all fear as much remains to be done. Let love be your guide as your journey continues.

We love you, dear children, and bestow grace upon grace to lighten your burdens as you journey forward to holiness.

Peace and love!

My dear children,

We receive such joy from those who come seeking peace ---- a peace into the hearts of whom we pour forth many graces. Bless you my children, who believe with such purity of faith and trust for your walk is that of holiness ---- a walk which must continue no matter how tired you become.

Earthly trials will sap your strength and disappointments will try to block your path, but the way is clearly marked by Jesus. Let your gaze always be upon Him and your hearts open to receive His words for you will never lose your way.

Through all that must come, remain firm in your faith ---- draw close to Our Hearts ---- the hearts that love you, as We are your refuge.

Peace, dear children.

November 3, 1997 (Mary)

My dear children,

You have been blessed many times for Our Words have flowed as the rivers flow into the oceans ---- one great depth into another. Yet, my children, you choose only to hear the gentle little brook which makes few waves as it takes its natural course of direction.

Those who hear Our Words must hear the underlying message ---- not pick and choose that which is meaningful but out of context. The depth of our messages is as vast as the ocean itself ---- comprehend Our Words for there is great urgency and little time. Our Words will test your comprehension and at times your very imagination ---- but, my children, Our Words are not mere words but grave cautions for evil abounds seeking your very soul. Hear and believe, little ones, and know, our faithful ones, you remain close to Our Hearts. Reach out, dear ones, to those who have been led astray for the heart of Jesus eagerly awaits their change of heart. In His Divine Mercy He reaches out to his people with an incomprehensible love so great He will snatch souls from the brink of the fires of hell itself if they but call on Him. Reflect, my children, on these words.

Love and Peace!

November 4, 1997 (Mary)

My daughter,

71

I caution you, my daughter, as a mother whose heart is full of love for her child and seeks to guard and protect the one she loves. Your time has come; you will be attacked as never before but let your heart not be troubled for you are well protected.

Remain silent in your times of trial ---- draw strength from Him whose arms are outstretched drawing you close to His heart. What is there to fear, my child, when one truly loves God? You must only seek to be one with Him ---- a bond that this world cannot break.

I have much to tell you, my daughter ---- not all of which you will write. Listen and discern, my child, as I your Mother now speak to your heart. My messages will gradually cease for that is as it must be. I have been allotted much time to be with my messengers. Now you must continue with even more intensity the responsibility I have entrusted to you. Bravely face the darkness for Jesus, the Light of Hope, stands ready to receive His Children. Do not be sad for I am still with you awhile longer.

I bless you, my daughter, as you in turn must carry Our blessing to others. Rejoice for a new day of hope lies just ahead. Peace!

November 5, 1997 (Mary)

My children,

My motherly peace I bring to you this day and ask you, My precious ones, to be disciples of peace and love. Join your hearts to Ours as in your daily lives you will touch many hurting souls ---- souls seeking the peace and love of Jesus.

So many waste this precious gift of life by placing time with Jesus far from their hearts and thus reject or do not recognize the gifts He makes available to each and every soul. Love Him who loves you ---- seek to abide with Him while there is yet time. Become the pure of heart into which His Divine Love will flow.

My children, He is extending every mercy ---- I urge you as the tears fall from my eyes to fall to your knees in gratitude for you as yet do not understand the magnitude of this great gift. Pray, my children ---- pray for this truly is a great time of mercy.

Peace and love.

November 6, 1997 (Mary)

My dear children,

I have chosen simple but meaningful words to relay my messages to you. In this means of communication hearts and ears long since closed to the real world of spirituality will be opened to respond more fully to the precious gifts sent by heaven ---- by My Son who reaches out to each of you with gentle compassion. He holds each soul with such tenderness that even the loving heart of a mother could not acquire the depth of His Divine Love

You have strayed so far, my precious ones, yet still His love and forgiveness remain unchanged. You are His and His you will remain until you choose otherwise. All is a matter of choice. There is heaven and yes, there is hell. So many believe they will have the opportunity to change before the Great Judgment ---- this is so foolish, my little ones, for you do not know when you will be called. Prepare now ---- much lies ahead and many will not be ready. Pray continuously for all life should be a prayer of thanksgiving . Let pure love be the intention of your heart for God in His greatness will honor such intentions. Pray more earnestly than ever, my children, for the evil of his world is deceptive and longs to prey on unsuspecting souls. Peace and love!

November 7, 1997 (Mary)

My dear children,

You come with so many questions ---- - questions that in the perfect timing of God will be answered. You wish Me to say "Yes" or "No" ---- "right " or "left", but I tell you it is your faith in the goodness and power of God that illuminates the course of your soul and thus the direction your life will take. Allow your hearts and minds to be opened to His love for it is in His perfect love that true knowledge and tranquility of Heart abide.

Do not dwell upon the coming events for evil will seek to destroy your peace. Times will be difficult, my dear ones, and others will be asked to suffer more than their neighbors, but it is all in God's Divine plan. Be a participant in life ---- not a specter (*a phantom / ghost*) ---- for all too soon you will realize that which you left unaccomplished. You cannot undo past mistakes but forgiveness is there for the asking ---- as great is the Mercy of Jesus.

Continue in developing a stronger prayer life for this is the true food upon which you will feed. Peace and love!

November 8, 1997 (Mary)

My dear children,

I desire to fill your hearts with true peace and tranquility, but you, my dear ones, must choose to allow Me to help you. True peace is achieved by abandonment to oneself with total dependence on God.

Trials and disappointments are inevitable in a world filled with sin, but one must overcome the seemingly insurmountable tasks at hand by placing all trust in God. He is the source of strength from which you will draw the courage to continue when darkness has covered your world ---- for darkness indeed comes ---- yet beyond the darkness lies such beauty and hope which springs eternal.

Listen well to my words and let them find meaning in your soul. Pray and contemplate for I have revealed much to you ---- you need but to open the door of your heart as the Lord of Love and Truth prepares to enter bringing eternal peace.

You are loved, oh little ones!

November 9, 1997 (Mary)

My dear children,

May peace and joy fill each heart as you gather to glorify My Son. I gather you this day and will present each one of you, one by one, as a precious gift to My Son who stands ready with His open heart to receive your prayers. Prepare, my children, for this is only the beginning of that which has be predestined.

You are chosen as vital instruments of peace. Each in his own way has become a beautiful thread being woven into the tapestry of life. This tapestry of which I have previously spoken is like the puzzle which cannot be solved without each individual piece ---- and so each of you, my precious ones, are the threads necessary to complete the beautiful design of life

` My dear ones. I feel the sadness and pain as well as the joy in each heart. Know I hold your heart close to mine ---- and My Son to whom my heart is joined will grant the desires of those hearts who obediently seek His Divine Will.

We love you, little ones, and bless you with our peace.

November 10, 1997 (Mary)

My dear children,

Let love fill your hearts as the joy which fills our hearts --- languishes in peace and contentment of our prayer filled remnant. Thank you, my precious ones, for hearing the requests of your mother which have rooted deeply within your souls. See, My children, how you are drawn closer together in a loving bond of peace --- peace that knows no distinction of race or wealth ---- only love ---- pure love.

Continue, my dear ones to draw closer to perfection in holiness as your souls seeks only oneness with God. Your strength will become greater as pureness of unity with your Creator becomes more and more important and life's trials and uncertainties gradually fade into the background canvass, upon which the Divine Painter has brushed the strokes of creativity onto the final portrait of your life.

Rejoice for beauty and joy surround you ---- look about you, my children, and comprehend the beauty of life. Know, my children, that suffering beautifies and purifies the soul which seeks this intangible unity with God.

Peace and joy, my precious ones!

November 11, 1997 (Mary)

My dear children,

I desire your firm perseverance in prayer. You must cast aside worldly desires and immerse yourself in oneness with My Divine Son ---- for all power to defeat the approaching evil lies within His holy Hands. As you draw closer and closer to our hearts you leave yourselves open to the scrutiny of your world permeated with the stench of sin. Know it is the Precious Blood of Jesus which is your armor against that which subtly encroaches upon your desire for peace and holiness.

Come to His fountain of mercy and forgiveness. My children, do not be afraid, for in your fear pride emerges keeping you from the healing presence of Jesus in the sacrament of reconciliation. Know it is to Jesus whom you speak ---- He who knows everything about you yet patiently awaits for you to recognize within yourself all that decays your soul and leads you astray. Seek His Divine Healing, my children, as He longs to draw you back to His heart.

Peace and love.

November 12, 1997 (Mary)

My dear children,

I come with love and the gentleness of peace to reassure your precious faithfulness to the Divine love of My Son. You are called, my little ones, to recognize the power and beauty of the purity of love which We seek to instill in your hearts ---- hearts full of compassion and love for one another.

Never feel abandonment, my children, for we bestow the grace of hope into each heart in which the Holy Spirit dwells. Seek the gift of discernment whereby your hearts will be opened and receptive to the graces which we desire to bestow upon each of you in abundance ---- abundance of which you have yet to comprehend.

Let the seed of faith take root into your hearts as it will be nurtured and grow. Others will be drawn to the beauty of your souls and thus Jesus who lives in your will be glorified. Praise be Jesus the Light of Love. You are the glow of His light --- shine brightly, my dear ones, for many will be led to the light of eternal life.

Peace and love!

November 13, 1997 (Mary)

My dear children,

Know, my children, that the times in which you gather in groups to pray are indeed special for your prayers form a forceful bond against which evil cannot penetrate. Always seek to be prayerful people of God for therein lies your peace.

Many attacks will come your way attempting to steal your peace. My heart is always open, my children. As you sense that which disrupts your peace, lay your head upon my heart where you will find comfort and tranquility as I will whisper the gentle name of Jesus and thus His peace will fill your soul.

I urge you, my children, to seek the peace of which I have long since spoken for darkness quickly comes upon your unsuspecting world. Be at peace for even the darkness cannot extinguish the light of hope. Draw close to Our Hearts ---- remain faithful, dear ones, as the Angels of God stand ever ready to defend your soul ---- the soul which seeks the salvation of Jesus. Rest now, as soon your strength will be tested! Peace and love.

November 14, 1997 (Mary)

My dear children,

I come with my heart so full of love for my children ---- all of my children. I am here to set firm your footing on the path to holiness for many have stumbled and lost their way. The desire of my heart is to present each of you to My Son, Jesus, who has commissioned me for just such a mission. We wish no one to perish yet many are unwilling to climb from the depth of self destruction ---- their desire for worldly pleasures blinds them from the light of truth and purity of soul.

I ask each of you to continuously pray for one another ---- binding yourselves to the cord of love, the end of which is firmly bound in heaven. It is our gentle tug of love each one feels as temptation assaults your soul. Hold tightly, my dear ones, as you draw closer and closer to Heaven's door.

Peace and love.

November 16, 1997 (Mary)

My daughter,

I come into each heart which seeks truth ---- truth in love and peace. My Mantle surrounds each of you this day as I gather your prayers and petitions and present them to My Son, whose merciful love has brought you together. You are the sheep My Son has gathered on this mountain ---- His pasture of loving grace.

Open your hearts and receive the blessings He extends this day. Unite yourselves in love for one another as Jesus hears your prayers and loves those whose childlike faith draws them to the fountain of His mercy.

Implore His mercy, my little ones ---- the hour grows late and many still wander in darkness. Be at peace and allow your faith to grow as you are never alone.

Peace and love.

November 17, 1997 (Mary)

My dear children,

You say how quickly time passes by and truly it does. I encourage you to be faithful servants of the Lord while there is yet time. All too soon you will be held accountable for the choices you have made ---- prepare yourselves, my children ---- ask for the gift of discernment especially now for you cannot avoid the pitfalls of life without such grace. Pray, pray, pray. Thank you for your precious gifts of prayer.

Peace and love. *(A personal message followed)*

November 18, 1997 (Mary)

My dear children,

I bring you the peace of My Motherly Heart. I am your safe harbor in the storm of life in which you now find yourselves. Seek the refuge of My Immaculate Heart where there is no fear or anxiety only peace.

Many will be coming as news of this place rapidly expands by word of mouth. My children are hungry ---- feed them the Word of God. Be compassionate and loving for by your actions others too will find Jesus as they see the light of His love shining brightly in you.

Peace and love, my dear ones as I cover you with My Mantle of Protection!

November 19, 1997 (Mary)

My daughter,

Embrace with all the love in your heart the trials and sufferings which come your way --- for you will receive the strength required to complete your journey. You are a link in the chain which must remain strong, for all pieces in the chain are dependent upon one another. Reread my messages, my daughter, when you are being tested and gather strength and encouragement from them. You are only asked to do that which you can ---- no more ---- no less. We are here , dear one, always by your side. Rest, that your health may return to you.   Peace.

November 20, 1997 (Mary)

My dear children,

Truly I tell you the time for decision grows shorter each day. Now more than ever before you must choose to live in harmony with the Will of God. Allow God to take His rightful place of first in your lives ---- willingly surrender all that which is within you to Him who wishes only to draw you close to His pure love.

My heart is filled with compassion and my eyes swell with tears as I watch My children in their humanity seek only to be governed by human desires of pleasure leading to corruption of body and soul.

Dear children, it is important you become aware of the intensity of these times. Many hearts which seek oneness with God. You will be tested to the point of near exhaustion but because of your childlike trust you will be given angels to guard and guide your every step ---- do not despair in times of difficulty for as gold is tested by fire --- so must you my little ones, be tested. Never fear but rejoice as you draw closer to perfection in His love.

Peace and love.

November 21, 1997 (Mary)

My daughter,

I have cautioned you of these difficult times in previous messages. The road you have chosen is not an easy one, but it is rewarding. The greatest rewards, my daughter, await you at journeys end not in this world which suppresses Godliness and finds amusement in those individual goals of holiness. Be strong in your faith and persevere in the goals we have set before you. Much good can and will be brought to fruit at the given time ---- God's time, which is always perfect. Love my daughter, those who seek to cause harassment and pain for though you sought to embrace martyrdom for love of Jesus, now you must realize martyrdom takes many forms. Rejoice as persecution comes. Know , my daughter, those who persecute will also encounter the risen Christ. Our love surrounds you and that which you wish to accomplish in this holy place.

Peace, dear one, ---- be filled with Our Peace.

November 22, 1997 (Mary)

My children,

We wish to bring you this day joy and the peaceful contentment that comes from knowing and trusting Jesus. Directions in life are so important my children, for by choosing the wrong path you become lost and confused. It is then your peace is attacked more severely and you lose focus of that which is now important ---- pure love and trust in Jesus.

You must allow all unwarranted rebukes and criticism to fall from your shoulders as rain drops fall from the sky. Know your faith and be prepared to proclaim and defend it. Be strong yet gentle and compassionate for many souls seek that which you now offer ---- a truly converted heart. Allow My Son to take the broken vessels from amongst you and repair them and fill them with His love. Rejoice and praise God for trials come and go but the love of Jesus remains constant. Do not fear but continually praise the name of Jesus. Love ---- unending love is our gift to you this day.

November 23, 1997 (Mary)

My children,

We bring you our peace to root in each of your hearts, minds, and souls. Yet far too many pray for peace but fail to recognize it and the true joy it brings. Your hearts must not be troubled, my little ones, for the peace and love of Jesus the Savior surrounds you and draws you close to His Heart which was pierced for love of you. Look beyond the littleness of your world and the small minds which seek only power and glory ---- but gaze with your eyes and hearts upon that which many cannot see ---- the realization that God the Almighty and Ever Living Father is truly the Creator ---- the Divine One in whom you trust.

Trust, my children, and accept that which must be for by trusting you faith grows and seeks only goodness and mercy. In all things give praise and glory to God and you in turn will find favor with Him who understands the trials you suffer and knows the great benefits they bring your soul. Rejoice, my little ones, as suffering out of love brings true joy. Peace and love.

November 24, 1997 (Mary)

My children,

I desire that all hearts be filled with love and desire for holiness. We are well pleased with the hearts who gather out of love to honor my request to praise Jesus and beseech His Divine Mercy. You, my precious ones do not as yet realize the power of your prayers as you gather in numbers to fulfill that which has been asked of you. Your faith blossoms as the flowers in Spring----bringing forth beauty and hope for the days to follow.

Do not become discouraged as darkness seeks to oppress you, but in faith and joy proclaim goodness and truth --- which brightens your path to holiness.

Bond together in common unity and strength for the Holy Spirit will direct your path of righteousness as joy and peace fill your souls. Never fear for you are greatly blessed. I bless you this day and draw you closer to the fountain of Divine Mercy.

Peace and love!

November 25, 1997 (Mary)

My dear children,

I seek to reach those hearts which have become as stones hardened to the Word of God and my messages of peace and love. You, my faithful ones, must out of pure love, open your arms and your hearts to the lost sheep whose blindness keeps them from the pasture which My Son has prepared for them.

Time moves swiftly, dear children, as you too must move swiftly. Prepare your hearts and listen closely as each of you is being called. Heed my words while the opportunity is still there. Pray ---- speak to Him who yearns to hear your prayers for mercy,

Destruction and decent lie close at hand. Life itself has now become a maize through which you must travel. Be wise, little ones, as you place your trust in Jesus ---- listen as He himself calls your name and directs your every step. I urge you in these most difficult times to stay focused on Him ---- for only through true abandonment of self will you succeed in obtaining true peace and joy.

November 26, 1997 (Mary)

My daughter,

80

I desire to console you, my dear one, as you embark upon a most difficult but rewarding journey. I urge you to allow yourself to rest in our peace for many obstacles will try and block your path of obedience as you follow the light of My Son's love. Fear not as the seemingly mountains of oppression will turn into valleys of peace and tranquility.

Justice soon comes. Be not afraid to proclaim the love and mercy of Jesus for you are now a loving vessel of peace. Do not reflect upon the efforts of your past for that is time wasted, but always seek the Divine Will of My Son ---- be a messenger of hope for truly hope is available to all who seek with hearts open to the truth of salvation.

You are blessed, little one, for you are greatly aware of the <u>Urgency of My Call</u> as your world accepts error as truth and thus many risk deception and the loss of their souls. Embrace those whose hunger has turned to pain --- for Divine Justice rapidly approaches.

Love and Peace.

November 27, 1997 (Mary)

My dear children,

Praise be Jesus who has richly blessed your country with countless gifts. Dear children, let praise and glory continuously be on your lips and in your hearts for the mercy of the Mighty One is boundless. In all things give thanks ---- in your joy and in your sorrow --- for pain and suffering cleanse and purify the soul and those souls for whom you suffer.

Let this day be a new day in which you resolve to follow the Risen Saviour. Be servants to one another ---- filled with the love and peace of Christ. Prepare, My children, for soon you will learn to give thanks in your time of want as the time of plenty draws to a close. Love, my little ones ---- love as you are loved.

November 28, 1997 (Mary)

My dear children,

I gather you close to my heart during these special times in which you celebrate peace and goodwill to all. It is the desire of my heart, dear ones, that each day be one of peace ---- each day you must develop habits ---- spiritual habits that help in your growth towards holiness. The material possessions of this world will soon pass. What then, my children, where has your true wealth been stored?

Hear me as I lovingly counsel you on this your journey through life. Do not delay in your preparations as I have cautioned you in my messages, but faithfully follow in the Master's steps. Carry your cross no matter what the cost, as each must bear witness to Jesus in the way chosen for him ---- by Him whose love will always be there to surround you with peace and courage. Fear not, for that which comes, comes quickly!

Peace and love!

November 30, 1997 (Mary)

My dear children,

I urge you in your daily lives to always make time for God. Love Him, praise Him and endeavor in all efforts to bring glory to His Holy name. My little ones, I tell you, you are loved and yet the depth of such love you do not comprehend, for God's love is unconditional, pure and holy. Strive for purity of heart and truly seek God's Will with a sincere heart which beats solely to love. You must decide now, my children, to pick up the Cross of Christ or reject it and Him whose precious blood was shed for you. Tears stream down your Mother's cheeks as I watch this world absorb your time and energy leaving you void and helplessly lost in materialism. Come, little ones, and rid yourselves of the burdens of this world. The hands of My Divine Son gently reach to grasp the humble soul which seeks holiness yet stumbles as the young child stumbles in his eagerness to walk. Do not fear, but trust in Him ---- take hold of the hand He extends to you. Walk beside Him now and you will walk with Him into eternity. Hear the Urgency of My Call. The hour grows late and my time with you draws to a close.

Peace, my precious ones!

November 30, 1997 (Mary)

My daughter,

You have been allowed a brief time in which to taste the bitter sweetness of the trials which have been foretold to you. Remain calm and with your faith abandon yourself in total trust to the Divine Will of God. You must be a strong and loving vessel of love which brings peace to the hurting and despondent souls of this world. Pray as you have been instructed, for there are many souls for which you are called to suffer. Never fear, my child, as We stand beside you guiding each step along life's path. Forgive the misguided, as you too, wish to be forgiven. The battle ensues with greater intensity.

Pray and prepare.

December 1, 1997 (Mary)

My dear children,

Prepare your hearts, for a great time of change soon comes. I urge you to reread my messages and discern that which has been revealed to you. Your time for decision seeps swiftly through the hour glass of life's unending challenges. Stand boldly, my little ones, in perfect faith and confidence in Jesus whose mercy is being poured out upon the thirsty souls bruised by deception of sin and arrogance.

Hear me ---- hear with your hearts where your faith must grow uncluttered by fear of the unknown. Truly I tell you, God exist ---- the Holy Spirit's presence is being poured out abundantly blessing so many souls with His special gifts. Believe as this is the time foretold to you in Holy Scripture. Pray for discernment as you read God's Word. Prepare, my children.

Peace and love.

December 2, 1997 (Mary)

My dear children,

Let your hearts be filled with joy as you rest in the assurance of Christ Jesus's love and the abundance of His mercy. Listen closely to the gentle whisper as He calls your name for you are summoned into the service of His Divine Kingdom. Prepare well your hearts----- for those who seek will surely find a love of such magnitude, that nothing can separate you from Him whose very life was laid down for you. Call upon Him always for He seeks to draw you close to His heart ---- to rid your soul of fear as the light of His love will shield your soul from the despair of sin.

Come to Him, little ones, ---- I urge you ---- do not hesitate. I am here, my children, to assist you. My hand ---- I extend to you ---- take hold and allow Me to present you to My Son. There remains much to do. Do all that you can ---- we ask no more of you than to share the love of Him who is pure love.

Peace and love!

December 3, 1997 (Mary)

My dear children, I desire that each of you deeply reflect upon your lives during this Advent season. Examine your consciences daily and resolve to allow me to help deepen your desire for holiness. I urge you to pursue humility ---- to choose your words carefully before speaking ---- and to forgive as you wish to be

83

forgiven. Do not speak out in anger but silently contemplate the love and mercy of Jesus ---- thus you will turn away wrath and help bring precious souls to Jesus. Let love ---- pure love guide you through this journey of life. It is wise to take more time in reflective prayer especially now so that you remain focused on the true meaning of the season. Resolve to be kind as kindness soothes many wounds.

Peace and love!

December 4, 1997 (Mary)

My dear children,

Praise be the name of Jesus whose love and mercy are constant gifts which He desires to bestow upon His children. Let your hearts be softened to receive these gifts as they are like the snow flakes falling gently from the sky creating a beautiful blanket which covers the ground. In time, the snow melts into the soil, so too, my little ones, the love and mercy of Jesus will melt into your soul refreshing it to bear fruit.

Trust, My children, and believe for you are not alone. Seek purity of heart and with a pure heart look about you. Your angels assigned by God are with you ready to assist in your daily lives. Call upon them as they too will pray with and intercede for you.

I, your Mother, bless you this day.

Peace and love!

December 5, 1997 (Mary)

My dear children,

Rejoice, little ones, let joy fill your hearts as Jesus the Savior desires to enter each heart that has prepared Him room. I desire this be the beginning of a new day in which you decide to live a true commitment to God in total abandonment to self. As you busily prepare for this beautiful season shopping and wrapping gifts, I ask you, my precious ones, what gift have you selected to lay before My Son, the Holy One, whose birth you will celebrate ---- perhaps an act of kindness ---- and hand that reaches out ---- a gentle smile ---- a warm embrace. It is these priceless gifts He desires from you, my children. Let this be the dawn of an endless season of love in Jesus.

Peace and love!

My dear children,

Seasons change ---- each brings its own beauty upon this earthly stage called life. So, too, each of you bring your individually unique qualities into this pattern of life. Know, my children, you are dearly loved as My Son has entrusted you into my care. I am here awaiting your response to my call.

Listen closely, my little ones ---- there is no fear or anxiety in my messages ---- only the reassurance of Our love and deepest concern for your eternal happiness. Always seek the peace of Jesus by abiding in His Divine Will. Be still, my children, as these times will test your patience and many small matters will attempt to steal your peace. Stay focused on Jesus ---- look above the things of this earth as I shower you with graces to withstand that which comes. Peace and love!

December 7, 1997 (Mary)

My dear children,

I urge each of you, my children, to rejoice in the goodness of God. Believe He is truly in control no matter what your circumstances in life may be. Be patient, my children, for by allowing His Will to become your desire in heart and mind, your spirit then becomes free to soar to greater heights of holiness.

Set for yourselves goals of humility and purity of heart where love will flourish. Prepare ---- pray and prepare! This is a time unlike all others ---- blessings flow forth upon all those seeking refreshment. I bless you this day as I gather you under my mantle of love and protection. Peace and love!

December 8, 1997 (Mary)

My daughter,

It is in times such as these you will require much strength for though your heart is willing, your mind seeks to control ---- thus your spirit becomes uneasy. You must read and reread my messages and comprehend that of which I speak. Pray and immerse yourself in Holy Scripture. Stay focused, my child, as the anxiety you allow to take hold, is not of God. We bring only peace and the confident reassurance of our love. Do not fear nor doubt but continue onward boldly proclaiming the love of Jesus.

Peace and love!

December 9, 1997 (Mary

My dear children,

I caution you to become aware of each day's distractions which draw you further from Jesus and the purpose for which you were created. Seek to form an intimate bond with Him whereby you will realize the necessity of deep and continual prayer ---- a prayer of praise and trust in the Holy One.

Many paths in life lead to materialistic fulfillment, but only one leads to eternal life. Choose wisely, my little ones, for soon all must account for their choices ---- both good and bad. Prepare your hearts ---- do not fear the total commitment of which we desire, but trust that We know what is best for you and freely surrender your will to that of the Divine Will.

Pray much and fast for such cleansing aids in the purification of your souls as journeys end approaches. Be ready and be prepared as the time of accountability now approaches.

Peace and love!

December 10, 1997 (Mary)

My dear children,

Peace and joy I bring to you this day ---- the peace and joy of Jesus. Do not despair in your daily trials but rejoice for great is the reward which awaits you. All must come to the realization that nothing of merit comes without sacrifice and obedience. Each must freely choose this path for nothing is unduly imposed upon open hearts which love and follow Jesus.

Life is a journey of joys and sorrows but all are required. Learn to embrace each for surely you will learn their importance as life itself is an enigma which through time and discernment you will learn to comprehend. You are dearly loved, my children, persevere a while longer as time grows short.

Peace and love!

December 11, 1997 (Mary)

My dear children,

In this season of peace, I urge you to contemplate the true meaning of peace as we wish you, Our Children, to experience it ---- for true peace in Jesus is complete trust. This is total trust which nothing can disturb. Walk with confidence, little ones, for love surrounds you and hope brightens your path.

Love much for pain can be healed by genuine love and compassion. There is no place for anger when you walk with Jesus ---- only understanding and forgiveness. This must be a journey of commitment ---- total commitment to the Divine Will. Times will become more and more difficult ---- but the justice of My Son will prevail.

Peace, My children, I bless you with my peace.

December 12, 1997 (Mary)

My dear children,

Praise be Jesus the Lord and giver of life. I urge you, my children, in these difficult times to come, to become little trusting souls who do not ---- nor will not ---- allow fear to take root in your souls. Be filled with true peace and joy for hearts must be made ready to receive Him who soon comes. You cannot escape the trials which come your way, but you can prepare your hearts by receiving the peace and love of Jesus. These are not just words that I often repeat but spiritual tools of survival.

Walk along the path upon which We have set your feet. Slowly, step by step, you will reach your own personal level of purification. In your humanity, you will tire, but by Divine Strength you will persevere.

Peace and Love!

December 13, 1997 (Mary)

My dear children,

I encourage you to pray much for all is not what it would appear ---- do not become lulled into complacency for all too soon your world will change. Be vigilant and attentive to My Words. The time of which I have spoken approaches. Pray and prepare! Arm yourselves with my rosary. Pray, my children, pray!

December 14, 1997 (Mary)

My dear children,

My heart fills with joy as you gather to pray and lift your petitions to Jesus. We do hear you, little ones, as your prayers become even sweeter as you struggle with daily trials ----- yet out of love you lift your voices in praise and gratitude to your loving Savior. I am with you and intercede for each one who calls for my assistance. Patiently endure that which comes. Prepare your hearts and those of the children as these times will not be kind ---- and yet they will be a time of great grace. My precious ones, you are dearly loved ---- in turn, I ask you to pray for the gift of love ---- unconditional love for one another.

Listen, My children, ---- hear the angels as they sing their praises in unison with your prayers.

Peace and love!

December 15, 1997 (Mary)

My dear children,

Your journey through this life takes many turns ---- it is a maze through which you must travel discerning which direction to follow. The peace and joy you readily seek in Jesus is the light which illuminates your path to holiness. Hold fast to truth for in truth you will find confidence in the righteousness of God.

My children, this life is but a moment in time ---- a brief span in which you are allowed to choose good from evil. Abandonment of free will, in return for life --- in the Spirit of God. Use your time wisely, for choices poorly made will reap the consequences of poor judgment. Hear and understand for free will carries many responsibilities. I reassure you of our love as I bless you this day.

Peace and love!

December 16, 1997 (Mary)

My daughter,

I urge you to offer all things to God in prayer. Many things are to be held deep within your heart ---- in that silent stillness of trust and obedience where you have prepared Us room. You become overly concerned with motives ---- why people come ---- what they will think. I tell you there is no cause for anxiety. My children seek hope ---- a small glimmer of the light of love to help heal the spiritual wounds inflicted by this uncaring world. You are a vessel into which has been poured love and compassion ---- now you must freely give that which you have been given. If it is but one soul which draws closer to Christ, you have not labored in vain! Rejoice in Our peace and love.

(Make known to My faithful remnant they are truly My little treasures of peace --- - the treasures which I present to My Son).

December 17, 1997 (Mary)

My dear children, I come as the humble Mother who desires to guide you along the path which leads to holiness. It is in the simple, uncomplicated way of the Saints to which I draw your attention. It is My wish for all of my children to draw closer to the majesty of God. Seek to recognize Him in the birds of the air ---- the flowers in the fields ---- and the faces of those whom He sends your way.

Hearts must be purified that eyes may see His handiwork woven through all of His creations. Be at peace as you seek God's will in all that you do. Make time now, my dear ones ---- prepare and be ready for the dawn of a new beginning quickly approaches. Trust in the Divine Mercy which flows forth from the hands of Jesus .

Peace and love!

December 18, 1997 (Mary)

My children,

I have repeatedly cautioned you of these times in which every effort will be made to steal your peace. Be firm in your commitment to Jesus that your strength will rest in Him and Him alone. Be cautious and wise yet loving and gentle in spirit. Many unsuspecting souls are being led astray and you, my precious ones, must pray intensely for the Divine mercy of Jesus.

Continue in your prayer groups as they are a source of immeasurable power which combats the evil sinfulness of this world. Be filled with hope as soon the Son will shine on a whole new world.

Peace and love, my dear children!

December 19, 1997 (Mary)

My Children,

Pray with great fervor during this special season of love and hope ---- sharing and sacrifices. My little ones, it is only that which you put into life from which you will draw your greatest rewards. I call each of you to empty yourselves of all negative thoughts, words, and deeds and, in turn, pray to be filled with the true joy and peace of Jesus. He comes, dear ones, to lighten your burdens and instill peace into every heart. You must desire His presence as He will not force himself upon you. I urge you to prepare your hearts now. Do as I have instructed you ---- prepare ---- pray and prepare. Let this beautiful season remind each one of you of the great love and mercy of God.

Rejoice and hold tightly to the promises of God as the time for which you have awaited soon approaches.

Peace and love!

December 20, 1997 (Mary)

My dear children,

I stand in your midst as the Loving Mother who desires to gather you into the peaceful serenity of My Immaculate Heart. Come to Me as you grow tired and weary from life's daily trials and I will offer you my peace from which you will draw strength. I urge each of you, my dear ones, to learn to walk in obedience to The Divine Will ---- seek to become one with Him whose love has given you the gift of life. Precious are these moments as soon they will slip through your hands as fine grains of sand. Be ready ---- be prepared.

Peace and love!

December 21, 1997 (Mary)

My children,

During this holiday season, I desire that you take time to look deeply into the faces of those whom you hold most dear. As you search each face, do you sense the peace and joy which Jesus brings or has the brightness of His light been allowed to grow dim. Have you, my precious ones, fueled the fire of Jesus' love within your families with hearts of compassion and understanding.

This is the time in which you celebrate peace. My desire for you, dear children, is to experience the true peace that only Jesus can instill within each heart. Trust, little ones, and throw open the door of your hearts and invite Him to enter. It is Jesus who will heal the broken hearts and refresh the dry souls with His healing mercy. Welcome Him with grateful hearts and allow the brightness of His love to emanate from each and every soul. Peace ---- peace, my children ---- trust completely as graces are being showered upon you.

Peace and love!

December 22, 1997 (Mary)

My dear children,

I come this day with joy in My heart for your prayers offered in loving obedience have warmed the chilled winter air making my mission bear the flowering fruits of

Spring. Do not become disheartened, my children, when it seems as though your spiritual life lacks growth ---- for spiritual growth requires much time and commitment. I tell you, out of pure love, it is possible to lead holy and prayerful lives while still bound to this earth for your spirit reaches beyond that which you can see into a realm of harmony with God. Do not seek to suppress your faith for truly I tell you all things are possible with God. As you learn to see with your heart your spirit soars and your faith expands seeking only holiness ---- an oneness with God.

Peace and love!

December 23, 1997 (Mary)

My dear children,

You have each been called to make decisions in life ---- decisions which will affect the final destination of your very soul. My dear ones, I urge you to keep uncluttered the prayerful communication between yourself and God. There is only one God yet many have unconsciously let materialism gain control of moral objectives. This must not continue ---- each of you must consciously make every effort to draw closer to God through humility and purity of heart. Time passes quickly and with it precious opportunities of conversion. You must seize every moment of life with grateful hearts and endure each trial with total trust and obedience. Hear my words that they will bear fruit in your hearts ---- fruit which you will one day offer My Son in thanksgiving. Make ready, my little ones ---- prepare.

Peace and love!

December 24, 1997 (Mary)

My dear children.

I invite you to join with me in the anticipation of the Birth of Divine Love. As my heart was filled with joyful expectation many years ago ---- so now I wish to share my joy with you. Come, my children, into the tiny stable in Bethlehem where the angels gather preparing for the birth of the Savior ---- the gentle Lamb of God. Hope soon comes to dispel despair and Love hastens into the world. Prepare now, my children ---- make ready your hearts.

Peace and love. *(Personal message given at this time).*

December 25, 1997 (Mary)

My dear children,

Peace and joy I bring to you this day as I the Mother of Divine Love hold God's precious gift to you close to My Heart. He is the Holy One ---- God, yet man, who comes to rescue His people from eternal darkness and suffering. He brings the light of hope from which springs forth joy and peace to comfort and heal his people. Dear children, my heart which is so full of joy continually rejoices in the greatness of God's love and mercy. Strive, dear ones, to be people of peace, humility, and forgiveness for then you draw closer to the unity of holiness for which you were created. Each new day will bring trials of various degrees ---- embrace each one for love of Jesus as your sorrows will be turned into joy. Do not seek to avoid sacrifices nor compromise your integrity for by focusing always on Jesus you will obtain His Divine Mercy and draw strength to persevere to journeys end. Hold tightly to these special moments as they are the gentle breeze before the approaching storm. Rejoice as you are greatly loved.

Peace, dear children!

December 26, 1997 (Jesus)

My people,

Hearken, My children, to the sound of My voice. You are My people whom I call ---- to love ---- to serve ---- and to draw others to the fountain of My mercy. Heed the words of My Mother whom I have sent to lead you to the sanctuary of My most Sacred Heart. She is the heaven sent ---- Holy One, who through humility and holy obedience is the Queen who lovingly reaches out with such gentle compassion to embrace each of My sheep and lead them to the fountain of My mercy.

My people, I love you and desire each one to be with Me in eternity. Do not fear nor be misled but come to Me and be reconciled as I seek to cleanse and purify your souls. Rejoice for I am with you always. Trust Me as I will never leave you but will continuously seek your eternal happiness. Let not your faith wither or be subdued by the errors of this world ---- I desire hearts filled with the confident assurance that My Word is True! As My promises to Abraham were revealed many years ago, so too, my promises hold true to those whose faith does not falter. Take courage, my people! This time of darkness soon fades into a new day of hope which brightens the horizon.

December 27, 1997 (Mary)

My dear children,

I encourage you to persevere in your prayer life ---- do not allow discouragement to penetrate the boundary of your faith for by your faith you will grow and develop the strength essential for spiritual development. There will arise many distractions along your spiritual journey but those who remain focused and committed to the praise and glory of Jesus will persevere. You are greatly loved and every opportunity of which you take advantage will assist in growth ---- spiritual growth and strength! We are here eagerly awaiting your call for assistance. Believe with all your heart as fear will find no resting place in your soul. In your eagerness to please Jesus, you will seek only that which brings Him honor and glory for you no longer will be consumed by self gratification but will seek only holy unity with the love of your Divine Creator. my children, you have embarked upon a great journey. A crown awaits those who persevere to the end. Rest in Our peace as love surrounds and protects those who in turn love with purity of heart.

Peace and love!

The following message was received on December 27th; however, Our Lady indicated the message was intended to be read on December 28th.

Sunday, December 28, 1997 (Mary)

My precious ones,

My love is like the container when filled with water gradually overflows onto the surrounding area. Gather My Son's sheep that they may drink of My Love ---- that nothing will be wasted as they will require this nourishment of complete and total love to refresh themselves for the journey home.

My Son awaits His faithful ones ---- let each drink his fill as the road ahead is an arduous one with many spiritual hazards. Be not afraid as We are here to aid in your preparation. I am your guide through this obstacle course of life. I am here to do the will of My Son. He calls you, My children, ---- listen well. Be wise but do not allow skepticism to block your path. I am here ---- reaching out to you ---- take my hand for together we will walk in the footsteps of Jesus for He has prepared the path for you. I am but a light which helps illuminate this path. Come, my children, ---- come and believe.

Peace and love!

December 29, 1997 (Mary)

My dear children,

Be at peace, my children as your prayers rise ever so sweetly before the throne of God. Know each heart is gently caressed to sooth away the aches and brokenness inflicted by a world of indifference. It is the purity of the intentions of each heart

93

which allows Divine Love to enter ---- to heal and to draw those receptive hearts close to His. Each one has been specifically chosen to fulfill a predestined purpose. Only by a continuous desire to deepen and strengthen your prayer life will such fulfillment be realized.

We love you, dear children and rejoice in your efforts to do the will the most Holy One. Yes, you will falter, but your desire for holiness will outweigh the obstacles strewn onto your path and with our joyful assistance you will reach life's goal of peace and joy in Jesus. I bless you this day as my heart surrounds you to comfort and guide you during these difficult times. Peace and love.

December 30, 1997 (Mary)

My dear children,

I urge you, my children, to abandon yourselves from the ways of your world ---- ways which bring short lived joys and frequent pains. Celebrate each new day of life as your first step towards eternal life with Jesus. The elusive peace for which you seek can only be found in the hearts of those whose thirst ----- for Divine Love draws them ever closer to the Heart of Mercy. Be patient, little ones and trust in Jesus for each day will bring its share of sorrows and disappointments. Focus on Jesus as His peace and joy will fill your soul with perfect contentment. Hear Me, my children, as you are being called to holiness.

Pray and prepare!

December 31, 1997 (Mary)

My dear children,

Know, my children, We are never far from you. You must trust in the love and mercy of God as trials of great sorrow will befall many. Your faith will be tested to the uppermost limits of endurance ---- no longer will you take for granted the simple every day conveniences of life. I urge you to seek humility and simplicity of life. Prepare now by making small sacrifices ---- by doing without some of the pleasures which have become habits of self-gratification.

Each day brings change ---- be vigilant, my children, ---- be prepared. You are greatly loved ---- do not despair but rest in the assurance that this love of which I speak brings only comfort and joy to those who seek peace.

Pray, my little ones, pray!

****

Messages from Jesus and Mary

January 1, 1998 – December 4, 1998

January 1, 1998 (Mary)

My dear children,

A new year is ushered in with joy and expectation ---- You, my children, anticipate various changes to be made in life, yet often fail in your good intentions as your commitments become burdensome ---- interfering with life styles. I urge you, little ones, to comprehend the gravity of these times. Do not fear to commit to the love of My Son for in so doing you will be assured peace in mind and heart ---- such peace will be your strength as times deteriorate. Seek Jesus as He eagerly awaits your return to Him ---- His love and mercy flow forth to embrace you, His precious ones. Come quickly ---- be reconciled ---- prepare. Peace and love!

January 2, 1998 (Mary)

My dear children,

I come to bring joy and encouragement to those souls seeking the love and mercy of Jesus. He is pure love ---- In His Divine Love He has sent Me to calm your fears and dispel doubt. Be open vessels, my children, into which love may be poured as you in turn will become His messengers of love. Seek to dwell in the peace of Jesus as there can be no room for hatred or anger if love is to survive. Forgive, dear ones, as you wish to be forgiven. As you seek My Son's mercy so must you be merciful.

Heed My words and prepare your hearts ---- pray with all your heart that none will be lost. Peace and love

January 3, 1998 (Mary)

My dear children,

Each one of you is being called according to your own special abilities to be messengers of Divine Love. Do not concern yourselves with the gifts of others, as you are individually unique ---- no one person is more important than another. You are asked, dear children, to concentrate on your own abilities ---- to perfect them as you strive to serve the Lord. Seek to find contentment in your position in life as God in His great wisdom has set the course each must follow in this great journey to holiness. Be patient and persevere. Peace, My children ---- Peace!

My dear children,

I greet you this day with My Motherly blessing as I draw you close to My Immaculate Heart. I, my children, am the refuge where you will find safety and contentment.

It pleases Us when you allow the Holy Spirit to work within your souls. Remain open to His call whereby you will become His fruits which will ripen as you place into practice true love of neighbor and obedience to the Will of God. Remain calm and stand firm as the evil weapons of the enemy are being hurled from every direction. Trust, my children, as your faith will grow and you will obtain peace --- - the true peace of Jesus.

January 5, 1998 (Mary)

My dear children,

I look about the earth seeing you, my precious little ones, searching for answers to life's questions. I see your struggles ---- the pain and suffering which each must bear in your process of purification. Know, my children, it is not a question of luck as some would have it but circumstances permitted by God to cleanse each of His children. He does not look upon you as rich or poor nor the color of your skin for all are the same in His eyes. More often, it is the poor who are rich and the rich who are lacking. Accept the role you have been given ---- each with grateful hearts knowing you are loved and will be rewarded according to that which has been done in each life out of love! Deny yourselves that others might see and believe. Pray that your journey through life would be like a beautiful flower ---- fragrant to be near and pleasing to the eye. It is your heart, dear ones, into which Good looks. May the intentions of your hearts be pure. Peace and love!

January 6, 1998 (Mary)

My dear children,

You are called to peace ---- to dwell in the Divine Love of Jesus. Seek with all your heart true humility and purity of heart whereby you will be drawn closer to the Divine Will. Desire to seek God in all that you do ---- let your thoughts be pure and the words of your mouth be selected carefully that they do not inflict wounds upon they neighbor. My heart grieves for those in whom fear has found root. Realize, my children, the love of Jesus has no limits ---- no boundaries. Love ---- Divine Love ---- reaches beyond human barriers to instill peace. Do not allow your heart to be troubled or your minds to fill with hypothetical questions for then what little faith you have acquired becomes buried under theological rhetoric. Faith, my children, is a beautiful gift ---- a gift which if properly nurtured will see you through this life's journey into the Kingdom of eternal life. Come, dear children ---- Our arms are outstretched to receive you. Peace and love!

January 7, 1998 (Mary)

My daughter,

You are an instrument of peace ---- a vessel of love. I understand the uncertainties you feel ---- Yes, even the anxiety which subtly seeps into the crevices of your faith. Be confident, my child, as there is still much to do and you must remain strong yet humble as the task ahead is great. Renew your strength through the Mass for there you become one with My Son as you dwell together bound by Love. Let your heart be light as you seek to serve Jesus for by so doing uncontainable joy will fill every fiber of your being leaving no room for fear or anxiety. These times will challenge even the most devout of my children. Beware, be strong and persevere. Peace, my daughter.

January 8, 1998 (Mary)

My dear children,

Much as been revealed to you through my messengers ---- yet many have turned their back on my call. You ask for signs and wonders that you might believe ---- I tell you, my children, signs and wonders occur each day but go unnoticed by most you, my precious ones. I urge you to take time from your day to abide in the tranquil presence of God through prayer. He yearns to hear the call of His children seeking the embrace of the Father's love. Set aside a few moments when your body is rested and your mind is fresh to praise and glorify Him Whom is pure love.

My dear children ---- you find no difficulty forming undesirable habits yet much effort remains to develop a binding spiritual relationship with God. Your faith must be nurtured if it is to grow ---- and grow it must if you are to survive. The hour approaches when you will reflect upon my messages and weep bitter tears for the choices you have made in life. Prepare ---- pray and prepare!

January 9, 1998 (Mary)

My dear children,

Let your hearts not be troubled or your minds become cluttered with unnecessary thoughts. Strive to live each day one at a time. You become preoccupied with that which is to come and fail to live in your present making the most of each day. I desire you to be prepared spiritually and physically without undo stress. Be calm, my children, and trust in Jesus for these trials will intensify yet all will be accomplished for the glory of God.

Rejoice as you travel upon the narrow path of salvation. Be firm in your commitment as We are with you guiding and protecting you each step of the way. This is the time for total conversion. No more can you stand in the middle of the road ---- it is either Heaven or Hell ---- the choice is yours. Be assured of Our unending love as we draw you close to Our hearts. Peace and Love!

January 10, 1998 (Mary)

My daughter,.

Draw close to my heart where you may unburden the cares of this world. You allow so many insignificant circumstances to influence your peace. You cannot control that which approaches, my child ---- rid yourself of doubt and anxiety as Jesus will see to all your needs. Be patient and allow Divine Wisdom to guide your path. You are but a simple messenger ---- a willing heart into which the seed of faith has been planted.

Let love guide your steps as you embrace the suffering of others. Seek to join your heart with Ours as true love and compassion are essential in this life's journey. Embrace with the arms of Jesus the hungry ones who seek His love and mercy. Rejoice, my daughter, as many hearts are now receptive to My Son's love. Follow the path laid out before you ---- do not deter from the narrow path but persevere to journeys end. Peace and Love!

January 11, 1998 (Mary)

My dear children,

 I invite you this day into the refuge of My Immaculate Heart where you will find peace and tranquility. My dear children, you will not escape the trials and heartbreak of this world ---- yet true peace can be yours. You must believe when asking for God's divine intervention, for if you ask not in faith by what means do you expect my intercession? So many graces are being poured out upon the hungry souls who out of pure love and hope seek spiritual consolation. My dear ones, in your human weakness you make something so beautifully simple become complicated and burdensome.

Divine love is not complicated ---- It is and always shall be an accessible fountain which beckons you to drink your fill. Cast off your cares and worries for God is in control! He hears the petitions of your heart and feels your anguish as you struggle to understand His Divine plan. Trust ---- trust, my children, as you will be put to the test. You are dearly loved, my precious ones. Let your hearts be still and rejoice in Him who is pure love. Peace and love!

My dear children,

Let it be by faith and faith alone by which you gather, seeking the peace and fulfillment of God's graces in your soul. You are called to this special place to pray ---- to rest in the peaceful serenity which has been provided by My Son. It is He who allows each heart to be open to His call. My children, you are greatly blessed yet many still dwell upon earthly gratification and miss the beauty which lies before them.

You are called to pray with great fervor that all hearts will be receptive to the Divine Will. My children, this is a peaceful journey into which each may find fulfillment and joy. Seek to join your will with that of Jesus for the peace you seek is not of this world, but of that which comes. Let all hearts prepare, for that which comes is but a moment away. Be filled with love that much fruit will bear witness to the praise and glory of God.

Peace and love!

January 13, 1998 (Mary)

My dear children,

I encourage you to walk with me along this path of life. It is a journey which all must take whether short or long ---- it is a precious gift which you must learn to cherish as each moment carries much meaning. Though at times you may struggle ---- all must be for the glory of God. Be quick, my children, hasten to my call, for as yet you do not comprehend the importance to my messages. My call is urgent. Come with joyfully expectant hearts as grace upon grace falls upon you to sustain you in these difficult times. There is much sorrow in your world yet hope remains alive and strong. Do not fear nor lose your peace for He who is pure love guards His chosen ones.

Pray and rejoice.

January 14, 1998 (Mary)

My daughter,

Be calm, My child, as you listen to My words for I desire your heart to be free of anxiety and the skepticism which surrounds you. Be at peace for there remains much to do and many sacrifices to be made. Allow your will be become one with His Divine Will where life becomes but a journey through time. Seek the peace of Jesus as all things then become possible. Do not despair as evil attempts to cloud your vision but in all things stay focused on Jesus and diligently seek to follow in His steps.

You must seek to remain strong in your faith as it will be greatly tested. Love much, little one, and forgive as the joy that comes will also bring pain.

Peace and love !

January 15, 1998 (Mary)

My dear children,

Out of pure love I come to you as a mother comes to the aid of her children. I urge you, dear ones, to be observant and discern the signs of your times for it is under the disguise of innocence that danger lurks. Time, My children, is so precious yet much of it is wasted upon idle pleasures that reap no reward.

I tell you, My children, you must seek a closer relationship with God for your strength to endure the coming events is a bond which God Himself will nurture if you but allow your will to become one with His. Live each moment as if you were in His presence for truly you are His children ---- the lives into which pure love seeks to dwell. Pray, dear ones, pray! Know that you are loved.

January 16, 1998 (Mary)

My dear children,

I come this day out of pure love desiring that each heart be entrusted to the Divine Will of My Son and the promises He has made to each of His children. My heart becomes heavy, little ones, as I sense the uncertainty which seeks to torment your souls ---- for you must not fear but walk confidently in the peaceful assurance of the love and mercy of Jesus.

My children, I tell you of this Divine Love over and over again and yet many hearts remain troubled ---- unsure and filled with anxiety. By what reason, dear children, do you fear love? Pure love is life ---- life in Jesus who continually watches over you with such compassion as He knows the intentions of your hearts and understands the frailty of your humanity. Be at peace, My children, for each day's struggles bring you closer to holiness. Trust in Jesus and persevere but a short while longer for all is as it must be.

Peace and love.

My daughter,

I encourage you, My child, to be strong both spiritually and physically as all your strength will be required as time draws closer to fulfillment of prophecy. It is in your weakness that We will draw forth great strength as you have given your fiat to the Lord. It is He who calls your name ---- He beckons you, My child, with His tender mercy ---- He draws you close to His heart still wounded by the sins of mankind. You are asked to suffer much as great will be your pain yet graces sufficient to sustain you during this trial will abound. Be at peace as joy surrounds you.

Bear in silence, My child, the wounds of indifference inflicted by those who doubt for the great awakening approaches as the light of His love will shine upon all hearts!

My dear children,

Know that each heart is but an open book, in which each page when read, reflects the choices which free will has made. I, the Mother of Love, am here to help each one write anew the pages of their hearts which My Son will receive with great love through My intercession. Dear children, do not allow these precious moments to slip by ---- moments of every day struggles and temptations without making a conscience effort to offer them to Our Lord. In all things seek His holy will whereby you, in turn, may offer your sacrifices united to those of My Son's sorrowful passion.

You, the precious ones, whose untiring love drives you ever forward are chosen vessels of Divine Love. This perfect love must be sought to be obtained. As the rains fall from Heaven, so too are the graces which ever so lightly touch the inviting soul ---- refreshing it with living water. Be not afraid , dear children, but place your love and trust in Jesus the merciful and loving Savior.

Peace and love!

My dear children,

I invite you, My children, to join your hearts with My Immaculate heart as we gather to praise and honor the Holy One, Jesus the Savior. Know, My precious ones, you are chosen to be the bearers of peace and love. It is through those open hearts in which the bond of spiritual unity will manifest the desire for holiness that hope will spring forth. Be the peaceful warriors whom We send into this final battle for souls for all are called yet too few respond.

Pray, My children, ---- be brave as fear cannot find a place of rest among hearts which belong to Jesus. He alone lightens your burdens and fills the voids of uncertainties and doubt. Let all hearts be light as true love engulfs you with Divine Love. Pray continually for discernment as true wisdom will enlighten the soul and brighten your path to holiness.

Peace and Love!

January 20, 1998 (Mary)

My dear children,

I gaze upon you so often through tears of love for though you hunger for spiritual food you find the nourishment We provide at times distasteful and bitter to accept. Each must learn to accept responsibility in life for joy and pain are often intertwined. You are called to pray ---- yet time for prayer is occupied by every day cares leaving only fragments of your day an offering to God. You are given signs and wonders yet still require more. At what point, My children is enough actually enough? I solemnly tell you, hearts must be prepared now, for soon all will witness the loving justice which hastens your way.

The Father patiently awaits your call for forgiveness ---- your earnest cry of repentance. Do not hesitate, My children, as these are final graces of great love which Our Lord has deemed worthy to poor forth upon His wayward children. Pray ---- -trust and believe as the gifts you are given , whether great or small, are priceless treasures from the Light of Divine Love!

Peace and love!

January 21, 1998 (Mary)

My dear children, I draw you close to My Heart where you will find the sweet repose of My Motherly love. It is in each day's journey the lessons of life become the reality which you must face. Do not be overwhelmed, My children, for though each day brings what it will, the peaceful tranquility of My Son's embrace will steady your steps upon your path to holiness. It is by falling, you learn to balance and then stand ---- so too, will you fall along your spiritual path yet in time the confident assurance of Our love will bring strength as you journey slowly forward. Accept what must be, dear ones, yet discern with much prayer for error seeks to weave deception. Let your life be bound with truth where justice and peace will prevail.

102

My dear children,

I stand in your midst eagerly awaiting your response to My call. Many hear yet My message becomes only words without meaning ---- without urgency. How My heart yearns to draw you close and whisper My words of hope and encouragement for far too many fail to recognize this critical point in time. Indifference grasps hold of your faith and you are left empty ---- void of all forms of faith ---- the belief in that which you cannot see. My children, look about you and this holy place for here We have chosen to dispense many graces. Breath in the tranquility which pours from Our hearts ---- let go, My little ones, of that which you have no control for by complete surrender of your human will do you obtain strength and the illusive peace of which you seek. Pray with your hearts ---- do not be lukewarm but allow the flame of your hearts to burn with the fire of desire for truth and love. Peace, My children ---- you are called to peace!

January 23, 1998 (Mary)

My dear children,

It is My desire that each heart be filled with the peace and joy of Jesus. You, My children, are the precious vessels chosen by Him into which pours forth a multitude of graces. It is you who are chosen and by His mighty and undying love, He guides your steps as He stands guard over your souls gently pulling you from harms way. Oh, My children, My dear children, hear My call for all must be messengers of the Divine Love.

I stand between you and My Son interceding on your behalf yet My time grows short and you must allow your faith to grow unhindered by the seeds of doubt and despair which envelop your world. Be strong ---- be reconciled! I urge you to seek God's gift of Divine forgiveness for by so doing you will be cleansed and made ready for that which comes. Do not take My messages lightly, My children, as the seeds of indifference are the weeds growing in the fields of the Great Harvest.

Peace and love!

January 25, 1998 (Mary)

My children,

It is with a joyful heart in which I receive your prayers and petitions for your hearts grow soft, My children, and My words rest gently with each receptive soul which longs for peace ---- the peace of Jesus. So many distractions cross your paths seeking to draw you further away from the pure harmony of life with Jesus.

You must be strong as the evils of corruption lie in wait for unsuspecting souls. My children, the obvious is not always the obvious and for this reason you must pray much that the gift of discernment will brighten those shadows of doubt causing unrest and discontentment.

Many souls now risk eternal suffering for they have willingly allowed error to become the acceptable way of life.

Pray, My children, pray!

January 26, 1998 (Mary)

My dear children,

Pure joy fills My heart as love and devotion to My Son surges forward in your world of uncertainty and confusion. Look about you, My little ones and see that all who gather ---- gather in unity and love of Jesus. Great is the grace which overshadows you for much fruit will spring forth from the purity of your hearts and your desire for holiness. Perfection does not come in this world, My little ones, but perfect peace can be acquired through the love and trust in Jesus. Great is the grace which overshadows you for much fruit will spring forth from the purity of your hearts and your desire for holiness. Though you may grow weary, it is but a test of your true desire to love and serve the Lord. Be at peace through all life's trials for though judgment comes I intercede for you before My Son, the Perfection of Mercy ---- as His Heart stands ready to receive His beloved children. Do not fear but trust and continue onward in the challenges of life

Peace and love!

January 27, 1998 (Mary)

My dear children,

My heart though filled with complete peace yearns for a total conversion of My children and thus My tears continue to swell within My eyes. My children, a great change is on the horizon and many of My precious ones still remain unprepared ---- desiring the pleasures of the world yet in their own minds they strive to walk a holy walk with God. Wake up, My little ones, for temptations are great and self denial scarcely exists but the flame of love of Jesus and His promises must never be extinguished. I call you to make more sacrifices whether it be in your consumption of food or the comforts in this life which you have allowed to become necessities!

Dear, children, hear your Mother for I caution you of the coming time of darkness and deep despair. Be at peace for though you do not know your future, He who is above all things holds tightly to the reigns of your soul. Let true love and

104

forgiveness be your constant companion. Trust, little ones, as we are never far from your side. Peace and love!

January 28, 1998 (Mary)

My dear children,

Take hold of the hand I outstretch before you that I may draw you close to Me where you will find the comfort of a mothers love. My little ones, you have come far yet further still you must go. Be the gentle dove My Son sends into this world bent on destruction ---- where pride and self worth have taken root. There is no room for pride where Jesus dwells and the fortune of man is not composed of silver and gold but by living in the Divine Will where true wealth is acquired.

Be ever so gentle, My children, and embrace the trials and sufferings as you would a loved one for truly these are precious gifts ---- you have but to open the eyes of your hearts to see the value each one brings.

Learn to sacrifice that others too may learn from your example.

Peace and love.

January 29, 1998 (Mary)

My dear children,

My call is a continuous one of urgency for you, My little ones, do not comprehend the deep despair which is to befall all of God's children. Even in your most vivid

imagination you are hindered from grasping the consequences of such a sinful world. We are not calling you to fear for these words must be spoken; however, My dear ones, each of you is being called according to God's purpose. Do not allow pride and your foolish nature to hinder your obedience to the truth. Live a life of joy in the Lord not a life founded on the pleasures of materialism for that joy will soon dissolve leaving you empty of peace and true happiness.

Heed My words and allow your hearts to be filled with the love of Jesus. I caution you, little ones, to prepare now for many unfortunate souls will cry out in fear and anguish. Though all must be as I have predicted, stand firm ---- believe and trust for God's mercy is great ---- His love is endless.

Peace and love!

My dear children,

The mist of uncertainty has engulfed your world where only glimmers of rays of hope penetrate the eagerly awaiting souls. These precious souls are My warriors who gather within the armament of righteousness valiantly grasping the sword of truth to make ready the coming of My Son. Be vigilant, My children, as each moment brings you closer to His return. Pure love and joy must rest in your heart for that which comes will be most difficult yet unimaginable joy is the reward promised to those who persevere.

I pray that you be kind and gentle of heart for you will obtain peace ---- the peace which only intensifies as you become one with Jesus. Rest easy, My children, for soon peace will prevail. Peace and love!

January 31, 1998 (Mary)

My daughter,

Come closely, My child, for My words are those which only the open hearts can hear. Do not become discouraged as your humanity seeks to gain control of your daily trials for it is through your childlike faith that We will accomplish great works where many hearts will feel the warmth of Our embrace. You judge yourself unworthy but judgment is not yours ---- for only through God's great love and mercy does true judgment come. Be aware of the pains of sin which pierce your heart, but be equally aware of the Divine forgiveness which mends the broken hearted. Let not your heart be troubled for I am here to strengthen and encourage you. As the rose is beautiful and fragrant that stem which leads to its flower is filled with thorn the wounds of which quickly awaken the soul and thus lead it back to purity and love. Allow your faith to grow as each trial becomes a flower which I gather and present to My Son. Peace and love.

February 1, 1998 (Mary)

My precious children,

Before you I stand gently gathering each of Our precious ones under My mantle of love and protection. Know, My children, no matter what your age, each is a priceless vessel into which pure love is poured to caress the pain of the wounds inflicted by a world misguided and bent on destruction. It is love, My little ones, which heals and therefore it is through love ---- Divine Love which We send you to be the victims of charity and compassion willingly surrendering your love to that of the Divine Will. Learn patience, My children, that aggravation and disagreements will melt into a pool of gentle forgiveness whereby each will learn to embrace one another filled with hearts of understanding and compassion.

Time quickly passes, My precious ones, leaving little time for decisions. Choose well, My children, for soon the weeds of the Harvest will be separated from the Grain of eternal life.

I bless you this day with My Motherly peace.

February 2, 1998 (Mary)

My dear children,

You have been granted the gift of life ---- the sweet breath of Divine Love breathed into your soul. It is in God's Master Plan you have been assigned a task and the means by which to accomplish His purpose.

As you continue through this beautiful journey, you by your own free will, are called to make decisions ---- wise decisions which can only be made by complete trust in the Divine Will. Not always do you choose wisely, but the intentions of the pure of heart bring joy to Him who ever so lovingly watches each small step of your life's journey to holiness.

Be firm in your faith ---- yet gentle and filled with compassion as the time approaches when you will reflect upon your life and the many small but ever so important matters left unattended. As you grow in faith, so must you also grow in wisdom. Wise is he who places his faith and trust in Jesus. Be well, My little ones!

Peace and love!

February 3, 1998 (Mary)

My dear children,

So busy, My children ---- time has become a priceless commodity ---- so valuable that to share such a gift requires great sacrifice. The beauty of sharing becomes burdensome ---- the time intended for joy becomes buried under personal desires for solitude with material pleasures. My children, you are witnessing a current of change in which many of Our children are floundering desperately trying to stay afloat. You are here to help one another ---- to be the ship which remains strong as it pierces through the waves of life's troubles and pain. Let your heart be light as I will help lead you to the safe harbor of Jesus where all will find true peace. You must learn to forgive and abandon foolish pride for only love ---- pure love ---- can mend the broken hearted.

Peace and love!

February 4, 1998 (Mary)

My daughter,

It is in your open heart, you must invite the poor in spirit, for their hunger is great as they seek closeness to God. Do not allow pride to draw you from the battle but receive My Son as often as possible for it is by His strength and His alone that evil will lose its power. There is much yet to do. Time spent away from My Son and His mission for your life is wasted. Be firm, My daughter, for what is and will be revealed to you will bring pain as well as joy.

This is a time of testing. You are well advised to stay close to your spiritual director for the years have brought him much wisdom. Do not fear to proclaim Our messages for through the gentle truth of Our words and your tears of compassion many hearts will be softened.

Rest in Our Peace!

February 5, 1998 (Mary)

My dear children,

I urge you to make room in your hearts where Jesus in His purity and Divine Love may reside. I ask you to examine yourself through eyes of Jesus. Where is the pain and sorrow which have inflicted your soul? Do not be afraid to reveal your wounds that Our Lord may bring His healing power. No longer try to hide the diseases of

your conscience for God in His power and mercy looks upon His children patiently waiting to rid each soul of guilt and shame for, My little ones, the healing begins. Your body is but a garment, hand made and perfectly tailored for each individual but through time will wear and become frail. The soul remains strong if well maintained but that also will become weak if neglected through poor spiritual habits. Always seek the peace and love of Jesus that you will walk in the confident assurance of His mighty power.

Peace and love!!

February 6, 1998 (Mary)

My dear children,

You have been summoned into the arena of life in which you will face unimaginable trials ---- trials which if not abated would draw you deep within yourself denying you the true joy and beauty of life. I have come that so many of

Our children would be released from the chains of depression ---- the darkness of the soul. I urge you, My little ones, to continue to proclaim the good news of Jesus for He alone is the pure light of love which illuminates those receptive hearts refreshing them with Divine hope and the gentle caress of tranquility. Your society has strayed so far, My children, that you have lost all sense of direction. Gaze upon the cross which rises high above the ground to remind you that as Love came to set you free so now you must renew your vow of love and draw others to the Fountain of Love where refreshment awaits. Know you are chosen ---- uniquely different - yet one in heart!

Pray and prepare!

February 7, 1998 (Mary)

My dear children,

You are Our precious little ones carefully chosen to bring joy ---- the joy of Our Lord to all the broken and fragmented vessels in which life has become difficult and despair the deeply rooted seed seeking to draw Our little ones into the darkness of loneliness and intense pain. Great is the responsibility with which you have been entrusted. It is by your childlike faith that fear will no longer find ground in which to grow for the love of Jesus and the truth of His words dispels all that is not pure and holy. Be brave, My children, for those whose hope is in Jesus will find assurance and peace and will confidently embrace the trials of this world with such warmth that all will melt into a fragrant pool of love from which the desire for holiness will spring eternal. Peace and love!

February 8, 1998 (Mary)

My dear children,

You are My dear children for it is through the hands of Jesus that I gather you under My Mantle of motherly love and protection. I do not come to cause dissension but to revive that last glimmer of hope which rapidly fades as the rays of My Son's love become buried under theoretical dissertations. I choose to speak simply and truthfully whereby all My children will understand. It is Divine Love which draws My Heart into unity with My Son and the purity of such love with which we pursue the misguided souls who choose to make something so beautifully simple so complex. My dear ones, where true love abides there is peace. Examine carefully your thoughts and words as they filter through your heart. Be kind and gentle and may your hearts be filled with forgiveness for much will come to disturb your peace yet you must be strong as the Holy Spirit will enlighten the minds of those who genuinely seek His discernment. Be at peace ---- trust much, little ones, as all will be tested.

Peace and love!

February 9, 1998 (Mary)

My dear children,

You are called to be the peaceful doves of My Son immersed in His Divine love. Humanity calls for peace, but fails to recognize its presence for you have become as the fragrant flower which sweeps the air with its pleasant aroma yet time too takes its toll and the fragrance is soon gone. My children, you are the flowers of the field of life placed into the care of The Master Gardner. It is through His expert care you are allowed to bloom again and again. I urge you to be humble that the fragrant beauty of His love will not fade as your delicate fragrance of childlike trust and peaceful submission to His Divine Will continue to flourish as journeys end approaches. This is the time of unity in which all open hearts will be bound with Divine Love. Persevere ---- pray much, My children, as the thread of discord seeks to flaw the precious garment of life.

Peace and love!

February 10, 1998 (Mary)

My dear daughter,

I urge you to bring to Me the words of your mind and heart that I might soften them before they are spoken. The trials, My daughter, will not cease nor the intensity with which they come but you must allow your heart to fill with compassion. You, Our little messenger, have accepted your gifts with great love ---- greater still must be the love which illuminates from your very presence for all must see as well as hear of the great love and mercy of Jesus. Be not quick to defend yourself from the arrows of ignorance and misunderstanding for Jesus in His perfect timing will put all wrongs to right. You are but to show kindness and mercy as all will learn one must be merciful to obtain mercy.

I wrap you in My Mantle of love that you may gather strength to be firm in your belief and with silent humility press forward as great are the rewards for those who persevere. Rest easy, My child. Pray much as darkness approaches.

February 11, 1998 (Mary)

My daughter,

Now is the time in which you must show great strength for soon My messages to you also will cease. You will be forced to rely on that which you have been fed and must in turn feed others. No longer will My words be so readily before you ---- the revelations of prophecy ---- for you will find yourself living that which has been predicted. It is time to prepare with great intensity. I urge you to be the bearer of My messages ---- to speak boldly yet compassionately. Speak of the great love and mercy of Jesus for fear must not find rest in your heart ---- only through peace and love can the seed of hope spring forth. *(There was then a long pause ---- the time of enlightenment approaches. The date in which the daily messages will discontinue was given.)*

February 12, 1998 (Mary)

My dear children,

As I prepare to take My leave from you, I wish to bless you with peace that all My messages will have taken root in your hearts and that you will more fully understand the great love and mercy of Jesus. Do not be saddened, but realize with grateful hearts the magnitude of the blessings which you have received. You, My little ones, have been blessed and too often you have taken these blessings for granted --- and so it is that humanity in it's weakness fails to see with clarity the approaching storm. You whose hearts have been consecrated to the Sacred Heart of My Son and to My Immaculate Heart must strive to live exemplary lives of holiness for the eyes of uncertainty will watch your every move and every word will be examined for truth. Strive to walk in the footsteps of the Master as He has cleared the way for you to follow. Focus on Jesus as you will see more clearly the path in the footsteps of the Master as He has prepared for you. You are dearly loved, My children --- pray with much faith as time grows short.

Peace and love!

February 13, 1998 (Mary)

My dear children,

Pain and sorrow are earthly terms which you have come to understand well as you struggle to rise above your human weaknesses. Many of My children wander in confusion without direction in life. They have piled doubt and dismay one upon the other forming mountains which they cannot scale for faith has been tucked away and not allowed to grow. Faith is life that seeks eternal union with God whose Divine Love encourages His children to be bearers of peace and love.

I am here, My children, at the request of My Son whose intense love burns with compassion as He watches the errors of humanity seeking to destroy the delicate souls of His creation. Dear little ones, I urge you to be at peace ---- there is a great wave of jealously and pride forming upon the sea of life. I caution you, My children ---- wiser is He who swallows pride and drowns in humility than He who seeks to stay afloat only to be devoured in the mouth of eternal damnation. Prepare ---- pray and prepare. Draw close to Him whose love endures forever.

Peace and love!

111

My dear children,

I come in peace surrounded with angels to welcome you, My precious little ones. In your haste you often fail to see the gentle beauty in life which God has graciously set before you. I tell you many times in each ones life the soft whisper of the breeze you feel against your cheek is the touch of an angel gently guiding your steps ---- reassuring you that you do not walk alone. You, My children, are greatly blessed by this alone for God does not send His children on this journey of life without companionship.

You are dearly loved ---- do not allow doubt to steal these precious gifts from you ---- be strong ---- be wise ---- be prepared Let your hearts be open to God's Divine Love as it is in this time in which He pours forth graces as never before! You will dream dreams as prophecy becomes alive drawing you to the fulfillment of your mission in life. I gather you close to My heart where you will find peace.

Be filled with joy as the brightness of God's love rests upon you!

February 15, 1998 (Mary)

My Dear Children,

Praise be Jesus the Holy One whose light ---- the light of love burns brightly as His precious children seek His most Sacred Heart. Little ones you are the sweetness which brings joy to Our Hearts for all your efforts to persevere have found favor with God.

It is in the small unnoticeable things of life ---- the spiteful word left unsaid ---- the feelings of anger and criticism which now you see as the tools of darkness being released in gentle understanding and all these help diminish the bitterness which sweeps-through your world.

Again I call you to be the gentle doves bound to Our Hearts for through true obedience and devotion to Jesus you become strong prayerful warriors who battle tirelessly for the salvation of souls. The intensity of your love must urge you ever forward ---- help bring Him the souls for whom He thirsts. Resolve, my little ones to forgive and love much as soon your turn will come to stand before the Lord. It is your Mother's prayer that you come before His throne bearing the precious gifts of souls whom you touched through the gift of His love.

Peace and love.

February 15, 1998 (Mary) - (Second Message)

Know, My children, we find great joy in seeing our faithful ones gathered in such numbers to praise God. As the suns bright rays break gently through the clouds so your precious prayers of love break through the tangled web of life's trials. No longer do you see them as unwanted sufferings but embrace them as the true gifts they are ---- tools with which you will build a stronger spiritual life. Many graces have been poured out this day ---- he fruits of which will soon ripen. As you come together in love and unity of spirit, legions of heavenly angels gather joining in your prayers of praise and glory to God. Here also My favorite sons have gathered ---- My faithful ones ---- listen well as their hearts are one with mine. I bestow upon each of you My Motherly blessing. Peace and love!

February 16, 1998 (Mary)

My dear children,

I search each heart for the quiet corner in which My words will fall undisturbed and unruffled by worldly cares ---- that small corner where together We will sing of the greatness of God ---- Our most merciful and loving Creator. It is in My Heart I have gathered My faithful remnant ---- My heart is the refuge where you may draw strength to combat the evils of moral decay spreading throughout your country.

You, My children, are being sent as a sacrifice of love for it is only through pure love can the course of ones soul be changed. By Divine Love, each was rescued ---- saved through mercy ---- so it is that each must strive to protect that which has been given. My little ones, you know My time here grows short. In these brief moments in time I have shared many things ---- I encourage you to read the messages ---- stay focused on Jesus where true peace lies. Be not disturbed but trust. Peace and love.

February 17, 1998 (Mary)

My dear children,

Through the purest love I come patiently calling all who will hear ---- all who willingly surrender their hearts to Jesus. I especially call the youth to allow Me to touch their hearts where pain and distrust have left scars which will not heal ---- where bitterness and sorrow have sought to destroy your peace. I am your Mother whose love continuously draws Me in search of each lost sheep ---- it is your precious soul I seek to guard and protect. Come, My children, into My arms ---- see the tears of joy which fall upon each lost soul that now is found. (Personal message: My daughter, you are a little mother called to embrace Our children ---- words are not necessary for your heart speaks for itself. Love, much as much will be required of you).

113

February 18, 1998 (Mary)

My daughter,

The joy which fills your soul is but a glimmer of that which comes, as many hearts are being softened ---- tears of joy will flow from many hearts as faith becomes more alive. Do not feel overwhelmed, My daughter, for I am sending My precious ones to help with this great undertaking. They will come --- as I have said it ---- so shall it be ---- both young and old ---- all will join together for the praise and glory of God.

I ask you to accept that which must be for the light of Jesus must shine brightly. This holy place will become a beacon in which many will seek refuge. All must become one family in Christ ---- unite yourselves in His love as mercy is there for the asking. Encourage one another, trust and love much.

Peace and love.

February 19, 1998 (Mary)

My dear children,

Today I desire a careful examination of each heart where peace and love must be allowed to flourish. Your hearts must become like the gardens in Spring where beauty has been planted and awaits but the gentle rain and the warmth of the sun to bring forth its harvest of delicate life ---- the fruits of your labor.

My children, do not be misled by My gentle words but search for their true meaning and pray that the eyes of your hearts will see beyond the closed doors of indifference. It is here fear and disbelief still linger causing doubt; the uncertainty which confines your faith and trust that truly all things are possible with God.

You have come to desire only comfort in your faith --not allowing for the miracles which do occur ---- the intensity of which shall increase in this remaining time.

I urge you, My little ones, to walk by faith for We are in your midst searching for the open childlike hearts into which we will pour great grace. Be wise, dear children, but in your wisdom do not restrict God's power by placing limitations for in so doing, it is you yourself who becomes restricted ---- limited by your lack of faith. Be bold ---- believe and love much.

Peace and love.

My dear children,

Your world is about to embark upon a great cleansing ---- a purification in which all hearts will awaken from their slumber of indifference to the realization that all are dependent upon God. I am here as the Mother who draws her children to safety before the approaching storm. It grieves My heart to see the fragmented dissension within your prayer groups for this is time wasted ---- - for all must be of one heart as all are part of the body of Christ. You are precious pieces in the puzzle of life ---- each one different, yet not one more important than the other.

My children, where is the injury and pain which you must bear? Come to Me that I may place a gentle kiss upon your wounds to sooth and comfort you in your afflictions. Trust, My little ones ---- allow humility to be the blanket which covers your soul keeping warm the fires of love and forgiveness, for upon these you will draw strength in your journey to holiness. Peace and love.

My dear children,

You hear the wind as it's forces echo as it brushes throughout the trees ---- the fields of wheat ---- the flowers sent to adorn the earth in garments of beauty yet simplicity. Still your hearts are not so easily moved for though the seed of faith lies deeply within your hearts, you fail to recognize the existence of that which you cannot explain as faith is but a simple belief in that which you cannot see. It must be allowed to grow unhindered by doubt and distrust.

We wish to pour so many blessings upon you, dear children, but you must ask in faith and believe with your hearts that Our merciful and loving God hears the cries of your hearts responding to each need in accordance with His will and the depth of your faith. What shall you do, My little ones, if the roots of your faith have not been allowed to grow deeply within your hearts? You will easily become uprooted and left barren to dry upon the parched indifference of this world ---- to be blown about as the shafts of wheat left by the Harvest.

I urge you to become the most humble ---- the smallest amongst you for you will go unnoticed by man but will find favor with God. The choice remains yours. The time for decision is now ---- where do you stand. I pray and intercede for you that you will walk in faith ---- in pure love and trust that Almighty God, the Divine Creator, will gaze upon His handiwork with compassion and gather you amongst His chosen ones to be a living witness of His love and mercy.

Peace and love!

My dear children,

We look about seeing Our precious ones bonding together in common unity ---- in prayer seeking truth and wisdom to know God's will. Let your hearts be light as joy comes to all those who search for peace ---- those who have opened the doors of their hearts to become Our silent yet power-filled peace makers. Much awaits you as you approach this the Springtime of life. All must learn of God's great mercy for in His compassion He leads you to His pasture of sweet repose where the flame of love burns ever so brightly.

Now, My children, you must chose as the delicate flower of life begins to wilt beneath the oppressive power of moral decay. Much has been said as My messengers have rallied throughout your world spreading My words of love ---- - hope ---- and peace. I call you to prepare ---- not to fear for where there is God there is no fear. Rejoice and be glad for soon all will feel the presence of God.

February 23, 1998 (Mary)

My dear children,

It is in the hearts of My children where I seek to dwell ---- to bring comfort and consolation as the path to holiness narrows. I have urged you to seek Jesus first in all things that peace may fill your souls ---- drawing you closer to the fountain of His mercy.

Through the Divine Love of God, you have been blessed with many signs and wonders ---- still many remain hardened. My children, pray the rosary as often as possible that your hearts and minds might meditate upon that which is holy. Leave no room for fear and doubt as in these times you must be strong. Have forgiving hearts for there is no time for bickering amongst Our people. You are the small glow of the candle emitting from the light of Jesus ---- together your light helps illuminate the darkness calling all who will hear of the great love and forgiveness of God. Do not slacken in your zeal for Jesus as great must be your preparation for Lent. I urge you to sacrifice more ---- to do penance ---- to be reconciled to Our Lord. Pray, little ones, with childlike faith for Jesus in Divine Love desires no one to be lost. Pray for an understanding heart ---- many souls hang in the balance ---- -each one of you is capable of making a difference.

I tell you, My children, how you live your life affects how others perceive you.. I pray that all will see love and compassion in each heart ---- as each has been given responsibility in life. Accept what you must, for there comes a great testing which you cannot avoid ---- confront it ---- embrace it as grace will allow you to overcome all things. Peace and love!

My daughter,

It is now in the intimacy of your heart I urge you to meditate upon that which has been revealed to you. These burdens will soon become as feathers which gently flutter through the air gradually coming to their place of rest. As you have accepted your simple role in life, you must gather physical and spiritual strength to accomplish the tasks which you have been given. As you feel in your heart, stress the importance of reconciliation ---- prayer and fasting for all must learn and willingly desire to become closer to God. You stand upon a new threshold of hope and enlightenment. Let all hearts be prepared for this time must be used wisely ---- no longer is there room for anger and conflict. All must become as one ---- one in

the body of Christ. Pray and prepare as the peace of Jesus will draw you to the compassionate realization of the times in which you live. Do not fear, but love and trust as we are near!

February 24, 1998 (Mary)

(Second message as we were unaware I would be in surgery the next day)

My dear children,

Time swiftly passes and many hearts remain to be touched with the gentle love and compassion of Jesus. Your responsibility grows as Our precious children will come searching for understanding hearts in which to share their joy and pain. I urge you once again to place Christ first above all things that His will becomes yours ---- that self is removed from your hearts leaving only the desire to serve others. I carry each of you in My heart where peace and joy may still be found. You are chosen to be children of Light ---- Divine Light and Love ---- - step out of the darkness, little ones, while the path to holiness remains brightly lit. The light of awareness is but moments away. Pray and be reconciled as the gentle breeze of peace will touch the softened hearts. Draw close to Our Lord, dear children, as He is the Mighty One who seeks to protect His children. Peace and love!

February 25, 1998 (Mary)

My dear children,

I call you to a deepening awareness ---- a profound awakening in each soul of the reality of God's great love for His children. I bring you messages of peace ---- of love and hope that all hearts will become fertile fields into which will spring forth new growth of forgiveness and compassion for one another. This, My children, is a special time of healing ---- of purification ----

a gift so great it defies understanding for only by accepting with child like faith are you given the grace to see and hear with simplistic assurance that all is as it must be. Fear and distrust have left open wounds which only pure trust in Jesus can heal. You have placed many barriers ---- false idols ---- before God, but His great love for you continues. He pursues your hearts with a Father's love seeking His precious souls ---- souls which soon will seek their place in His kingdom. Pray and persevere as soon you will be called.

Peace and love!

February 27, 1998 (Mary)

My dear children,

The trials of life pull at you from many directions. We see your struggles to maintain balance ---- to maintain strong footings in your faith by not allowing the distractions of life to weave their subtle webs of oppression and confusion. This, My children, is a constant battle, but one in which these enemies of destruction will truly be defeated through the present awareness that Jesus has conquered the enemies of the flesh and calls you to trust totally in Him. Talk to Him ---- walk with Him ---- love Him and you will find yourself drawing closer to His Divine Love and Mercy ---- to the refuge of His Most Sacred Heart.

It is my prayer for you this day that the veil of fear and uncertainty will be lifted from your eyes that no longer will you fear that which you cannot see nor understand. My children, what is there to fear when death is but the door which opens to eternity. Be at peace, My little ones. Give Me your petitions that I may lay them before the throne of My Son, sweetening them as I intercede for you.

Peace and love!

February 28, 1998 (Mary)

My dear children,

I your Mother, yearn to draw you close to My Heart where the reassurance of peace and love continuously beats for you ---- for your total conversion. It is time, My children, to awaken ---- to become aware of the many signs which God in His Divine Mercy has allowed in order to show His displeasure towards His beloved creatures who willfully choose to ignore His love.

The slumber of indifference has lulled many into complacency. This, My children, is a false sense of peace. The weight of sin has become an anchor which neither allows you to move forward nor backward but remain entrenched in disobedience. My children, so many souls are in danger ---- they have lost their way - choosing to follow a path well worn by selfishness and pride.

Pray, dear children, ---- extend your hand to them while clinging tightly to the rope of salvation as you seek to spare your brothers from the depths of the abyss! No longer, My children, allow pride to rear its ugly head for selfishness must fade into selflessness as the light of pure love shines brightly upon you.

Pray from the heart that your heart will at last find peace.

March 1, 1998 (Mary)

My dear children,

Praise be Jesus. In these times of turmoil when hearts lie broken and confusion seeks to steal your peace ---- know it is Jesus who stands in your midst caressing each heart with great tenderness and compassion. Your life is delicate as the flower whose petals form from the bud of infancy into an array of beauty ---- - vulnerable yet boldly allowing its beauty to be enjoyed by all. So, too, My little ones, each petal of your life as it unfolds brings in itself a stage of life ---- of growth and maturity. In Spring, the youth of life, your hearts are filled with expectations of great accomplishments ---- yet too often you fail to recognize God's hand in your life ---- thus you tuck away gratitude for that which you have been given. Mankind, in error, fails to acknowledge God and thus in the Autumn of their years the petals of life wither awaiting only the final moment until they fall ---- no longer beautiful but dry and void of life.

My children, many are in the Autumn of their years yet because of their great love of God, their beauty has not diminished. As these precious petals (souls) fall, they are gently caught in the loving hands of Jesus. It is He who breathes new life into His children that they may dwell with Him forever. Pray much, My children.

Peace and love.

March 2, 1998 (Mary)

My dear children,

In this special time of grace, many hearts are being purified ---- cleansed to bear true witness to the love and mercy of Jesus. I am gathering all of My faithful ones ---- those who seek the refuge of My immaculate Heart for there must no longer be barriers of dissension but only the embrace of pure hearts ---- each bound

119

tightly to Divine Love. It is time to put aside differences ---- to allow wounds to heal especially those within your own families. Each must be a vessel of peace emanating the compassion of Jesus. Learn true forgiveness whereby you will reach a degree of holiness through which others will see and feel the presence of God's love. Do not delay, little ones, for the remaining time must be well spent. I love you and encourage you in this your journey of life!

Peace and love.

March 3, 1998 (Mary)

My dear children,

Pray, dear children, with your heart for it is in private moments when hearts are joined as one that prayer becomes a weapon of power. It is heart felt prayer which allows faith to grow whereby the mountains of disease and injustice are cast off ---- no longer binding but freeing its victims to gratefully acknowledge God's love and mercy. Learn, My little ones, God does exist and His heart is moved with pity for His children who seek Him with pure and loving hearts without selfish motives.

I urge you to continue in prayer ---- call upon the angels and Saints ---- - the Heavenly courts for all are eager to assist you. Believe and trust and your prayers will be well received as I your Mother know your hearts and lovingly intercede for you. Rejoice as We rejoice with you. Peace and love!

March 4, 1998 (Mary)

My daughter,

Pray for the grace to love ---- to love well ---- unconditionally without reserve. Remain focused on Jesus whereby peace and understanding will filter into your heart. My children hunger for answers to life's many questions and thus they will seek those whom they feel have been blessed with special gifts. You know this to be true. It is in these times in which you embrace others you will be greatly tested as no longer must they see you for you must die to self, that Jesus may dwell within you.

Your world soon embarks upon major changes. I ask My children in their preparations to return to the use of holy water in their homes. Bless yourselves frequently that your thoughts and words will be pure and pleasing to God. I urge all prayer groups to stress the importance of holy water for this is a powerful source of protection now and in the times to come.

Always encourage others, My little one, for the power of the Holy Spirit descends upon God's people as they will proclaim His glory now and forever.

Peace, My daughter. Prepare much as holiness requires great sacrifice. Continue onward in humble obedience as the awareness of My messages penetrates many hearts.

March 5, 1998 (Mary)

My dear children,

This is a most holy time in which I call you to reflect upon your lives ---- the condition of your soul for Divine Love has come to heal. He softly calls each of you to walk in His steps ---- listen with your hearts has you must be still and contemplate the words which He speaks to all hearts. Do not fear, oh little ones, for He has come to gather His precious children in all their brokenness and pain. He seeks not perfection but only open hearts in which He may pour His love ---- His peace.

I pray with the love of a mother's heart that the awareness of these times in which you live will arouse all hearts and will stir within each soul a profound desire to be holy people of God. As each is chosen so too must each respond. Pray for discernment as much remains to be accomplished.

Peace and love.

March 6, 1998 (Mary)

My dear children,

I continue to come out of deepest love for My children for many hearts remain heavily burdened. Though in your hearts you seek to live holy lives, the words from your mouths and your actions betray your human weakness allowing pride ---- distrust and envy to disfigure the soul which cries for mercy.

My children, My heart grieves for you who struggle with such intensity to believe and trust yet you cling to old habits which have scarred your faith. The innocence of infancy where childlike faith and trust abounded has long faded and been replaced by skepticism and uncertainty. Hear My words, dear children, as Divine Love seeks to restore the innocence of youth.

You are living in the time of the great Harvest when all souls must be enlightened. Love and forgiveness are not mere words but conscious acts which all are called to perform. Where the seed of compassion has been planted, love ---- true love ----

grows with roots deeply embedded in the Divine Will leaving no room for the weeds of fear and doubt

Many souls hunger for truth ---- I urge you to put aside differences ---- - to become humble for in your humility others will see the light of love and hope will emerge once again encouraging all to seek God's love and mercy. Peace and love, dear children.

March 7, 1998 (Mary)

My dearest children,

As My time with you grows short, I wish to draw you close to My heart ---- the heart which beats as one with My Son. It is He who in His goodness and mercy has allowed My stay ---- a time in which graces have flowed and hearts have softened that all will beat as one. Life, My children, is a time of joy ---- joy in which you love beyond the glitter of materialism and seek with humility the simplistic reality of Christ's love. It is here, My children, where you will separate the wants from the needs. God is mighty and capable of all things and in His mercy He meets the needs of His people. I urge you to trust Him without reserve for He alone knows that which is best for you. His love is total ---- pure and unending. He reaches down to you, little ones, so lovingly as He gently wipes away each tear. It is not pain and suffering He desires for His children but in the greatness of His love He allows that which purifies each soul that by embracing each trial you become a precious stone ---- priceless and irreplaceable ---- a treasure so great you would drown in tears of gratitude if you could only comprehend the magnitude of His love. Be strong, My children, as you are called to live your life in love ---- not fear. Peace and love.

March 8, 1998 (Mary)

My dear children,

Throughout the world I have come to reinforce that which has been foretold many years ago. I am a light which shines brightly upon the path which leads to Jesus. In all ways, My children, My mission of love has been but a simple awakening of hearts ---- hearts fallen dormant through neglect ---- now reawakened ---- aroused through true conversions to become strong yet gentle voices of love. It is those voices which have assisted Me in My mission which now must echo throughout your world.

I urge you to be strong ---- well versed in your faith. Seek reconciliation often as you know neither the date nor hour in which you must account for your journey through life. I encourage you to be obedient, yet joyful, as you in trust and desire of heart, are being led into the pasture of holiness. Follow the path which Jesus

122

has walked being confidently aware of His Divine presence. It is the awareness of holiness which draws the soul to seek union with its Creator.

May the love of Jesus take root deeply within each heart as the realization of the signs of the times becomes more and more evident with each passing moment. Pray, My children, for evil wears a cleaver disguise and many fall unwittingly into its snare . Pray with your heart for in such times enlightenment and knowledge shall prevail for Jesus reveals to His chosen ones that which dispels the darkness of sin. It is through prayer and trust in Jesus that evil shall be defeated. Peace and love.

March 9, 1998 (Mary)

My dear children,

I desire to repeat My messages of peace and hope as the trials of life beat down upon you. It is as though , My children, you wander scorched by the sun's rays ---- tired and helpless to defend yourself. Reach out, My children, to the hand outstretched before you as I will lead you to the oasis of My Son's love and mercy where you will find refreshment.

Here you must gain strength as the hour is close at hand when your very faith will be tested. Have no fear, My children, for many graces are being poured out upon God's people. I urge you to pray and prepare.

Peace and love. *(Personal message given at this time)*.

March 10, 1998 (Mary)

My dear children,

We wait in the silent stillness of each heart which through trials and obedience has persevered in its efforts to draw closer to God. My children, My prayers for you have stormed Heaven's gate as many are unprepared spiritually and physically to meet the challenges ahead. The time quickly approaches when I must step aside as prophecy unfolds to a greater degree. My children will scatter in fear and confusion, but My faithful remnant will remain strong and unshaken by world events for they have sought the protection of My Immaculate Heart. I urge My little ones ----those who have strayed and have become entrapped by the enticements of this world ---- to search their hearts for true peace and wealth are not of this world but of that which soon comes. Prepare your hearts now in service to the Lord where true peace and riches beyond measure are being stored in the treasure chest of His love.

Peace and love, My children.

My dear children,

Peace and love I bring to you this day that each heart will become a willing vessel where the tranquil assurance of Divine Love will dwell. Message upon message We have heaped upon you filling your minds and hearts with the awareness of God's great love and mercy. Many have chosen to become complacent and idle in their faith allowing it to grow weak from neglect. Allow the encouragement We bring to rekindle the flame of faith that it will become bright and vibrant ---- a source of encouragement to others.

Each must assume their role in life ---- accept responsibility, My children, for human will seeks to excuse error for lack of knowledge, but I tell you the awareness of that which comes has been revealed to you. In your attempt to excuse error, you compound your sin by allowing injury to fester ---- to become a vile disease that only reconciliation can cure. Sin has reached such an epidemic proportion that God must cleanse His people to halt the spread of its disease. Be at peace, My children, Pray ---- love ---- forgive and be reconciled. Peace soon comes.

March 12, 1998 (Mary)

My dear children,

The words of My Heart reach out to each of My children to embrace you with peace and understanding that My messages will become alive and bear fruit. My children ---- many times your spoken words have become instruments of destruction. You speak ---- then think and thus remorse follows for you have inflicted injury and harm upon the character of another. Be humble, little ones, for materialism ---- the decorations of life ---- are but surface ornaments beneath which lie the disfigurement of sin.

Your hearts are called beyond this world where you must rise above temptation and evil which strikes from every direction seeking the destruction of your soul. It is through My messages of peace and joy that hope becomes alive ---- strengthened to do battle with the forces of evil. It is through Jesus ---- through whose love comes salvation that each soul is allowed the awareness of true love and peace. You are His children ---- whom He watches ---- gently urging each to pick up their cross and follow Him. There is no other way, My little ones, which leads to Heaven ---- all must bear that which has been allotted to them. Divine grace is the strength which lightens the burdens of life. In the quietness of your heart, beseech the Lord for in His mercy and tender unending love, He blesses His people. Take that step of faith while there is yet time.

Peace and love!

March 13, 1998 (Mary)

My dear children,

I come once again calling each of you to quiet your hearts and let the cares of the day become as drops of rain which fall cleansing ---- yet nourishing the soil which will bear new growth. Listen, My children, attentively for I speak My gentle words of encouragement ---- slowly ---- to nurture the soul which seeks union with God. Do not, My little ones, hurry through My messages as you hurry through life ---- for the simple beauty of God's creation goes unnoticed ---- - as does the simple wisdom of My words.

Out of pure love I have come to be the Mother into whose arms you may come to seek comfort. I whisper subtle warnings ---- yet console you in your times of un-certainty . You are never alone, dear children ---- you have but to let the scales of doubt fall uncovering an open heart into which We will pour forth love and peace. Rejoice as the simple awareness of Divine Love brings hope to conquer the darkness which comes.

Peace and love!

March 14, 1998 (Mary)

My daughter,

Be still, My child, as I speak to your heart which needlessly races to accomplish more than is asked of you. You are called to be gentle and loving ---- a compassionate dove of peace. There will be many wounds, dear one, but none that will not heal if placed into Our hands where We will sooth away the pain. These are but the trials of which We spoke ---- - obstacles placed in your path to destroy your peace. It is in these times you must rely upon your faith and trust in Jesus as He allows only that which you can bear. You heard His words ---- -"Has your burden become too heavy" ---- you looked at His nail scarred hands and were ashamed of your weakness. Be brave, little one, for in such weakness comes great strength for the awareness of His love and mercy defies the human mind. Be at peace as the journey continues but awhile longer.

March 14, 1998 (Jesus)

(This was an unexpected message for a young retreat group from Douglas, AZ. I had gone to confession and was praying in front of the Blessed Sacrament when my heart was being prepared to receive these words. I came home, stopped by the Chapel, and went to get my notebook to write. I was instructed to go directly to the computer and begin typing the dictation.)

My precious children,

In each struggle through life you face decisions ---- decisions which must be made with a heart prepared with love and founded on truth. Each of you are here to experience the profoundness of My love and of the gentle caressing of My Mothers compassionate intercession for Her children. You are not here by accident, My children, for in My plan of life each one is called but many fail to respond for the ways of the world still hold tightly upon the strings of their hearts.

I knew you before you were conceived ---- I saw you in your brokenness as I hung from the cross on Calvary and today ---- this night, I call you by name. Into each heart I come searching for a willing spirit that comes to me in love ---- the sweet innocence of a child's love for its parent.

The journey ahead is filled with distractions ---- all meant to weaken your desire for holiness, but you, My children, are mine ---- I have claimed you ---- with Love I paid the price for your soul. It is you now, My children, who will be asked ---- will you outstretch your arms and receive this gift ---- for be warned, it does not come without a high price!

How much do you love Me, My precious children?

March 15, 1998 (Mary)

My dear children,

You live in a special time of great grace ---- a time of preparation for that which soon must come. My call goes out to My children throughout your world in search of hearts willing to sacrifice and perform acts of penance in reparation for the evil which has sought to destroy hope and love. I call all who will listen ---- to hear and react out of childlike faith ---- by living My messages. Yesterday is but a time in history ---- once here ---- now gone ---- only the memories linger. How many yesterdays have you allowed to slip by without a simple kind word ---- some encouragement. So many despair, My children, for life is not always so kind but you ---- because of your faith and trust in Jesus, you must be kind. You have been taught by the Master Who is Divine Love. The pathway to Jesus is well worn, My little ones ---- it is narrow and its obstacles are many, but He who outstretched His arms for you upon the Cross awaits His children. Do not fear this journey, but be aware of the great battle which ensues about you. Let the love of Jesus shine brightly for in His love you will find the power of peace.

My dear children,

I call you to receive with an open heart all that has been entrusted to you. You have been blessed with many signs and wonders ---- still many refuse to accept their authenticity. Each must pray and discern for themselves as We do not ---- nor will not ---- force Our will upon yours. You remain free to choose until your last breath on earth. I urge you to become aware of the subtle changes in life and examine their meaning as knowledge abounds now in your lifetime more than ever before ---- it must be controlled though, My children, and used wisely for man becomes proud of His knowledge and thus pride becomes His downfall. Pray much during this holy time that you will abide in the Father's Will ---- freed from the world's enticements. Peace and love.

March 17, 1998 (Mary)

My dear children,

My call goes out to all those who will hear ---- for indeed My call is a call of urgency. Too many of My children have been caught in the web of doubt as their Bibles lie dormant and dusty upon the shelf. How, My dear ones, are you to learn ---- to be prepared when God's Holy Word remains but a book which many possess but seldom read. I encourage you to walk with Me through the pages of time as slowly We will uncover truth in prophecy. All has been laid in place as chapter by chapter will unfold the mysteries of God's great love and mercy.

I am sent by Divine Love into each heart that will accept Me as the gentle Mother who flies to the aid of Her endangered children. Beware of false prophets, My children, that you will not be led astray for the evil one seeks to devour those lukewarm souls ---- souls again caught in the web of uncertainty. Be bold ---- be brave ---- as together we reach journey's end. My children ---- Jesus knows each heart ---- there are no secrets. Surrender your will to His while time permits. The trumpets sound.

Make ready, My precious ones.

March 18, 1998 (Mary)

My dear children,

I come in your brokenness to heal and restore your faith made weak by a world which seeks to smother the life of the Spirit within each heart. My dear children, I do not come to chastise ---- to scorn ---- or to instill fear, but only to encourage by My love the gentle awareness of God's presence.

In His greatness, He desires to enlighten the souls of His children drawing them back to Him ---- all the while purifying them and enlightening them with hope and peace.

All that which lies before you shall soon take form as the veil of the curtain is about to rise on the destiny of mankind. I urge you to pray with greater intensity that strength and perseverance shall dwell in each heart longing to walk in holiness.

March 19, 1998 (Mary)

My dear children,

I invite you into My heart ---- a heart of peace ---- totally void of anguish and uncluttered by worldly distractions. peace for Jesus in His Divine Love and mercy does not impose Himself upon His children yet it is only through Him can true peace be found. The desire of His Heart that you love Him is not an obligation ---- a restriction ---- a condition upon which you must meet certain demands ---- It is simplicity of heart ---- a deep hunger for holiness that only abiding in His love can bring. His love is like a series of notes when played well become a harmony of inexplicable joy.

I tell you, My children, time is too short to dwell upon that which attempts to steal your peace. Do not, dear ones, make this journey through life more difficult than intended ---- for each day brings that which is specifically intended for that day --- - no more ---- no less.

I am here to speak to hearts prepared spiritually to accept and acknowledge My words of truth. Prepare with intense prayer and obedience for the enlightenment of that which follows must awaken all hearts.

May you find happiness, My little ones in knowing you are dearly loved.

March 20, 1998 (Mary)

My dear children,

There is a wave of sorrow in My Heart as My time with you grows short. You are My ---- dear ---- children whom I have nurtured but a short while yet you are strong enough to stand for the common bond of love ---- the love of Jesus ---- unites you one to another. My precious ones, do not fear the unknown ---- but continue onward with the assurance of Divine Love's unending compassion for each one of His beloved children.

128

The trials of life ---- those times of pain and suffering which can take many forms, are an intricate part of this life's journey. They are a means by which you obtain great grace ---- and thus through grace, you become led upon the path to holiness.

I urge you, My dear children, to bear your crosses with joy as you trust in Him upon whose cross you now gaze. I solemnly tell you, little ones, you have come upon holy ground. This place has been chosen ---- not by man ---- but by the hand of God. All is in place for the angels of the Lord stand ready to defend that which is His. Let fear and uncertainty no longer control your lives ---- rejoice for the awareness of Our presence will be experienced by many. Prepare your hearts to love and forgive as only through true conversion can peace be obtained. Peace and love!

March 21, 1998 (Mary)

My dear children,

This day you are called to that moment of decision ---- the moment in which all must choose the course of ones soul. We have urged you ---- encouraged you ---- consoled you and above all ---- loved you with such depth of emotion that should humanity comprehend the reality of such love it would expire ---- unable to contain itself ---- overwhelmed by what had been revealed.

It is your Mother's prayer that each soul seek eternal life with Jesus. Joy beyond words awaits those souls who patiently and in quiet humility await the day in which they will enter into the light of eternal love and peace ---- where all, at last , are one ---- united with Jesus!

I caution you, My children, do not continue in idleness and self-gratification for your world has chosen an irreversible course of self destruction. One plague upon another has been unleashed ---- - you have, by your own self induced wisdom, unwittingly engaged the gears of self destruction.

This is a final time of great grace in which Divine Mercy seeks to rescue ---- - to restore respect for life. Take heed, My children, hear with your hearts the gravity of My words.

Peace and Love!

March 22, 1998 (Mary)

My dear children,

In joyful harmony the angels sing as We receive your humble prayers and petitions for you have responded to My Call. You gathered in love ---- out of this

129

love shall flow forth seeds of faith nurtured by trust in the presence of God and the reassurance of His compassion for His children. It is by your childlike desire for your Father's approval that you obediently seek to grow and accept His Will. My beloved children, the pathway to My Son is well lit but many fail to see for they seek only out of idle curiosity ---- the whim of emotion completely unfounded on faith and thus no matter how brightly shines the Light it becomes only a distorted shadow for again humanity seeks to explain that which it cannot, and all vision is impaired. My children, I urge you to comprehend My words for they are truth and in truth you shall awaken to the realization of God's Divine Love. It is time, dear ones, to prepare ---- to forgive ---- and to love much. Pray from your heart as I intercede for those who seek the love and compassion of a Mother's heart. Peace and love!

March 23, 1998 (Mary)

My dear children,

I have come to prepare the tender hearts of My faithful remnant who will meet with courage the challenges about to befall your world. The line has been drawn as good and evil maneuver into position for the final battle. You , My precious ones, have been well armed with truth ---- the Word of God which will be your strength during these trying times. I have sought to instill peace and love that you may face the enemy free of fear and anxiety for you are now warriors of love ---- Divine Love!

It is in service to My Son that your heart will seek the lost ---- disillusioned ---- to bring comfort as each of you are now messengers entrusted with compassionate hearts which We will use to draw souls to the fountain of Divine Mercy ---- here, My little ones, hope comes wrapped in Pure Love.

Be brave for their is nothing to fear. Life continues as it must ---- eternity awaits. Prepare ---- prepare ---- pray and prepare!

Peace and love.

March 24, 1998 (Mary)

My dear children,

We draw closer to the moment when these particular daily messages shall cease. I draw each of you close to My Heart that you may feel My warm embrace and experience with unquestionable certainty the love which has urged Me in tireless pursuit of Our beloved children. I have through repetition relayed message after message that you, dear ones, might comprehend with great certainty the inevitable consequences of sin as mankind, by free will, has disregarded God's laws and has become inflated by pride ---- envy ---- and the desires of the flesh. It is by the

130

mercy of the All Loving and Just Father that his children shall be allowed the great grace of the awareness of soul*. I urge you to prepare, My little ones. Seek the heart of Jesus for in His Most Sacred Heart is that peace which each soul yearns to possess.

I love you, dear children, and I will hold tightly to the reigns of your hearts until you either embrace Our love or reject it. This is a crucial time for mankind. Pray, My children.

*(This was understood to be the forthcoming "warning" or "enlightenment" of conscience).

March 25, 1998 (Mary)

My dear children,

You are the precious stones polished to adorn the Throne ---- the flowers picked from amongst the weeds. You have in essence been prepared to perform a great task in the coming era of life ---- a new beginning for most ---- yet, a time of great sorrow for those who willfully sought the path to destruction

You have received many graces through these messages and others. It is in these coming times you must rely upon the great mercy of Love Himself as He now calls His chosen ones to hear and live the words of encouragement and love which have pierced the hearts of His beloved children.

My dear little ones, walk confidently on the path of righteousness as Truth has prepared the way. There is nothing left unsaid. You are prepared to recognize the signs of the times without fear for you know that Jesus is Lord of All and soon comes to claim that which is His.

You are the stars of joy shining brightly in the darkened sky. Let your light, which is the light of Jesus, never be extinguished as many will come stumbling and crawling ---- for the path, though well lit, is filled with cunning arrays of distractions meant to discourage and extinguish the desire for holiness. You are strong ---- believe and trust for Divine Love has sought and claimed that which is His. Be at peace, My dearly beloved children.

(Note: Our Lady indicated that this message was the last <u>daily</u> message for the public. Notice - Our Lady did not say good-bye as had been anticipated. She instead briefly repeated Her words of encouragement while reiterating that we belong to Jesus - "we are His" - and, as such, must stand and be counted as loving peacemakers - willing to forgive others out of love for Her Son as time, indeed, is short. It has been discerned that periodic messages for the public may still be received. The following messages confirm this.)

131

This message was received while praying the Chaplet of Divine Mercy at the small shrine. It was intended for those in attendance --- all in attendance, as Our Mother said we each have individual roles to perform.

My children,

What has kept you away little ones --- We have patiently awaited your return. See how life can pull you from every direction --- distracting you --- permitting peace to be disrupted as priorities have been rearranged. My dear ones, it is in this place --- a place of prayer where hearts --- broken hearts will be mended and faith restored.

It is a role of great importance which has been entrusted to you --- each of you. You have been chosen to fulfill a great mission --- a mission of sacrifice. We have examined your hearts and found them to be willing instruments which We will use as Our people come. It is a time of many graces --- graces which will exact a toll upon each of you. It is the Lord Jesus who calls you --- hear well, My precious ones as you are vessels which We have filled in preparation for the times to come.

It is with joyful hearts We have received you this day.

May 18, 1998 (Jesus)

My children,

I gaze through time eternal in search of hearts willing to unite themselves with My Will. These precious souls are in the fields harvesting the crop --- preparing for the fulfillment of prophecy. They work diligently seeking those grains (souls) which have fallen --- left unnoticed --- buried beneath oppression or selfish desires which prohibit the fruition of the soul. I have sent My Mother clothed with the burning desire for souls to draw each of My children back to My Heart of Mercy.

Look about your world and observe the depth of decay. Know, My children, I do not look upon you with eyes of scorn or contempt but with Divine Love and forgiveness. Come back to Me now while there is yet time, for soon My Justice shall strike. You are called from the darkness into the light of My love to be My bearers of peace and joy. Pray with sincerity of heart and I will hear and answer you. You must be cautious and vigilant, for many are being deceived through a false sense of peace and security. Invoke the presence of the Holy Spirit, for He will dispel doubt and instill peace within each heart which seeks holiness.

Be at peace, My children!

May 28, 1998 (Our Lord)

My daughter,

So much, My child, is yet to be accomplished. There are many hearts remaining to know My peace as they hunger and thirst for purpose of life. Be not afraid as your journey intensifies, but calmly draw close to My Heart. it is I who fills you with strength whereby many souls will find sweet repose.

Listen well to the words of My Mother. She is the Holy One, the Anchor, who remains firm in Her constant desire for souls --- an ally like unto none other. She is Queen yet Mother of all. Follow Her guidance for She will truly lead you to peace, My peace. Tend My sheep as many will gather.

August 5, 1998 (Our Lady Speaks)

My dear children,
You see the sun as it rises majestically in early morning silently making its way into the sky. So, too I call you, My Little one, to allow your soul to climb ever so silently to spiritual heights of holiness. It is not by the roaring thunder of approaching storms, but by gentle sincere persistence that each soul valiantly makes its way--- soaring above the temptations of this world seeking unity --- that purity of heart --- which draws them closer to Jesus. Be encouraged, My children, for I, your Mother, stand closely by to encourage you through each moment of life. I entreat you to bear your cross with holy dignity, for by your example, others will seek the fountain of My Son's mercy.

Come, My children, and allow me to caress your wounds for it is only through true devotion to My Son can true peace exist. Already the rumbling storms approach--- I call you to peace--- such peace is not a mere word, but a necessity for spiritual survival. Hear Me well, little ones, for much meaning lies hidden in My words. I bless you this day as I draw you close to My heart. Peace and love!

September 2, 1998 (Mary)

My daughter,

This journey upon which you have embarked is one of fragile dreams bound tightly with Our love --- that strength which allows you to grow and mature in your faith. That which you have been allowed to see is very real and carries great responsibility for you will become the eyes of many. We have chosen Our little ones throughout your world as each must awaken to the urgency of Our call. The

133

world with all its false idols is on a rapid course of destruction --- there are all too few of Our children prepared for that which is soon to be unveiled.

Pray intensely, allow these remaining moments of your life to be prayerful vigils which will strengthen Our children with the serenity of Our love and peace. Be courageous warriors in this battle for souls as We stand ready to defend all that is Ours. Be at peace as Divine Love conquers all!

Peace and love!

October 13, 1998 (Our Lady Speaks)

My daughter,

Soon the light will shine brighter, that all might see the sin scarred crevices of the soul wherein lies ones deepest secrets. Ponder in your heart the signs of these times. Be still and unshaken by rumors, for in this place to which you were called shall spring forth unmistakable healings of soul and body. Criticism and skepticism you shall not escape as each must be borne for the greater honor and glory of God. Believe and place total trust in Jesus. All must see that by Divine purpose pure love has come to conquer fear and instill peace in each heart.

December 4, 1998 (Mary)

My dear children,

Peace I bring to you this day wrapped tightly with threads of love spun upon the Master's loom. This peace is likened unto none other for it is the calmness that soothes the anxious hearts and allows the spirit to rest uncluttered in the tranquility of the Divine Will.

****

134

Messages from Jesus and Mary

January 2, 1999 - December 31, 1999

January 2, 1999 (Jesus)

The following message was given during private prayer time after a rather intense spiritual happening in which a small group from Nogales and Douglas had gathered on the mountain to pray. It offers an explanation in a simple form of the power of prayer and how we are each called to believe and trust totally in our Lord Jesus Christ. It is recommended that this be read slowly that one may concentrate upon its meaning.

Each soul upon whom My Spirit rests is given many graces. It is in these times *(while resting in the spirit)* when no longer is your human body in control for the spirit within continuously searches until it finds the Divine Will and thus you rest outwardly, but inwardly the spirit.... Your spirit, soars to new and far greater heights of prayerful communion...... thus enabling you to accomplish that which has been predestined. Do not dwell upon the mysteries of this life but rather place your trust in Me.

January 13, 1999 (Jesus)

I wish you to plant a garden of souls. Sow each seed with loving kindness and I will send the gentle rain of graces which will awaken the dormant seed as it takes root in My Word. You are My gardeners and I am the Master of the Fields. Tend well the fragile souls... shower them with kindness that they may know beyond doubt that it is I who call their name. My shield of love and protection I freely give as My love knows no bounds. The stormy battle for souls intensifies. Be vigilant with quiet hearts that listen for My voice. I speak to all souls... be patient and trust in Me.

March 19, 1999

(Our Lord has a message for us...he is extending the invitation, an R.S.V.P reserve space via penance.) (The following is our Lord, in a gentle but firm voice clearly spoken)

"I invite all of you to walk with me and to share in my passion. Look deep into your hearts. Will you respond to this call? Pray for conversion to my Sacred Heart and that of my Mother. Do not fear my children. Do not fear things in this world. Many things are coming, but I will give you strength to endure them all. This Lent is very important. My children, have confidence and strength in me. I have given you each a cross of Love. I will speak to each heart you will know my voice. Listen. Accept my way, walk this path. There will be much pain and sorrow, but also much joy. There is a brilliant light. Many are coming to me". *(some sobbing, as though the passion itself were being experienced)* "No, No," *(As if in much pain and anguish)*... "they will endure" *(said with a sense of resolve or resignation)* "Following the Commandments and walking in my way will lead to paradise.

Endure my children, much will come soon."

May 28, 1999

The following messages were received Friday evening after the last decade of the Sorrowful mysteries of the rosary.

"My children,

Do you really think you could stay with me beneath My cross? Do you, My children, have such courage ? - - - And yet I was left with just a few. My children, I ask of you to draw closer to My heart. You, My precious ones, will not survive if you do not surrender your will to mine. I am Love ---- pure Love! I call you to be courageous, yet gentle of heart. You do not know what lies ahead, so I have come with My Mother to strengthen you that you will not falter or lose hope. Trust Me! The way will grow more difficult.

Be at peace. I do not leave My children without comfort."

(After original message above, Jesus said) – "My grace ...... My blessing is upon each of you tonight. Be bold - be brave - be gentle!"

May 29, 1999

(The following message was given to a visiting group from California. This message was received in the Chapel while praying for the intentions of this special group who had traveled a long distance with hearts filled with love for Our Lord and His Blessed Mother)

"My children,

Do not feel disappointment in your hearts if you do not receive a special message for you have My special blessing this day ..... for you have come from far away to honor Me and My Mother. All my children I gather in My most Sacred Heart. Remember, My children, it is never I who turns and walks away from you. It is you, in your moments of weakness who turn and walk from me. Turn and gaze upon Me ... My heart on fire for each of you. See My eyes as they search each soul. What more, My children, do you need of me? Ask in your hearts, and I will hear and answer you. I bless you..........."

(Note: There was some discussion later that evening as to the frequency of messages we have been receiving. Certainly our Lord and Blessed Mother have showered us with such graces for a reason. The intensity of their love for all of their children becomes more apparent as we watch these "signs of these times". This morning's scripture was the twenty first chapter of Luke. I believe that speaks for its self.)

June 12, 1999

(The following message was received Saturday evening during one of Our Lady's Call to Conversion retreats. The message came very soon after the Sacrament of Reconciliation.)

"My precious children,

I gather each of you close to My Most Sacred Heart. Join with Me this day as I stand in your midst ---- My eyes searching each heart. I desire you to be bold and to feel My gentle peace, for you are being sent into the world which does not know My peace.

I bless you --- I love you --- I cherish you and I await you!"

(Note: During the laying of hands Saturday evening Our Lady blessed all of those present. She caressed each person by gently holding their face in Her hands. It was our Mother's gentle reminder of Her "very real presence" as She leads us all to Jesus.)

June 17, 1999

(The following message was received during the Thursday night vigil in the presence of the Safford, Arizona retreat group.)

"My Children,

What do you seek of Me, My children? You come with hearts so broken. Yet I, My precious ones, will mend each heart.

Listen to Me for My words are true. My love for you knows no bounds. Come freely ---- without fear for My arms are outstretched to receive you. You, My children --- My precious children ---- will be like the leaves of the trees which are dormant as faith in many lies dormant. I am the rain that comes to refresh the earth and your souls. As the leaves spring forth from the trees, so too, your faith will blossom.

It is I who will nourish each soul!"

June 25, 1999

"My precious children,

Know, My dear ones, that you have found favor with My Son. He has examined each heart, and though weak and lacking in humility, He embraces you with His strength. Rejoice, My children, ----- through your prayers and sacrifices, My Son accomplishes His plan of Salvation.

Do not be deterred from this holy path, for that which lies ahead, My little ones, words cannot describe. For you are still children, and that which is ahead you cannot comprehend ------ such grandeur ---- such love ----- such peace. I urge you now more than ever before ---- be vigilant and wise, My children, for the light of these times soon dims. You will need all the graces that are being poured out upon you. Be My courageous little ones for into battle you are being sent. Fear not, and let love be your weapon which destroys the enemy.

I bless you for you are Ours ------ Our little ones! Go now filled with courage and confidence for we stand guard over that which is Ours".

July 10, 1999

(The following Message was received Saturday evening during the "laying of hands" at "Our Mothers call to conversion" retreat.)

"My children,
The battle has begun ----- a line has been drawn. Where do you stand, my children, for by the choices you make you either choose life in Me or forever away from Me. Do You love Me as I love you? Will you choose sacrifice or pain if it brings souls into My Kingdom? I need you, my children, so much to return to Me.

Always let love --- pure love --- be more and more that desire of your heart which will bring strength to endure in this life. Many paths are so difficult, but nothing, My dear ones, is impossible ---- for I can do all things. Learn to always trust Me, love Me and walk this path to Me."

July 10, 1999

"Oh My beloved children;

Praise be to Jesus Who has sent Me into your world to guide you into a journey so filled with opportunities. Opportunities My Children, to draw others to the Mountain of Mercy. This place that My Son has chosen; this place where so many hearts will be healed.

Continue little ones in your undertakings. Cling closely to My mantle for I, your Mother, I am you refuge. Together we will journey to the throne of My Divine Son.

Hear My words for truth must always be heard and spread throughout your world. Do not falter from this path for ahead lies glory. Welcome my children into the service of My Son. I bless you, each of you are mine. Be at peace".

July 15, 1999

"My beloved children,

I am in your presence. I seek only your hearts. Join Me here - with your heart - united to mine --- for you know not the importance of what I ask. Time now is not your friend. You must use each moment wisely. I will shower you with graces. My manifestation you will see!

I am preparing my remnant ----- your bodies will tire, but your spirit will grow stronger and stronger. *(Brief dialogue in tongues)*. Prepare now.

You have heard My words many times. You have heard My Mother as She encourages all of Our children. Be not afraid. The time comes when you will be tested --- some beyond their endurance. Pray for My children ..... pray. Trust Me! Stay with Me this night ----- let us be together while time permits."

July 22, 1999

"My dear children:

You are so blessed ----- never take for granted these graces. I, your Mother, wish only to protect My children. *(brief message in tongues)*.

My precious little ones, please pray for peace --- peace in your families --- peace in your Country --- peace throughout your world; but, My children, the peace for which you pray must begin in your heart. Look to the valley below --- one light shone through the darkness and then another. Look now, My children, --- so many lights! You, My precious ones, are the glow from the candle of My Son's holy light --- one light is dim, but together your lights will brighten this darkness.

We come with reassurance of Our unending love, but you must be strong. Our presence here will soon fade, but the seeds We have planted in the fertile fields of your hearts will grow for so many of Our children (spoke in tongues) will not be lost because the word of My Son will permeate the air. He awaits all of His children ---- His patience ---- His love, and His mercy are yours, My dear children. You must be strong and you must --- you must believe that My Son's mercy will embrace all of His children.

139

Come to the fountain of His mercy --- come here, My children, the signs and the wonders you will see. Trust always in your loving Savior for he truly has claimed you. You are His.

Be at peace, Oh precious ones!"

July 30, 1999

"I hear your words, Blessed Mother" (Pat)).

"My beloved children,

I your Mother, the Mother of Mercy, have come to you this night asking for your most earnest prayers. The trumpets, My little ones, will soon be blown. The Father will call His Angels from the North, the South, the East and the West. Soon you will be left with only that which has been instilled in each of your hearts. Dear ones, do you not recognize you have been given so much because so much, in turn, will be required of you. The Chariots stand ready. The angels hold tightly to their reigns. Pray, trust, and pray without fear, but with great confidence in My Son's Divine love and mercy. *(Tongues)*

I wish your hearts to burn with passion --- passion for souls. What else matters, My children, -- but that which lies beyond this life. Prepare and persevere, for never, My children, <u>never</u> will We leave you. Rest always in Our peace. Do not search this world for peace --- for Our peace is not of this world. I bless you this night, for you are My precious ones -- My prayerful ones. Cling tightly to My rosary, for by praying, you constantly ask for My intercession. How can a Mother say no to the children She loves".

August 1, 1999.

"My beloved children,

I, the Lord your God, rejoice this day for each heart I have searched and found much pleasure. This is the beginning of your journey to My Father and your Father. Feel Our presence in your heart. We will always be the strength that you require.

Rejoice and be glad for joy truly has come to our hearts."

August 6, 1999

"What do My children see? Do they see only a statue or do they see a Mother whose heart burns with love and compassion for Her children. My children look, but they do not see *(Pat cried)* ---- they listen, but they do not hear. Prayer is a

140

conversation --- do you wish Me to answer? You call Me to intercede, but still you do not wait for My reply. My dear children, what more do you wish of Me? The gentleness of a Mother's hand across the brow --- across the cheek of Her precious ones. Do you feel the love? Must I tell you time and time again to pray with your heart, for We see the intentions of your heart. We see the times your minds have drifted off to worldly things and We are no longer important.

My Son, My beloved Son gazes upon you, My children. He gives you every opportunity to come home --- come home to Him. This is an invitation this night to come home. He stands at the door, His arms spread wide to embrace you with His love. Do you accept His invitation? Help My children -- none must be lost. All are called. Support one another, encourage each other --- love each other".

August 13th, 1999

"Oh My precious children,

See how God has sent the rains to refresh the earth; so, too, My Son has allowed Me, your Mother, to send forth the graces to refresh each soul. As the soil receives the rains and springs forth the seeds of both flower and fruit, so with them lie the weeds.

My children, the graces that We give you, as they sink deep roots in your soul ----- they must bear good fruit; but, unfortunately, little ones, the weeds of doubt ---- the weeds of confusion intermingle with the graces of God. I tell you --- be patient. Never cease in your prayers for a great responsibility has been given each of My children. Go into the fields now while there is still time. Gently sift through the souls of My beloved Son. Carefully nurture the flowers --- the souls who hunger for righteousness --- the souls who hunger for My Son. It is not an easy task, but one for which you are called.

Pray that My Son will send His Spirit to guide you --- to fill you with discernment for time approaches, My dear children, and many are not ready. Many parents have not prepared their children. All must know of My Son's great love and tender mercy. The invitation still stands while there is yet time; for Love, true Love will never close the door of hope and never lose hope, My children for We will not forsake you.

What do you wish to offer My Son this night? Will you give Him your heart? And I, if you so will, shall take each heart in My hands and bring them close to My heart and say to My Son, "Here, My Lord and My God, are the fruits of the field."

August 14, 1999

"My precious children,

Praise be Jesus. In your presence He stands this night. He is the Holy One, He is the Lord. He welcomes you, My dear children ----- He calls you to come unafraid with much trust. I, too, stand in your midst - arms open wide to receive you into My heart ---- the heart that is joined with My Son.

Tonight, dear ones, you have been awakened --- awakened to what lies in this world. It is from this world We call you to live --- not as a child lost and searching its way in darkness; but, We call you with such love into the light of our hearts that beat with joy for We see you come with so much, My children, ---- <u>so much</u> to lay at the throne of My Son. You do not need to carry these burdens, for My Son, your Lord, My Lord, stands ready to assist each and everyone of His children. Ask Him ---- call upon His Holy name. He is your Lord ---- yet, He is your dearest friend. One like Him you will not find on this earth.

Set your goals high, My children, ---- high beyond the world you know --- for in so doing, you will leave behind the cares of this world for the joy of Jesus will fill your heart!"

August 28, 1999

"My beloved children,

Test and trials you shall not escape for I have touched each and every heart and have chosen you for purification. I accept your hearts --- the work of your hands --- for the harvest is ready, and My workers are so few. I send forth My Spirit to rest upon you, My chosen ones. Call upon Him for He is the guide ---- listen to Him ---- reject not His counsel. I have not called you, My children, unto a path smooth and without ripples, but I call you unto a path strewn with many obstacles.

Reach out your hands --- assist one another --- for together the harvest of souls must be completed. Time comes when all must be prepared. You are not alone --- feel the Love that surrounds you."

August 28, 1999 - Second message

"Listen, my children, to the words of My Son. Tonight We have gathered each heart and each heart We bury in the recesses of our hearts protected by Divine Love. Be strong -- be bold with love --- for Love as it was meant to be is your protection. You are blessed. Realize the gifts that you are given ---- nothing must be wasted. Time ---- time, my children, quickly passes.

Work diligently for your reward lies in heaven."

September 10, 1999

"Awaken, My Children. Rise up and remove your soiled robes of complacency and indifference for tonight I hand you a new garment --- a garment of truth and justice.

As My blood flowed forth from Calvary's cross to cleanse your soul --- to refresh you --- I now ask you to place upon your body this new robe --- tonight ---- spotless, for it has come from My hands. By this robe and the mission to which I send you, all will know you are Mine.

Gaze about you, my children --- not with impatience --- for you know not what comes; but, see the pain in your world and with great love accept this commission into My service. Love Me as I love you and many souls will be touched as that precious seed of hope will be planted in their hearts. Could your world exist without the sun? My children ----- without hope you cannot exist for hope fuels the fire of love --- a love so intense. This love is My gift to you. Use it well. Do not horde and hide the gift, but spend it freely as freely it is given to you!"

September 24, 1999

(The following message was dictated by Our Lady after a rather lengthy personal communication in which She spoke of preparing Her children to recognize the errors of this world and how to counteract them through the word of God. She calls for obedience to God through abandonment to the superficial ways of " a world bent on self destruction". She stresses the importance of unity in faith where the disease of pride is exposed as an abscess which eats away at the soul decaying all that it touches. We must be vigilant and guard each of our senses so that we do not become deceived, but instead become bold yet gentle warriors of love and peace through Jesus.)

"My dear children,

I am gathering My faithful remnants throughout your world each being directed to a Holy place devoted to My Son and His Divine Will. Allow Me, as your Mother, to direct your steps along this journey, for in so doing, I will cover you with My Mantle of love and protection while deepening your faith and total trust in Jesus. As Our hearts beat as one, so you too, My little ones, must learn that total dependency upon God whereby your heart will beat in unison with Ours.

Your world has fallen asleep lulled by pride, materialism and greed. I have come to awaken you --- to sound the alarm to return to My Son where His merciful heart awaits the repentant sinner. He desires only that which is best for you , that which restores your peace and allows your sin scarred souls to heal. Come now My children, bathe in the spring of Mercy and receive your gift of salvation".

September 26, 1999

My dear children,

Learn from My words. I am but a Mother Who comes out of love for your (Our) children. She, a mother, does not forsake her child but continues to reach out her arms to embrace --- to love --- and to forgive. It is through forgiveness that you shall grow. It is through unconditional love that you must learn to come to Him *(Jesus)* through trials and tribulations. Love as you know it is not the same as Our love, for Ours is already unconditional. I await for all My children when they struggle for they have not learned to love My Son *(by total trust and abandonment)*. The choices in their lives must be sought with such intensity to draw away from this life's false gods so that they may have the true peace which only Jesus can give. I watch you with My heart ---- My heart of thorns for the pain which you feel, but I give you My heart and ask --- will you give Me yours in return?"

September 26, 1999

"My beloved children,

I have been with you these few days. I have examined your hearts and found them worthy --- worthy to receive My words. No longer must I call you children who stumble and fall, but I call you to maturity of faith for I have entrusted into your hands a great mission. It is not the time to turn back --- it is the time of great joy for the doors of My heart are open. Extend your hand as Mine is outstretched to you. Take hold and feel the strength of your God. Trust Me for I have not misled you.   I have always been with you. I have watched you grow, but understand with such growth ---- if your heart remains pure ---- your responsibilities will increase.

I call you to deeper prayer. I call you to reconcile all differences for I will purify and purge all My servants that they will be ready for these most difficult times. Rejoice for you have chosen not to reject Me, My beloved children, and I will always be at your side."

October 1, 1999

"My dear children;

I wish to breathe upon you this night My heavenly gift of love and peace. Let each breath resuscitate your mind, your body and your soul. I wish to fill you with courage. My messages to you have forewarned of these times and yet you seem so surprised. Have not my words found roots deeply within your souls. I pray, my children, that you will not falter as more and more difficult times shall come your way. Be armed with truth ---- with God's Holy words. Cling tightly to My rosary and pray that each moment will enlighten your hearts--- for each moment---- once spent is forever gone. Trust My Son for His love is beyond all measure. His mercy is always there for the asking. You must take advantage of each moment, as time quickly passes and your mission to reach souls is great----- for the enemy strikes at your heel, but do not fear ----for. My foot shall crush the head of evil. Be at peace my beloved children".

October 17, 1999

"My beloved children,

Take courage for you have come to the Fountain of Mercy. Here Mercy looks at the purity of each heart. He sees the pain and sorrow --- yet, be filled with joy for My Son sees each heart and each heart He takes in His most holy hands. He is life eternal and has created you to be His children of light and love. The distractions of this world are many, but you are called to a path of holiness ---- a path that I have been sent as a light which will brighten each step. Dear ones, I ask you to hear the urgency of My call for truly this is a place of holiness -- a place of healing. I ask simply that you open the doors of your hearts that Jesus may enter where He will abide with you and you with Him. Rejoice for the love He pours forth upon you is the strength to endure the trials ahead --- so many --- yet, I tell you, with much faith ---- much prayer ---- much fasting ---- you will become strong and vital instruments of His peace. Never fear, my children, for God is always near. He has sent his angels to guide --- to guard and protect you. As a father loves and protects his children, so too, Our Heavenly Father does so much more. Allow Him to love you. Learn to forgive for in forgiveness comes true peace and joy as My Son has intended it to be."
(A brief personal message from Jesus followed by our Mother's words). "The time of great purification comes. This is a time also of joy for from the rubble will spring forth the seeds planted by Our Lord --- a rebirth. Not only of this earth, but of all of God's children. Follow Him ---- love Him ---- and obey His commandments."

November 3, 1999

"Repeat these words to my children that they may hear and take heed to the importance of what I say. It is only through the Divine Love and Mercy of My Son that I have been allowed this much time with you, Our beloved children ---- for these are grave times and great measures are required to strengthen and build up the body of Christ. I urge you to rely upon Me as a source of encouragement and strength for by My gentle spirit you will find comfort to deal lovingly and compassionately with your brothers and sisters in Christ Jesus.

This is a most difficult task ---- one which requires a humble spirit that seeks only God's Will. I encourage you each day to strive to detach yourselves from all pride and the materialism of this world and to attach yourselves to God's Divine Will which is true and total perfection. Holy and pure you are called to be ----- a little light flickering in the darkness now, but gradually as you draw nearer to Jesus

145

through true and total conversion, that light of love will shine ever more brightly in your lives. The light of Jesus which you now carry shall be a beacon to draw others from this world of darkness and despair into a world of faith, hope and love.

Pray, my children, and make sacrifices for many souls cry out to the Lord for help. Be His willing servants ---- His instruments of peace ----- and joy will fill your heart and those you touch."

November 12, 1999

"My dear children,

I wish you to bring to Me, your Mother, this night all your pains --- your sorrows and your sufferings, and these, My beloved children, I shall gather as I move amongst you touching each heart as I go. I shall take all of these into My heart and from My heart shall flow the healing balm of love. I am preparing you, my dear ones, as now is the time that you prayers will be put into action. Pray with much intensity --- yet a gentleness of spirit and My love shall support you in these times which come. You are called to do the will of My Son. Each heart is now ready. Children --- hear your Mother ------ a Mother whose love would not allow harm to come to one She loves so dearly. As My Son has placed your care in My hands, know I shall not fail you. Trust now more than ever before --- let your faith become alive that all who hear --- all who see -- will know that Christ, My Son, dwells within you. You are loved. Be strong ---- be strong ---- be strong!

We shall not fail you!"

(Visual after message): "Don't understand --- fire --- wall of fire --- people --- pull them through."

November 13, 1999

"My children,

I have placed into your hands the staff --- the staff of leadership and guidance. I now ask you, can you drink from My cup? ---- for your responsibilities are great and only by drinking from My cup will you fulfill your mission in this life. It is your choice. If you so choose to drink from this, My cup, grace upon grace will come to sustain you. Taste the bitterness of life ---- yet know that My true presence sweetens the cup from which you shall drink. Choices, my dear children --- so many choices. How do you choose? Pray before you answer for you know not what "yes" would mean. Truly you must understand, once mine ---- always mine."

146

"My beloved children,

You are My faithful remnant --- My small but faithful ones that I call into the service of My Son. Do not lose hope or become discouraged for your numbers shall grow and you will rely one upon the other ---- for you are all a part of a magnificent plan formed long ago. Each of you has been called ---- so long ago, my children ---- before you left your mother's womb. All was predestined! So now I gather you --- each of you (personal conversation in tongues) for you have a great task ahead. You have barely seen or heard the greatness of what comes ------ - the graces My Son shall pour out upon this holy mountain.

I ask you now to begin preparation for this coming Advent. Prepare your hearts to be gentle --- loving --- and filled with compassion. So many will come. You must be prepared. Know you have found favor with My Son and this night I bless you as I gather each of you into the folds of my mantle where I shall keep you secure and free from the evil that shall come against you. Stand firmly, my dear ones, for My Son is your strength ---- rely solely upon Him. I bless you, my children. I seal you with the sign of the cross."

December 11, 1999

"My daughter,

Write these words that I have placed upon your heart that you might remember them ----- tell them:

You have found favor within My Heart for my words have become seeds planted and nurtured within the fertile recesses of the grounds of your hearts prepared by Me for just these times. You have not shirked your responsibility but have embraced it with faith and obedience to my word.

You have accepted the call ---- the cross ---- you have heard my voice and responded to its calling out of obedience. I call you My warriors ---- gentle and peaceful, yet filled with the spirit of My unconditional love. Become bold yet gentle warriors of love and forgiveness and through you I will work many miracles. See the fruits that now blossom into strong witnesses of courage; courage to carry the Gospel as they journey through this brief but necessary part of life.

My children, do not flee from the uncertain --- the distasteful aspects of life --- but rather with much courage and strength strive to understand with My heart the pain and suffering which life deals to all of My children. No one escapes --- but great grace of acceptance allows you to grow in holiness and gentle spirits where true love conquers all! Prepare yourselves with reconciliation that the light of Divine Love will strengthen you to persevere for the journey with a true holiness that forgives and gives you the grace to embrace all things in my name. Never forget, I am always with you. Trust Me and abide in My Holy and perfect Will.

Be at peace, my beloved children."

December 17, 1999

"My dear children,

The peace of My Son I bring to you this night. You are My special ones for you hold a place within My heart. Your hearts We have searched and now We rejoice because you are Ours. My children, I ask you now to look with the eyes of your hearts for I shall bring My Son to this holy mountain! *(It has been discerned Our Lady is referring to the infant Jesus).* Believe that We are here ---- do not let your faith be clouded by doubt, but know that you have been told what is true.

Rejoice with Me *(slight pause for private message)* My children, for tonight My heart beats with such love as I gaze upon the works of your hands and see the tenderness of your hearts. Receive my blessing, my precious children."

(Note: Our Lady indicated She wished us to receive this very special gift with great love and much faith for we can only "see" with the eyes of our hearts.)

December 24th, 1999

(Christmas Eve - The Friday night Canyon Rosary: Immediately after the rosary, Our Blessed Mother requested the front row of chairs be removed from the Prayer Room. She then called for the children present to come and be blessed. She specifically stated we were not to awaken any of the sleeping children. She then said) :

"I bestow My special blessing upon these special little children. I take each of them and bless them with the sign of the Cross that they may grow strong and pure of heart in service to My Lord and Your Lord".

(Pat) She now calls each of us to come to receive Her blessing. (so as many as can fit around this area --- She is here) This is Her gift to us this night. We will each be anointed* with the sign of the cross. She said that any religious articles that you are wearing or have with you - She will bless. She asks only that you take this blessing and pass it on to those who were not able to be here tonight or to any of those in need of a tender - loving touch. Pass on this blessing for it shall be as if She personally had held each of them in Her arms.(C a n   e v e r y o n e   f i t ?)

A song was sung in tongues followed by its translation:

"I call you all my precious children ---- I call you all into My Heart. Do not my dearest little children let fear or doubt cloud that which I send into your heart."

(Pat relates) *Receive the anointing of the Mother as She blesses us in the name of the Father, the Son and the Holy Spirit. (While resting in the Spirit:)*

"My children, --- Each day for one week at the hour of three o'clock recite the Divine Mercy and I shall come with Mercy Himself --- My beloved Son. I shall hold Him in My arms for all to see. <u>Look with your hearts</u> for you are blessed this night. Look, My children, feel Our presence."

*(Note: After listening to the audio recording of this message I questioned the word "anointing". Our Lord explained) --- "Even though Mary is not part of the Trinity as we know it, She is the spouse of the Holy Spirit, the Mother of the Son of God and hand picked by God the Father Himself as His chosen servant who is now elevated to Queen of Heaven and Earth. She indeed used the word "anointed / anointing" for as graces pour forth from My hands through Hers, so too, the power of anointing is also given in special circumstances <u>as I desire</u>. I need not explain all things to you, My child, for I wish you to ponder and discern on a more spiritual level rather than confine yourself to the simple aspects of life as *(Further clarification was given on other issues at this time)* you now know it."

December 25, 1999

(After the Chaplet, we processed up the hill to the Grotto. Upon reaching the Grotto, we knelt to receive our Holy Guests. There was such a brief timing between their visual gifts and an unfortunate leg accident. We all needed to regroup and discern what we were to learn from all of this. It was the unanimous conclusion as Our Lady asked us to "see with our Hearts" that our fixation with cameras and actual photos was not the given priority. We were missing the true meaning of the message of the "gifts". Our hearts turned to deeper prayer and many graces followed throughout the week).

December 26, 1999

"Allow Me, My children, to take you back to the manger where My Son was born into this world --- for tonight in My arms I carry the One of whom you spoke. This child destined for such greatness, who must bear much sorrow, I hold in My arms. Today -- not a day of sorrow --- but a day of joy --- a day of anticipation for the greatness that My Son shall bring ---- that He shall bestow upon His people. Many times I have asked you to look with your heart --- to feel with your heart, and now, as you honor me in prayer, I will pass amongst you holding My Son who shall bless you.

Rejoice as We rejoice. Thank you, my children, that you have heard My words --- that you have heard the call and that you obey out of love. Receive this gift --- for My Son comes to each heart."

Gifts of the Holy Spirit

Wisdom, Understanding, Counsel, Fortitude, Knowledge, Piety,
and Fear of the Lord

(Pat) These are supernatural gifts which dispose the intellect or the will to act upon the assistance and light of the Holy Spirit, and reside with the confirmed soul as long as he remains in the state of grace.

(Note: In reference to Our Lady's gift bringing Her Son (the infant Jesus) for the period of one week from Saturday December 25th to Friday December 31st, there were some questions as to if there was a particular reason for this "seven" day period. During the visitation of December 27th, Our Lady indicated each day represented a "gift of the Holy Spirit". She said this was a time of grace in which the Holy Spirit desired to bestow His special gifts upon all those whose hearts were pure and sought only to be united in love and devotion to God. These gifts are ours for the asking; however, much faith and obedience to Gods Holy Will are the "keys" which will aid in unlocking this great treasure chest of graces. Believe and trust for God is full of love and mercy --- He searches each heart ---- nothing is hidden.

"Give thanks with a grateful heart for His mercy endures forever").

December 27, 1999

"Look, My children --- gaze about you. What is it you see? A cross --- a statue --- a chapel --- what is it, my children? I call you to look --- to feel --- to embrace all that We give you. Each day receive a gift --- a gift of the Spirit. Strive, my children, during this special time of grace ---- to do the Will of My Son with a pure heart. Seek forgiveness as you must always seek to be in the Divine Will. My children. How much We love you. Did I not say I would be here with My Son? Then look --- look with your heart -- for truly We are here".

December 28, 1999

"My precious Children,

I thank you for coming here this day for truly My heart is filled with joy as well as that of My beloved Son. My children, I look at the hearts who should be so full of love and gratitude and yet, you allow your minds to control your hearts --- numbers are not important*. We look for the hearts, dear children --- do you not know the power of one pure heart that prays and cries out to God for mercy. Do

150

not concern yourselves with the little things, but concentrate on improving your relationship with God. In time all things will become clear. Be at peace as I bless you and leave you this day".

(There were just a few present for "Their" visitation).

December 29, 1999

"My children,

See how My Mother holds Me so tightly in Her loving arms --- so too, My children --- We wish to embrace each of you. We bring you Our peace and Our joy. Do not allow your hearts to be burdened by all the trials of life --- for even the leaf as it falls from the tree is not wasted --- for there the ground is prepared for new growth and thus, My children, the "circle" of life is unbroken. There is no beginning --- there is no end --- only a perfect circle" *(said very slowly).*

"My beloved, when you come into My house to adore Me --- what do you see --- but a perfect circle ---- "LIFE". I am perfection. I love you, My children and I bless you as I take each of you into My heart. Be at peace".

(Personal note:) So bright -- the lights were so bright. I was allowed to kiss the child Jesus who The Blessed Mother held in her arms. Those in attendance watched me partially raise (not levitate) up from the floor unassisted to embrace the child).

(Orientation on tape followed by: Confirmation from "M" who stated The Blessed Mother said we could touch the face of Jesus. A brief message followed given to the person by The Blessed Mother. [D said] " I was allowed to hold the baby Jesus." [This person was visibly overwhelmed with emotion]. [L said] The Blessed Mother was seen in front by the altar with rays of white light streaming from Her hands towards [J]. This also was the first time [J] has spoken with what was felt as a special message for someone sitting close by in the Chapel).

December 30, 1999

"Oh, My little ones that gather to pray in this holy place. I greet you with My love --- with the love I hold in My arms *(Jesus).* Today, My children, I gather you securely beneath My mantle for I must, as gently as a Mother can, forewarn you, My children, that prayer must be a most important part of your life. We have spoken of what must come and today I whisper into each ear that you are loved and that each of you has a great responsibility --- a roll which I will teach you to fulfill. Please trust Me for I am the Mother who would not allow Her children to be misled --- to be harmed. I stand guard over each of you. My weapons I extend to you. Take the rosary and My scapular for in them lies the power to defeat the enemy. I do not come to bring fear or anxiety but to bring joy for the peace of My Son shall reign in your hearts. His peace will see you through these difficult times which approach --- but love, My children, as you have never loved

151

before. Put aside all indifferences --- all unkindness --- and seek a compassionate heart that beats with love --- the love of My Son. You have but to look about you and see there is so much to be done and so little time. My precious ones, allow Me to prepare you with a heart that will never give in to the ways of a world bent on destruction. Be at peace for only in peace will you survive. You are My chosen ones --- My small but power filled prayerful ones. I bless you as the tears of joy stream from My eyes down My cheeks embracing each of you, My beloved children."

The Seventh day - 3:00 pm Chaplet/Rosary

December 31, 1999

Tongues .... "I greet Thee, My Lord and My God...."

"My children,

I stand before you this day --- this final of the seven days to express My gratitude and My intense love for each of you. This day has much meaning for in each heart this day has been placed a special gift. In just a moment I will send the Holy Spirit to light the flame above each of His children. Be at peace and be assured that each one here shall have at least one flame glowing from the top of their head. My gifts I have freely given --- I now ask you in return to so give them to others for My children are so in need. Listen to these words before you commit yourselves. If you choose to accept these gifts knowing full well they are to be shared, I extend to you the pen of Divine Love and ask you of your own free will to reach out and write your name across My Sacred Heart. Will you do this for Me, My children?

I stand before you with My Mother and I have asked My beloved St. Joseph to join us this day as each of Us at this moment extend Our blessings upon you. Rejoice for the graces you have received are unheard of, My children. You are truly blessed. Follow Me. I go before you ---- take courage. Come follow Me!"

****

Messages from Jesus and Mary

Messages - January 14, 2000 - December 29, 2000

January 14, 2000

"My dear children, *(Blessed Mother)*

I ask you to take My hand this night and I shall lead you onto the path of Divine Light where the peace of My Son shall embrace you. I hear the questions! ---- yes ---- your very thoughts. In my messages and in My Son's there are questions. You ask <u>what is this staff</u> My Son has placed into your hands? .... what else My Child, but the Word of God! He spoke as the staff was raised and the seas parted; and -- as the staff struck the hardened rock and waters flowed forth ---- so My Son wishes you to take this staff of His Holy Word and strike the hardened hearts of His children. Reach out to them with such love and tenderness for in so doing --- by your example --- their hearts will melt like the snow as the temperatures rise. My children --- My dear children --- be at peace for you are loved."

(Conversation in tongues)

(Jesus) "My children,

Never be afraid to speak My Words for My Words are truth. Take courage, trust and with confidence heed what I tell you. My Mother is your greatest and most cherished possession on this earth. I gave Her to you and She has graciously watched and cared for each of you. Honor Her as My Mother and your Mother."

January 28th, 2000

"My children,

To walk down the path of life, cling to My hand that is outstretched. Open wide your hearts for I shall pour forth into each heart that trusts in My Son an abundance of graces -- an abundance of peace. My children, how many times I come to you and gather you beneath My mantle. How many times I've embraced you and yet you have not felt the Mother's touch. Receive Me now as a Mother who longs to bring the gentleness of peace and understanding into each heart.

Do you know, My children, what you witnessed? *(This is in reference to the above statement in which many were amazed at what they felt they saw.)* My dear children, all things --- I repeat --- all things are possible with God! Seek Him in everything you do -- everything you say and in so seeking you shall find courage and strength to endure not only the simple everyday trials but the heavy crosses that each must carry. Trust -- trust -- believe and trust. My hands I outstretch and call you beneath them for My blessing. This night as in many nights --- I come and I bless. This blessing is for courage, courage My children. Be strong, hold tightly to the promises of My Son who loves you far more than simple words can say.

Be at peace and rejoice, my children."

(Comments from "M": This night we've been given the graces and wisdom so that all the questions in our hearts will be answered. Pat's message seems to tie in with so much of what we've heard over the last three or four weeks. Have courage to step forward with whatever the Lord in leading us to do. To have faith, courage and strength to move forward and that we will or have received wisdom to understand whatever it is we've been called to do in our lives. The message to walk forward -- to walk straight ahead -- walk in faith -- seems to be confirmed over and over again in the last couple of weeks. What a beautiful evening tonight.

(Comments from "T": As we were finishing the regular Canyon rosary, I saw a brilliant flash to my left. My eyes were closed but I knew it was in front of Pat who was sitting about ten feet from me. Marie had asked us all to pray the prayer asking for a "spiritual communion". As we finished, Pat asked for the lights to be turned down. I could tell she was in deep prayer and was experiencing something very spiritual. As I watched her I felt a familiar pressure building in my chest and closed my eyes praying for discernment. When I looked back at Pat she was being lowered to the floor by Jerry and Delia as she rested in the Spirit. As I moved closer to her and prayed I saw on her face the beauty of someone in true peace. As I watched and prayed the following words came to me:

"My little ones -- Do you see what is before you? Do you see with the eyes of your heart? The flower in front of you has bloomed because of her acceptance of graces. The graces I pour into each heart. Do not doubt what you see for I stand before you. Open your hearts my little ones.

Be at peace in My heart."

(Each of the above individuals is under the direction of a "Spiritual Advisor")

The early year 2000 messages given in February, March, April, [one exception] and May [one exception] cannot be given at this time.

April 7th, 2000 (Lent)

"My daughter,

These are my precious children that I have gathered as the sheep of my pasture.

These children must - as all my children - be purified. Tell them not to fear, but as I emptied Myself upon the Cross, I call them to empty themselves of all that is not of Me. I am Divine Love and Mercy. I give this mercy freely to each of my children; but you, little ones, still must learn that mercy does not come without forgiveness. They cannot be separated. If you wish this mercy, you too must learn forgiveness. You have said yes to this Lenten Journey --- dig deeper within the recesses of your hearts that forgiveness will flow forth to your families --- to your friends --- to all in need of that forgiveness ---- Then, my children, come into My open arms where My forgiveness awaits you."

May 26, 2000

"Oh, My little lambs,

I greet thee this night with a joyful heart. Thank you for the children (there were many little children in attendance) ---- thank you for opening your hearts to My Son. Oh, my children, how do I make you understand the power of these prayers. If you could only comprehend such power ---- a weapon thrown against the enemy ------ Listen, children, pray --- pray until prayer becomes a beautiful melody --- a melody that resounds --- stirring the heart of My Son. Prayer is communion with God. Be joyful, my children. Let the melody of your prayer always be in your heart for as it is in your heart then there is no room for the evil one. Try -- just try to understand that trials must come. Pain and sorrow are but gifts if accepted and offered to My Son.

I caution you, my children, --- do not be lulled into a false sense of peace and security for these walls too shall crumble. It is only with the peace of My Son that you shall persevere. Love one another as you are loved."

June 2, 2000

(Pat) (Since receiving our Lady's message of May 26th, I have been praying for discernment as to Her words "for these walls too shall crumble". This morning after the Sacrament of Reconciliation just prior to Mass, She began speaking and instructing me as to the meaning of these words. I will not reveal at this time all that She said as I must first seek guidance from my Spiritual Director; however, the following message was dictated just prior to the Chaplet of Divine Mercy and does give insight as to Her meaning. Please pray and discern as with all messages that the Holy Spirit will enlighten you).

"My daughter,

I have allowed you this time to ponder My words "for these walls too shall crumble" so that you may grow in deeper faith and understanding to contemplate God's plan for your life and that of all of His children. Too many of my children dwell only upon the physical realities of this world not realizing the greater depth of My words --- those for spiritual health. Surely, as it has been written,

155

catastrophes shall come bringing great destruction, but all shall leave this world as God calls. I am here to guide you and to calm your fears, but also to awaken you to this false sense of peace and security wherein you allow yourselves complacency in your spiritual prayer life. You build with straw upon the sandy soil and thus as the winds blow --- bit by bit --- the structure weakens and the walls crumble. My children must grow and mature in prayerful love and obedience to God. He is the foundation upon which you must build then nothing shall steal your peace and destroy that which has been built on faith. Believe and trust! If you truly do as I have instructed, your lives will become strong and healthy instruments of God's love and mercy. Peace, My children."

June 9th, 2000

(The following message was received during the Friday night Canyon Rosary with approximately 30 people in attendance including a family from the Phoenix area. The mother of the family has had severe back pain for many years which was the result of a bone mass which had been twisted somewhere in the pelvic area. The Lord has been doing wondrous things for her including realigning the pelvic area to where she now has approximately 90% reduction in pain and is able to lead a very productive life. Glory be to God! Please pray that the Holy Spirit will enlighten you with the gift of discernment as you read the following message).

"My children,

Humble yourselves before Me, the Lord your God, and I shall look with compassion and mercy upon you and draw you into the depths of My Sacred Heart. How many times, my children, I ask of thee to trust Me and yet the words have not penetrated your hearts for fear and anxiety still trouble your souls. What is there to fear when I am with you? I have walked this path in life and now, my children, I call you to follow in My steps. To follow in My steps you must abandon yourselves from all the ties of this world --- for in the world love as it was meant to be is but a shadow --- a fleeting shadow. Do you wish to do My Will? --- Then learn to love ---- learn to forgive and then life becomes a joy. For you are My children chosen for a great mission, but you too must be purified; but, I shall pour forth showers of graces to strengthen you as you journey through all the trials --- through all the obstacles of life. Take the hand that is outstretched before you for it is My hand My children, and I shall not let you stumble. You are mine."

(Note: During the course of the evening after this particular message, there came another message - unusual in the fact that there were phrases in tongues followed by what was discerned interpretations of these tongues - until the complete message was given. This took us by surprise; however, in reading 1 Corinthians 14:13 it would appear that this does happen. After the rosary, one of the prayer team members* approached me and said we were "asked" to placed our hearts into the hands of our Blessed Mother, who in turn would take them to Jesus. This was followed by a very spiritual laying of hands at which time the Holy Spirit poured out many of His gifts).

This particular prayer team member had also received a message from Our Lord during the week prior to the Canyon rosary and that message was read. It appeared to confirm other messages that been received as well as reveal other areas in which the Lord is directing us. We pray that the Lord will continue to use His servants for the praise and glory of His holy name! Amen.

June 14, 2000

(The following message was received just after the "laying of hands" with a retreat group from Safford and the surrounding area. Fr. Bob (Spiritual Director for the retreat) began the evening with a prayer to the Holy Spirit. It was a beautifully spiritual evening as the Holy Spirit manifested His presence amongst the group. The brief message which follows was written down by a prayer team member as it was being given. As no audio recorder was available for accuracy, we particularly request that one prays and discerns when reading the message. As is usually the case, the message began in tongues followed by):

"My precious children,

You fill My heart with joy this night for you come into the presence of My Son who stands in your midst. We look into each heart with love. No, little ones, you are never alone. Take courage and trust in My Son. Walk with Him --- talk with Him and He shall bless your life with the joy of His presence. Peace ---- all children of My heart."

(Note: Received scripture John 14:25-2 7):

"I have told you this while I am with you. The Advocate, the Holy Spirit -- that the Father will send in My name. He will teach you everything and remind you of all that I told you. Peace I leave with you; My peace I give to you. Not as the world gives do I give it to you. Do not let your hearts be troubled or afraid".

June 16th, 2000

"My daughter,

Speak these words to My children. I am the God of mercy and justice. I am not mocked.* I come for each heart seeking repentance -- true repentance in the hearts of My children. Into each repentant heart I shall infuse My Divine strength which will enable each soul to persevere -- to calmly and boldly proclaim My words of

truth and mercy. I came into your world to redeem My children --- to save them from their sins --- from the terrible pitfalls of their sinful ways and yet today I still come for My children who still do not hear My words. Dear children, My love is so intense as I gather you deeply within My heart. I shall do all within My power to continue to draw you close to My heart that you will feel this mercy and you will turn from your sinful ways. I have sent my little prophets and those too you mock. What shall I do, My children, but continue to persevere as I ask you to continue to persevere.

Love and forgiveness I freely give. This love and forgiveness I ask of all my children to be their gift for each and everyone of their brothers and sisters.

Hear Me while there is yet time for My mantle of love covers you -- protects you. But My mercy, My children -----do you understand? --- My mercy at some point will be withdrawn and then you shall face My justice. <u>Be not afraid</u> --- Heed My words for you are dearly loved."

(Note: After careful discernment among members of the prayer group, it is felt our Lord is referring to Galatians 6 wherein He specifically states (verses 7 & 8), "Make no mistake: God is not mocked, for a person will reap only what he sows, because the one who sows for his flesh will reap corruption from the flesh, but the one who sows for the spirit will reap eternal life from the spirit. Let us not grow tired of doing good, for in due time we shall reap our harvest, if we do not give up. So then, while we have the opportunity, let us do good to all, but especially to those who belong to the family of the faith." (Translation taken from the Saint Joseph Edition of The New American Bible)).

July 7, 2000

"My dear children,

I bring you peace as you gather in unity --- in prayer joining your hearts, your minds and spirits in praise of My Son and in honor of your Mother. This peace with which I greet you is not a peace which you as yet understand. This peace --- with the peace of My Son ---- is a uniting of your hearts to His Divine Will.

My children, your spirit is never at rest for it continuously seeks the Creator with such hunger --- such love --- to be reunited with Him.* My beloved children ----- My little gardeners ---- see the souls I have sent your way. Cherish them --- nurture them --- be instruments of God's love so that no one will be lost. Pray --- pray, My children, --- fast and do penance for many of My Children have forgotten that these are essential in obtaining that peace which My Son desires each of His children to experience. Great things are on the horizon.

You must be spiritually prepared. Live the love of Jesus. Remember these words ---- for in difficult moments ----they shall be your consolation".

July 9, 2000

"My beloved children,

158

Here in this holy place I greet thee gathering each of you beneath My mantle of love and protection. I desire this day to take the thread of Divine love --- more brilliant than the stars at night --- and weave it into the hearts of all My children. I seek pureness of heart for without such pureness the thread becomes coarse and through poor choices made by My dear children We are unable to draw you close to our hearts where we wish you to dwell.

Purify your hearts through frequent confession --- then the coarse threads become brilliant golden fibers which slide easily into the needle of Divine love. Allow your hearts to become softened through true devotion to My Son then We shall draw all hearts close to Ours --- already united as one.

We bless you this day, oh dear children. Be at peace."

July 14, 2000

(A Special Invitation From Our Lord and Blessed Mother)

(Blessed Mother) "My dear children,
Be at peace and filled with great joy for tonight My Son extends to all of His children an invitation to a great feast --- a banquet prepared for all those He loves. See the table set before you -- magnificently set -- fit for royalty --- fit for the children of The King. See the platters that overflow with love, joy, <u>peace, humility,</u> and <u>forgiveness.</u> See the goblets into which He pours Divine Mercy brimming to the top. Oh, dear children, welcome to the feast ---- taste and see the goodness of the Lord for there is room for everyone. You have but to accept His invitation. Know you are dearly loved."
(Jesus) "I am standing at the door and I shall personally greet each of My guests. I shall show them to the seat selected just for them. Come My children -- - do not be afraid --- come now --- come to your Lord."

(Note: Please refer to Matthew 22:1-14. Again, this is a matter for personal discernment; however, it would appear Our Lord is inviting us to the Wedding Feast of the Lamb. Notice the servants were dispatched to summon the invited guests to the feast, but they refused to come. His servants were then sent into the main roads to invite everyone they found - good and bad like until the hall was filled with guests. At first reading this may appear as <u>all will be seated at the Lord's table</u> until we read further that one particular guest was not dressed properly - his garments soiled (sin) and "He said to him, "My friend, how is it that you came in here without a wedding garment"? But he was reduced to silence. Then the king said to his attendants, "Bind his hands and feet, and cast him into the darkness outside, where there will be wailing and grinding of teeth. Many are invited, but few are chosen." Does this perhaps tell us we must continuously stay focused on Jesus - seeking always to do His Holy Will and to abide in His Grace through the Sacrament of (frequent) Reconciliation. We must guard our soul -- it's our most priceless possession).

July 21, 2000

(This particular evening was quite beautiful as there were many in attendance from various areas of Arizona and all had joined together in "one" heart to praise our Lord and honor our Blessed Mother in prayer and song. We marvel at the working of Jesus and Mary as many people will say "they don't really know how or why they are here", but they've found themselves in the presence of such peace and joy that they know it was God's will that they be here. The following message was transcribed from an audio tape used to record the message as it was being dictated This particular message began with an unidentified strong male voice perceived perhaps to be that of St. Michael He has spoken only once before that we can recollect).

"Behold, children of God, the Queen of Heaven and Earth is in your presence. Heed Her words".

"My dear children,

I am here this night sitting amongst you and I call you as a mother calls her small child to come and sit by My knees as I tell you a story --- a story of love. You, dear children, have been planted as a garden --- a garden for a King, and yet, little ones --- what has sprung up in this garden but the thistles --- the thorns of pride which tear at the delicate blossoms of your soul. The time is now to weed out these undesirable elements in your life and it is only by recognizing that sin takes many forms can you understand that God awaits you. He awaits you in the Sacrament of Reconciliation.

Oh children, never lose hope ---- cling tightly to My hand for I shall always lead you to My Son. He is mercy and love and forgiveness. He but awaits each of you to come into His presence. Be not afraid, but be aware that life itself --- the journey it entails --- is filled with so many little weeds of discontent -- of jealously -- of envy --- and through your pride has found root and your peace flies as a feather in the wind -- flitting here and there but there is no rest. This is not the peace of My Son. His peace is eternal --- it is devotion to His Will --- His will that will fill you if you but ask. Precious children, hear Me. I will wipe away each tear --- I will place each tear within My hands and take them to My Son ---- tears of your repentant love for Jesus. I tell you these things that you may place them

deeply within your heart. Nurture them --- do not forget --- you are in a great battle. The enemy strikes swiftly --- you must be prepared. I bless you with a Mother's tender love.
Be at peace."

July 28, 2000

(The following are three messages received during the Friday night Canyon Rosary. It is very difficult to inflect onto paper the great emotion in our Mother's

voice as She was indeed quite intent in relaying the urgent need for family healing and reconciliation. The evening was beautiful as Her message touched many hearts and "healing" began. As with all messages please pray to the Holy Spirit for the gift of discernment as you read the following. Once again, Our Mother was introduced by a strong male voice; however, as you may discern for yourselves, it is felt perhaps this may have been St. Gabriel as the word Messenger as mentioned. The messages began as follows):

"Daughter of God, Be not afraid for I too am a Messenger. I am the Messenger that came before the Blessed Mother and here I stand this night at Her side. Fear not but hear Her. She comes accompanied by the Legions of Angels from Heaven and here in your midst stands the Queen. Pay Her heed and great reverence."

(Blessed Mother) "My dear children,

I come this night asking for your hearts into which I shall pour My Son's Divine Mercy. I ask for the gentleness of your spirit that I may fill it with His peace. How long have I been with you, oh little children of My Son and what have we accomplished? I have called you to be children of peace and yet peace must begin in your homes -- with your families. How can this peace (long sorrowful pause) how can this peace be shared My children --- when there is no peace in your home -- where there is no love --- no trust? When you do not pray together you do not allow peace to find root within your hearts and within your homes. Do you understand children that the mission before you is grave requiring you to be strong. <u>Your peace must begin in your homes.</u> Love one another -- cherish one another and then that peace shall overflow as a river of love reaching all hearts with whom you come in contact. It is not something with which you walk out a door and greet your brother and sister and say "I love you -- peace be with you" for then that is <u>hollow and without foundation.</u>

There is <u>much, much </u>more I wish to share with you, but you must learn as a child beginning to walk <u>how important love within families is</u>. It is the structure upon which love for others is built. If My Son does not have first place in your home then, children, has Our time with you been wasted? I pray not for I do not come to scold you as a disobedient child, but I come to call you to reflect more on your lives. Examine your lives for tonight I look at many hearts --- hearts here praying --- singing --- yet, hearts that are <u>empty</u>. Allow Us to fill those hearts with love --- a love that will heal the wounds in each and every family and then, My children, -- then you will be ready to arm yourselves with God's love and go forth into the fields, for yes, the Harvest is ready, but the <u>Harvesters must be prepared</u>. I love you, little children --- come now --- come --- repent --- come for the door remains open but a short while longer. You have been so blessed. Do you realize the gifts you have received these last three years? Be at peace --- I love you, My children --- be at peace".

(Jesus) "If you do not listen to the words of My Mother then She shall no longer appear!"

161

"My dear children,

I am with you this night to announce a great gift from My Son --- a gift I must explain in earthly terms --- for to tell you as it is in Heaven -- you will not be able to comprehend its magnificence. My Son Holds in His Holy hands a scroll - not of parchment - but of fibers formed in Heaven ---- gold in appearance - yet the light shines brilliantly through and on this scroll are the names of His children ---- each name lovingly and with such tender care embroidered with threads of love. As He unrolls this scroll, He asks each of you, dear children, in the quietness of your heart to listen --- listen for that still - quiet - voice which calls your name. You are His precious children.

Know that gathered around My Son are all of your loved ones and all the Saints that have been praying for you --- praying for your name to be placed on this Scroll of Eternal Life. Dear, dear children, what you have received from My Son --- His love --- His compassion and Mercy has allowed your name [you] to join the Heavenly realm of Saints. This, dear ones, is a gift but yet one which must be *earned ---- so little My Son asks --- love Him --- trust Him and obey Him and through your consecration to the Holy One. You shall have your name embroidered on this Scroll.

Be at peace and find such joy this night ---- for healings have begun allowing your journey to My Son to become a reality."

*(*Note: It was further explained (through various teachings of the Saints) that Salvation in itself is an unearned gift we receive through acceptance of the precious blood of Jesus --- what we are allowed to earn is the "interest" on our spiritual account which elevates our place in Heaven).*

August 6th, 2000

(Consecration to God the Father)

"Be filled with great joy for I stand in your presence receiving your heart and taking it into My own where I shall love you and protect you and heal your wounds. Rejoice -- rejoice My children, for you have honored My Father and this day He shall bestow upon you His blessing. Receive now the blessing of the Father for you are surrounded by His angels. Fear not but feel His peace!"

August 25th, 2000

(Oh dearest Mother, we love you)

"My dear children,

Tonight My request to you is as follows --- husbands pray for your wives --- wives pray for your husband and together pray for your children for truly all are children of God. But not all of His precious children --- His beloved sheep --- graze in His pasture.

You look with wonder at the signs you see and in your heart you ask <u>what do you wish of me --- what does this mean</u>? I tell you - you shall see far greater signs than those that have been revealed thus far. You must pray My children, for only in prayer will you obtain the strength to fully understand what God desires to reveal. Yes, you are dearly loved and yes, much will be required from each of His precious children.

Pray --- pray --- pray --- for you know not the day or the hour and you must be prepared. Gather My Son's children deeply within your hearts --- your wounded hearts ---- forgive and love as Jesus forgives and loves. I bless each of you this night as My heart goes out to all of our children who struggle.

What did you just pray, My children? Did you say "I love you oh my God"? Do you mean that --- do you truly mean that? Then amend your lives, little ones. There is much work still to do."

September 1, 2000

(This particular evening was comprised of a somewhat smaller group; however, we always believe our Lord has just the precise individuals He desires at each gathering of prayer and we are particularly noticing the increase in the number of children attending the Rosary. How They love the children - we know our Lord and Blessed Mother look upon them as little treasures .Perhaps we as parents and grandparents need to look at them with the eyes of our Lord and see them as the truly unique "gifts" they are.)

"My dear children,

Speak of your love for Jesus to Me, your Mother, and I shall rejoice with you in praise and prayer. Prayer --- prayer from the heart is a most beautiful fragrance that silently rises before the throne of God as though carried on the wings of His angels.

My dear children, many times I have spoken of prayer --- of love --- forgiveness --- penance ---- sacrifices and many of you have heard My words and have obeyed --- yet, there are those who "hear" only! They do not heed My words! I have requested from My Son additional graces for these precious children that the flame of love for My Divine Son will burn so intensely in their hearts that no longer shall they be lukewarm but be on fire for love of Jesus.

I know, dear little ones, how difficult life must seem ---- so many trials ---- so many temptations ---- so much pain --- yet, My children, this is as God deems it

163

must be. I do not ask you to understand God's ways for His ways are not your ways. I ask only that you trust ---- trust as never before --- for the trials shall increase but so shall the graces to get you through this journey of life.

Be at peace ---- I love you, My precious children!"

September 8, 2000

"Oh My precious children,

I thank you this night - for the precious gifts you have brought your Mother --- for your hearts ---- those hearts so full of love ---- so filled with so many everyday cares. Dear children, I accept these gifts with great joy. Allow Me to present to you a small but beautiful gift. Will you take My hand this night? Come walk with Me ---- see the sun about to set and yet, there is still enough light. For ahead of us ---- see the trellis of roses ---- smell the fragrance as we enter beneath the beauty of the flowers. Catch the aroma of the Jasmine --- the gardenias.

Look about you children. See how the garden is perfectly laid out. See there are no weeds. It is a thing a sheer beauty --- of sheer beauty because it has been nurtured by the graces God has bestowed upon these precious flowers ---- the souls that have sought Him --- that have loved Him --- that have followed His Will and been obedient to His commandments. What lies ahead? See the little garden --- where the flowers are beginning to shoot up --- not yet fully formed. Those, My children, are the ones in need of prayer, for they have not as yet asked God for His graces. In asking God, He does not refuse.

Pray, pray dear children, that these precious seedlings will become beautiful flowers in God's garden of souls. Let us leave now, but I ask one more gift of you this night. <u>Let the words from your mouths, be so tender, and be so humble, that you shall soften the hardest heart. Melt it into a pool of love</u> ------ for Jesus".

September 15, 2000

(A Message from Our Blessed Mother and Saint Michael)

(St. Michael) "Children of God,

I greet thee and I speak these words at the command of My Lord and My God. The daughter through whom these words are spoken is no longer in our presence. She has been taken beneath the mantle of our Holy Queen to glimpse the journey that lies ahead. It is not for you to question what lies ahead but with much faith - grasp hold of the shield that lies before you for I have been sent with my legion of angels to guard this holy mountain. This is holy ground and I shall defend it. Listen ---- listen, Children."

(Blessed Mother) "My precious children of love,

164

Have no fear as you listen to these words for they have been spoken but to make you aware of the greatness of your responsibility for this mountain is a mountain planned for greatness ----- for God's purpose.

I tell you now to fill your lamps with oil ---- to fill your sacks with grain ---- and be prepared --- such love ---- yet such responsibility. Feel the presence of the Holy Spirit for He is your constant companion ---- your guard and your guide. Know that St. Michael is always with Me ----- always at My bidding and that of My Son. Listen carefully to all you have been told. Children, trust ------ discern ---- trust------ believe --- for this is real.

The graces you have received and shall receive shall sustain you. Never walk in fear, but walk in the light and hope of Jesus."

September 17, 2000

"My dear little children,

I gather each of you into My heart where I wish to teach you how to live your lives for Jesus. It is so simple if you but open your hearts. Love My children -- -- love as you have never loved. Forgive - for you cannot love without forgiveness.

Times as you know them shall rapidly change. You have been planted on solid ground. Let your roots grow deeply within the soil of Divine Love. As you grow and mature in your faith, you shall find yourselves walking and living in the Divine Will of My Son.

Be at peace, My beloved children."

(There was just a slight glimpse of a hand with the thumb, little finger and the one next to it barely touching ---- the index and middle fingers were raised as if a blessing was being given. A small portion of the wrist was also visible with a faint mark in the wrist area. It was obviously a male hand leading me to believe it was Jesus}.

September 22, 2000

"My precious children,

Look before you and see the Mother who stands holding in her hands a rosary of roses --- for I greet thee this night as the Queen of the Most Holy Rosary. See the roses in My hand ---- how, My children, do you pray such a delicate rosary ---- for each is a tender, delicate blossom unique in itself. I Tell you My Rosary is made of tears ---- the tears of My children and each tear has been turned into a pearl ---- each one different --- for each of your tears are formed by sorrow --- by joy ---

165

none are alike, thus none of the pearls are alike.

My children, I desire that you encourage devotion to My Holy Rosary --- for many have forgotten its power ---- many except the one who tempts the soul -- who seeks destruction of God's children. He knows the power! You must seek out those who do not know of this powerful weapon. Teach them, My children, for these times which come require weapons far greater than missiles and bombs. They require Love ---- only through Love will you survive. I beg of thee, My children, do not fear, but trust and pray for these are times which require great concentration --- much effort on each and everyone's part --- for yes, you each play an important role! Be faithful --- try, trust and believe for God shall prevail. Even in the darkest moments, the light ahead is the glowing crown of salvation --- – persevere without fear. Love much --- forgive and I shall keep you close to My heart ---- for each day as you know it I make another rosary formed of the new tears of My children.

As I touch each precious bead I bless you and I give you a special grace to endure --- to endure to the end. Praise be Jesus for His love and mercy endures forever."

September 29, 2000

(Brief visual): (Do you wish me to tell them what I see?) ---- We're above a beautiful garden once again. It must have rained for flowers are heavy with dew – moisture ---- rain drops. They are bending over just slightly, yet the aroma is still so beautiful. We are like these flowers --- the rain is the graces that God pours forth ----- our souls so weakened at times that we, too, bend upon our Lord for the weight is so great and only He sustains us.

"My dear children.

The Son --- My Divine Son --- has broken through the darkness and the despair of your world and has illuminated and refreshed the parched souls with rivers of mercy. These parched souls are those who have suffered the oppression and the aggression of evil --- yet --- they are the souls that cling so tightly to the slimmest thread of hope --- trusting and believing in the word of God. These are the souls washed in the blood of the lamb --- groomed and perfumed to join the holy --- just warriors of Christ the King.

Listen to My words --- ponder and discern for I am gathering those perfumed souls --- those souls being purified --- and --- those souls yet to be purified by the Fire of Divine Love. Be reconciled to God. Draw from the fountain of His mercy and drink the cup of His forgiveness.

Be at peace, My beloved little children."

October 6, 2000

"My daughter,

Be still, My child, and listen as the leaves dance amongst the swaying branches of the trees where sunlight inches its way through the thick woods producing images and shadows as God paints His master piece for all to enjoy. You have sought solitude and refreshment of body and soul -- thus God has allowed this special grace (saw white image come through bedroom window) that your heart might remain with Him to be strengthened by His Divine love.

You now must carry this love and disperse it amongst His children that they, too, will feel His peace and seek to abide in His Divine Will. Yes, My child, the trials will always be with My little ones --- like shadows --- there but seen only when the light permits.

I encourage you with a Mother's love to bear all things in love for the sake of Love Himself who bore all things out of love for you.

Pray for My sons, much has been entrusted to them and many are fragile, especially now as the enemy seeks to thwart My plans of triumph. Pray ---- pray -- -- pray."

October 13, 2000

(There were many new faces joining us during this Friday night's Canyon Rosary. People are responding to our Lady's call to prayer from various locations throughout the surrounding area. It would seem (as a gentleman visiting the Shrine earlier in the day had stated) "we are all being called to stand in the gap for our fellow brothers and sisters". The following message has been transcribed from an audio tape used to record the message as it was being dictated. As with all messages, we urge you to pray to the Holy Spirit for discernment as you read the following):

"My dear children,

Reflect in these changing times and recall My words to you to pray and be reconciled to God. Oh little remnant of My heart, you shall not escape the afflictions of the impious souls consumed with envy, jealousy, and hate. You can, however, through fervent prayers, beseech God for extra graces for those poor souls lost in the darkness of materialism and modernism. Ask God through true humility --- for when you ask for another --- especially, My children, for one who has inflicted pain ---- God rejoices in your heart ---- He hears your prayers ---- and moved with mercy --- He shall extend His hand to touch all those souls.

As My heart was pierced by the sword so too shall your hearts be pierced by the sword of Divine Love of My Son. Dear children, remove all bitter thoughts from your mind -- for these thoughts when left unchecked open old wounds and thus you carry the scars of un-forgiveness. This is not God's plan. You are a child of God. God forgives --- so you, too, must forgive.

Come under My mantle this night and I shall bless each of you as I intercede for the petitions buried deeply within your precious hearts.

   *I love you, My dear little children."

(Note: *There was just a slight change in tone which seemed to imply our Blessed Mother was whispering these words into each individual heart. There was such a sense of peace --- a warmth --- as we experienced this particular "I love you, My dear children". A few people came forth and said they felt our Lady's particular mention of interceding for those petitions buried deeply within our hearts was an answer to prayer for them as it was a confirmation of what they were asking Our Mother to do).

October 20, 2000

(Mary) "My precious little ones,

Seasons change ---- they bring what they will ---- the trees dressed in bright colors ---- the flowers now reclining into the cool earth - resting until they are called again to bloom.

The soul has no season with God. Everything remains constant. It is not God, My Children, but man himself who by his own free will either clings to God and His Divine Will or chooses the ways of the world and turns his back on <u>truth.</u> God is <u>truth.</u> Choose to live in His truth and your soul will continuously rest in the Spring time of God's love and mercy.

Do not be afraid, oh little children, for God loves His little ones and He shall send you grace upon grace that the flower of your soul will bloom --- re-bud --- and bloom again and again. Be at peace, oh little flowers that I gather this night.

My children, do you think that your heart goes unseen? No --- but each heart is nurtured with the tenderness of a loving Father and He shall always protect that which is His own. You are called --- you are chosen --- and you are His."

(Jesus) (Short greeting of message not recorded on tape)

"I beckon you to My heart. It is here I shall place each of you to guard and protect you. Never ever doubt My love for you --- for My life was <u>given</u> --- <u>every drop of My blood was shed for you. Does that not tell you how much I love you?</u>

Come as I call you ---- come ---- come, My children."

(Messages and Experiences)

(Sunday, October 22, 2000: During the Divine Mercy Chaplet in the Chapel, I experienced a familiar sense of something about to happen. This is somewhat described as though a warm blanket has been placed around you and a strong sense of peace begins to penetrate your body. I have been very tired lately and as I recognized what was happening I asked the Lord to please let this day pass without any additional spiritual situations. In other words, I said "No way, Lord - not today" and I tried to intensely focus on the prayers and gradually the feeling left me. At the end of the Rosary, three different people mentioned they felt something special was going to happen that day. We will never know because I said "No", but knowing that God can take any situation and turn it into a greater good, perhaps His purpose was achieved in another way. I sincerely pray that is the case).

(Tuesday, October 24, 2000: We received a call from a Priest in Mexico who indicated he felt he was supposed to come "lay hands" and pray over me. He arrived with six very spiritual prayer warriors and we all knelt in the family room to pray. The power of the Holy Spirit was very evident. During the course of the prayers, I rested in the Spirit and relayed the experience of "the golden rose". A beautiful image (in lights) appeared holding a beautiful long stem golden rose. The people in attendance said I reached out my hand as though to take something----I thought it was going to be the "rose"; however, to my amazement, it turned out to be a golden thorn. I was told to take that thorn and place it in my heart (for Her heart, too, was pierced by the thorn of love). She said this thorn would give me strength as well as strength to those I touch and we are to continue to pray for each other that the bond of the strength of our prayers will not be broken. It was the discernment of the group that my "no" to Jesus represented the thorn and when I placed it in my heart, I experienced the pain of sorrow that perhaps our Lord feels when each of us in our own little way also say "no" to His Holy Will for our lives).

(Friday, October 27, 2000: The Friday night Canyon Rosary was particularly beautiful. Perhaps because of the intimacy of a smaller group. Again the power of the Holy Spirit was amongst us and the following message was received. The message was transcribed from an audio tape used to record the message as it was being dictated. As with all messages, please pray to the Holy Spirit for discernment as you read the following):

"My precious little children,

Come beneath My mantle and feel the warmth of a Mother's love for her children. Listen closely and hear the beating of My heart for each of My children. Rest assured, oh little ones, that We are always with you. We come securely wrapped in the graces of God. These graces He pours forth upon each of His children according to their needs. Many of you have faced such trials and your hearts have been broken -- your spirits weakened --- but I tell you children to face these trials with the confident assurance of God's intense love. Be like the tree of which Jeremiah spoke. The tree whose roots reached down into the river firmly securing it for nourishment that no matter what happened --- the storms that came --- the drought --- the roots reached into the depths of the river and thus sustained the tree. My children, your roots must reach down into the river of Divine Mercy where you will drink continuously upon the Mercy of God. You are loved --- you are asked but to trust and be at peace as you find patience and humility which God shall entrust to all of His precious children."

(Second brief message followed): ("I'm sorry" - then dialogue in tongues)

"My daughter, I ask of you to tell My children of this golden thorn for even though you felt the pain for your actions you also felt the Mercy of God. Teach them that God loves them even though we cause Him sorrow. There is His Mercy ---- His love."

November 3, 2000

"My dear children,

I bless you this night as I place a kiss upon each heart to sooth away the cares and anxieties in your lives. My children, this is an oasis of peace. Unfortunately many become distracted by the mirage of worldly deception and thus what they believe to be true soon fades before their eyes. Each of you has a particular purpose in God's wondrous plan of salvation. Be strong, My little children, for you are loved and much strength will be given to you for through this very oasis flows My Son's river of Divine Mercy and peace.

Come, little ones, without fear --- come beneath My Mantle -- that which will protect you. Trust in My Son in these most difficult times --- you are His beloved children."

(Note: Three important confirmations were given this night. During the course of the Rosary, long before the Spirit noticeably came upon me, I peacefully sensed many "beings" coming into the back area of the room where I was somewhat secluded. I was later told two very special people were praying that the Lord send His angels to guard and protect me as one of the persons who usually assists me during these times was unable to be by my side. Also, after the message, it was quietly indicated, a very blessed individual had sensed a "river of lights" which may confirm "the river of mercy" flowing through this oasis).

170

November 4, 2000

(A small group from Nogales had come to pray the Rosary and visit the Chapel. In the group was a child suffering from diabetes which was already attacking her body. She came for prayer and the following is what took place after a rather intense request to our Lord to hear the prayers for the child).

"My dear daughters,

Because you come in such a peace and with such pure hearts seeking healing -- know that I have heard your prayers and that I shall answer your prayers. I ask you to have much faith and trust in Me for I am your Jesus of Mercy. I love all of My children. I want each of you to experience My spirit that I have sent to rest upon you to feel the healing power I have sent to you this day. I have held this precious little child in my arms. I have raised the hopes --- those hopes that you have sent to my throne into beautiful balms of healing love. Graces shall flow upon you from My throne -- through My wounds to touch and to heal.

Trust Me and receive My peace."

November 10, 2000

(As this particular message was replayed just prior to transcription, it was interesting to note certain phrases which have been periodically repeated throughout Our Lady's messages. Numerous times we have been asked to "listen" and not just to listen, but to "listen carefully". We miss or fail to comprehend the simplicity of Her statements. We seem to be in a hurry to hear what She has to say next and we glide over the importance of Her message. We ask that as you pray for the discernment of the Holy Spirit prior to reading the following, you also pray for a quiet peaceful heart in order that you might really hear what our Lady is telling each and everyone of us).

"Listen carefully, My children, for tonight from My hand flows many graces ---- gold dust --- which My angels carry to each of you, My precious children, for these times are grave and many hearts are wounded and filled with sorrow. Through these graces you shall receive much strength --- but, tonight ----- a special gift----- a blessing from My Son for He shall take the golden dust from your hands which you shall hold out before Him and He shall bless you that all shall know that you are His.

Little ones, My precious children ---- how many times have I told you ---- you are loved and that this is a special place designed by the hand of God. You are chosen and given much responsibility.

This special blessing this night will give you that strength for it comes from the hand of Our Lord, My Son, who loves you unconditionally. Come just as you are ---- bring to Him your pains --- your sorrows --- your joy ---- your illnesses. Allow Him to touch you. Come with much faith for without faith, My children, even My

Son cannot touch the hardened hearts. Relinquish your will to His Divine Will and find that peace which He wishes all of His children to experience.

Beloved children there is much to do ---- much to do and you feel there are so few, but I tell you all is in God's hands. Trust Him ---- rely in His wisdom and in His mercy. Do what you can, and I assure you, He will do the rest."

(Note: Two other member of the prayer group were blessed earlier in the day with experiences involving the color gold. Their own personal "gifts" this day help confirm tonight's

November 17, 2000

"You who watch over this daughter ---- place a crucifix in her hand."

(This voice preceded the message from our Blessed Mother and is believed to be that of one of Her angels which accompanies Her during these special moments).

(Blessed Mother) "My dear children,

Allow the peace of My Son to fill your hearts as I take you on a walk along the seashore. The sun sends its rays shinning like precious gems -- the brilliance of such surpasses the imagination of each and every artist for none can capture God's majesty for He is the Master Artist. *(Tongues).* Look, My children, do you see the imprints in the sand as your feet press into the wet sand? These imprints --- the trials --- those burdens of life which weigh heavily upon your souls ---- feel the water as it rushes to meet you --- to cool and comfort and to cleanse the sand from your feet. This water --- the waves which come in to cleanse the sand --- is the Mercy --- the Mercy of God who comes to bring comfort and refresh your hearts and soul. Look behind you now. What do you see? The waves --- God's mercy --- have washed away the imprints in the sands as His Mercy shall wash and cleanse your very soul. <u>Do not ignore this great gift of My Son's Mercy</u>. Continue in your prayer --- in your prayer from the heart for through such prayers you shall mitigate God's Divine Justice.

Peace. little ones .... peace."

(Visual) He (Jesus) walks upon the water --- His arms outstretched.

(Jesus) "Trust Me, My children --- do not be afraid --- come forward --- come forward for <u>I am Mercy.</u>"

(Note: The following morning (Saturday) we had two visiting priests who wanted to celebrate Mass in the Chapel. The priest who gave the homily referenced Jesus walking on the water and how He beckoned Peter to come forward just as He beckons each of us to focus on Him and <u>come forward</u>).

November 22, 2000

The message began with the usual greeting in tongues followed by "I love you."

(Mary) "Beloved children of My heart,

I greet thee with such joy this night. My daughter has come that you might hear My words of love. I am the Mother of Mercy and it is mercy I wish to share with you this night. As I look amongst you --- gazing intensely into each heart, I see the cares - -- the anxieties of your lives and wish to replace them with peace and with the joy of My Son. Beloved children, never doubt that you are loved beyond measure -- the fountain of Mercy flows deeply for each to drink their fill. Come without fear for I hold the golden cup in My hand. Take this cup -- dip it into the fountain of My Son's Mercy and drink that you may be healed.

Little ones, let your thoughts be so pure and your actions so humble that they will melt the most hardened hearts and all will see the love of Jesus within each and everyone of you.

Trust Him for He calls you ---- He calls you His own."

(Jesus) "My children,

You have heard the words of My Mother -- the most Pure One. She has told you many times not to fear but to trust in Me -- the Lord Your God. Know that I am always with you in your daily lives --- as you gather to pray --- as you gather this very night. I have heard your prayers -- I have seen the intentions in your hearts. I have come to gather those precious petitions and as I gather them I place them within My Sacred Heart. I bless you this night -- children, My children."

(Note: She came in beautiful white - not exactly a color, but glowing like stars all twinkling together and this time She held a bouquet of roses. She had a cup and She was holding it out. I don't know why She was holding it out to the people. That's all I remember. Did you see the cup? The tape was then played and Jerry asked for discernment. A lady with very special gifts was in attendance. She saw the gold cup and indicated the bouquet of roses were gold. Another young man in attendance gave a detailed account of how he felt the "cup" was a symbol).

December 1, 2000

"My dear children,

I greet thee this night as I have greeted thee many times with love and tender compassion. This season is one of great joy. It is a time to reflect and meditate upon the greatness of Our Lord and the love He has for all of His children.

I ask you, My little ones, to listen carefully to these words and discern their meaning. Come and sit beside the fireplace decorated so beautifully with ornaments of the season. Watch the flames of the fire as they dance with a rhythm ---- a rhythm as though they are responding to a silent melody. Draw closer to the fire --- feel the warmth from the flames. Now ---- step back and you feel the warmth less intensely ---- step back still further and you are unable to feel anything because you have distanced yourself from the fire.

This fire is Our love which continuously burns for each of Our children. Draw closer to Our hearts for in drawing closer to Our hearts your heart will be filled with peace and tranquility.

I invite you to warm your very soul in the Devotion to the Sacred Heart of Jesus. Walk in His truth, My children ---- follow in His footsteps --- boldly yet humbly carrying your cross which one day you will lay at the foot of His throne.

Be at peace, My precious children ----- be at peace."

December 15, 2000

(Our Lady opened the message with "My dear children". *She made reference to whispering our love to Jesus ---to withhold nothing of ourselves as Jesus in His great love for us withheld nothing ---- even His very life).*

(She spoke of the "Flame of Divine Love" *burning within Her womb and of His longing to make His presence known to His people ----- the anticipation of the birth of Christ).*

(She then spoke most eloquently of St. Joseph and invited us to be imitators of his love, patience, kindness and total trust in God. We were asked to say a special prayer in honor of this very humble saint following the Rosary which we did. She also said the following is for next Friday December 22, 2000):

"I wish you to place a table in front of My statue. On this table place your special religious items which you wish to be blessed. During the Memorare, I will personally bless them." *(The following applies for Sunday December 24, 2000, 3pm Rosary),"* I wish for you to do something special for My Son. Place on the altar a gift for Him that comes from your heart. During the Memorare, I again will come and bless them and give them to My Son."

174

What a blessed evening! There were many people in attendance each bringing the religious items which they wished Our Blessed Mother to bless. As per Our Lady's instructions on December 15th, these items were placed on a table by Her statue as She requested. Everyone was very reverent considering such a large group as the presence of the Holy Spirit was very evident..

"My beloved children,

Thank you for responding to My message with such great faith. It pleases Me to see so many precious items placed before Me ---- some with such meaning ---- those memories ---- cherished possessions. I most gladly bless each and every item that you have brought and I ask you to reflect --- what have you brought? Did you choose that which you highly value or did you choose the lesser of your possessions? I say this in preparation for Sunday when you shall gather with your gifts for My Son.

This is a great banquet. Would you bring your very best -- for your gifts are for the King of Kings --- the Lord of Lords. What would you serve a most distinguished guest? Would you bring your <u>leftovers</u> or would you bring the very best that you have? He asks of you the very best ---- your heart.

My children, do not lose focus during this Holy time for truly God must come first. No <u>leftovers</u>, My children ---- only the very best you can bring.

I rejoice with you this night. Know that I have placed a kiss upon each who come with true belief. I have also placed a kiss upon those (who do not believe) that they might believe. My blessing, My children ---- the blessing of your Mother."

(Reflections: After hearing the message, the word "leftovers" kept coming to mind. I personally recognize I have been so busy "doing" God's work that I have often failed to have that personal relationship with God that He desires of each of us. As one beautiful lady said "she prays she will become more like Mary than Martha." That seems to say it all. Although both of these women became Saints, Jesus said Mary (in choosing to sits at the feet of her Lord, to spend time with Him) had chosen the best of the two. Perhaps we need to ask ourselves - which do we choose to be ------ Mary or Martha. The choice is ours).

(Our Blessed Mother has stated she will come and bless any religious items brought to the Friday night Canyon Rosary at Mary's Knoll on December 22nd. A table will be placed in front of Her statue and She said the blessing will occur during the praying of the Memorare. Also, on Sunday, December 24, 2000, in the Chapel after the 3:00p.m. Chaplet/Rosary, She requested "gifts from our hearts" to Her Son be placed on the altar in front of the mural of Jesus. She will also bless these gifts during the praying of the Memorare).

(There will be a basket placed on the Altar for those wishing to place their petition ("gifts") here for the special blessing. All those petitions will then be placed in the Jesus stocking and taken to the Manger as our gifts to Jesus for the coming year. Think of what you might wish to offer Him. Listen to your heart----- a simple promise of an act of "kindness" would be a wonderful start. They will know what lies in your heart ---- no further words are necessary).

December 29, 2000

The following messages were received during the Friday night Canyon Rosary. It was another beautiful evening as guests came from Phoenix, Tucson, and the surrounding Hereford area all uniting to praise our Lord Jesus and honor His Mother. It was a blessing to have Basil (along with his trusty guitar) with us once again after a long absence due to illness. The following message was transcribed from an audio tape used to record the message as it was being dictated.

(Unidentified - but probably an angel) "Awaken oh children of God and show great reverence for the Queen of the most holy angels stands in your midst surrounded by Her court. Hear the words of the Holy Mother of God." *(On a few other occasions, the presence of our Blessed Mother was announced by an angel).*

"My beloved Children,

Praise be Jesus! I wish to tell you of the great gifts which you presented to My Son and how they were received." *(There were some individuals who were in attendance at the December 22, 2000, Sunday afternoon Chaplet/Rosary)* " My little ones, who witnessed the glimmer of lights and these lights were My angels who took these gifts as I blessed them and carried them to the throne of My Son.

How pleased He is with your gifts ---- but, I ask you, dear ones, to look at these gifts as you would the candle whose wick burns with a soft gentle glow. Think of your gift as a candle. The wick is your commitment to keep these promises --- these gifts to My Son. Little ones, let the flame of your intentions burn so brightly that God will see the purity of your heart and know as He looks upon the light of your gift He sees how much you love His Son.

Dear ones, I could tell you so much, but you are not yet prepared to receive such knowledge. Let it suffice to say you are Our chosen little ones entrusted with much. Your pockets have been filled with coins of great wealth --- for they are love and they are the Word of God which have filled your very soul. Spend wisely these coins. Do not horde them, My children, for they are gifts for all of God's children. You have received much wealth; therefore, much is required of you.

Peace, beloved little ones. Call upon the angels and the saints who are here to assist you. Ask, My children, and you shall receive."

****

Messages from Jesus and Mary

January 5, 2001 - December 28, 2001

The following messages are repeated as private revelation. They are of a similar nature to the 1997 - 2000 messages that were approved by Pat's former spiritual advisor. He was aware of their distribution as "Private Revelation" and the messages being published at no charge as book one and book two under the title "A Call of Urgency".

Father Louis Hasenfuss, Pat's previous spiritual advisor died suddenly on February 28, 2000. We all miss Him. Pat's new spiritual advisor became Father Henri, the newly elected Prior of Holy Trinity Monastery located in Saint David, Arizona. Before Father Louis death Father Henri was the immediate superior under Him and was familiar with the situation. On April 3rd, 2001, Father Henri Capdeville confirmed he gives his permission to publish current messages on the same basis as Father Louis. Father Henri has reviewed the 1999, 2000 and the early 2001 messages and has found nothing contrary to church morals or church teachings. Any formal publication of these messages are presented as "Private Revelation", and should be discerned as such.

The Diocese of Tucson has issued a private letter on this matter. Because we are not asking the church for any interpretation or approval they have stated it is not an issue with them.

It is to be noted that currently most of these messages are given audibly --- that is they are orally spoken in a distinctive voice through one individual while in a spiritual state. To date, there have been at least four different sources of spoken words. Starting mainly in January 2001, these messages have been followed by an "allowed oral response" to what the messenger has been given visually to witness. Many are now on file on private audiotape.

January 5, 2001

(Blessed Mother) "My little children,

Seek Him Who is truth. Run eagerly after the Heart of Hearts that burns continuously with love for each of His children. As you prepare to remove the decorative ornaments of the season -- the trees -- the lights -- flowers and, yes, My children, even the manager scene placed in a most prominent place occasionally caught by the eye and felt by the heart. So too these memories of this Christmas shall pass as <u>shadows</u> as have the memories of the many Christmases long since passed.

I am here to remind you that God's great gift of salvation is not seasonal, My children, nor can it be purchased with great wealth. It is a gift received *(freely)* only by a pure and humble heart which seeks the face of God . Obedience to His will and the acceptance of His mercy *(the precious blood of Jesus)*.

Let the peace of My Son fill your hearts with strength and joy as you call upon His most holy name." -------- (*long pause* -------- *Voice now believed to the that of an Angel)*. "It is most important that holy water be placed in this room --- a crucifix be placed in this daughter's hand and each who guard her test the spirit. For this is a time of great deception and all must be protected."

(Blessed Mother) "The shadows, My children, are also the souls who seek your prayers. Speak My child, what do you see?"

(Visual-Pat) " *They have no forms or faces ---- just grayish images and they're crying out to us. Help us --- pray for us. And I see some as we pray ----- light --- the lights --- they are transformed into a light of sorts --- not brilliant as when our Blessed Mother comes, but they've changed in appearance and I understand that they've been released and God is calling them into His Kingdom. They rise with such joy. They hear the sounds ---- voices ---- yet, not voices ------ it's so beautiful. Each one is greeted by a choir ------ so beautiful --- and the joy. The joy shines so brilliant. We must pray for these souls for I am told our time shall come and we shall be dependent upon the prayers of these souls for whom we have prayed for many (here) will forget us as our time approaches, but God has made provisions and the Holy Souls shall pray for us."*

January 12, 2001

(Personal message after a somewhat unsettling day)

"My little daughter with the wounded heart ---- you who care so much for the smallest of God's creatures ---- do you not realize this is the heart which God uses to gather souls? When you offered to Him everything -- did you not think there would be some pain -- some sorrow or only your joys? Little heart, you know better. Realize this day - - through its gentle sorrows to your heart --- has brought a soul a great gift. Teach others to realize that the smallest offerings in life when joined with the Passion of My Son bring to His heart a tender awakening and He reaches out for those souls who have neglected Him ---- who have lost their faith and thus have turned away from God. It is in all suffering --- no matter how great or how small that God greatly rejoices and accepts all such gifts for His plan of salvation."

"My dear children,

I have called you to be warriors through the strength of God's graces -- yet only by accepting the afflictions of a heart pierced with love --- an indescribable love for souls ---- will you be able to only slightly realize the intensity of the desire ---- that hunger within Almighty God for all souls. Pray that you might understand

178

My messages regarding these souls and the responsibility which you share not only for the souls here at this very moment --- but those who have gone before to be purified in the fire of God's love.

Pray, My children, listen ---- open your hearts and listen for truly God speaks to each heart. You have only to listen with much faith. You are His children --- the children He calls by name. Listen --- listen for there is much that He wishes from each of you for each brings their own gifts. God desires you heart. Listen -- hear Him --- hear Him --- have much faith. Little ones, if you truly wish to please your God in true service to Him - ask only that you be allowed to do His Holy Will. Ask nothing for yourself except that which pleases God."

January 19, 2001

"My precious children,

Am I not the Mother that has loved you --- that has nurtured you with the milk of truth and forgiveness? Yes, My children, I am here and I wish for you <u>to listen carefully and discern</u> for what shall be told to you is of great importance."

(Pat) "Yes, I see ----- but, it's so dark I can barely ---- (unfinished) She comes in the brilliance of the lights --- very large ------ very beautiful. I can't see what's in Her hand. A ball? No, a globe ------ a globe of the world. She's holding it securely in Her hand and it's turning very slowly. Such a sense of peace. There is a large figure of a man ---- brilliant ---- and He's calling Her and She fades ---- and the ball --- this globe begins to spin. There is nothing to control it ---- spinning -------- She's back. In Her hand again She holds the globe but She also holds a key. This key is to unlock our hearts that we will allow Christ to fully reign in our hearts. I understand it is some type of warning of things that must come but great peace will be with us the peace of Jesus to see us through this great storm that approaches. She says to be at peace and to fear not for after the storm comes a new dawn from which will blossom the peace of Jesus."

"My little children,

I have allowed you to see this night so that your soul will be refreshed as the Holy Spirit comes to permeate each heart with the Light of Divine Love. This light ----
-- the rays---------are arrows now mounted into the bows of the angels who stand in your midst. If you really mean it, open your heart ------ they shall then send these arrows deeply within to fuse the fire of Divine Love that shall strengthen you. Oh, little children, --------- so much love ------ so much love We have for you. Yet, the world still tugs on the strings of your heart in such subtle ways. You truly do not understand how many neglect My Son ---- how many are indifferent to this

great grace He has bestowed on His children. They have turned away ---- for The Way of the Cross ------- the way of penance and sacrifice does not appeal to their taste. Without your devout prayers, oh little ones, so many will lose their way. Pray now with your Mother as I intercede for you before My Son. Offer your prayers now filled with life defining love that these precious little souls will not be lost.

I cover you with My Mantle and those that have consecrated** their hearts to My Immaculate Heart -- I gather and tuck within this Heart that is eternally united with Jesus."

(* In discerning, perhaps the spinning globe designates the approaching storm).

(** As She was saying this, the prayer group (in the other room) was praying the Consecration to the Immaculate Heart of Mary).

January 26, 2001

("Thank you for this gift this night, My Lord and My God")

"My dear children,

Praise be Jesus who has allowed Me to be with you these many years ------ Who has allowed Me to come to Our oasis of souls. Daughter ---- look now but do not repeat ---- *(Private visual followed which seemed like a long period of time; however, it lasted approximately 30 seconds of our time).* My child ---- God is so merciful that with many prayers what you have seen may be mitigated."

" Oh little children,

You are being refined and fine-tuned as precious instruments sent into the Harvest. Yet, My heart is heavy this night for I must tell you as a Mother gently tries to persuade her children ---- to steer them on the proper path. O fragile humanity ---- stubborn and impatient. You hold onto the world with one hand and the other you reach out for God. God did not hold back --------- He gave all and He requires all from you! It is time ---- it is beyond time to make choices in your lives ------ to rebuild broken relationships -------- to reach out to those whom you have wounded with your words or with your actions. Precious little children, hear the pain in your Mother. I weep for those bound to the world with self-love, but -- − I rejoice in the abundant mercy of God for all of His children!"

(Visual: Pat) (Now?) "It is very bright --- almost too bright to look at ---- there are two very large angels (I think) and in front of them they hold a torch --- no, a stand with seven torches on each stand. It's like a curtain that's being opened -- −a veil ---- There is a lamb -- a lamb on the altar --- more beautiful than I can describe. Then there's our Mother --- hands folded on Her chest -- head bowed in

180

great reverence. The altar seems suspended and in the back --- almost around the altar --- four, five, six (I appear to be counting) --- 12 chairs --- 12 more -- kind of like thrones and there are men (I believe) sitting on these thrones praising God ---- praising the Lamb. Beneath the altar flows a river --- a river of red. It passes beneath the angels holding the torches. It seems to be suspended in air -- but beneath -- there are all the children -- reaching up to God. This river -- like red rubies glistening so brightly --- slowly falling on all of the precious children. I believe they are martyred. (There is no response to my questions) I can only assume perhaps they are being cleansed by the blood of the Lamb. (No need to fear, Our Lord is with us).

(After visual was over further clarification was given) "We shall see greater disasters than these and there will be no holding back the hand of Her Son. She calls us to pray -- to pray and to pray. Even though there is a warning there is never a sense of anxiety or fear. There is just a tremendous love and tremendous sense of sorrow because there are only a handful of warriors fighting a battle against many, but that will be sufficient if we persevere and be true to our Lord."

January 28, 2001

"Children of My Mercy,

Do not fear the approach of difficult times nor the seemingly insurmountable obstacles which shall befall you. Be of great faith --- free of despair. This is My holy mountain ---- a beacon ---- a lighthouse in the desert ---- a desert of souls. Come to Me in faith and complete trust for though the darkness shall come. My Divine Light shall erupt as a volcano of hope touching each soul who clings to the promise of My Mercy. Mercy, My children, is your hope of hopes. Trust Me as I thirst for all souls, the lost -- forgotten --- the abandoned ----- all souls.

You are My little faith filled instruments which I send out into the ocean of souls. Drop your nets and love and encourage each soul by your actions of obedience, faith and love in My Mercy. This is your time, My children, to follow Me. Do not detour because of difficulty of understanding for to fully understand is not your gift -------- your gift is that of faith ------- faith in what you do not see but believe. Trust Me ------- love Me. I hold you in the palm of My hand.

Rest is My peace."

February 2, 2001

"My dear children,

I come to you this night with a heart much lighter than when we met before, but yet there is still much to do -------- for tears still cloud My eyes when I see My Son left alone in the tabernacles around the world ---- lonely --- yet, loving waiting ------ waiting for you, My children. You speak of Him, but you do not speak to Him. He is your friend Who calls you to keep Him company (if only for

181

a moment) and that (when) you come to Him ---- you are real and without pretense ------- for there are those who profess to be Christians ---- who profess to love God yet it is pretense of wasted energy for their hearts are void of love and trust in My Son.

I asked that you set aside time on the third Thursday of each month to console My Son, and I love you, little children, for you have tried so hard to obey My wish. Little ones, this is far greater than you can see for you do not realize the souls which cry out to you ------- crying for prayers. They await the call from God to enter eternity.

Pray, My children, pray and sacrifice for only by these means will you accomplish the purpose for which God has sent you here. So much confusion in your minds ---- *(you ask)* Why here? Why not, My children. It is God's choice."

(Visual-Pat) " I see ---- there are two people --- a man and a woman (very petite and very beautiful --- it appears to be Jesus and Mary) --- yet there is no air of majesty. There is simplicity. There is warmth -- there is humanity --- yet, there is Divinity" (I do not know how to describe, but Our Lord is saying) "Come to Me in your simplicity and I shall greet you in simplicity for love --- Divine love ---- My love ---- will reach out to you on any level, but the simplicity of a child ---- a child that trusts ---- brings the greatest joy to My heart." *"They speak, but I do not hear. They glance this way -- nod, and smile and He says;"* "Mother, My pure persistent Mother ----- How can I deny you these your children?"

February 9, 2001

"My dear children,

Praise be Jesus Who has allowed Me to be with you --- to come into your presence as you feel the presence of your Mother. Oh My children, I look into each heart and I see all those hidden emotions ---- the hidden pains you fear to reveal, but I ask you this night --- do not fear, My Son --- bring to Him all that lies within your heart so that He may touch and heal the wounds before they fester --- before they cause destruction. My heart is filled with emotion this night for look what is beside Me, My children. Look closely and see not only was My Son pierced for love of you, but My heart as well has been pierced with love for all of My children.

I ask thee this night to learn a lesson --- painful though it maybe. Pride disguises itself, My children, and it has scarred many souls. I speak of spiritual pride. You become so absorbed in this prayer and that prayer ---- your brother or sister is not doing something correctly ------- According to whom, My children ? God or to you? Beware of this trap. Do not allow yourself to be caught for it is painful, My children ---- painful for these wounds to heal --- for spiritual pride affects the lives of so many others. I encourage you with so much love to turn towards God and in turning toward God ---- pray, be obedient, My children, reconcile yourselves to the Lord your God --- sacrifice and do penance------- for you are called to holy children of God. Some lessons are painful, but those which inflict the most pain have the most lasting affect. I love you, little children --- you who strive to follow My Son. Do not fear what the future holds for He who holds the future holds you in the palm of His hand. What you shall now see --- pray much, My children, for it holds much meaning."

(Visual-Pat) "The curtain opens. It is so bright. It looks like an immense cube -- clear -- a large cube --- a square. A square -- transparent -- glittering. It's like a rainbow of colors. Very tall --- very large --- like crystal (I can't tell if the colors are from the bevels in the glass). They are gold and green, shade of blue -- a dark gold --- hum ---. topaz -- purple (I can't describe the others). This massive cube turns and there are three big rectangles standing on end -- white -- maybe a precious stone ---- hum ---- Each side has three ---- twelve in all. They open ---- they're doors! They're doors opening into a city of crystal. We can't go in yet. We have to wait --- more prayer --- more sacrifices ----- until God calls us and then we can enter the city)."

February 16, 2001

"My beloved children,

The trials of life have tossed you about like a tiny ship dragging its anchor on an angry sea --- unable to steady itself. <u>Pull up the anchor,</u> My children. With great faith turn into the storm. You falter, My children, even as you hesitate to face the storm for you seek compromise with God. God does not compromise. He loves you, but He does not compromise. You hold on to God and yet you still cling to the world for you see a false sense of security. My children, in doing this you become lukewarm. Lukewarm leaves a bitter taste in the mouth of My Son.

I have been with you, Oh little children, who are trying so hard to follow My Son. I am the Mother who lovingly mends the tattered patterns of your lives with the golden thread of patient love. My children, I have come to instruct you ---- to <u>draw you close to God</u> that you may become His obedient children. Do not only read My messages, but practice them --- for I wish <u>to draw you closer to God.</u> Through love and forgiveness may you be reconciled with God."

Visual: Our Mother sits on a chair of stars. She is dressed in a coral colored robe with a blue mantle and across Her lap She is sewing a big rug (?) a quilt -- a tapestry. There is no end. Oh, My Jesus ---- they are all faces --- they are souls. She's patiently stitching them one by one. These little souls through the wear and tear of sin are starting to unravel from this beautiful tapestry. But She is there unconcerned with the length of the quilt. She concentrates on each precious soul with such tender care. Beneath the quilt/tapestry there is an hour glass and it's sifting through very quickly. Mother, it's sifting through ----- there are so many --

183

there is not time. She looks and I hear Her say "pray and watch as you pray". *There are golden threads -- there are no hands. They are going to each soul as far as I can see. They are mending the quilt --- this tapestry of life. She looks again and She says* "the name of this thread is prayer. *Now you see the power of prayer".*

February 23, 2001

(Tongues) Holy Mary --- pray for us.

"My dear children,

The light of Divine Love has illuminated the path upon which you stand. It is a path well worn by the disciples of love which have come before you. I call you My disciples of love ---- I have called you but you have not <u>heard</u> My voice, but it is the spirit within you which has unmistakably recognized (My voice) and thus has responded.

Dear little children; We invite you this Lenten season to walk in the footsteps of My Son. Reach deeply within your hearts and expel all that is not pleasing to God and ask Him in His mercy to unite that which remains to the Passion of His beloved Son."

"Dear children, you have been called here to receive many graces and in receiving such graces you are asked to go forth sharing all that you have received with those precious souls still searching yet not knowing for what they search. You are now little lights in the darkness. Little lights illuminating the love of Christ. In extending Our invitation to you for this journey------ remember that <u>you will walk with Jesus</u> ---- you will not escape the burdens of the crosses. There are no short cuts in this journey ----- as you might say ------ there are no <u>end runs,</u> but the reward is great and it is everlasting if you but persevere.

These next few weeks I shall take you on a journey ----- a journey through the Passion of My Son. I ask that you pray much --- receive the Sacraments ---- especially reconciliation ---- that you might <u>worthily receive My Son</u> for He is your strength. Without Him you cannot survive. Prepare for this journey for many souls await your positive response to this Our invitation."

(Visual): I see --- am I to share? It appears that there is a long winding road --- not a modern road but a road of pebbles and stone with jagged edges and curving. There are souls ------ different colors of lights ----- not color exactly. grays, some lighter tones ---- some darker and each one has a cross. There are footprints embedded in the stones. Each one of these souls is diligently trying to step in these foot prints. They are the foot prints of our Lord. There are walls all around this narrow area and yet there are so many souls. I see there are some that are very bright (oh, my) their cross is red. I believe these are those that have been or will be martyred. As I look there are also little souls little forms ---bodies --- and their crosses------------their crosses are so large. There are larger forms

184

and their crosses are smaller. And our Lord says:

"I give to each only what each can bear. The silent little souls in your world often carry the largest cross for their heart knows nothing but love for Me and doing My will. They seek no attention. They seek but to quietly go about doing My will. Yet, I do not judge for those carrying the smallest cross are just as important. All are necessary."

(Visual continued) Way, way in front of the line, as far as I can see, there are beautiful, beautiful people. Very defined features --- faces just glowing. They are the Saints. They are encouraging all of these souls and the souls are not burdened by their cross. They are singing. They are praising God! Their hearts are so full of love. In the crowds there are angels and in their hands ------ their hands are extended and they are cupped as though they are holding something so precious. He's stopping and he's looking at me. He's turning so I can see what He's holding in his hands. (long sigh --- crying) It's a child --- it's a fetus --- -it's an aborted baby. It never made it ---- it's his Guardian angel that's so tenderly carrying that child to God! Why is he still looking? I don't understand! This little speck of a child looks at me. (gasp) ------------- It's my grandchild. It's my grandchild. (much emotion) It's ok. God has him ---- it's ok now.

(Note: It's so important that we never cease praying. Be diligent for we never know who our prayers will touch. How many relatives we have that we may never be aware of ---- how many children that never made it?)

March 2, 2001

(Message began in tongues as usual).

"It is time, My children to come with Me. Take My hand ---- come beneath My mantle. Listen --- hear ---- and see with your heart."

(Visual): It's very dark ----- now, I can see. It' about late afternoon. It looks like Our Lord with some of His disciples (I believe they are His disciples). They are walking, but more like climbing. There is a slight incline ----- a hill---- shrubs and some trees. It's a location up above a town or village. In a not too distant area, Our Lord has been talking as He has been walking ----- sharing things with His disciples. They come to an area with some rocks ----- appropriate for sitting. They come to a rest. Something has happened. The lights --- it's getting darker --- not night dark ---- but the sun instead of brighter in the sky is lower. The images are still clear, but the time frame has elapsed. I can't tell how much. Jesus has obviously been talking. It must have been a difficult conversation as the disciples have taken other positions. I see two sitting. One with both elbows on his knees, the knees slightly apart. His face covered by his hands. The other is sitting ---- just staring into space. There are two standing. One is by a tree, his arms wrapped around the trunk of the tree, his forehead pressed against the tree. It looks like his legs are shaking. He's kind of sliding down the tree. I see him take his hand and raise it to his face to wipe the tears. The other just stands very

*emotional --- obviously trying to comprehend what Our Lord has said. I think there were others in the group. I see the back of some. They're going into a slightly wooded area. It's hard to determine for what reason. It's getting darker and perhaps cooler. Maybe they are going after some fire wood, but I think it's an excuse to hide the pain that they are experiencing. It's difficult to put into words. They look back and still seated is Jesus. He turns His head just slightly (in my direction). I can't move. His eyes are like pools of love. It's so different than before. It's love yet there is such determination in His face. I know there is a message in this, but for now I can only describe it as best I can. ***

He turns His head back now and He rises to His feet. There are two angels behind Him ---- adoring Him ----- praying; and as Our Lord has stood up, He raises His arms and prays. I'm not allowed to hear His prayer, but it would appear He prays for those He loves --- those disciples that are now lost in their sorrow. There is slight breeze with an aroma I can't place ---- pleasant in a way --- not like a flower --- just different. I am told <u>it is the aroma of tears and sorrow ground with love.</u> It filters through the air ------ it's a time a great sorrow ---- lack of comprehension. They (disciples) are there (physically), but yet they are not there(spiritually). Poor precious one --- they love Him so much --- it's difficult for them to believe what they have heard. "There must be something we can do" (that's what they are saying) "there must be something we can do." There is nothing ---- and Jesus heart just melts for He loves them but He wants them to understand the fate that shall befall Him).

*Note: There is such sorrow in Our Lord for His beloved disciples as they must also endure His Passion in their own way. They can only cling to "hope" that Jesus will be resurrected. Jesus also looks at us with sorrow for we have the benefit of "knowing" that He suffered, died, and rose again. Why then do we behave as we do ---- too often caught up in our own little world of "feelings" --- too tired, too hot, too cold etc when we should be centered in Christ serving others and praising Our Lord.

(Our Blessed Mother continues ...)

"My dear children,

There are many things I wish you to see and many lessons I wish you to learn. What did you see when you looked into His eyes? You, My child, described them as pools of love for you knew it is these eyes that look into the soul and expose it and see each heart and open it to where it lays bare before you *(allowing us to see our sin and its affect on our soul).* You were captivated by the eyes of love --- unable to move ---- certain that if you but simply breathed --- your lungs would expand and burst because you would be inhaling Divine Love ---- and, the soul within you would want to be united with its Creator.

Patience, little souls, be patient for this love you are as yet unable to understand ----- but, as you continue this journey with sorrowful joy you will have your heart filled ever so slowly with the tiny particles of this Divine Love ---- gradually each heart will be filled to its individual capacity to understand.

Peace, My little children, for the journey shall continue. Pray, trust, sacrifice, My children, and above all ---- love My Son and in loving My Son, forgive ----- Forgive ---- forgive". *(Prayer group could be heard singing "I Exalt Thee" in the background).*

March 9, 2001

(Visual): I hear a voice. "Come pray with me ". *It is our Mother. She is in a small room. There are no inner doors in this house. Someone has taken off a cloak and hung it in what looks like a doorway so that She can have Her privacy. The room is very dark with the exception of a beam of light coming through the ceiling material or there is an opening way high on the wall I cannot determine which it is. That's the only light. The light shines upon the Mother who is on Her knees on a stone floor. There is not much furniture in the room. She just kneels on the floor --- Her hands are in front of Her. Her fingers are kind of locked together in front like She is trying to keep them from shaking. There is no color ---- everything is gray... different shades. It is a sorrowful time. I hear Her. In between between Her prayers are kind of like muffled sob She falls back on Her knees and sits on Her heels and I see the face, the face of suffering. I want to go ---- just to put my arms around Her. When I look beneath this suffering and this pain ---- there is a beauty I cannot describe ------ there is just indescribable beauty. There is a message to the beauty.*

(Our Mother says.........)

"The beauty My child tries to describe is obedience and love. Out of obedience to the Father, Our Son has been taken away. Out of love for you, little children, He freely went. Comfort My Son during this His time of sorrow by loving His Father who sent Him and by obeying His Father's Will."

(Note: I don't see anything else. I hear people in the next room ---- sounds like mostly women ---- should they go in ---- should they be with Her? ----- no, they decide ----- it's best to leave Her ----- that's what the Mother wants. The room is back. Our Blessed Mother lies prostrate on the floor. She's praying --- I hear ------- "Most loving Father in heaven, hear the prayers of your lowly servant" ----- (it fades).

March 16, 2001

(Visual) I've been here before ---- some type of a building ---- it's still dark and I'm standing in front of a large door. The door is opening (I don't want to go in ....I don't want to go in). There is a light ....it's warm ... it's OK now ....it's my Guardian Angel. We're going through the door. There is a large area facing the doorway as we enter. It is perhaps a meeting room or living area

..... it's just different from what I am used to .... there is a hallway just inside the door which runs both left and right with the large open room just beyond the walkway ....directly in front of the open door. There are men ...... looks like they are resting ... they are jeering "so He's a king" ....so He's a king" that's what I hear them saying.

My Angel leads me down the corridor to the left. It's dark but there are torches/candles along the wall to provide some light. I'm not certain where I'm going or what's beyond the wall. I'm holding on to the wall ....it's wet like it was Before .....it's damp wet ... not from rain .... and now I know where this is going, but it's ok this time. I'm going down this narrow passage .....I'm trying to go, but I need help ....There is a small hand being held out to me. It's the hand of our Mother. She's going to take me this time. We're walking but I'm still holding to the wall. She has my hand. We're coming to rooms, sort of like rooms which are all blocked off. There is one ..... and ...we're stopping. There is just an opening that you can see through, but I can't quite see. It's dark ....there is a bench (looks like a stump of wood resembling a stool) and I am told to take this. So I pull it over and I am standing, but I can't see .....then ......there is .....Oh (long sigh) .... there is a light and I see Jesus. The light shines on Him.... just barely ......very dim ...... and He's been so badly mistreated. They have His hands bound way up above His head and His body is stretching as far as He can. They've got this piece of wood under His feet and His toes can barely touch it for support. He's so uncomfortable. He's so much in pain ....and there is a stench ......an awful stench ....They have done awful things ...awful things. Oh Jesus ....I've done this.... I'm so sorry.

"Tears, My child..........what shall you do with these tears? Add them to the multitude of tears My Mother has shed for all of mankind. You little one can only see the external ....the swollen battered features......the gaping wounds and, yes, you can even smell the odor of excrement to defile the flesh. But, I have allowed this journey to draw you from the external into spiritual reality. The swollen disfigured features .... the gaping wounds are the afflictions (sins) of the soul. The odor is the decay of pride and self-righteousness which have attacked the soul. My children, My precious children, I am the <u>Physician</u> that has come to heal the wounds with the balm of My love. Children, Oh children, I can heal the wounds of your soul if you but trust Me and come to Me. Come to Me through the Sacrament of Reconciliation. Do not delay, as many do, in seeing <u>The Physician</u> for this disease is terminal. Time swiftly passes through the hour glass of life. Hurry, My children, hurry."

(Commentary: Through sorrow, pain and suffering .... love must come before all. We cannot survive unless we <u>love</u>).

March 23, 2001

(Visual): I can see everything. It's early morning ... the sun is just beginning to come up above the hills in the background. It's quiet .... I can hear the birds singing in the trees ....it appears just to be an ordinary morning.

It's a town now.......... I think it's a town with very high walls of stone .... stone paved streets and pathways. I can hear the carts as they are being pushed along the stones. It looks like vendors are setting up for their sales for the day. There are stands of fruits and vegetables. One little store has leather sandals ...... just various leather goods. The vision begins to fade .... it darkens .... it would appear to indicate a lapse of time.

The sun is up a little higher .... I'm guessing it's about two hours later in the day. There are lots of people now .... their voices resemble a humming sound like swarms of bees. I can't make out what they are saying ....just a lot of excitement. They are on both sides of the street just waiting for something. There are people up above on the roofs .... the roofs are flat and the people are looking down. They , too, are waiting. The people have strange looks in their faces can't describe the look. Not a look of excitement exactly ...it's just not a pleasant look. The Lord says to be at peace. "Their look is not important ....concentrate."

All eyes turn down the street. Way in the distance there are men on horseback in uniform .. .. I think ...men walk beside them and behind them. I can see a light. Things are no longer in three dimension .... nothing but a series of lights now .... mostly grays as has been before. The light that comes closer is a soft, pleasing light .... oh, my ..... oh, my .... I'm so grateful I cannot see .... It is Jesus. He has no shoes, but I can see His feet .... even His feet are all wounds .... I can see the bones in His feet. He's walking and he's forced to step in all of this filth which presses into the wounds in His feet ....He's going to fall .... He 's falling into this filth .. but .... He looks this way ..... and ...... His eyes .... say .... everything. His eyes say I love you and I love them. And, I will forgive them if they but ask Me.

He says to look beyond the exterior .... to look at those who persecute Him with pity for they do not know what they do. No disdain must come from us who love our Lord. Look with love and pity.

"My dear children,

(Mary) You have been allowed but a shadowy glancea glimmer of the perverseness of evilhardened hearts …..senses dulled by hatred and injusticebut you little ones are God's chosen children. The mission before you is so great for you have been given this opportunity to look back and see … not to make these same mistakes. Unfortunately, little ones, these lessons are not well learned and only through

time …….much patience and perseverance ……will you come to understand the depth of the Love of Jesus.

Yes, My Son did walk these paths strewn with filth, but the filth you saw was not the filth that brought Him so much pain. It was the hatred, the oppression ....the Anger .... all of those things He trod upon because they are the poisons into which the arrows have been dipped to pierce the hearts of His children.

I tell you now to go as did My Jesus ...... meek and humble of heart ......into the arena of life....... filled with peace .... that peace of abiding in the Father's Will."

March 30, 2001

(Visual: I am shown what looks like the sky ......it's dark ....although I don't see any stars. It's like a canvass ready to be painted. I'm starting to see images and outlines, but nothing is clear. It's like a camera that's not in focus. I can't see........now ....there are many roads .... all of stars .... going in different directions. I'm standing before one and it's so beautiful... .I'm just looking.....it's so inviting ....I want to go down ....but I can't. It's not the right one. It's a false beauty. It's a worldly beauty. It's not what our Lord calls us to..........can't go down that one ......have to look for another one.

There is a path ...... lots of people ...... kind of a narrow line. There is no pushing ...no shoving .. ..just calm. It's hard to describe, but it's like a river that's flowing undisturbed It's so beautiful. It's almost like a costume party. It's very odd. The ones in the front I can barely see. They are wearing some sort of robes ...... something just very old. In the middle where I appear to be there are just different styles of clothing. These people (I'll call them people) are all different sizes ... even children. I see people in uniforms ... all kinds. I can't describe what they belong to or to whom (country). There are people in habits. I would say they are monks . I can see some with collars (I know they are priests). There are Sisters in habits ….some are strange ...really old ...but I know what they are. I'm watching history.

These are all souls. I see them …..they all bend down and they reach for something. It's small and they pick it up and take it in their hands. There is a burst of light like millions of stars exploding. I can see faces. And the pieces of whatever they are holding ...they've turned into crosses. I am told to look towards the front of the line. Now it all makes sense. There is Jesus. These people have picked up a splinter from His cross. They are walking in the footsteps of the Master.

I've never seen this before .... there is our Mother ... I'm sure it's our Mother and She is behind Jesus but in front of the people and there is a cross ....there is a cross ....it's not on Her shoulder exactly as Her hands are in front kind of holding

Her robe so that She can walk. There are little angels .... they look like little babies ...chubby with wings ....and one has got his little body and wings between the cross and Her shoulder. He's supporting the cross ...... there are others that are helping. The cross is clear. It's like crystal clear and I'm watching and at the very bottom.... I see drops of water (?) .... looks like water.......and Jesus says:

"These precious souls have chosen well. They have recognized the beauty of the cross and they have embraced its pain and suffering as one embraces a loved one. As for My Mother's cross ....Her cross .... Her cross is the cross of tears that She shed then and sheds now for all mankind. With each tear that falls upon an unrepentant heart .... many graces will flow to that soul to enkindle in it the desire for My Mercy. Pray now during these last few weeks of Lent that many souls will receive My gift of Salvation."

April 6th, 2001

(Just prior to the visual, the audio tape picked up " <u>water, need water. I'm so thirsty ...must keep climbing"</u>*. There is a hill and there are a lot of people around the hill ...... lots of people. They don't go all the way around. I can't see anything on the other side of the hill. Maybe they can't stand over there. There is a path leading up to the top .... kind of like a semi circle .. like there are two ways up, but they are all connected. It's strange because I'm looking down and there are so many colored "tops" ......must be head-dresses, but they look like a field of flowers ....but ..they're not flowers .... they're not flowers. Where is Jesus? .... Where is Jesus?*

There is a line of troops between the people and an area not quite on the top of the hill and I see coming through with an escort .... it is Jesus! He's no longer carrying His cross. His head is bent way down ...... it's hard to breathe .....so hard to breathe. There is a man and he's on a horse and he says "yes". Now there is a woman ....they are letting this woman through.... it's Mary. Her eyes are so swollen...... so full of tears ... but she has to be brave ...."I have to be brave for My Jesus". She says .... "Son" .... and Jesus turns His head. His hair is all matted with blood. His eyes are caked with dried blood and tears and yet ....He sees ....(we then heard the word) ..."Mother". That's all they can say, but their eyes ....their eyes embrace even though their bodies cannot ......their hearts ....their hearts that have always been united are still bound as one. She has been sent back now and they take Him and they have laid his cross on the ground. He obediently lays on His cross. His mutilated body is just waiting. They grab his hand ... it's His right hand and He sees the nail ...... and He says nothing. They place the nail on His .... (looks like His wrist).... and I hear the hammer on the nail ..... He moans and moans. Then, He hears His Mother and She is weeping. He cannot do anything but be silent. He will not moan again. They take His left arm and (what are they doing???) ..... they are pulling it ..... it doesn't fit .... what are they doing? ....(long pause).......It's finally secured to the cross. Only tears fill His eyes .... no more murmuring. He doesn't wish to cause any more pain to His mother. They stretch His legs .... (there is a large man sitting on His shins to straighten His legs so the nail can be driven into His feet). He just

191

lays now. His body secured to its final physical torture. I'm looking for the eyes .... He always calls us to see His eyes. There is no hatred .... there is no anger ..... there is only such compassion. The sky turns a strange color. It's gray now and the people ... they become like lifeless grayish statues. There is no more movement everything fades now and our Lord says:

"Looking with the eyes of love is a gift bequeathed by the Father for those who seek truth. Without the eyes of love you cannot see the heart ....especially the hearts ....those hearts entangled in ignorance and self righteousness. These hearts have been bound with ropes far heavier and stronger than those used to restrain your Savior for their restraints are those of pride and injustice.

I call you ....those who stand with Me .... to go as gentle doves carrying My love and forgiveness into a world which does not seek My mercy. You, My children, must be merciful. Your pain and rejection I shall receive as a fragrant offering for all souls for whom you pray."

April 20th, 2001

(Pat) "I do not recognize you. Please identify yourself." I am but an angel of God sent to prepare the way for the Most Holy Mother. Each heart must now be ready to hear Her words for She comes to bring love, healing and peace into each heart. Listen as the Queen approaches."

" My beloved children,

Know that these spiritual works you have done during this Lenten season ----- your increase in prayer, sacrifice and penance have not gone without notice, but have indeed produced great fruits. Many souls have been graciously infused with blessings from Our Lord -------- graces to strengthen them for the time approaches when these precious souls will find their cross heavier and heavier ----- yet, through the prayers of the faithful during this past season, God's grace has showered them with strength ----- for not only has their cross become heavier, but their faith and trust in God's Holy Will shall be tested.

These are times in which many will be tested. Times My children, that hearts will awaken, where you no longer must be absorbed in self. For I tell you will not bring joy and by your constant application of self-will delusion invites confusion. God's rightful place in your heart must come first. Embrace the trials before you for you are My little warriors of love. I have given you a gentle spirit and patience to persevere. Trust, My children. Look at Our Hearts eternally united* in love and find healing and comfort by Our example of obedience to the Father's Will.

Remember, My children, unless you make a conscientious effort to empty yourselves of all that which would distance you from God, you will be lost in a pool ---- stagnated in a pool of self-love. Stay focused on My Jesus. His gentle

Shrine view

Fr. Bart Comforting

I

Prayer team in Mexico

Prayer team in the chapel

Part of our prayer team

Child and friend praying at station XIII

Pat praying with child

Hope with child

Fr. Greg – St. Andrew the Apostle Church

Fr. Louis and Fr. Henri – Holy Trinity Monastery

Deacon Joe presiding at Sunday Divine Chaplet / Rosary

Visiting Bishop Rafael from Ecuador and clergy.

Our Lady of Guadalupe grotto built by John and Daniel

Mural at Mary's Knoll   Artist – Donna Raemaeker

Dan made this quartz Crucifix   Pilgrim Cross at Mary's Knoll

Photos of Mary at Mary's Knoll taken minutes apart

Light in the Sky

At least angels - un-retouched

Angel of Revelation

Revelation XII Photo taken above shrine

Our Lady clothed in the sun image above the shrine

Taken off of live video tape near small shrine

Compound image off video.   She came in a shower of light.

Station of the Cross XIV on the Shrine is a tomb.

Two hearts that beat as one.
One heart that fills the air.
One heart that shows we care.
Each time we adore Our Lord
the lifeless thorns which
have pierced His sacred heart
take on new life.
Reparation for sins brings
new growth for hope and
blossoms into love.

Early Cross construction

Chapel interior

The Founders

gaze will penetrate each soul with waters of purifying love. Be brave, My little children. I bless you this night. Look and see how much we love you."

(Visual: I see a display of lights all around two very brilliant "people". I know they are Jesus and Mary. No longer in sorrow but in radiant attire and their Hearts ----- flowing from each Heart--ribbons (?) --- strings (?) but they are floating down to all these souls below. As these souls reconcile themselves with God. I see a little heart that attaches itself to this ribbon and it gently floats up. One by one ----- millions of hearts flow into the Hearts of Our Lord and His Mother. It's almost as though Their Hearts are super imposed one on the other. I see flames and thorns. It's like all one Heart, but I know they are two separate Hearts. They receive the hearts of their children with such tenderness and with such love).

(Note: * We will attempt to have someone in our group sketch what the perception was in the vision. It became so clear as to how the hearts actually appeared to be united as one. The two physical bodies actually disappeared leaving only the two hearts. The Sacred Heart of Jesus became much larger - the outline of a Heart completely surrounded by brilliant white flames. The Immaculate Heart of Mary then became the center of our Lord's Heart and the two pulsated as one heart. It also became clearer that as we walked this Lenten journey with our Lord, He was calling us to bring comfort to Him through comforting our fellow brothers and sisters. He always directed our attention away from the physical (sufferings) to the mercy which <u>always</u> remained in His eyes. Perhaps we need to "look" more carefully to "see" the needs of others by looking with the eyes of Jesus). *Sketch in center insert was done by Martha.

April 27, 2001

"My dear children,

Persevere in your efforts to achieve humility. My Son is well pleased with such souls and will immerse them in His Fountain of Mercy. Your world mistakenly believes humility to be a sign of weakness. I tell you it is a sign of great strength for to be humble is to conquer pride and recognize your dependence upon God.

My children, blessed are those who accept with love the wounds inflected by ignorance and lift up each erring soul before the Throne of God's mercy imploring His compassionate grace to change arrogant hardened hearts into willing receptacles of His love. Pray with joyful hearts no matter what your circumstance in life might be for such prayers are treasures stored for you in Heaven. Be at peace."

(Commentary: How challenging it is to find that little corner of our soul in which God has planted a small seed of humility. How can we as mere humans even remotely hope to nurture this "virtue" unless we are permitted through God's grace to recognize our many weaknesses and call upon God's mercy to love and forgive one another that we may grow strong and healthy in our faith? We cannot

grow if our words and actions do not coincide with God's Holy Will. God does call us and, yes, He often calls us to be last that others might be first !)

May 4, 2001

"Children of Divine Love,

Reach out and take My Hand for many of Our children stand upon the precipice of hope ------ daring to hope but confronted by human frailty ------- an inborn weakness that only the Spirit of God can successfully confront. Take hold of the Word of God and cling to its promises and your faith will burst forth as does new growth in the season of Spring. Dare to be bold ------ to reach for that which you cannot see ----- trust in the abundance of God's merciful love and compassion.

Your way has been well prepared ---- the path made ready. In time you too will see the individual care God has given to each of His children. His angels are continuously busy guiding and gently encouraging you as you face each hurtle of life.

I have spoken before of the world of spirits and the constant battle which rages for souls. This is real, My children ----- not something derived from an imaginary Story book. Salvation came with a price ---- paid in full by the precious blood of My Son, Jesus. Yet, it still remains a gift which must be accepted to be effective. Look about you ------- how many do you see that understand the role God has asked each "performing" God's work ----- and how many would be "spectators" of the "performance." Use your time wisely ---------this is not a rehearsal. Many souls depend upon your prayers for the courage to step from the audience onto God's stage of life. Pray ------ pray --- pray!"

(Commentary: I strongly believe Our Lady is reiterating Her pervious comments in other messages regarding our reluctance to "make a commitment for God". We have a tendency to want to "wait and see" before actually making a decisive commitment to God's calling in each of our lives. It is obvious the false gods of materialism strongly bind many of our brothers and sisters and it is only with constant sincere prayer are we as warriors for Christ able to help break the chains which hold many souls as "prisoners of the world". Let us be consistent in our prayer life always seeking the Will of God and following the path to holiness which He has laid before us. We all fall, but God is always by our side to bring us once again to our feet to continue this journey to which He has called us.)

May 11, 2001

"My dear children,

I come in the gentle breeze barely discernable, yet ever so slightly caressing each tender soul with love. It is with such tenderness you are called to radiate the warmth of selfless love. As you join your hearts one with another, you form a blanket of self-sacrifice which suppresses the cold selfishness spreading

194

throughout your world. Tired and spiritually hungry, My children roam the world .... the spark of joy no longer gleaming in their eyes .... for My Son walks unrecognized amongst His people. It is His peace and joy of which you must be receptacles ....willing to be poured out as a libation upon hurting souls.

It is a time for wounds to heal. Forgiveness is the soothing balm which heals. As you, My children, forgive .... you draw closer to the selfless love of which I speak .....for this love is the love of God. It is the journey for which you are preparing. Take courage for God in His infinite mercy shall lead you Home."

(Visual: Saw large undefined area in various shades of gray. One by one bright lights appeared ...... just a speck at first then gradually it was as though someone had turned on a light switch and the whole area was becoming brighter and brighter until it was dazzling. The word joyful came to mind. Then I heard, "It is the conscious decision of one soul to forgive which ignites the flame of love into a spontaneous explosion spreading the light of God's peace and harmony into an otherwise dark and joyless world.")

May 18, 2001

"My dear children,

Times such as these cause My children to ponder reality and question spirituality to such a degree that life becomes a struggle of uncertainty. More time is needed in prayerful communion with God to renew and strengthen the foundation of trust in which God displays His mercy.

He invites you to a feast .... a great celebration. You are welcomed in your joy but especially in your bruised and brokenness. He asks only that you come for He delights in His beloved children who show loving trust in His forgiveness and unconditional love. Do not be afraid, My children, to accept God's invitation for it is an invitation written and sealed with the precious blood of Jesus. The heavens proclaim the glory of God as each precious soul is seated at the Lord's Table of Salvation."

(Commentary: After prayerful discernment regarding this particular message, it is felt our Blessed Mother is referring to the "Mass" as the supper to which we are all invited. What joy should be in our hearts to know that our Lord personally invites us to feed upon the "Bread of Life" daily so that we may receive the nourishment and strength necessary to perform our tasks in life. We are never left alone; on the contrary, we are well fortified to face whatever obstacles may befall us if we but only accept God's "invitation" for spiritual renewal.)

195

May 25, 2001

"My dear children,

I call you to greater prayerful contemplation of life. Each day God allows is a precious opportunity to more effectively utilize the time He allots in each life. The moments of anticipated joy in the expectation of a new life (birth) and the sorrow in impending loss (death) all form intricate threads woven into the delicate predestined tapestry of God's creation. Each day God presents His children with a treasure chest filled with graces to fortify their soul to meet each situation that life may bring. He is the loving Father who speaks to each heart .... to love and console as each soul requires."

(Visual: I saw our Blessed Mother dressed in vibrant "lights" of light pink and blue. She was bending down just slightly holding a beautiful box or treasure chest in Her hands. It looked like souls of children all gathered around Her. She opened the box so that all could see its contents. Everyone looked inside, but by the expression on their faces they did not understand. She smiled slightly and She and the chest became even brighter. I was led to believe the chest contained the irreplaceable treasure of "time". How we spend it while on earth determines its value in Heaven.)

June 1, 2001

(Recipient) ......I hear your words...

"My dear children,

Praise be Jesus Christ who has allowed my presence with you this evening. I gather each of you into My heart that I may remind you of the great love of God for all of His children. Many have forgotten. How is that My children when you see the envy and selfishness in your brothers and sisters but fail to see it in yourselves. Have I not taught you well? Have I failed you as a mother?

I do not come to scold but to renew and refresh the instructions of God's love. Children, do not lose hope for God has given you a life line ....a life line of mercy and forgiveness... grab hold while there is still time. Children, there is so much to accomplish ....so much that We ask of you who truly have consecrated your lives to the Sacred Heart of My Son and to My Immaculate Heart. You must .....you must look at your brothers and sisters until" *(at this particular moment it was a though She had started to say something, but the conversation changed into "tongues". It was most interesting that at this precise moment the obvious sound of birds chirping was recorded on the tape which was extremely unusual as it was late in the evening and the room in which the message was received could not possibly on its own pick up such a sound. The message then continued)* .... (I will not repeat.) "A gentler tone perhaps, that you will not be disturbed. You must look until you see the Spirit of God in each of your brothers and sisters. This lies covered ..... but you are called to uncover............ to

196

search until you see as God sees ….. *(tongues)* …… for only then will you find the true peace of Christ………. only then will you find your feet firmly planted on the road to holiness." (Do I repeat?) … *(tongues)* ……

"My children, I do not come to scold …… truly I do not …..but to bring you love and the awareness that lives must be changed. There is an uncontrolled epidemic of pride, envy, anxiety and frustration that is running ramped in your world. Unless you learn to trust in God there will be no cure … for God is the Physician that heals and brings peace into each heart. Remember these words……..listen carefully …….. Now, what do you hear ?" *(The group in the other room could be heard on the tape singing "Master…… Savior" which obviously Our Mother wanted us to hear ……soothing words of healing).*

(Visual): (So loud ……. it's like stampeding animals across the prairie ….. it's so loud. I can't see anything. Oh dear Jesus …… they are horses. There are four horses ……. they are huge. Their riders are angels set for battle. Each horse is a different color. Prepare your hearts …… prepare your hearts …. pray ….. for they come. They have been released. There is a paper (?)… it has been opened … it has been pried open There is a … uhmm ……stamp. It's a gold'ish stamp….ah….it has a marking on it …….a throne ……very vibrant ……very ornate ……it's wax (can you feel the wax …..feel the indentations ……. feel the throne …….It's God's throne. (Once again we were able to hear birds chirping in the background) …….. don't touch …… don't touch. He has released the four horsemen. They ride into our world. God is our strength. He is our joy and our trust. There is no fear … for we each bear the mark of Christ. The angels will pass over us. They are coming …….cannot stop them ……. no way to stop them).

June 10, 2001

(The following message was received Sunday morning during a "sharing" session of Our Mother's Call to Conversion "gathering" at Mary's Knoll. Many people shared their beautiful experiences and the blessings they received through the peace of our Lord and Blessed Mother. More than once, people remarked of the joy and tranquility they witnessed in the "team members" as they evangelized our Lord's love and mercy through not only their words but also their actions. This particular message was received as the power of the Holy Spirit came upon me and I rested in the Spirit. As you will note, it is very brief, but very profound.)

"Little children,

Many times We have spoken of this journey, but you perceive it as a line from one point to another. It is, however, a perfect circle. From Me you come ………to Me you return. You may turn your back and walk away, but keeping walking, My children … for you will in turn walk right back into My arms."

197

June 15, 2001

"My dear children,

You are called to be children of God .....filled with His love and wrapped in humility ...... Humility ignores reputation for true humility is the reputation, which speaks silently for itself. It is the light of God which shines brightly in each Soul ....each soul which seeks to obey and abide in His Holy Will.

Little ones, you seek to uncomplicated your lives, but instead you further complicate them for in your earnest efforts to make positive changes in your lives you fail to seek God's wisdom and His loving mercy. You exclude God from your decisions and therefore your lives bear little fruit. You look at weakness as failure. Does the sun not shine upon the weak as well as the strong? Are you still placing limitations upon God ....that He in seeing the pure intentions of your heart will not transform your weakness into a beautiful metamorphosis of a grace filled Life?

My prayer for you this night is that you will have a complete metamorphosis in your lives in which the fruits of the Holy Spirit will root deeply within your hearts and as He shines His light upon you, you will bloom in darkness and in light.

Peace, My beloved children ..... peace."

(Visual: Saw lots of the color blue ...... then wings ...... butterflies. The blue butterflies will come and they will signify to many the presence of our Mother.)

(Special instructions were given regarding the Crucifix held during the time the evening message is being received. I was informed this particular Crucifix has a special significance as it was given to me by a holy priest (Fr. Edwardo) from Mexico. I was instructed to offer a special blessing that night while placing the Crucifix upon each person's forehead and was further instructed to continue to use this particular Crucifix in our prayer ministry. Just prior to completing the blessing, I rested in the Spirit and the following was recorded.)

(Angel) " Do not take this blessing lightly for it is one especially bestowed as a gift from Our Holy Mother. Rejoice children for you are blessed. Receive this blessing that it will bring healing into your lives and increase your faith."

June 22, 2001

(The following message was received during the Friday night Canyon Rosary. It was a beautiful spirit-filled evening with many special blessings from our Holy Mother. There was a rather diverse group this evening with people coming from Phoenix, Nogales, Arizona and Mexico, and El Paso, Texas, along with our regular participants. At our Mother's request, the special crucifix was used to extend Her blessing and it was powerful. We were especially blessed to have Lety, a visionary from El Paso, pray with us and share some of the messages our

*Lord and Blessed Mother are giving to her regarding these times. We just thank
our Lord and Our Dear Mother for showering us with such graces).*

(Pat) "It's very bright, Mother...... so many lights ......so beautiful"

"Children of Our Hearts,

You are wrapped in the splendor of the Divine Love of My Son and He in pouring
forth His love into your soul shall beckon you into the abode of His Sacred Heart.
Rest in His heart .....away from the chaos of your world ....for tonight is a night
of grace.

You have been called to be Our little servants of mercy for into this valley and
upon Our Mountain of Mercy shall spring forth a river of living waters. Many
graces shall flow .....many gifts shall be received. Blest is He who receives yet
in a humble heart remains unaware of such graces. He becomes like a sieve into
which the graces are poured, but they are dispersed with equal measure. Seek
such humility that you might ask nothing for yourselves and then you shall be a
blessing to others."

*(Visual: "It's very bright and it looks like it is on top of a mountain. It is taking
shape ...... lots of light ......brilliant like crystals with prisms but on the inside there
is a heart of rubies. I see lots of souls beneath the mountain and I hear a voice."
"Come to Me ......all those who seek My peace for My Sacred Heart awaits you".
"There are all of these little lights all heading up to this beautiful, beautiful heart
and as each one enters the lights become stronger and stronger. The whole sky is
radiant ... it is radiant with God's love."*)

(Mary) *Yes ....the little daughter??? " Tell them My little daughter does not
hallucinate ..... for I have been with Her and I shall remain with Her........ for I
shall take her home."

*(*This final passage refers to a terminal cancer situation of the mother and sister
of two of our weekly prayer members. Helen, who took the revelation photo at the
shrine, made her final journey within 24 hours of this message).*

June 29, 2001

*(Visual: The message began as usual in tongues). " Yes, ... Mother, all I see are
just millions and millions of stars. Yes, ...a book??? I see a large book. I cannot
describe the size .....it is immense. It is brilliant. It almost looks like a bluish
color, but very, very bright. There is no title on the book only faces ...... countless
faces. I see a hand ......it's opening the book. I can't read it, Mother. I don't
understand it. (it was obviously a foreign language) The printing then changed in
appearance and I was able to see clearly. I was, however, instructed to remain
silent regarding its title, etc."*

"The hand turns the page again and it looks like what we would call an index. I don't know how to describe it otherwise. They are all names ......everyone is a name .... a chapter in this book. I'm glancing through the index. I see these names that have a special mark (for lack of a better description). It indicates "named by God". These names take up just a little space in the book .... a precious soul no one wanted. It didn't make it into this world, but God loved it so it has its own special place.

I see other names ... the chapters are longer......maybe indicating a length of life. Oh, Jesus, the book opens to My name. I hear ......"read". The page turns. It's today as I remember it ... as much as I can ... I'm waiting for the next page. No, I must wait as we all must wait. This is a precious gift to know that we are all in this book no matter how short or how long our life span. Every detail of our life is carefully recorded. Yes, carefully recorded ...... for the Author is God".

"My children,

You take a book and quickly lose interest......... so you flip through the pages and, yes, you even go to the last chapter to see if it's worth reading. Life is like this book, but My children, you cannot skip each page. Each page must be lived as God has intended ... .for each page contains vital information .....the statistics of your lives. The last chapter will come, but only after the entire book has been completed. My little children, a book written in the obedience of God's Holy Will is a story well worth reading.

How shall people respond to your book. Will they see God's hand in your lives or will they want to skip through the pages to the final chapter. Cherish each day that there will be no need to skip through (it) .... for life .... your life .....is contained in this book. It is a gift given by the Father for you, My children, who have been redeemed by the Son."

July 6, 2001

(Visual: I saw the Blessed Mother in the most beautiful iridescent shades of pink (the first time I can remember seeing Her in all pink). She had a lantern in Her right hand and a rosary in the left hand. The rosary was made of rose buds but more like a precious stone than an actual flower. The lantern was very bright; however, as I was allowed to see inside, there was neither a candle nor oil to cause the lantern to illuminate with such brilliant light. There was nothing other than light itself. There appeared to be something similar to fireflies emitting from the lantern. These little lights turned into much smaller lanterns which were placed into each of our hands.

Our Mother's lantern appeared to light a stairway of stars leading to Her Son. I was informed the smaller lanterns placed into our hands were to be used to "search" for souls in need of Her Son. She said), "Never fear for this is the light of God. He will remain with you as He in return asks all of us to remain with Him. Use your lanterns to seek the souls in need of Our Lord's mercy. The only thing that will diminish the light of your lantern is fear ...... for when fear comes you fail to trust in God, and your light will become dim and ineffective in seeking the souls in need of God's love. As your faith matures, the light of your lantern grows brighter .....for it is a deterrent of fear itself and thus only the peace and love of God remains.

Remember, My children, perfect love casts out all fear."

July 13, 2001

This is not a message from Our Blessed Mother as we are more accustomed to receiving them, and perhaps that makes what I am about to say take on a different tone – like someone ringing a bell very loudly and saying <u>wake up!</u>

The days leading up to the Friday night rosary were a little different than usual. It is difficult to put my finger on one particular thing – it was as though something was missing, but I could not accurately discern what that "thing" was. It was a busy week with lots of mental annoyances; however, we've been through those before and Our Blessed Mother has always been there to guide us along the right path. This time, however, there was a <u>major</u> difference.

Friday night came and we had a beautiful diverse group of people all gathering to sing and pray the rosary. I took my usual place in the back area and prayed with the group waiting for the time She would come and reveal Her message to us. That time did come and She did speak However, I was the one gently "hit between the eyes" when I heard Her say – <u>"My child, you are not prepared"</u>. To me, that said it all. I finally realized what that "thing" was that was missing earlier during the week. I had lessened the intensity of my prayers in trying to do what I thought needed to be done rather than spending the quality time with God. I compromised! I didn't even realize that there was indeed a message – a very powerful message – for myself in particular, but perhaps for everyone else in general.

Friday nights in this Our Mother's house are special and that particular word can in no way describe the magnitude of the blessings we receive by having Her presence here with us. This should take on a whole new meaning of prayer. Are we prepared to the best of our ability those days before the rosary. This is not a monotonous prayer we recite, but a song from our hearts – as we along with the Blessed Mother walk through the life of Jesus. He is with us – His Spirit is within us. Have we "cleaned house" in preparation for honored guests, or perhaps, sometimes do we allow ourselves to become preoccupied with life and compromise leaving God on the "short end of the stick". Our Lady certainly made me aware of my shortcomings or at least some of them. I realize even more so now that I cannot function and be a true instrument of Our Lord and Blessed Mother unless I have my intimate moments with them in prayer.

In saying that there was no message tonight – simply meant I could not "see the forest for the trees". *We do not function if we are not prepared and the only way we can work towards this goal of preparation is through prayer. God bless you!*

July 20, 2001

(Visual: It looks like a valley, but it's not a desert ... it is an orchard with all kinds of trees filled with fruit. (Personal ... I have Your hand) ... don't understand what I am supposed to see. We're turning around now ... so pretty ... "Look ahead." *There are mountains. It's our little mountain. I see the Cross. We seem far away. I can just make out a chapel and the statue of the Blessed Mother. Looks like something growing on the mountain... it's almost like a blank . . . can't make it out ... it's moving. Oh my, they are people ... . lots and lots of people.)*

"My dear children,

Praise be Jesus, My beloved Son , and Our Savior for He has entrusted you and those who come with a mission of mercy... for this is a holy place and to this holy place shall come those who hurt .....those who are unloved ..... those who are distressed with life. We ask you, dear children, to be little Missionaries of Mercy.

I wish to tell you of greatness. This greatness of which I speak is within each and everyone of Our children ... .but each must wait for that precious moment from God. As He speaks, each precious soul matures and ripens like the fruit from the trees which you just saw. This gift of greatness is, My children, the gift of humility, trust and simplicity .....all graces from God. It is a gift given to each precious soul who will open their hearts to receive it. Greatness ..... this greatness ..... does not deem itself worthy of applause or of earthly recognition. It seeks to go unnoticed ... hidden in the shadows until God calls ... for as He calls … the power of His presence enlightens each soul with such strength to go forward to embrace the hurting .....the lonely .....the forgotten. That, My children, is your purpose here ....for this, Our Holy Mountain, is a refuge for souls. It is but one of a few scattered throughout this world. I call you to pray and prepare … for you will require much strength! Trust in My Son as I encourage you this night and bless each of you, My precious, precious children"!

(Special instructions: We were asked to form teams with various talents ... those who can be of service in specific areas when necessary. We must all seek to be in a state of grace as we will be working with souls in need of God's mercy. This will help us in times to come. All those with special talents (gifts) will help us function more smoothly ...... for God's plans are great and He is giving ample warning ...... we must prepare now......we must prepare now!)

July 21, 2001

"Welcome, My children ....filled with joy. I thank you that you are here .... that you have opened the doors of this building and that you have opened the doors of

My heart. I await you with such love. Rejoice now ....feel My presence as I am before you........... feel My love. Children this is a time of joy and a time of opening hearts .... a time of renewing life.

I bless you as I gather each of you into this heart that I have asked you to enter. Let your heart be as one .....one in unison ......one in love with My Sacred Heart. Sing and praise Me for I am your Lord...........I am your God and I shall bring healing and peace into the lives of those who come.

My peace is with you. Lift up your arms......... lift up your hearts. Be filled with My joy .... be filled with My peace as I bless you and gather each of you holding you tightly ..... holding you My children ...the children of My heart. Come closely to My heart and see My Mother .... My Mother who intercedes for each of you ...... My Mother who cries with joy for the hearts that are here today.

Oh blessed little children .... receive the graces that shall be poured forth this day. Receive all that I have for you......... for no heart shall leave here empty! Each heart shall be filled to its capacity ....filled with My love ....filled with My peace .... for you are the children of My heart. Sing and praise My holy name for I, the Lord your God, have spoken and so shall it be."

July 27, 2001

(Visual): I see three fields .... there is a stone wall separating each field. We are in the first field. There are so many beautiful flowers. They are all wild flowers. I hear little giggles .....there are children........some are barely able to walk ...... they are so happy! They are picking these flowers and clutching them in their little hands. I hear birds ......birds singing in the trees and butterflies alighting on some of the flowers. Such a sense of peace. *There is a big burst of light ....pinks, blues, gold and whites. It's towards the end of the field. All these little children are trying so hard to get there. They are tripping and yet they get up giggling ......they are having such a wonderful time. They've got their treasure in their hand. They are running. It is Our Lady ..... can't see Her face, but I see a beautifully delicate hand. It reaches down and accepts all these little bouquets. It's amazing ......they all fit into Her one hand and the look on the children's faces ....a smile that goes from one end to the other. Their eyes are like stars that are just dancing. They are so happy. That field is now gone.

In the next field there are people of all ages. Some are picking the flowers ...... enjoying the scenery, but others are in such a hurry. Where are they going? It appears they are in a hurry to go nowhere. You can sense the difference .....there is a sense of anxiety .....nothing that resembles a tranquil surrounding. It's like rushing to get somewhere, but they don't know where. They walk right past Our Mother. They don't even see Her. Oh, My Jesus. We've come so far yet we've missed everything.

The other field now ... It's better. There are people of all ages. They are all picking the flowers and watching the butterflies, listening to the birds, gathering their bouquets ..... and, yes, they see Her. The older ones pick up the younger ones. Their little chubby hands holding their little treasures and even though I can't see Her face I sense a joy She feels for I hear "These are the children who have heard the voice of My Son ... His sheep who have returned to His pasture of peace and tranquility".

"My dear children,

Contemplate with great joy the love of God and the sweetness of His mercy as He prepares to receive from each of you that simple gift of selfless love which you offer with all your heart. God is so great .... His love for you so intense.....but you are not quite ready to understand and accept the magnitude of what He has for You .....for in your lives you fail to see the beauty ....the true presence of God in the smallest and in the weakest of His children. You hear whispers whispers that penetrate your ears but cause uncertainty ..... for these whispers turn to shouts .... disturbing your peace for you have not committed yourself totally to God and therefore, what you hear is a battle that rages for your very soul. Be at peace, My children, and trust in My Son for He is your strength. He is the one that loves you beyond measure. Be simple little ones and in true simplicity you shall find God and uncover the purpose He has for your life."

(*Note): On July 29, 2001, at Saint Joseph's Home, Our Lady confirmed She at times comes as "Our Lady of Lights". *During this visit, which followed a blessing of a priest, She also said* "This place too has much meaning ..... it is a place of refreshment and peace".

August 3, 2001

"My dear children,

All praise and glory to the Spotless Lamb of God Who sits upon the Throne calling each of you into His pasture. Praise Him as He calls you in song .... it is such a beautiful melody that only you can hear and detect your own name. Listen ....do not be afraid to listen .... do not be afraid to open your hearts and accept responsibility for God calls because He is in need of your service *(implies He requires the assistance of our free will to accomplish His purpose)*. Listen each of you, My precious children, and allow these words to penetrate deeply within your heart.

I come to give you a message this night ....Yes, I come to this Our holy house ...... but it is not just here, that My messages are sent throughout the world ....

for there are other places designated to be My little Centers of Mercy. My Voice spoken that you might understand ....floats as on the currents of the Wind ...... up and down ..... as the current directs.......but, still My messages reach the hearts of all of My children. I have revealed so much to you .... how much

204

more can I tell you, little ones, for <u>those words</u> I have already spoken .... <u>many have been filed away</u> ....perhaps as a treasure, but as such a treasure it must be opened, enjoyed and shared. Your responsibility is to share but with a gentle loving heart that says you are loved. That is most difficult when the opposition faces you with words .... with remarks .....that tear at your peace. But, hold tightly to Christ for His Spirit which dwells within you will fill you with every competence to gently and lovingly lead souls to the glory of eternity with God.

They read and ponder ..... for you shall find many times I have repeated My messages ....changing the words just a little but leaving its meaning in full view. <u>Wake up,</u> My children, <u>wake up</u> and prepare for this battle for souls. Allow the Holy Spirit to touch and refresh your lives each day. Become the simple ..... humble..... souls which are the secret weapon of My Son. They leave no scars, but the power is so effective. Love one another now as never before for the journey and this mission shall take different directions and I call upon each of you ... .especially the most timid soul ..... the soul that I hold so close to My heart (to strengthen it...to fill it with love and to set it on fire) ....to bravely go forth and proclaim God's love and Mercy.

I bless you this night as I leave you with My angels singing sweetly to refresh and encourage each and everyone of you. I love you, My children."

(Short visual): (A lesson in humility ... our pride cautioned us by publishing this visual one can expect ridicule). I'm looking down and it's so cute because it looks like children, but they are not all children. They are making paper airplanes. I'm watching and sure enough they are tossing them into the air and you see the currents take them one by one ...... lifting them higher... .some lower ......but sending them in all different directions (once again, we could hear the sound of birds chirping in the background). These are our Lady's words .... "We are the messengers." .

August 10, 2001

(The following message was received during the Friday night Canyon Rosary and has been transcribed from an audio tape used to record the message as it was being dictated. The use of long dashes indicates pauses in Our Lady's conversation where She may or may not interject "private" phrases not intended for the general public. This particular evening was interesting in that a number of people were "moved by the Holy Spirit" to make comments as to how this message was interpreted by them. The music was particularly uplifting and we once again thank Basil and his famous traveling guitar for being a part of this beautiful evening. As a matter of fact, we wish to thank all our Lord's and His Mother's faithful little groups that gather not only here but throughout the world spreading a blanket of prayer to cover all the hurting and lost souls in need of a tender touch of "spiritual love".)

"Listen, My children ……. calm your hearts …..clear you minds and come and sit around Me for I wish to relate a simple story that you might understand ….. a story no matter how short or how long God's Will for your life upon this earth might be ………. there is a treasure. Look, little daughter …….. what can you see?"

(Pat) "I'm not sure it's …..hum ….. it looks like a baby, but it's all wrapped up. I can't describe it. It's an unborn child ……. that's what it is. Look at the hands …. tiny little hands …. one little thumb sucking in it's mouth ….the other clenched."

(Mary) "I tell you a story in a way that you may relate …..for I have often spoken of treasures. Listen carefully . see the tiny clenched hand of this unborn child about to make its entrance into this world. It comes … a precious gift from God and the hand is still clenched. Why………why………for inside the hand is a very minute little chest unseen by the human eye but the child clutches this tiny chest. This chest remains with each and every one of you from the moment of conception ………through life ….. and finally until you come into the sweet refreshment of the Kingdom of God . The treasure ……. a chest of treasures that only God can see …….. for as each soul matures ….. the chest becomes larger and changes from the simple innocent child like chest into one that has matured.

My children, you often search for God's treasures. Do you not realize that God's treasures often remain hidden until the time He deems most appropriate. The chest in each precious hand become more and more ornate as it draws closer to Jesus ….. to His love and to abiding in His Will. The beauty that only God sees, My child, it is meant to be (hidden) ……… for if one could see the treasure that is held within the hand …………. pride would enter in and the treasure would become tarnished. Realize now, My children, that the treasure within each chest is not the treasure which God has given to you, but it is your precious treasure to God Himself. Oh listen and understand that you are God's precious treasures and what you bring to Him are the graces that have been accumulated from God through your life …….graces that shall in time bring glory to God.

Understand, My children …….bear your sorrows and your crosses …..your joys and your sorrows …….for each are tucked within this precious treasure …this box that becomes a precious gift to God. There is no value, My children, for these Gifts … . when given from the heart are priceless treasures to God and as one day you present them before the Throne of God …….. each one shall be opened in His presence and shall turn into a crown which will adorn His Throne".

"Take My hand and walk with Me that I May show you the greatness of what is to come. Are you tired, My child ?……. then let the love of Jesus refresh your soul that you may see what He wishes you to see ……… that you may speak the words He wishes to be spoken. Look briefly ….. but for a moment"
tongues ……………*(personal message of praise).*

(Visual): The message began in tongues. " I cannot see it, Mother...... I can't make it out ...... it's a strange shape"

"My child,

I have chosen you to be child like ....in simplicity that what you see and what you try to explain shall be understandable to all My children. Concentrate now .....tell Me what you see!" *(Pat) "Looks like a key ...... all different sizes and shapes of keys".* "And what, My child, do you believe these keys are for? .... (what do they represent?) Let Me help you. There are many different kinds of keys ..... many sizes and shapes as there are many different sizes and shapes of Our children. <u>The importance of the key is that it unlocks the Tabernacle in each heart!</u>

You saw a key last night *(This was at the 3rd Thursday of the month 3am Chapel vigil)* ... You wrote *(made personal notes)* ...... for the key does unlock the Tabernacle of My Son ...... the other keys unlock the door of the heart (of His children). Have you seen My Son as He knocks upon the door of the heart? ...... *(Saw an old familiar picture which depicted Jesus knocking on a solid door)* ......for there is no knob and there is no keyhole (visible upon the door). The answer, My child, is that each heart does indeed have a keyhole in which My Son places His key .... but it is only the keyhole of <u>free will</u> that allows My Son to enter. So simple, My child ..... is it not? Then why ...... why are so many of My children struggling? ....because they have let senseless ambition close the keyhole to their heart. They have become intoxicated by worldly desires and no longer seek to entertain such a Guest as <u>The King of Kings and the Lord of Lords!</u>

Speak softly to each heart that these hearts will once again receive the tender touch of My Son and there shall appear the keyhole in which He places His Divine Love .....to heal and restore your (their) faith. You must allow God to enter before He can heal you. He draws you from this world into the next by simplicity.....by desire for holiness. Empty that which remains of yourself and truly God will fill that with all He intends for your very soul and its salvation.

Believe and trust as a child that holds tightly to their Fathers hand ....trusting ....loving......... always <u>unafraid</u> for their Father is there holding securely to the hand that reaches up to Him."

(Personal) "Rest now as I will speak to your heart and yours alone for you have so much to do ...... little daughter who sees the lights"*

*(*Note): Often Our Lady comes as a Lady of lights ..... just a brilliant silhouette of colors impossible to adequately describe. An attempt to describe such attire would be garments of precious stones .... so bright yet barely discernable to the human eye.*

August 19, 2001

(Visual) (Pat) "It is our Lord upon the Cross. Oh, most loving Lord! ...You who hang upon the Cross yet smile so sweetly upon us" ... (Jesus) " Tell My children that upon this Cross I do hang, and yes, I do smile even in My pain and in My sorrow ..... for My children are just that ...... they are My children. *(Saw blood running down the Cross).* Come beneath My Cross for here lies the healing power .... My precious blood that has been shed for you and for all My children." *(seconds later)* "You are weak, My child, but I am strong and My strength shall see you and all of My children through this journey. Cling to My Cross .... Cling to My Cross!"

August 24, 2001

Greeting in tongues ...(Angel) "If you but realized Who stands in your midst, you would be on your face for the Queen of Heaven is in this room. Glory to God that He has allowed Her presence with you. Glory to God .... The Mother of God comes to you, little children of God."

"My dear children,

I have observed many actions this week ....many trials of health ......family problems and financial problems. But, I have taught you to cling to My Son for these are things of the world.........and these shall pass .... as your body shall pass........all things, My children, shall pass. Your joy is in the One Who sent Me.........Who sent Me to love you ..... to remind you of His love.

I caution you for I notice many times you wish to criticize .... to jump to conclusions. Many times you say you love God and yet someone passes by ..... perhaps reminding you of a pain in the past and you ignore that person. Is that truly what God would have His child do? No! This is not any easy journey, but I have instructed you and I have prayed to My Son to fill your hearts with so much grace that you will see only Him in others ......that you do not return pain for pain .....sorrow for sorrow .... but reach out with His love and His forgiveness .... for only then will wounds heal. Contemplate, My children, the goodness of Our Lord. Look at your life. See where you wish to consult with Him and Him alone .....and say <u>My Lord I need you. Only you can help me </u>and then <u>trust Him</u> .....<u>trust Him</u> .....for anyone who calls upon His name ..... He hears and He will answer.

There is so much doubt and so much fear in so many of our children .... that is why you are so blessed. I know of all of your pains ... your sorrows and your struggles .....and yet.......... <u>I know you are capable through God's grace to love and to help heal the wounds of others."</u>

(Visual) "I see it. I don't know what it is, but it's very, very big and there are baskets all around it ...... baskets of yarn. It is an ancient loom ......because the yarn is being woven through strings coming down and across. Each piece of yarn represents our life that is being woven into this tapestry. It is so beautiful. It must be our Mother (doing the weaving) but I can only see Her back. She reaches down and picks up a ball of yarn and looks and gently places it back into a large green basket (green denotes the color for hope). She asks us to pray ... to pray for conversion. For this yarn (soul) .... the one that is knotted and gnarled, will not slip through the loom, as it has not found its way to our Lord .

Our Lady says to continue to pray for these souls. She continues using the loom carefully picking beautiful colors (all souls) and then She reaches down and picks up this ball of yarn that was once so gnarled and matted, but now because of prayer .... our intercessory prayers .... it has been made ready to slip through the loom of this beautiful tapestry.

We must always pray for even as She so simply symbolizes the power of prayer, we can never comprehend the souls that will be saved because we prayed .... <u>we asked our Lord for the conversion of sinners!"</u>

August 31, 2001

"Oh little children,

Slowly, ever so slowly, God is molding you into the person He wishes you to be. He takes pains and great joy with His handiwork as He gazes upon His children.

Think, Little ones, of a person who takes a piece of wood, a sharp knife and with a great deal of patience ... gently whittles the wood until it becomes an object of art transformed not from gold or silver, but from the simple common wood. This, My children, is how God wishes you to be .....simple, yet with great potential to be beautiful works of art reflecting love........ His love .....through obedience to His Will. For God, too, gently whittles away the imperfections of each soul ... transforming them into precious treasures.

My children, I know you take great joy in striving to abide in God's Holy Will; but, God sees the souls still in need of sanding and polishing..........souls that have not yet understood - <u>God comes in distractions</u>! Our children seek silence ..... the solitude of God's beauty .....to be one with Him .....and, yet, they must learn that <u>God allows disruptions so that you may grow and thirst for His presence!</u>

Be steady as the helmsman that guides the ship along the calm seas and the rough sea ....focusing always on what lies ahead *(personal ......tongues)*. You must remember, Children, that life is like the sea .....very unpredictable. But, God remains constant and He wants only the very best for each of His children. Trust Him in His mercy and in His forgiveness .... that you will be unshakeable.

209

Remember, My children, that God's voice is heard even in the greatest storm, for even in the eye of the hurricane there is peace. Seek God's peace.

I see tonight there are those who come to My home and I welcome them. They are My children. I wish to dispel doubts in their hearts that they may be filled with the Holy Spirit and the grace of God shall penetrate their very souls."

(Visual) [Pat] " You'll have to help me. I can't tell if it's two things ...... if it's the sky and water, they look like they are so close together. But, I see a morning sky ... I'll say the sky is beautiful, but coral colored ..... and the sea is calm. There is a large boat. I don't know if it's a fishing boat because it's an ancient construction. I do see nets in various places but it's not a fishing expedition as we know it. There are a number of people on the boat and all of a sudden there is a noise. The wind ..... the wind is picking up and the sea is starting to move..... large waves come into view. The people are not concerned ... there is no fear .... no anxiety, but the water is coming across the deck of the ship. They (the people) remain very calm. There is a loud noise. I think it is some of the sails perhaps rolled up and hitting the poles as the force of the wind blows them and the waves against the ship. Still there is just peace ...... oh ....I see only from the back ...... a man with His hands on the wheel of the boat. There is a mark on each hand. I know it is Jesus. That's why they are not afraid. Jesus is the Helmsman of the Souls. It is still very loud ..... but even through all the noise, I hear "Peace, be still"! The water calms ..... the sky becomes blue .... a few clouds as the sun burst through them. The boat is gone. It was so tranquil .... so must it be when we believe in Jesus .... the peace He gives to each of us."

(She so simply symbolizes the power of prayer, we can never comprehend the souls that will be saved because we prayed .... we asked our Lord for the conversion of sinners!)

September 7, 2001

(Angel) "Has thou forgotten! Where is the crucifix that goes in this ones hand?"

There was a fairly long pause. (Months earlier we were instructed that the "special" crucifix used to give our Lady's special blessing is to be placed in my hand as the message is being received ... . it had apparently been laid upon my chest instead. It should be noted that we try to have those familiar with this "special time" be present as often as possible. Sometimes during the overwhelming gift of the moment we become so intense in prayer (alleluia) we have "senior moments". "We shall wait then." *An even longer pause until the crucifix was placed in my hand.)*

"My dear children,

I invite you this night to come with Me ..... to remove yourself from everything that does not pertain to My Son ..... that does not pertain to prayer and love of neighbor for you are gathered here as My beloved children .... children which I am preparing for a great race. See the athlete as he prepares and conditions himself for a great race ....strengthening his muscles and his endurance that he may compete to the best of his ability.

You, My children, are also athletes but an athlete for souls. I ask you to prepare as you would be running a race to condition yourself to endure for the race is long and you must be prepared. Pray, for through prayer comes strength that will nourish your soul to persevere. Children, as you run this race, do not look over your shoulder .... for over your shoulder is yesterday and as you concentrate on yesterday you stumble through the precious moments of today!

Think of Me as the Mother who prepares the child for a great race .....but the child is still a toddler. Do you not think that I would scurry to prevent harm from befalling him .... so I your Mother constantly scurry after you. You are Mine ...... placed into My care. I am your Trainer .... to strengthen your Soul .... to prepare you for this race of life for the starting line is conception and the finish line is the arms of Jesus!". *(Tongues ... followed by a brief private message).*

(Visual): "There is something like a racing area in the center and everyone is lined up. There are different shades of lights ... perhaps different nationalities (I can't really identify them). There is a bell that goes off and everyone starts out in this race, but you can't exactly see the competition. The competition is *time! You're only allowed so much time to complete your race. The stadium is full and there are voices and they are so encouraging. They are saying come on! ... come on! just a little further .... come on!. It's Jesus .... He's waiting.. come on you can do it .... don't look back, just put one foot in front of the other .... keep going. Then you sense someone has fallen. You can't leave him have to stop, that's what God wants. Let me help you ...... he slips his arm over our shoulder and you keep going ...... it's hard, but you keep going. It's a race for souls. We are all in it ..... we are all accountable. None must be lost!"

(Private message with visual).

(*Commentary): All through this particular message as we were trying to transcribe it, in the background we kept hearing this strange sound. My husband called the prayer warrior who was in attendance as the message was being dictated and asked if she was wearing a watch or anything that might have a "ticking sound". She replied "no". We finally realized as we continued transcribing the message, the ticking sound was that of a clock. There was, however, no physical clock to be found to make that "tick-tock" that mysteriously was heard on the recording. The rest of the tape was examined and found to be normal. Only this particular message had the sound of a clock .... our competition is the race of "time".

September 14, 2001

Tongues ... "Yes, My Jesus." ... *tongues* ...

"I, the Jesus of Mercy have come to you My children who show mercy. Mercy is a gift .... yet a gift which is learned. As a child who receives a new toy, he must learn how to play. .... for you My gift of mercy is much more significant. For to learn is to be in yourself merciful. You come .... you pray for your needs and those of others, but it is to My merciful heart that all these petitions are gathered and sorted and here I look about and say, My children, be My little missionaries of mercy. Where ever you come from ..... where ever you go .... you are mine .... My little missionaries of love."

(Visual) "I see people marching .... banners flying .... children .... life .... a march for life. A march for souls, but people are not cheering .... they are very rude." "What is Life they say; what is life? I cannot see it, therefore it is not life". "But God says". "My children you march for Me .... you march for My unborn children. Receive My blessing for there shall be many times .... many times in your life which shall seem like a trial .... a trial for life. Stand up for truth and justice for soon there will be no place to stand, except before the Throne of God.!"

(Mary) "My dear children .... filled with uncontrollable emotion. Take My hand .... rest your heart upon mine for together we must sort through this day. We must sort through the events that have happened and are yet to happen! Remember it is up to God to disperse His graces as He sees fit. You wonder at times.... for you say" " I don't comprehend .... I don't understand Lord, My human frailty blocks my understanding .... help me, heal me."

(Jesus) " Child ..... the one who receives grace oblivious to such a great gift is the one chosen by God. For this one has been made into a garden in which the seed of grace has been planted and nurtured by God himself. There is no need to worry My child. (private reference).....(Message then continued).... For you My children .... have you not read? .... I shall lead you through the valley of the shadow of death for I am with you. You know that life is but a temporary moment in time .... it is like a shadow which casts an image upon the world .... gradually in time it fades .... but it fades into eternity. It grieves My heart that as yet so many of My children do not understand the importance of mercy .... for without My mercy there is no healing of the wounds ....there is no chance for that final moment as you stand before Me to come into My Kingdom .... and you .... you must not judge. Sorrow and pain I understand ..... judgment (our human tendency to judge) you do not .... for that has been reserved for one and one alone. Believe and trust in Me your Merciful Savior ..... for the wounds of the past shall heal and new wounds shall open .... but those too shall heal .... for those who love and trust in Me are My children chosen from the beginning of time. *The little box you clutch in your hand is precious to Me. For I know one day you shall reveal its contents before My throne, and together We shall go through each moment of your life. Be

212

simple .....forgiving ...... as your wounds heal. This shall become easier, for together you and I shall walk the path that leads to eternity."

(Note: See message August 10, 2001 for reference of "little box").

(Visual): I see a rainbow (actually two rainbows) ...... one crosses the other. The tips of the rainbow have been straightened ... not remaining arched or curved as a normal rainbow. I see bits of ..... I don't know what to call them . perhaps glittery sparkling precious stones similar to confetti .... just so beautiful. I understand that they are the graces that are falling upon this valley. For as I look .... the rainbow has formed a perfect cross. Its center is a circle..... the circle of life .... it is Jesus. The rainbow is His promise ...... cling to Him .... for He is truth and in Him can be found nothing but truth!

September 21, 2001

"My Dear Children,

You hear the whirling sound of the wind as it gathers strength .... becoming louder unleashing it's power to all in it's path. Yet the gentle breeze .... still in itself wind .... catches the fallen leaves .... and gently brushes through ones hair and against the cheeks .... a kiss from God.

Each of you have faced obstacles and will continue to face many more in your journey to holiness. Some exude great efforts to withstand the underlying currents which attempt to draw you beneath the vibrant rays of hope ....burying you under layers of disappointment and discouragement.

You reach for support .... an unshakeable and indestructible strength beyond all strengths .... the Hand of God! He waits for you My children to open your heart and outstretched hand. The hand which reaches out in complete trust fits perfectly and confidently into the hand of the Father.

Out of holy love do not be afraid to place your hand in the hand of your brother and sister in Christ. The circle is your reminder from Jesus .... from Him you came .... to him you shall return.

The simplicity of God's truth is our courage to journey to the cross! Fear not impending disasters .... for you are the fertile ground from which shall spring forth new life .... precious and holy .... obedient to God's Holy Will. "

September 28, 2001

(Pat) *Mother ..... why so dark? All in dark blue .... not black but dark blue. A veil covers Her face......very soft. (I understand .... tongues).*

"My dear children,

213

Beneath My veil My eyes are filled with tears to cleanse and wash away mans inhumanity to man. But through My veil, I see the eyes of My Son .....the eyes who hold back the tears. Yet there is a special mixture. One of utter love .....the other compassion. But I, as the Mother looks closely at His eyes and see there is more. For what lies there is beyond description......... shall I say ..... but a glance from His eyes would grasp the heart. A heart that would repent and be contrite.

My precious children, you have experienced much and have met much confusion, but tonight listen carefully to My words .... for their meaning is of most importance."

(Pat) (Tongues) .... now? There is a shadow forming ...... a very large shadow ... the time of the day makes little importance ... for coming into view is the biggest bell I've ever seen ..... a bell ..... it has a crack down the side ..... it is very old ... it reminds me of something ...... the Liberty Bell ... which rang out for peace and justice in this world. There is no movement there ...... all it quiet. But now a burst of light comes and there are bells ... all different chimes ... all different sizes ... all ringing all over the world, and I hear our Mother say:

"Come, My children as one people under God. This is your chance .....this is your opportunity for grace. Kneel now and take between your hands the rosary.....the most powerful weapon .....and as you hold it ....lift it before My Son, and say Mercy My Jesus.....Mercy once again on your people; and, yes ... .tonight I too, shall kneel with you and pray for mercy ...... for that final chance of Divine Mercy."

(Visual): "I see a very large pitcher ...... older and different in size and shape. I then see all of these bells. They are all going into this pitcher and they are becoming liquidized (similar to melting metal). I see a hand that grabs a hold of the handle of the pitcher and pours it, over this huge bell. The mixture is faith and trust ..... that our country will once again be one nation under God. The bell rings ..... it is not a loud, loud ring ... it is a ring of peace. God draws us back to peace as He meant His world to be. Praise you My Lord"

(Commentary): It would appear each bell represented a Nation/Country and as our prayers for peace penetrate the entire world All the bells would then become one liquidized molted substance of love molded once again by the Master Potter. The regular evening scripture reading was from Laminations 3; Verse 18-23.

October 5, 2001

(Pat) " Oh Mother...so bright and beautiful. You come to us in rays of colors and an unusual scent ... a scent only of Heaven .....for the Queen of Heaven. Mother, ...are you saying there is a special blessing for each of us tonight ...... a blessing of healing that you would take the beauty of your lights ...... the aroma of Heaven ...... and mend the broken hearts? I think that is what I hear you Say......but the voice is so delicate ......so loving! Do I hear correctly, Mother?"

"My dear child,

I have come this night as the Lady of Lights and yes, I am scented with a gift from Heaven to touch all of My children. There are so many wounds to be healed ..... but yet My children, the beginning of healing starts with God ..... with relinquishing your will to His Holy Will. Lay before His throne the virtues of love ..... your penance ......every most difficult thing you have done for love of God. Lay them before His throne, and then My children, the path before you will become as brilliant as My attire. There will be lights of pink, and blue and white, silver and gold ..... for you will have relinquished the ways of the world and you have sought the rewards of Heaven! This is holiness.

Each one carries their precious treasure chest immaculately laid out with tools ....with tears ..... with love ... for you must be ready at a moments notice when God calls you. Keep looking forward for My loving Jesus stands waiting for each of His precious children."

(Pat) "It is so bright, but the beauty is so simple ..... to see the glimmering lights of the Queen of Heaven lighting our path to Heaven. How does one describe lights of such beauty ..... lights of such joy.... lights which welcome us .... call us .... and yet guard us because we are the property of Her Son! She is the Mother Who will defend Her children".

"I have much more to tell you .....much more shall come ....but it shall be at My time..............the time chosen by God .... not at your convenience! Be strong .... be faithful and be patient for God has much to teach you. Rest now, prepare .... for there are many souls which require God's healing power. You are being sent as instruments to love .... tired though you may become, you shall be filled with joy when you see the results of God's plans.

 Rest and prepare".

October 12, 2001

(Conversation with Samuel)

The following message is somewhat unusual in that it is the first message in which I have actually received a direct message (conversation) from Samuel, my guardian angel. The particular Scripture which I thought I had (personally) discerned to read 1 Samuel 2: 1-10, was read before the Rosary, and I thought it had no further meaning to the evening; it was just a beautiful reading. Our faithful group of prayer warriors were in attendance and the evening began beautifully with song. This message is of such an unusual nature we urge you to read it slowly, carefully, and with much discernment from the Holy Spirit. As you read the first part of the message, you will understand it is more of a conversation rather than an actual message which we have previously experienced.

Tongues ... (Pat)..... In the name of Jesus, My Lord, identify yourself.

215

"I am He whom you have called upon this week in a most difficult time. I am the one who never leaves you. I am He of whom you spoke. Greetings, my child, from Samuel! I have come at the bidding of My Lord and God to comfort you, to encourage you through these difficult moments of decision ..... for truly you are free to choose ..... to follow or not, but, my child, follow you shall .... for you have been marked by God His servant .... His messenger. Shall I tell you this week when I held your hand .... when I wiped your tears .... when I took you into my arms. Listen and remember, one thing, we discussed love, we discussed memories and we discussed money."

"I asked you to walk in a familiar room, darkened .....totally without light .... to carefully touch those things that came within your path. There were many large objects, child. What room did you choose?" (Pat) *"I chose my mother's bedroom because I was so filled with uncertainty and disappointment."* "And beneath the darkness what did you feel?" *"I smelled my mother's clothes ..... the perfume she used to wear and I remembered all the times we shared."* "You will help many .....for this journey takes place in every life .... for all will lose those they love and what is left but ... memories. Did you notice you did not need the light? Memories.....don't require light. What would you choose, little charge of mine? Would you choose the memories of clothes long worn.........slightly scented with an old perfume .... or would you disregard and seek something of a worldly value that brings no meaning to life? Finally...... my little charge..... you have found peace for you chose well!

"Tell them not to be afraid of the darkness for beautiful memories lay tucked away in a garden lit only by the stars............the stars of God. I shall continue with you ....to journey's end. Confide in me. I long for our conversations. Little daughter with so much to do ....pray .....and pray intently for your world shakes as it has never shaken before............ let there not be fear in the darkness nor fear in the shaking but true joy in knowing that God is always in control. His you are ..... His you shall be .... mistakes, yes, you shall make, but God will help correct those. Be at peace and let love ....just love .... rule your lives."

(Commentary): He (Samuel) has light brown hair and blue eyes. He wears a cream colored robe with a darker sash around his waist. He has such penetrating eyes. There leaves no doubt in my mind that God has sent His angels with one purpose and one purpose alone to bring us safely back to Him.

October 19, 2001

Message began in tongues..........

(Jesus) "Daughter of My Heart,

It has been awhile since we have spoken one on one ..... but tonight is our night ..... for we have much ground to cover ..

I waited for you last night ..... resting quietly in My Tabernacle ...... I waited to

216

hear your voice ....to call My Name .....My Jesus .....and then the joy of being exposed for all to see .... for all to see My love for each of My children. Do you not think I am unaware of your being tired? For I have given you much responsibility .....but the work must be done and the harvesters are still few. My children brought joy to My heart ..... for few in number they seemed, each seat was completely filled. The songs ... .the sounds of Heaven's choir ..sang the whole time .... the whole time that you praised Me .....the whole time that you sat quietly ..... and just looked at Me as I looked at you.

My children, if you only knew how strong.....how strong this is.....this force which comes into your life ...... the power of My presence ....you would not miss a day to come to speak with Me. Time now is at a great impasse   not undefeatable ..... but at a great impasse ....for your world fears ..... and it should not fear. For where I am there is no fear. In one hand there is love ....the other hand holds fear. It is like mixing oil with water .... they do not mix .... so I take from you, if you so choose to give Me, your anxiety and your pain and allow My love to remove any fear in your life ..... to bring only peace ..... only joy.

And I wish to speak of My Mother. She is always with Me. She was with Me as a child as We sat in grassy knolls and pulled the stems from the field and made great treasures of something so simple. She is here with you now helping to plan your treasures for the day that you will be presented to My Father. My Mother and My Mother alone, holds the key to My Heart. Honor Her .....love Her .....do not disrespect Her. I will not tell you what such actions shall bring should you dishonor My Mother........... but think of the times when She is with you when you feel Her peace and Her joy .... and remember .....that She is My Mother .... My Mother whom I gave to you.

Let us go to a great banquet tonight. Dress in your finest affair *(attire would seem more appropriate .... but is that where the Lord is leading us?)* and bring one gift and one gift only. What is your finest affair *(Perhaps more discerning is required for obviously our Lord is not referring to an actual wardrobe, but something of far greater meaning. He challenges us to "think" as He did His disciples over two thousand years ago)* your humility.....your gentle Spirit ...... your love and your patience. What gift do I ask ... but your heart wrapped as you so desire. Lay it in a box of beautiful flowers ... .tied with ribbons .... and as I greet you...........take your gift to the table prepared for such *(gifts)* ....and then, as the evening progresses, when I call your name ..... go to the table .....pick up your gift .. .and walk side by side with your loving Savior, for we will be heading to My Father and your Father. Be filled with peace and only My peace will do ....for so much distracts your world .....that you must trust Me .....you must believe Me ...... that no matter what .....you are mine! I bless each of you, My dear children, this night."

(Commentary): (Pat) "It's (banquet) by invitation only ......not everyone can get in ...we'd better get ready. Our finest attire ... only our best will do for Our Lord."

October 26, 2001

"My precious children,

I look about your room where we are gathered and see the faint sparks of light........ but enough light to brighten the path that lies hidden .... the path to your soul. Hear Me My children, for God loves His children and wants none to be lost. You must seek simplicity .....but you do not understand. Simplicity is relinquishing yourself to God .....you hold on to nothing but God. When you reach this point in your life .....when you are able to let go of worldly attachments and seek only to be in contemplative prayer with God ..... then you have relinquished your will ....for your will then has been given back to God by your free choice. *(Tongues)*. What should you care when others seek your will .... for your will no longer belongs to you .... you have freely given it to God. What else can they take, My Child?

We see you as beautiful vessels designed by the hand of God .... filled with His love .... filled with all He wishes for each of His children. You may not find as you look within each vessel what you had planned to find there ....but it is what God has deemed necessary for your life."

(Pat) "The vessels I see are newly made, for there is still a form of clay on the tools used to design the faces ..... so many names ..... because they are not all the same. God's artistic plan is amazing ... so many diverse groups... yet, I am led to believe they do represent us. We are His vessels chosen to be used as He has deemed it must be."

(Jesus) "I have asked you as gently as I know how not to fear, for these vessels which in turn we shall call a "life like vessel" are no different than life as you know it.............for each will eventually break or end as all things eventually end. Finding the peace of Christ removes all fear.......... for where you go, My children, depends on your choices in life. If you have given your life to Him ... rejoice ... for He rejoices with you. If you have rejected Him then weep .... for He weeps with you. He is a God of love............. a God of mercy and He has chosen and He wishes to teach you through patience .... for it shall require much patience to learn the simplicity ... .the relinquishing of your life itself ...... that you might find eternal peace with God. But it is a time of great joy ....each lesson is to be looked forward to .....more and more to learn .....more joy to absorb .... for God truly awaits you .....arms spread wide to receive you. Loving children who carry so much practice this lesson .....practice until you feel you are ready to face God .... for face Him you shall!

Each day ... at peace and without fear for as you grow in learning God's purpose for your life you shall feel nothing but His Divine Will........   His Holy Peace"!

(Visual): The wagons ...... not ordinary wagons ... power ... I sense such great power, and the vessels are in the wagons. They (the vessels) are being

218

knocked against each other. Oh God ...we have so little time to make repairs ......
so little time. The horses race ... but I know not where ..... I don't know where.

November 2, 2001

"My most precious children,

Pray and as you pray ask Jesus for that special grace to see your soul the way He
sees your soul, that you might look without fear but with great joy and gratitude to
Our Lord ....Pray and begin to make changes in your lives .... for My
Children .... I tell you as I have told you before .....time is of a critical nature.
You see the plight of your soul and now you have the responsibility for your own
Soul ......and the graces you have received have enlightened you to realize your
role in the assisted salvation of others. How, My children, would you experience
joy if you had not tasted disappointment? Now your world shall taste much, but
you shall be prepared .....for you who choose to listen to My words to hear the beat
of My heart .... shall be the true Missionaries of Mercy."

"It starts here, My children ....right here in this family.........My family of
warriors. You are strength for one another. Realize life does not simply revolve
around you and your individual problems .... for if you have truly surrendered
your will to God .... everyone has become your family.........their problem is your
problem............ together all shall be accomplished for your common bond is My Son
and He shall unite you .... even stronger than before .... for I said time is of a
critical nature. Believe Me, believe Me .....and pray ..... but see the joy that lies
beyond, see the grace that God has allowed you. Are you special? You are My
children and you have a job to do........but all My children are special and all
hearts must be aware of the need to abide in God's Will. There is no other way.
Listen as He speaks to your heart .... love Him ... love Him."

(Visual) "I can't see ...... it's dark ... it's forming ...a huge ...... huge heart.
It looks like the Sacred Heart of Our Lord ...but He wants... (private). I see the
Heart above the mountains and it is fragmented ...... it's breaking in tiny pieces
and I hear, I hear Jesus say" "This is My Merciful Heart and those whom I have
chosen. Those who treat Me with luke warmness cause My Heart much Sorrow
...... for you have been given such special graces, and I expect, for I have chosen
you ...to hear My words... to mend your ways ... .that My heart will be whole
again For I love you and My Mercy is there for all of My children."

*" It seems to be a whole heart now ......it is beautiful. I see people praying. But
I sense differences now. <u>They pray with their heart! They pray with sincerity.</u> This
way His Mercy becomes an ocean to cover all His children."*

219

November 9, 2001

"My dear children,

This is the time when impatience is stirring the kettle of destruction...........and hearts which belong to My Son are finding themselves longing for spiritual graces. Disruption and chaos spill out all over your world ......and if it were not for deep spiritual roots........one would easily be swept away and tossed into the kettle.

You, My little prayer warriors, must not let down your defense, but pray with even greater fervor ....for your trust is in God. He alone shall sustain you who are faithful to Him. Let your sufferings bring you joy as the flames of Divine Love purify your soul. Be at peace   for God sends His angels to guard His precious souls."

(Brief visual): "The sky was gray but there was a bright smoky vapor which seemed to be coming from some vessels. I believed these were not positive signs as we might see them because the smoke arising from the vessels was of an ominous nature. The sky became very murky ....,.then all of a sudden the vessels appeared to be pouring their contents upon the earth ......it was as though everything was boiling. Everything then became cloudy and faded away."

November 16, 2001 was a private message.

November 23, 2001

(Visual): "I see a very large area ...... there is very little light ..... it's more grayish. I'm waiting .... I can see images and little flickering lights ..... they look like candle lights. I must be standing high on the mountain or hovering above .... the valley is filled with lights and as they move closer to the mountain, the lights become brighter. Everyone's moving .....there are a lot of souls in the back .....they have a light, but it barely flickers ..... it barely shines. Some try to step forward, but they can't .....they quickly draw back and their little light is so dim. It appears these souls are heading toward a building on the mountain. It looks like the Chapel, but it's kind of like a Lighthouse .... a safe harbor for souls. I hear like a wind but nothing is moving....... and I look again and they are the wings of angels. They are gently nudging each soul closer and closer to God's mercy. I hear a voice" ....

"My dear children,

The light which each soul carries is faith. As each soul draws closer to God, it is filled with peaceful confidence to accept the graces which God freely pours on each of His precious souls as He so desires. The flickering lights in the distance are those souls unable to make a commitment to God and His plan for their lives. You must pray that each soul be filled with faith to such a degree that it will lovingly and confidently seek to have a heart that burns with such intensity for holiness. The lights you see above the mountain ......the golden lights, My Child, are graces which await the children who come in faith ... for God will not allow them to leave empty handed. I bless all of My children this night."

November 30, 2001

"My dear children,

As you prepare to enter into this joyous Advent season, I ask that you re-commit your love to God and to your neighbor and with Christ like patience restore peace within your families. Trials and temptations shall always be with you, but those who truly know the peace of Christ shall prevail against all adversity.

There shall be times in each life when prayer becomes difficult. There is a dryness within the soul that it cannot discern which way is Jesus ..... for often He hides that you may become stronger in your faith. I ask of you .... in these moments ..... when prayer is most difficult ...... simply repeat the Holy name of Jesus ...... Jesus ....Jesus. Gradually your soul will be consumed by a burning desire to draw closer to God and the soul will find refreshment to renew its prayer......" (dialogue in tongues) ...."May I repeat?"

"My children, this is a season which should be filled with great joy and yet the stresses of the world interfere with Gods plans for your lives. It is a time of sacrifice and of deep prayer that you may stay focused on Jesus .... a Holy time, My children .... a Holy time. You will weather many storms ... as you hold tightly to the hand of Jesus. Trust God ..... and as you trust God ... come beneath My Mantle, for I am the Mother that shall lead you to the Sacred Heart of My Son!

I desire a table to be placed next to My statue and once again I will bless all the items people shall bring the Friday before Christmas. I request also that this particular night be all candle lights and that the prayers that are said will be said from each heart. Sing ... sing My children, for God loves to hear you praise Him.

A basket shall be placed for gifts to My Son beginning the first Sunday of Advent and it shall remain in the Chapel until Christmas morning. I shall come that Sunday before, during your Chaplet and Rosary, to bless each and every petition .... each and every gift to My Son."

(Pat) "Mother, I have been praying and I haven't heard anything........."

(Mary) "Yes, My child, your prayers have not fallen on deaf ears. Tell My children I am well pleased with their perseverance for the Third Thursday Vigil and their efforts shall not be un- rewarded. You may end the vigil at 11:00 (p.m.) ....I ask that you spend at least fifteen minutes prior to the Chaplet in

221

praise of My Son. As your group grows, we shall resume the 3:00 (a.m.) vigil. I bless you for your efforts .... for your love for My Son and for myself.

One more thing I ask of you..... you try so hard to do the impossible.... I want you to do the simplest task with such great love that it will be worth more in the sight of God than conquering the impossible."

(Visual): This particular evening I was allowed to see a visual while still in prayer in the privacy of the back room. The visuals are normally recorded on the audio tape; however, this did not occur as my husband discerned the message had ended and was preparing to play the tape for the prayer group. The following represents what I was allowed to see. The sky was very bright with many, many stars .... and all at once, there appeared what seemed to be a large cave .... not dark and dingy ...... but an area of lights .... for sitting in the cave was our Mother ......once again all in lights of pink and blue; however trying to describe the lights as one sees them is very difficult as they are so brilliant that the color itself is so soft yet still slightly distinguishable. She appeared to be with child ..... and the stars (probably souls) became shooting stars that darted right into the gently outstretched hand of our Mother. It seemed as though She took a piece of Her mantel and carefully wrapped each soul as a gift. She then placed each precious gift beneath Her mantel until all the stars (souls) had been accounted for .... these "gifts" are obviously in preparation for the birth of Her Son .... they are the "gifts" we each shall bring to be placed in the *Chapel basket and later to be placed in Jesus' Christmas stocking. The stocking will be placed in the manger on Christmas morning. As our Mother said in Her message above .... it is the simple yet sincere gifts from our hearts which please Him (Jesus) the most.

(*Note): We encourage anyone out of the area to either mail in their petition gift to be put in the chapel basket or send them via the email prayer line available in our web site.

December 7, 2001

"My precious children,

I invite you again to take a walk with me along the star lit path to peace and serenity where you can hear the chimes of the angels voices as they praise Almighty God! Yes, we have taken these walks before, but each time you renew your steps into the footprints of the Master, you draw a closer understanding to His love for all humanity. It is most difficult understanding God's love for humanity but, you are children of God and you shall persevere and this knowledge shall be imparted into each and every one of your hearts where peace and unity as God has deemed from the beginning shall come to pass.

You look and see disaster and destruction, but what has come is but a joyous rebirth of courage ......courage to go into the Harvest .... to reap the seeds that have been planted for this is your mission. You become one with Him in Whom all things have their origin .... you become a part of Divine Love.

222

Now we still walk .....notice the stars ... how brilliant they are. The ground about you is well lit. We are on a treasure hunt for memories. I see you reach down and place something into your pockets ....these things we shall discuss at a later time. I see one of you has found something so precious .....come show ... your Mother. It is a button, My daughter, and what significance is this to you?"

(Pat) "I had a beautiful party dress made by mother and somehow I lost the button that held the bow and I was so distraught ... and I cried and I cried. Mother, I've ruined My dress ...... and my mother took a button from her dress and gently sewed it on to mine. My mother gave me her button; but, Holy Mother, most importantly she gave me her love".

"Yes, most important of all is love ..... how we find it and how we share it brings such joy to God. We will turn back now, but there are many other stories to tell. It is so important for My fragile children to have little treasures for little treasures become of great wealth as time passes by ..... be blessed this night .... as I gather you all beneath My mantle and as the stars shine upon us, My Son smiles with His blessing upon each of you."

December 14, 2001

"My dear children,

I call you this night to a peaceful quietness, and yet I call you to a great expectation. I desire that you ask of God for that special grace to find joy ... His joy .... in sickness or in health. The joy of which I speak is indescribably beautiful, for it cannot be described in your human terms .... it is a joy that is filled with strength and with courage. Can you find joy in difficult family situations.............. in occupations with are filled with stress .... and simple little children, can you find joy in making order out of chaos? What We have called you to is to be simple .....child like ..... obedient servants of God. In being a servant of God, you think not of yourself but take great joy in serving others. What better time, My children, than this beautiful service..a service that you are called to observe during the Advent season ....a service to a King about to be born .... a King who will serve. My children, I feel His heart beat more and more rapidly within Me as His time approaches when birth of Divine Love will come upon this earth. Oh little ones, come with Me and rejoice. Put aside all that tempts to disrupt your peace, especially nowwhen God wants only peace in your lives. Turn from temptation and rejoice in simplicity of love .of the little things in life that God finds most pleasing. Here we are gathered this night... .soon to prepare for a most glorious event. My children, I ask of thee to pray .... to prepare your hearts .... to be willing to lay your heart before the Throne of God as your gift to Him! Can you do that .... you can only try .... for no more is asked of you than to try!"

(Visual): " There are all sorts of stars .... all shinning....... glimmering ... once again like jewels and I see our Mother sitting on a .... rocking chair..... it's all in

lights .... so beautiful ... so serene. I can't make out what She is doing, but She is busy with Her hands. I (now) see ...like shooting stars and they go to what appears to be (I would say) Her lap: And She takes each one ...... and She is reaching down and brings up what looks like .... I'd have to say a piece of fabric ...... but again, it's all in lights. And She takes this little star and I'm led to believe it represents a soul ..... and She wraps it with this beautiful fabric of light......but there is no bow ...... there is no ribbon (to hold the wrapping to the package). She takes Her hand to Her mouth and places a kiss upon Her fingers and then touches the little box ... the little soul ..... and seals it with a Heavenly Kiss. She then takes that little box and tucks it beneath Her mantle and one by one ...... so quickly it seems ...... each little star finds its way in Her lap ..... .and She repeats and She repeats ... and She wraps each one as though it were the first .... with so much love .... and each time She secures it with a kiss and tucks it beneath Her mantle ..... and She says" "These are in preparation for My Son. I shall present each of His children wrapped with My love before His Throne ... *(Tongues)* ... Receive the blessing of the Father, Son and Holy Spirit. Rest well, My children, for the angels which surround you sing in glorious harmony to the praise and glory of God."

December 21, 2001

(The following message was received during our beautiful Christmas gathering during the Friday Night Canyon Rosary in which our Blessed Mother came and blessed all the items which everyone had brought and placed on the tables next to Her large statue. Everything was aglow with the soft lights of candles while Christmas music could be heard sweetly playing in the background. It was an absolutely holy evening.)

([Pat) "I will say it just as you say.

"My dear children,

What if I ask you this night to take My hand .....without seeing ..... without expecting anything .....yet, you know deeply within your heart that you hold the hand of your Mother. This is as it was with Jesus ...whom I took into My arms and bathed Him in My tears of joy ...tears of joy .....and I glanced at My dear Joseph ....who stood there so in awe ... not knowing what to do. I held out My hands with this precious gift from God and I could scarcely encourage this holy man (Joseph) to take from My arms the Son of God .... to caress against his chest

to feel the beat of His heart. It was at this moment that I took My hand and placed it in the infinitely small hand of My Holy Son.

This is our gift to you this night .....for as you allow Me to take your hand .....I tell you the Power of the Holy Spirit will come upon you ....and you will be taken back to that precious moment in time when the Son of God held the hand of His

224

Mother! For you, My children... .your hands are larger I ask you to believe that I take My fingers and gently weave them between yours .....for this is an embrace from Mother to child!

I realize it is somewhat difficult for many of My children to comprehend that anything so beautiful could be possible in this world .... but I tell you .... you shall never reach the degree of intelligence that will allow you to understand the smallest detail of God's plan for your life .....for you shall always walk in Faith .....you shall be kissed from time to time with precious gifts........with butterflies of blue ......with pictures in which you see our image. Do not allow yourselves to become discouraged, but cling tightly to your faith for all are gifts from God and must be received as such. He loves you as a most tender Father and has permitted this evening as one of special joy to allow Me to come into your presence and bless the objects which you have brought forth for My blessing. I thank you above all for your faith for you shall always walk by faith. Everything you do in life is done out of faith and trust in Almighty God. We bless you. Know that all that have come that are ill ..... I have personally touched and prayed an intercessory prayer before My Son. ... The children, I always bless as I bless and keep all children close to My heart.

Be at peace now for surely you know that God loves you. You have a mission, My children, and by the power of God and the strength of His love, you shall accomplish that which has been assigned to you."

(Note): There was a silent, if I may say "holiness" right after the rosary. We sat silently contemplating what we had just heard. Then we heard the most beautiful "Ave Maria" being sung that echoed throughout the room. It was the climax of a most enchanting evening!

December 23, 2001

(This message was given by Jesus during the song and prayer conclusion of the 3pm special Sunday Chaplet of Divine Mercy and Rosary gathering. The large petition basket as requested by Our Blessed Mother in Her message of December 7, 2001 was overflowing with petitions in the form of gifts to be placed in the upper grotto for the baby Jesus. With some audio difficulty these words which we believe to be accurate were transcribed from the recorded audio tape.)

"My Children,

I thank you for gathering in such numbers as My Mother stands holding not your basket my children .... but a basket woven of gold. The hands of my angels gather each petition and place it into this basket of heavenly vibrancies. My gift of which you give to me.

It is time now to rejoice ..... for my angels ..... their heavenly court ....surround this chapel with such joy..... for the faith which you have brought. Little children of much faith .... I gratefully accept your gifts ..... and I shall honor them as your Lord and as your Savior. Precious children ...... the Queen, My Mother, extends this basket to Me. It is the one which will be carried to me .... on Christmas morning. My words are true ..... I have heard your hearts and seen your needs. I reign now upon you showers of graces. Golden graces from the golden basket."

December 28, 2001

(Commentary by Jerry): The following message is from Pat's guardian angel "Samuel" who was first heard on the message of October 12, 2001. Although initially of a personal nature, as with many messages this is another example of how God is further teaching us [the community] to ask for His help through the angels in troubled times. In this message as Samuel confirms "Tell all of our children". We have discerned to pass on the value of this personal message. You are also encouraged to discern as you read the following taken off the audio tape as it was dictated thru Pat. Note that Samuel calls Pat "My Little Charge"

Tongues (Pat) "I recognize thee. But in the Holy Name of Jesus by the power of His Precious Blood identify thyself."

"My Little Charge,

It is I Samuel. Why have you remained hidden .... seeking a place where no one could find you? Tell me my child ... for we share much. Is it that you think I do not know the burden in your heart ... the joy, the holy reverence you were allowed to witness as the veil was lifted from your eyes. Little child of God this is your gift, but one in which in time all will share."

(Pat) "Am I to answer you? For you know my heart is no longer within me For I send my heart before My Lord to lay prostrate before him .... to adore Him .... there's nothing within me ...... nothing within me ..... I have given him all and yet I want to be so quiet ...... that nothing will awaken Him within His Mothers arms ...... and that I may be still with Him just a moment longer. I have experienced nothing like this before .... with such holiness and such reverence that my feet floated across the floor. I have been here yet not here ...... my body is here but my heart is somewhere elsewhere ... it is so bright and the lights are so beautiful ...... but they are so soothing ... and the aroma holds me .... holds me .... the aroma is so intoxicating. I feel I cannot continue the conversation. Oh praise be My Jesus ...... praise My Jesus."

(Samuel) "Little daughter it is true .... your heart has been taken as you asked it to be taken .... before the manger, before the new born Lord .... but it has been split into many pieces ....many tiny hearts filled with love that shall be returned to you ....to be distributed to those whose hearts are so heavy. Do you not realize there were many who felt the heaviness of the holiness of this time and yet, knew

226

not what to do. We are here but you fail to call us .... you fail to send us....... to do your bidding. Send us to Our Lord that we might Adore Him as you rest. <u>Send us to those who are dying that we might comfort them in their last moments.</u> Send us to those hearts that are so broken that we might pray with them and share a token piece of your heart with them . Tell all of our children that we stand ready to be used as warriors .... to be used as gentle souls to console. <u>But you must ask ... you must send .....we do not go without your permission</u>... give us thy order ... send us, and we shall boldly go ....we shall wave the banner of Christ ...and we shall go into the fields .....and we shall prepare the hearts so in need of healing. What a time this has been a special time ....a time of quiet reverence .... a time of learning ... a time of sharing ..... a time my children of forgiving. Do not hold on to those moments of un-forgivingness ... .for God shall call you when you least expect. We stand guard this night awaiting your command .... little charge of my heart where shall you send me what is my duty for you this night?"

(Pat to Samuel) "With a mission of mercy to *Cindy's family, that you may begin healing, say your prayers to Almighty God. Unite them I pray. Go my dear friend .... be about Gods business."

*Cindy died during the week without her family near.

****

Messages from Jesus and Mary

January 4th, 2002 – December 30th, 2002

January 4, 2002

(Tongues) "Children of God, I welcome you!...........(tongues) .... By the blood of My precious Son which flowed from Calvary .... (tongues).............. I cover thee .... (tongues)........ by the power of the Holy Spirit ....(tongues) ....I shall open each heart to hear the word of God ....(tongues) .... I do not ask that you believe ....I ask only that you <u>listen and hear My words!</u> .... (tongues) ....time passes quickly................(tongues) .... much too quickly .... (tongues)......... My children, My time here has been well spent .... (tongues) .... many lessons have been given ..... how much has been comprehended? ..... (tongues)......... that is up to each heart ....(tongues) ....open your hearts this night....... (tongues)....... listen well to My words for My Son has sent Me .... (tongues) ...... and I am here to deliver His message".

"My precious children,

Those who come with imperfect hearts open to the will of God shall be filled with the perfect wisdom of Almighty God. I see the hearts of those who are here this night and I smell the fragrance of pure love ..... love which has allowed God free will in the lives of His children .... for unless you relinquish your free will your love cannot be perfect as He the Lord your God requires. Listen, My children .... these words are not difficult to understand, but difficult to place into practice. I am here to assist you............to hold your hand ....to wrap My mantle around you.............that you might fully understand and be at peace. For when you fail to relinquish this .....your will to God .... He is unable to strengthen you......... to give you the grace ..... to pick yourself up when you have fallen......... but when the joy of coming to God........with your heart and your hands ..... finally materializes in your life .....you truly understand ....<u>Thy Will Be Done!</u>

There are many messages being spread throughout the world during this time of great grace. It is your responsibility to pray to Almighty God for the intense ability to discern what is of God and what is not... remember the Word of God is Truth........it has not changed from generation to generation. Read....... learn......... comprehend .... for all will be as it has been written."

Visual: [Pat] "I see a great book with many men (I think they are men) standing around the book. As it is opened, each one (of the men) comes and reads the

228

words which have been written in that particular section. They step back ....
another comes and reads and explains the words which have been written ......
he steps back .... again and again this is repeated. The pages of the book turn
...... the men come and they read ...... explain and praise Almighty God. Finally the
last pages are opened. An elderly frail man comes.* He is illuminated ......
but not like Jesus ...... not like others I have seen ...... and he reads and he reads
and this shall come to pass ...... and at last the book is Closed .... nothing more
to be added nothing to be deleted. This is God's Holy Word ...... these are His
chosen ones who have explained each book of the Bible. It's the Bible as it was
meant to be interpreted. It is closed now...... but I hear open and read learn and
believe .... learn and believe!"

(*Commentary: It is believed the elderly/frail man was / is John the Apostle).

January 11, 2002

"My beloved children,

Once again I come to greet thee ..... to bring Our love and Our peace ..... to heal
the wounds of your hearts .... to restore peace in your families. My children, We
observe you moment by moment......... day by day.......nothing goes unnoticed. If I
were to tell you it would be like a joke as you would say in your terms ... the times
you strive so hard for holiness .... and turn around and do just the opposite;
but, there is no laughter there is only deep sorrow for you My dear children. Much
encouragement is needed for responsibility shall never lessen but increase and you
grow tired and you grow bitter ....but these are just trials for the grace of God
shall overcome all things and great joy shall come into your life. As the suns shine
its brightness, the sky shall be illuminated and you will see the glory of God.
Look up, children ... .look up and see ...... God has so much for you and yet you
ignore the small things, which are great miracles. Let Me help you. Start slowly"
...........tongues ......

(Commentary by Jerry: This explanation involves discernment to publish the
following prayerful conversation below from Pat. Notice the conversation coming
from Pat is given in a very personal way [which would appear her very soul
speaking to God]. The conversation then appears to come from outside means
coming from far beyond what she was initially trying to express to the Blessed
Mother. First when Pat asks, "Mother may I speak" she is getting permission to
put these words into spoken words to be given to the community. Otherwise as in
previous similar situations it would be a time of silence or private tongues.
Observe when Pat asks how she can help her brothers and sisters the flavor of the
conversation progresses into answers. The conversation then leads into a direct
touching scenario of how one might find a means of relating to God. It is indeed
touching!)

(Pat) "Mother, may I speak?

*How can my heart contain the love of my Lord? I feel it will burst ...... my feet
never touch the ground. The wind swirls around Me, but I never move. I feel
nothing about me but my Lord. Where am I Mother? Where have you placed
me? Where have you taken me......that life no longer holds me.......... that I wish to
draw so close to you. The warmth from the sun compares nothing to the
warmth of Your heart. The beauty of the earth holds nothing to the beauty of
Heaven. The fragrance of the flowers holds nothing to the fragrance of
Heaven. All these things I smell and see and long in my heart to be with Thee;
but, here I lie ...... here I lie unable to move ...... unable to come to Thee. What
good am I Mother......what good am I? How can I help Thee.... how can I come to
my brothers and sisters and tell them of such great glory of God and say it is
time......it is time ....conversion must come in all lives! Whatever you are
doing......take time for God! There is nothing to compare in this earth with what
lies ahead. Forget the troubles.....forget the pain.....forget the suffering......for they
are wrapped as precious gifts, but they are given to us here to enjoy, and yes, I
say enjoy .... for that is as God meant them to be ....to offer the precious
treasures......the treasures to Him before His Throne ...Mother what is
wrong.......my words .... my words will not cease......for I long not to be within me
but with you. My heart cries to thee. I will love and I will do thy will. Forgive my
weaknesses......forgive my indiscretions ......forgive those times when I have
turned my back on my brother and sister......when I should have embraced them
in my arms. Forgive me Mother......plead for me before thy Son ....My Jesus
I would not offend Thee My Lord whom I love with all my heart. It is my heart I
give to Thee this night. I would sing a song of such beauty if I could sing.......I
would praise Thee with such eloquent words if they were mine to use......but I
am but nothing....I am no one, but your child, who hides within your heart and says I
love you! Send to me what You will. Give to me what You will... .for all you give
me I shall share....I shall share with joy.......I shall bless as You would have me
bless... .speak as You would have me speak ....only take my heart, for it hangs but
by a thread.......a thread of love!"*

(Jesus) "My child,

This thread of love which you describe is like an umbilical cord .....one attached to
bring nourishment to the body .....the other (the thread).....to bring nourishment
to the soul. Though one is cut ... .the body continues to grow and be nourished.
It is the thread of love.....the invisible thread of love which is never cut and
continues to draw you to My Fountain of Mercy."

January 18, 2002

*(Pat) "Holy Mother......I did not think you would come tonight. You have been
with me all this day and I kept telling you, I don't know how to say the words you
wish me to use. Mother of My Lord and God.......I am thy servant."*

(Mary) "My dear child,

It has been difficult, especially for you this week, for the hearts which melted together last week have remained bound as one. Your words were sweet, My child. They were fragrant as the flowers ..... they were all those things you said you could not do........you could not say .....but see the power of God........and how He takes this child and molds it to His perfection.

I have gazed around the room this night .... and I see many........ many of My beloved children.....who have come... .and I have watched that seed of Divine Love sprout from within their hearts into the tiny seedling which it has become ....and I will continue to watch..........for these are My children, entrusted with a great mission of My Son. You ask .... tell us what to do, Mother ....what shall we do next ..... which way to go......... what material to use..............and I say to you.....you are the children of God ..... He has entrusted in each of you the ability to make decisions. He has placed in your heart the desire for prayer to commune with Him. Use these gifts, My children. You hang as a child hangs upon a mother's apron strings .... not wanting to lose balance .... not wanting to let go of security. We will be with you. You think your work is finished ?..... this beautiful gift.....these Stations of the Cross shall truly be well known .....but I tell you .... <u>roll up thy sleeves</u>............ <u>put on thy sturdiest boots and take a great stance for the road ahead requires much climbing</u> .....it is steep .....it is difficult .....but the job ahead shall be accomplished.

I wish for you to take a break .... let's take a coffee break .... but instead of coffee I offer you the fruit of the Spirit of Patience. Eat heartily that you will grow strong.....that you will grow wise and that your hearts will be filled with love. There will be less questions, but many answers .... for God shall give you a great gift ..... a great gift of knowledge. Pray, My children. Do not be afraid to pray." *(Tongues)...*

(Pat) "*I see it ......yes, there is a very large hedge......a very large hedge ...... kind of like a square. It is a beautiful, beautiful garden... but the hedge is shaped funny ... but by the entrance, there is a most beautiful statue of Our Lord and Our Dear Mother. Our Lord is bending on one knee. His hand is reaching out to the water which flows just so gently from the fountain....... and the little animals come because they see what I did not see......They are not statues......it is our Lord and our dear Mother......and She asks (yes, please) (She asks if I would like for Her to take my hand because we must walk through this hedge.) It is light. I believe it must be the morning hours because the birds are singing and the sky is beautiful. There is such a freshness in the air......and as I walk, I feel a sense of peace because our Mother is there. There is no fear...it is beautiful. It's a maze ...... that what it is......we have to get to the center ...... make a right turn ......and it's like a tiny area all of lights...of beautiful lights. But the lights are a sense of peace... a hunger in the soul...... a hunger of which I want more. I want more Lord, I want more... is there more? And we continue walking . She smiles and leads me down the walkway into various little rooms...... five rooms, six rooms, all different ... all radiant. But its not the body that feels these things ... it is the soul.*

The soul that cries within us. God allows us to see with our souls the beauty which lies before us. Allow us to feel these things My God, that we might truly be Thy servants... filled with Thy love. The last room (I'm not ready... I can't make the last one). It is so glorious......so glorious."

(Mary) "My Child .... each room is an area..... an interior area of the soul..... which through much prayer and deep love for God ..... you shall reach ..... and you shall attain the sanctity to which God calls you. Persevere..........I shall always hold your hand. It is when you are ready that We will continue the journey. Enjoy God's goodness...........His blessings .... this night.

Next week, I shall tell you the story of the "broken cup". Bring all your problems as well as your joys, for by evening's end the cup will be filled and brimming with the graces of God."

January 25, 2002

(Note: This promised message is a follow up from the previous week's message. Pat's oration continues to be expressed with more depth and knowledge. All italic text type is Pat.)

(Pat) Tongues "My Lord, what has Thou done......where has Thou placed me this night? I feel as though we walk together, but it is not familiar......and yet I know with you beside my side... my heart rejoices. There is no fear......there is only joy. Mother, I knew you would come. So much has happened. I have felt so unprepared and yet by the Power of the Holy Spirit... My dear Jesus... My holy Mother...we shall begin as you say."

(Tongues) "I see.... I see the brightness of the lights....... I do not continue! What is missing, My Jesus? I knowest if Thou wouldst hear me. My hands come empty before Thee. How can that be? [The sacred crucifix had fallen from Pat's hand] Where my heart is always in my hand before Thee. I do not feel my sacred object. I shall not continue for the Lord said instructions have been given. Where is the crucifix? [The crucifix was then placed back in Pat's hand] It is a peace now ...... and I hear very clearly.

Dearest Mother......You have called your children here this night to reveal a special and holy gift. Take each and every one of them who have come with a heart ready to please and to receive. I feel the warmth of your heart as you see so many of your children gathered for this moment... a cup...... a broken cup. How shall I describe it, Oh Mother...... the cup in which you intend to be revealed to your children? Take My hand slowly...... that My words will be those of the Spirit of God...... I remember messages ago when many souls walked along a narrow path....following the footsteps of Your Son......who upon His shoulder carried a most heavy cross.... but pieces...... broken pieces ..... as broken pieces of our lives fall and we must retrieve them. We saw them, Mother [the souls] ...... we saw them

232

walk...... we saw them bend and with great reverence to pick up a tiny obstacle in their path....... and as they picked it up it became a cross upon their shoulder."

(Mary) "All these pieces...........these tiny fragments of holiness have been gathered .... .fitted perfectly together ...... sealed and secured with Divine Love..............for the cup, My children is not a mere cup........it is a Chalice formed by the Splinters of the Cross of My Son. It is now brimming with forgiveness for those who seek His pardon ....for those with contrite spirits .....their pieces fit neatly. Isn't it a joy, My children, to see small puzzles of life unveiled.... that you may be a part of God's plan of life. Come now............ . prepared......... and drink from the cup of Divine Love .... when the cup is no longer broken......... when the cup is the Chalice of Our Lord .... into which His precious blood is placed to heal the wounds of the souls of His children. You have but to make the effort to come as a holy child to receive the great gift of God. Do not be afraid, for this is a time of joy. Come all My children."

(Pat) "My Lord...... I dare not come before Thee. I approach the cup of Thy love and my lips quiver for I am unworthy to receive Thee. My Jesus, how can you love so much when so much as been done to you......... for sins have broken the cup... but repentance has restored the cup of Divine Love. My God, my hearts burns with love ..... what shall I do......where shall I go now. I find my Jesus!!! Let all of your beloved children come to Thee in the sacredness of your heart ...... having drunken from the cup of Divine Mercy...... inebriated with love. My Jesus... My Lord, gather each of us... let me not be a selfish ignorant child that wants all, when my body cries for all. Lord God, give me everything ...I will take everything ...... I will do everything for Thee......when I am nothing and can accomplish so little. But together... together if we all come, If we all accept Thy mercy and Thy cup of love . [Here Pat appeared to drop into deeper ecstasy] My Jesus, look..... look at the souls that shall come ...... souls who love you...... souls who know and seek your mercy...... to seek to eat of Thy flesh and drink of Thy blood...... to be holy and pure in Thy sight. My dearest Lord, bless these your children and as they come to drink from your Chalice, brimming with hope... brimming with forgiveness ..... .may their cares, their worries ...... all that keeps them from you ... dissolve into a pool of nothingness...... for your blood is the blood of God that has sanctified us and made us your children. Praise you My Jesus. Bless each of your children ...... give them strength to grow in love for Thee. For there are no more words ...... my words are useless...... and my words fail me... but my heart burns and continues to burn. Oh, Lord, Thou art my love. Draw me to Thy Heart with all my brothers and sisters. Open wide Thy heart, My Lord, for many shall come.

(Tongues) As we drink... the blanket of your love and forgiveness shall cover us that we might remain your true children ...faithful ... and true ... until at last you say" . "Come home ....My dear ones....... come home."

(When Our Lord speaks of "the decay of the body" He recognizes that many of us are experiencing the pain and discomfort which is a natural evolution of age and with others who are experiencing disease, pain and suffering at a younger age. Read how the great gift this can be to Our Lord. In the second part [Pat's words] we emphasize that the spiritual relationship of Pat with God continues to be a remarkable expression of personal prayer and hunger to be with Him in the next world. Because of her personal exposure to what lies in the hereafter, she simply longs to complete her temporary stay in this world as we know it. Much of this message pertains to all of us in reference to how we respond to the requests of Our Lord.)

(Pat)...... "A great burst of light" .

(Jesus)   "My child,

I am with you and all of My children gathered here this night.......... for I have seen the sorrows of the hearts and I have seen the decay of the body. I wish to speak with you..... that each may understand that their pain and suffering is a great gift to Me if they so choose to offer it to Me. I need you..... I need My souls who will place themselves as victims for those children who do not realize they run quickly into the abyss of eternal damnation. It is hard........ I know My children, it is hard..............when you feel so weak and I ask so much.....but it is My strength that I shall give thee. Offer what you can with great love and that will make all the difference. If it be but a little that you can give Me each day............ give it to Me with great love and I shall take and use your precious offering as a treasure .... a treasure that will capture and hold the souls bound to be lost. <u>We do not give up my children.</u> We call upon each and every one of you as a source .... as a source of great strength that you do not realize you possess. This is why you must pray...... you <u>must</u> speak to Me. You say".... "I cannot pray .... they are just words .... senseless words that I read from a book.....what does My Lord obtain from this?" "My child, speak your heart."

(Pat) "My God...... how can I speak ... for to whom do I speak ... for Thou art the Trinity .....Father... Son... and Holy Spirit ...and I ......I am ......who knows who I am... but a soul that seeks to love Thee... that seeks to draw closer to your heart. I want no more than to be near your heart...... to draw others to the Fountain of Your Mercy...... and yet, and yet My Jesus, I feel so worthless. I lie helpless ... unable to say great things... do great things... .. accomplish great things......but You, My Lord, it is you I wish to see. It is you I call my "Love" ...... the Love of my heart to be joined with you forever...... and this world holds me, Lord. This world holds me as an anchor about my neck and I cannot flee from here. What is it My God ......what is it that Thou would have me do...... an unworthy soul can accomplish so little? But I crawl as a toddler...... learning to place one knee... one little hand in front of the other...... and I crawl to Thee ...... and say" "My Jesus... whisper in my ear" ...... "Who am I that you should love me... that you should open your heart to receive a mere baby who has so little to offer... but

234

whose heart burns with fire when I come close to Thee. I burn...... I burn, My
Lord ... for it is Thee I want... and no matter of whom I should read I cannot
compare to precious souls...... precious Saint. I can only be myself and have my
own hunger and my own thirst in my own little way...... and My God... it is Thee
who I know will renew and make this world a better place......but these precious
children ...... those that say I know not how to pray ... they have but to listen to
their heart. Words are not necessary...... for one heart speaks to the next ...... and
surely, My God, it is Your heart that understands each beat of ours."

" Precious Jesus......Oh Our Lord...... grant us the strength. Grant those the
strength that come especially this night... and those that cannot make these
prayer meetings and think that they have no part when my God you have sent your
word throughout the world...... not by our means...... but by your mighty hand. So
all are part of our gathering... all are part of this group...... Our Lady's Group
...... who prays to Thee Almighty God, in thanksgiving for your Mother who comes
to us so gently and so sweetly, and says" "My Son, calls you...He needs you ......
He loves you. Do not be afraid to face the challenges ... to face the pain... for it
is all part of a glorious crown that one day shall be placed upon your head."

"Tonight there will be a great change for many of your children. For they shall
thirst and hunger for your heart as never before. Words will not be necessary ......
but the look on their face ...... their actions ...... the gentleness of their eyes
......shall say"...... "My God ...... I shall walk with you. To the very end ... I shall
walk with you. And you, My Lord, will be there ...... the gate will open and Your
arms will be outstretched ...... for we have followed your path." " Never fear.
When you are called to great things for God ...... for He shall always give you the
means by which to accomplish His mission."

February 8, 2002

(Mary) "My beloved children,

Once again we begin preparation for these forty days of Lent .... each requiring
much preparation. My children you have seen by example how the evil one
attempts to destroy and disrupt. This is a warning of that which is to come. I ask
of thee this night to pray and renew your consecration to the Sacred Heart of Jesus
and to My Immaculate Heart daily that you may receive spiritual courage and
strength for the journey ahead." (Tongues) "I give to you this night two words;
first, <u>sacrifice</u> .... a pearl of hope .... second, <u>penance</u>...... the precious gem
of reparation. Use these diligently during this holy time and you shall be a source
which God will use to help pursue the souls for His Kingdom.

(The following segment pertains to the recipient of the message (Pat); as you will
note the inference to "child". It also later refers to the general public, meaning
"children").

"God does not interfere with your lives, My child, as you so thought. My poor

235

child, you become so confused .... but still speak for there is more for others. You (children) are asked to commit yourself totally to God. You cannot choose God and the world ....only one choice may be made. When you become tired, disillusioned, dissatisfied with life .... I beg of thee to immerse yourself in prayer ..... and come .... hide beneath the Tabernacle of My Son ....where you may receive courage and He shall see His child and all the children who will obey My request. Strength only comes from God .... do not be misled especially as the trials increase .... for God has great plans for those who come...........for those who pray ....for those who seek His mercy..........for you are the children who trust .... who are faithful and that is what He calls you to be .... His faithful little children! I will walk with you through this Lenten journey for attack after attack shall come, but be assured that God has sent His angels to guard you carefully ..... to give you courage to persevere."

"Watch the steps before you. Trod only where the Master has walked ..... as I have told you, it is well illuminated .... bend and look........do you not see the stains upon the stones? They are stains of "love"... and the others you see ....they are the faithful Saints uniting their blood and tears ..... when faithfully following Him to journeys end. That is where we shall go. We shall go as a family united in Christ. One will be strength for another .... the journey is difficult and will be made more so because of the sin that has immersed itself in your world. It is a time for courage..... and you are My courageous warriors....... armed with My Rosary and My Scapular and great faith. Oh, My children, it is time to take My hand now as the journey soon begins. We must not be late. God is expecting us!"

(Pat) (Visual) "I see an open hilly area. It looks like someone has built a large bonfire beneath a large slab of wood. It looks like something that would be an old fashioned sacrifice of years ago. But I recognize these people. My Lord, I see...... these are people I know. I don't understand. It is very large... this sacrificial table. I don't know what else to call it. There is someone there ...standing above these people. An angel ... but ... it raises its arm with a great weapon ready to come down upon these people...... and I hear.... "Do not touch these .....with stay thy arm for they are Mine." I hear the voice...... I recognize the voice...... but it's a Lamb...... a beautiful white gentle Lamb. There are no weapons raised. Everyone has been released. We are to follow the Lamb ......   — the Lamb of God." (Tongues) "I see... I am to wait until later." (This would indicate either a follow up or some type of connection to this Lenten message.)

February 15, 2002

(Jesus) "My children,

If you could only see the result of My suffering, you would unite everything in your life in union with My Passion. But you are sensitive child like creatures....

.who must be led firmly but gently through this great time of Lent .. I gather you here that you might join together as families united for truth .... families united in the holy love .... families united in willing sacrifice. Many times you have been told to follow the steps .... the stones upon which My blood lays after centuries. It is still visible. That My children is where we shall go tonight and each night of Lent, stone by stone. It is the only way .... it is My way and I desire your will ..... I desire your free choice .... *will you walk with Me? Will you join with Me in My suffering and in My sorrow? Will you gain souls for the Glory of My Kingdom .... will you say yes? It is too much for such frail ones to say yes , to so much so soon! But your heart will be awakened.... your heart will be filled with the knowledge of where you shall start. Start slowly that you are not overwhelmed ....as fear will not creep in and destroy the beauty. Sacrifice where is the beauty of sacrifice? It is buried in humility! Just the slightest glimmer of pride fights the humility for which you are called. Humility is like a fog in which you are lost as a tiny boat ...... floating with no direction no sense of where you are going of where you have been. The little boat is pride. Look as you pray for that slight glimmer ....that slight opening of pride in which the fog parts.....and your sails shall burst as a gust of wind and draw you through. Oh little children do you think that I would leave... .leave you helpless and lonely..... the One who loves you more than any other ..... not I My child.... for you are My children. I ask much of you I know, but much is required .....but in tiny increments.....slowly you shall accomplish..... all that My Will requires."

*(*Note: On February 17th, Pat said "yes" and made the intense walk of suffering and sorrow over the mountain path at Our Lady's Shrine.)*

(Pat) "May I dare to approach Thee? I was humbled and I feel lost, and out of control. Where My Jesus do you wish me... when you know that I wish to be with you....... and yet ...... and yet the chains of love keep me here. How My Lord can such a useless instrument be held so long when my meager offerings ...... my meager sacrifices..... are so insignificant in my life. I can see ...... I can see Lord Jesus only so much ....not as you see... for you see how everything comes into place. For we try to make it and make it where I wish to join with you... in all the pain and all the suffering ...... step by step...... on all of those stones which contain Thy blood. I know Lord Jesus where I head and I know that one who tempts and torments me. I cannot...... I am not worthy...... and yes, I am not worthy, but through Thy love and through Thy grace you shall take me and all those who believe in Thee, into the tiny opening where that gust of wind shall send us all sailing along that path to Calvary...... and there we shall lay our lives upon the bottom of Thy cross and let Thy precious blood flow and cover us that we may be precious children of Thee. Oh, My God...... my precious Jesus, you are my all ...... my love......what more can one say whose words are lost in eternity...my useless words."

(Jesus calls to) "Samuel" *(Pat's guardian angel responds)* "I am here, My Lord."

(Jesus) "I command thee to guard this one .... to protect Her during this most difficult time."

(Samuel) "My Lord and My God .... my little charge shall not escape my care. I do all for Thee. This one entrusted to me I shall protect .... I shall watch and I shall guard .... and then My God ...... My God ... .I shall return her to you safely, and that she will hear once again, the whispers from your lips as she praises you with all her heart."

(Pat) "If I may be so bold, My Lord. The evil one has tormented me and I do not know why Thou allowed it. I know, My God, that it is for Your praise and for Your glory, and I accept deep in me, for I am so weak. I do all for your glory ...... all for your children. I love them all, for I fear not for Thou art always with me. I do not fear to touch .... and love ... for they (His children) must first touch you ... You stand always between me and those that come ...... for you are the Lord ...... the God of healing ...... the God of mercy. My Jesus, My Lord ...... let me not fail Thee ...... let me not fail Thee My God ... for I shall truly die ...... oh remorseful soul ...... to fail Thee but one time."

(Jesus) "I bless you little child of mine."

February 22, 2002

Tongues (Pat) "Maria...... Mother......... I can't see. Help me... ... there is something on my eyes that won't let me see .... thank you (our Mother uses what appeared to be a part of Her mantel to wipe my eyes)..... it's all red ...... your beautiful mantel, is all red. I'm sorry! "

(Mary) "My dear children,

You have been entrusted into the care of unconditional love. You have been placed in My hands as we take this journey through history's darkest hour. Are you ready? Then we shall go. Take my hand as I have asked for I shall light the way along the path ..... and what is it you see that causes such alarm. Yes ... .the insensitivities of poor decision which caused the pain and death of My Son. But it is not a time in which you are called to fear... .for God never causes you to fear. He causes you to recognize the indiscretions in your lives ....the sins which mar the soul and must be cleansed and purified. Together as we take this journey .... each and every one of us look down Do you see in between the little spots

of blood of My precious Son? Those little spots that you see are the drops of blood, which indicate the sins He bore for you. So, you see ..... we take a journey of pain ... . and yet a journey of such great love ... that yes, once again, I must say, you can never understand until you come into the Glory of God.

As you take My hand, I ask you not to look back .... for then you will become concerned over those whom you love in this world and wonder .... will their steps be following yours? Do not let your thoughts linger here, but look ahead for God's love. You shall see.........."

238

(Pat) Tongues " Mother... I see many people way ahead and yet, how is it possible that you hold <u>each</u> hand? There are so many things that I don't understand and I can't tell people that you can hold everyone's hand at the same time...... but you do ...... and we are all walking in the steps of Jesus. I see three crosses... and lots of people gathered beneath. But it's like the sun has burst above the cross and all Heaven has opened up ...and there are so many beautiful people (I think they are people)... saints (I know some relatives) ... and there is Jesus. Now Mother... you have a gray dress on... but you're standing up there in gold. I'm confused, but it's so beautiful and it's so real and I know anything is possible with God. I pray it is not my <u>sins</u> that have darkened your clothing... but I feel that you have chosen to walk this way. And each of us ... as we take your hand... our sins, have caused your garments to darken. I'm so sorry ... but I see ahead...... and I know that once we get to Calvary , where Jesus is... He's on the cross...... but yet high above in full glory, waiting, smiling, beckoning us. Now I know how all this comes together. I know that suffering must come, and I thank you. I thank you as I praise My Jesus ... My Jesus ...Oh Mother, I wish that I could tell of such love. You give me so much. You put so many words into My mouth ...... cannot the words which describe the beauty I see ... be placed upon my lips ... so that I might whisper them to the whole world? If not now, perhaps in time!"

(Mary) "My daughter, everything in God's time........great joy shall break through all sorrow. God's love will permeate the air as a fragrant aroma of purification. All will breathe and feel the love and peace of God." *(Brief unprinted message continued......a personal conversation).*

March 1, 2002

(Mary) "My dear children,

I have much to tell you during these next few days.....much to say that requires your attention. Listen well as I explain. Each day God is revealing a piece of His puzzle .... an unfathomable design of this *(puzzle)* ......indescribable, yet you play an important role .... for each of you are different........ you are uniquely precious .... and you bring before the Throne of God precious gifts and in so doing God is able to work wondrous deeds when you have willingly suffered during this time and in the time to come. For many have been exposed to what lies ahead and the importance of complete obedience to God. How precious the gift, to walk the pitiful Passion of My Son, to see the suffering ... ... and yet I ask you to savor delicate flavor..... of suffering spiritually for souls. Each time I ask of thee to join with Me........ you notice there is a fragrance........ there is a flavor .... sometimes bitter....... sometimes sweet .....but together it makes a beautiful aroma in which God uses all of your gifts..... all of your efforts......... no matter how small, to sweeten the suffering of My Son's Passion. Each time you say yes .....you say yes to God .... you say yes to souls that would have been lost, had you not been willing to offer some suffering in their place. My heart rejoices in such a time when I must walk with you ....for it brings back a time many years ago when We walked alone ... .just He an I .... for only We knew God's purpose .... God's plan. Today you are blessed for you are permitted to join in the journey for the salvation of souls."

(Pat) "Oh Mother....... I have been there before...... so many times...... must I repeat... for all have heard ... what they have done to my Lord...... having been forced each time to take this darkened trip... this murky path deep beneath the crowd where the moisture and the stench are unbearable. My Mother... I cannot help...... I can only look for such sorrow and such misery in my heart ...... and find that I am lost... and there He stands... He is swollen and still filled with love and compassion... still holding no guilt nor distaste for what has happened and what shall happen ...... and all this comes from His free will and that is what He asks of us...... freely join Him. What portions are we allowed to see Mother? I know not...but I beg of thee for the courage and the grace to respond in the spirit of holy love ...... the spirit of holy love from our Lord, that we would gladly follow Him wherever He goes and every steps He takes... that we would bear every wound ... every insult ... every humiliation ...... for He is our Lord and our God. Oh Mother, I feel your presence and I feel your strength... and yet I feel the strength from my Lord gradually fade. He struggles... He struggles now... for His final journey... for each and everyone of us. Let us praise Our Lord with all of our hearts. Let us offer everything in our lives from the tinniest to the greatest and my Lord let this help heal the wounds of thy foot... of Thy shoulder... of Thy back... of Thy face... of Thy arms... Thy hands. Thy hope is to wipe away the tears, the tears that burn your eyes, the tears of abandonment. My God help us to love you more, to serve you."

(Mary) "Much will be required and much strength will be given .... for each shall experience .... in their own way..... a portion of the Passion of their Lord. Praise Him .... love Him.....thank Him .... for He loves you....... He loves you so much."

(Apparently from an unidentified angel) The following message was given in front of the Holy Mother statue after the Rosary and taken from script notes.

"I say that all men must pull together for the hand of Christ has been held back for so long. It is given in love not in fear..... review your life ....make changes where necessary but come back to God......... He is your only chance of survival. Listen between the words of Our Lord's and Our Lady's messages for there is a great puzzle. Each person represents a piece of the puzzle. Only God knows how it will come together........ You must prepare to be melted and molded .... as God so desires so all fits together .... for His will. We stand besides you..... we will help you..... we will guide you and guard you."

March 8, 2002

(Mary) "My dear child,

I have come this night..... not to increase your sorrow .... but to awaken you to joy. Through your trials you have listened to my words..... and the sensitivity of their meaning has found a place in your heart. All of these things must be as God has predestined .... but each of you My children are a part of a great plan of salvation..... for as you listen and hear My words .... the scales fall from your eyes and you see the need for repentance and reparation .... for the sins that have caused such anguish and pain for My son. Yet this, too, is a great miracle..........and now you see........... you recognize a role you play ..... an important role. God has measured precisely what each one will carry ....what portion of My Sons Passioneach shall see *(visualize)*. I caution you to do as I have Instructed to obey.... to fast.... to do penance and to sacrifice. For all of these lead to the mercy of God and through His mercy comes an ocean of forgiveness for all souls for whom you pray."

(Pat) "Oh, Mother sometimes it is so difficult to understand. I want to be prepared...... I try to say things just right... to tell them so they will know how much love there is...that's how much God's mercy is not being taken advantage of. We fail to call upon His mercy ... perhaps because we consider ourselves so unworthy. Oh, we are unworthy......but the Lord has called us to drink at His Fountain of Mercy and I come and I bring all who will hear these words, to drink, to be filled, to be purified. For it is true the battle does rage... and it will, but we are brave warriors; aren't we mother? We're trying."

(Mary) "My Child,

Let your heart be filled with peace..... for what you are experiencing is emotionally difficult to convey .... via words to those about you .... but you shall try, and through God's grace, they shall understand. It is more important for you to remain at peace.......... for then God's precious blood covers and seals you and keeps you safe within His heart. For you must reach and touch many with the words My Son and I give you to speak."

(Pat) "Oh Mother I wish I felt more competent. But I shall try and I shall trust and I shall believe. For I know that God is always with me...... You are always with me...... my Jesus ... always... always beside me. And yet, I have weak moments, when I step backwards and lose my footing...... and there you are ...... bending down ... reaching...... to assist me once again, as you reach and assist each and everyone of your precious children. Lent is a time that many people place different meanings upon." *

(Mary) "What I offer you and have offered you from the very beginning is but a taste.......... it's the sweetness of a love that shed every drop of His blood for your eternal life. Be at peace all children of God .... for we still journey but a little while longer."

(*Pat's Commentary: We as Christians hold various views of Lent and just what that may entail for each of us. It has become more and more evident during this walk with Our Lord that Lent is a time of Mercy. Never more, in my very brief awareness of the Mercy of God, and what that really means, has Lent taken on a more enlightened meaning. I have personally always acknowledged this was a time of .... at the very least...... doing with less. It has not been until the Holy Spirit has brought me the awareness that it is a time of Mercy...... yes, doing with less personally, but more importantly doing more for our fellow brothers and sisters. It is an eye opening experience and personal belief that Lent is a life long process of doing for others. Perhaps, we have just become more lulled into conditioning ourselves for forty days of our meager sacrifices and then "business as normal". I feel more than ever before we are living in the time of Christ's mercy and we had better re-evaluate our thinking along these direct lines. We too, are Christ's messengers of mercy......... that's twenty four hours a day......... seven days a week. What a sight that would be......... a world of Christ's mercy and peace! God bless you now and always!)

March 15, 2002

(Mary) "My dear children,

I call each of you this night to join with your Mother..... to join your heart with mine... .that we may draw strength from one another for that which is about to come. I spoke of this Lent and what it would entail..... it has been a different journey for many .... but it has not been a journey without pain and without suffering. You suffer in many ways, My precious ones ....the suffering of the mind.....the suffering of the heart.....the suffering of the body. In which do you suffer and in which part of this part of this suffering do you joyfully offer to My Son? We have watched you through this journey, but not only us... but those whom you cannot see have observed all your actions........all your struggles. You have not gone through this alone. My dear children, choose your words in a loving way that your actions may exemplify your words.....meaning you say what you mean. Truth has been tested more this Lent than in the last few years. It is time that you, My beloved faithful warriors face anxiety and all its complications and lay each and everyone before Me and My Divine Son. You are My warriors and through you actions many conversions will take place. You must be faithful ...... you must be persevering precious souls of God. He comes first and then everything will fall into its proper place. Perhaps not as you would have chosen ....but as God has deemed appropriate for this time in your lives."

(Mary) "How many questions .... I am besought by so many questions".

(Pat) "Mother, why has this happened ..... .why has this been allowed?" [Her own response] " For the grace of God.....that is all you need to know."

(Visual) " I see a hill...... not exactly a mountain ... and it is not really steep... just taking its place coming into view...... not much to look at ... just stones and plants... not a thing of real beauty as we might think of it...... and there is a large

242

rock... a stone, perhaps, but not large and upon I t sits our Dear Mother. She is all in lights...... not as bright as I have seen Her before but Her head is down and I cannot see Her features In the distance, way in the distance. I see three crosses...... they are very faint and I know they are crosses. Our Mother...... gently, slowly lifting Her head. I can see distinctly the eyes... the eyes that say so much but still She calls us with just the motion of Her eyes. The eyes are different than I have ever seen...... they are very intent...... very strong... yet filled with so much love and I understand It's our Dear Mother's preserving love for Her children that gives Her the strength and courage to call each of Her children throughout the world to come ...... to walk in the steps of Her Son.... for soon the crosses will be more visible and the time will be more difficult as well. We must join together... hold on to one another... be strong... be faithful as our Dear Mother has asked. Mother, Holy Mother of God... of such love and of such strength... we will not fail Thee, but follow Thee where ever Thou shall lead us."

April 5, 2002

Jesus speaks...

(Jesus) "My children,

Risen, risen I am .....now and for all eternity. My great joy is to have each and every heart united with mine ....where the fires of Divine Love shall purify each and every soul........ for I have come to set the captives free .... and yet..... there are those who chose to remain shackled to this earth. They reject my gift of salvation.....for the world and all it holds..... holds them as well."

It is a difficult thing I ask..... but choices must be made. My Father sent Me .....it was my choice .... now, it is time for you to choose between the world and the false glamour it holds..... or to serve your Lord who promises you trials, sufferings and disappointments on this earth, but great glory in the world to come. My dear children, these habits have dug deeply into your souls. The envy, the jealously and the pride! I detest pride and I will take each of My servants and squelch the pride that seeks to grow and make of them new creatures........ a new beginning... a new

purification..... for only in humility ...sincere humility ... no false fronts. For I see all and total devotion I require . that I may send healing into each life..... healing that will begin a new life ... a new journey   one without shackles one with only joy and My peace shall dwell in the heart of all of My children. I thank you for taking this Lenten journey with Me. I thank you for the struggles..... the difficulties which you endured in My name... for blessed are you who are persecuted for My name sake. For truly you shall receive your reward in Heaven."

(Pat) Tongues.........

(Mary) "My beloved children,

243

Do not think that I was allowed to come into this world to spare you the trials and disappointments of life? But on the contrary …. I was sent as a gentle loving Mother to take your hand and lead you over and through these difficulties …….. where together we shall go to My Son. Trust and pray and praise My Son …. for His love shall be with you now and throughout all time."

(Pat) Tongues... "I am so confused, My Mother, I wish to speak. I see myself at the tomb of our Lord and as I peer in ... it is barely light ... I see where My Lord was laid and I know He no longer resides there, but has truly risen. And now, Oh Mother, my spirit no longer wishes to stay ... and yet there is an anchor tied upon me ... and what am I to do Mother... what am I to do? Everything is contrary to what I believe I see .... I wish to be with Thee... but look at me, I am shackled ... this anchor just holds me here. What good am I with so many trials where I have failed Thee ... and failed those I love and yet You leave me here and you speak to Me of such beautiful things ... and so unworthy am I, that I should flee and hide ... but you draw Me ... LOVE draws me forth and I have no choice. I have no choice but to hear the words of LOVE and meekly come begging forgiveness for myself and for all those whom you love. I am wounded as my Jesus says ... a wounded Dove [references private message of April 2nd] and I try to fly. But my wings will not carry me ...... I stumble ... I drag my wings. I try My Lord and as you place your hand upon my head I feel the warmth and healing of your love. And though I stumble and fall, I will always feel your love. I will never feel rejection... as all your children who stumble and fall must know that they are not rejected but they are loved and they are consoled. Oh Mother of God, take me into your arms for now I feel so weak but yet I feel such peace ... a peace that was lost and now returns ...... for my God stands guard over all His servants ...... His angels He has sent to protect us ..... and my dear Samuel (my guardian angel) I have put you through so much and yet you hold tightly to me and I know that you guarded me and protected me as God has commanded you. My Jesus ... my love ...... it is my heart I lay before Thee. Do with me what You will ... and as I grow stronger, help me Lord to be the servant you wish me to be, that others may see the light ...... your light still burns brightly... for it is hidden but for a moment from the eyes of men. But from the eyes of God it is a "flicker" that shall turn into a flame of love.

I pray that many shall be allowed to see a glimmer of what lies ahead ...... how many changes we would make in our lives ...... I pray My Lord ...... let the scales fall from the eyes of your children ... that they may seek and seek only to do Thy Will ...... abide with Thee always!"

April 12, 2002

(Samuel)

The message began in tongues as has been our normal means of greeting; however, this particular time one is able to denote "two" distinctive tones of voices which implies a conversation between two individuals.

(Pat) *"If this be Thy will...... I ask you to cover us Oh Lord that it might truly be of Thee......Yes, I hear."*

(Pat's guardian angel) "Do you not recognize me, My Child .... it is I, Samuel, the one in whom God has placed the care of His little child .... you are my "charge" and God's child. I wish you to come with me. I know that you see now and smell the aroma of the flowers. Come sit beside this tree. Sit and be still. What is it I hand thee........ a rose...... a beautiful long stemmed rose...... now describe the rose with your heart....... not you eyes."

(Pat) *"It is obviously a rose. It looks like it's red and beautifully proportioned ...... not totally opened ... ... just so beautiful and so fragrant, and I am running my fingers down the long stem ... very carefully ... for I know there are thorn's. I feel the brush of the leaves as they touch my hand."*

(Samuel) "Now take one of the petals from the flower, place it in your hand and crush ..... crush it so that there is nothing left. What do you feel........ what do you see?"

(Pat) *"It's a limp moist petal ... ... but it still smells so beautifully. I don't understand the meaning, Samuel. I've had a difficult week."*

(Samuel) "My child .... many have had a difficult week. Let me explain. In God's garden grow many flowers .... some from the most beautiful roses ...and some from the most fragrant of all flowers. When you take the petal, it is a time of trial........... a time when God seems so far away and yet He remains constantly with you .... but the fragrance never leaves. It is you, little children of God, who remain dormant as God waits patiently for the springtime of your soul .... when new shoots shall arise from the ground. It is time now to rest, for those shoots will soon require much care and you and all the children who form the bouquets for God will nourish these shoots as God has so directed. These are the words that My Lord has commanded that I reveal to you. Oh little charge, when you feel so lost..... when you asked Our Lord this day to place His arms around

you........to squeeze you that life no longer would remain here .... you think that He did not hear ....for He sent me this night that you shall remain........and you shall be comforted .... but rest, that strength will return when time comes, so quickly now .... so quickly......... . rest. Lay you head upon my shoulder and you shall sleep."

Tongues...(Pat) *"If it be Thy will. By the precious blood of Jesus, I ask you to cover us Oh Lord. I truly believe in Thee."*

April 14, 2002

(Jesus speaks)

Tongues.........(Two different voices as though in conversations.)

(Jesus) "My child,

Go and write of My Mercy..... for those who still do not understand that My Mercy is in such abundance and they (His children) come with such little faith. Tell them to open wide the doors of their hearts that I might pour forth My Mercy and there it shall stay and there it shall bring peace and joy into their lives. Come freely..... come joyfully.....dance and sing before me.........for today is a holy day .... a day I have poured forth much healing........ much joy into the souls of My children. Without such faith.....without such trust.....what shall hold My Mercy? Write, My child. The instrument of My Mercy is the body itself.

Come before Me. Empty yourself, that I may fill you with such joy and such peace. No longer shall you doubt ... no longer shall skepticism fill your hearts and your minds ...... for I am the Lord your God ...... I have spoken... and so shall it be!"

(Pat) "And what of the children? ....My Lord, what shall I tell the children?"

(Jesus) "Touch the children .... Thy hand shall be filled with My Mercy and My Mercy shall flow to their hearts ...."

(Pat) "Oh, My Jesus ......Oh, My Jesus".

April 19, 2002

(Mary speaks)

(Mary) "Oh my dear child, I desire that you speak these words to My children that they may hear and have them buried within their hearts .... that they may know of the Mercy of God and of His great love for each of them. Earlier tonight, My Son's message was relayed." *(the audio message of Sunday, April 14, 2002 was replayed before the Friday rosary).* "He calls you to accept His Mercy........He calls you to listen .... as I call you to listen. Hear with your words hear those words with your heart ...... not only your ears ....for ears can deceive but the heart remains true. *Tongues...............*

There are so many of our children who do not approach Our Lord......... who do not call upon His Mercy ....because they find themselves in the pitiful state of unworthiness and fear the Lord will turn His back and have nothing to do with

them. But I assure you.........when you call to My Son ....He runs.........He runs to you with His Mercy to bless you and protect you .... He asks only that you bring a vessel for Him to fill and fill it He shall. What is the largest vessel that you can bring ....the soul. You must take every moment slowly .... to empty yourself of all that displeases God. For in so doing.......... you make more and more room for God's Mercy to fill your soul. Oh, precious children of God ....the depth of

God's Mercy, you shall never understand on this earth. But let us begin as little children.

Make a little room which we shall call your soul .... and as you empty and discard all these things you have carried for years, God will fill that with an abundance of peace and of His love. This is your own <u>private Mercy room</u> where you and Our Lord meet and join hearts to pray for all the souls throughout the whole world. As it sounds so simple .... I tell you it takes time .... it takes a life time to truly rid yourself of years of neglect when God had no place in your life and you wish to do this overnight .... to make this Mercy room for just you and God .... where joy will abound. For you will speak to Him as you speak to your Father and He will talk to you as He does His child. The Mercy room brings comfort .... but it brings even greater strength for there you learn the value of souls......... and in learning the value of souls......... you learn that Mercy and forgiveness are an important part of each life. How difficult to forgive when we have been so wounded, but the joy it brings God is immeasurable.

Take this day .... this very moment.......renew your love and commitment to God..........that the bond of love will become so strong, that souls throughout the world will find this same Mercy and this same peace .... for it is God Himself who sends such a gift to all of His children."

(Pat) "It looks like a blackboard. But it is probably the sky ... and all of a sudden there are these little lights ......(I need help Mother to describe such lights for to say they are like the little lightning bugs that we capture as children) ...... they flicker on and off. They are so similar but yet they fall from the Heavens......... millions...... probably billions...... all landing on each soul. God allows Me to see this little light..... like an invitation......... perhaps each individual name on their "invitation" , <u>a name written in the precious blood of Jesus.</u> The invitation is written on such a material I cannot describe. For it seems to seek what's within the body and there rests within the heart. My Lord says...... <u>He has invited all to receive His Mercy.</u> It is up to each and every one of us to choose this precious gift."

April 26, 2002

(Second message - from Mary)

(Pat) Tongues

(Mary) "My Dear child,

Do not worry this night........ that your voice is not as it has been .... it's an offering to God. Because of this suffering......... others will come and bring their minor offerings to Our Lord......... and many souls will be saved.

How it (the day's severe wind outside) blew......... and how objects were tossed to

247

and fro. Was it not your soul ..... also that was tossed to and fro? That was the grace of God .... that allowed such motion .... such disruption in a normal day. So that you might know that He is always with you through every circumstance of life. There is no soul which we shall let go. The wind blows this way and that way .... and you feel caught .... not knowing your trust in Our Lord wavers ever so slightly .... not like the storm..... but like the breeze in the trees, and of the wind of the fields .. it's ever so slightly when any disturbance threatens your lives.

Children, you are the beloved ones of God and you feel this anxiety .... in these moments of uncertainty .... call upon Him... . and in moments, moments of time .....you will feel the hand of God, rest upon your shoulder ...... to renew with His strength and His love. I tell you to pray..... pray your rosary.........wear your scapular.......... keep holy water in your homes and bless them frequently....... for the battle approaches .... the battle in which the children of God must be prepared without fear... but with total trust in the mercy of God. Yes, there are many things you do not understand .... the simple trusting in God and His Holy Will, will bring everything into His light............ that you may see, the purpose of His plan. Keep the word of God ....cling to it and upon it's promises and boldly proclaim them. For they are from God .... He will not let you down. He has given you these powerful tools........ to strengthen you through this journey........and yes......... and yes I repeat, the battle comes ... the wind shall blow ....but you shall stand firmly on the word of God.........strengthened by His love and by His mercy. Do not fear little children ...... do not fear, for God is with you ....He is your strength ....He is the peace which comes into your lives, especially at those moments when anxiety tears at your very soul. Take time to be with God. Allow yourselves to be so quiet that even a tiny pin dropping within a room will go unnoticed. Listen for the voice of God .... very softly ..... and you must be prepared....... you must believe that God talks to you ....that He encourages you......and that he loves you, as a Father loves his children. Jesus does not remain away, but embraces you .... feel His strength ....rely on the strength of God .... for in so doing peace shall fill your life. Strength shall come to endure all adversity ...for God alone is the Holy One. He is the Lord and He shall protect those who are His own."

April 26, 2002

(Jesus speaks)

(Pat) During the afternoon of April 26th, I was a little late in arriving to pray the Chaplet of Divine Mercy. We were expecting some very special guests from Tucson. I was not certain if they would be staying for the Friday Canyon Rosary and I decided to try and make time just to say a little blessing with them. This sounds not too unusual except I had just returned from a doctor's appointment as the antibiotics I was taking had caused a slight problem with my being able to eat or talk. Through God's grace, these beautiful people started praying for me and I experienced the most beautiful presence of our Lord.

As sometimes happens, there was a beautiful dialogue in "tongues". At the time this was being experienced, everything was being spoken and understood in our natural language. It is a complete language of "love" with tender" advice" and discernment. One can only rest in the spirit and feel the true presence of God and know without a doubt He is in control.

Jesus spoke of His children, especially those who bask in the light of His love and return that love to others. The <u>Son</u> filled the Chapel with such radiant glory and it was impossible not to cry and shudder under the power of such Divine Love. It felt as though a great and brilliant Host had completely enveloped each of us. We cried with tears of love and gratitude.

Our Lord often speaks of the Glory which awaits those who trust in the Holy Name of Jesus for it is He who paid the price for our redemption through the shedding of His body and precious blood. What more could we say than "Thy Will Be Done". He did say; "Our health would greatly improve through a steady diet of forgiveness, patience and humility". We can only be healed by going to the Great Physician to receive our daily dose of the fresh fruits of The Holy Spirit. It is like a beautiful salad flavored with the sweetness of Divine Mercy.

He calls us to be bold ..... to act without fear......... for the only weapon we need is trust in the precious name of Jesus. His blood leads us to our own personal Calvary. Let's take each others hand and follow that path which leads to the Cross. Together we are strong for we are bound by the love of Jesus .... bow your heads and hearts in prayer...... sing joyfully to the Lord our God.

May 3rd, 2002

Mary speaks

(Pat) On May 2nd Jerry and I returned to Northern Illinois for our annual visit. Around 3:00 p.m. today while sitting in a chair in the family room of our home in Elburn, Illinois, I began to hear a familiar voice and quietly gathered my blessed candle, notebook and pen and headed to the bedroom where I would have privacy for what may follow. My husband was taking a "command performance" nap on the sofa at the time. What was also interesting was the "feeling" he received upon awakening to open the bible and read Jeremiah 26 while I had slipped out of sight. He simply woke up and turned to this particular passage. It may not have any connection with the message I received; however, those knowing my husband are aware he is not a particularly frequent reader of Holy Scripture. Be what it may, we urge you to pray to the Holy Spirit for discernment as you read the following.

The message began in prayerful tongues........I know the word "Mother" was mentioned numerous times.

"My beloved children,

Gather tonight as a family in prayer for the world and those who inhabit it. Long for peace and tranquility ....beseeching Almighty God for His mercy as corruption and destruction seek to permeate the slightest crevices of the soul. Confusion sets in and disrupts peace......... the peace of Jesus.

Where lies true peace, but in love and forgiveness. You are being choked by pride and unholy desires of the flesh .... disguised as tastefully delicious delicacies at the expense of your soul. My children, when you truly trust in God, you plainly see how evil and sin coupled together distort truth. Through God's grace you are given the discernment to see through falsehood with penetrating eyes of love... the eyes of Jesus.....not judgmentally..........but with the eyes of the heart that continuously prays for sincere and lasting conversion.

My Son asks for simplicity of the love of God .... where a holy serenity of obedience calms the disruption of a world lost beneath a darkened veil of want (selfishness).........and needs (charity) subtly surface ...... and the fulfillment of God's plans become an incomprehensible light which transposes good from evil.

Arise, My children, to life with God .... not to unhealthy impromptu urges which confuse and mislead ....but cling with unquestionable faith to His unending mercy............surrender your free will and you will be enraptured in the calming peace of Jesus".

(Commentary): Just a personal thought. Picture yourself standing before God each day of your life and without fear discuss the day...... your accomplishments ...... or lack thereof. Did you do the best you could, but most importantly did you do all out of Love for Him who Loves us so very much? Let the Love of God always be our goal! When we fall short of our goal, let us remember He still loves us. We haven't failed until we stop trying. Even then He continues to call our name until at last we finally "hear" and say "yes, my Lord... I am coming!

May 10, 2002

(Our Lord speaks)

The following message was received after much conversation with our Lord which has been on a somewhat intensely personal nature since our arrival in Illinois. Many conversations are not recorded, for to me they are just that – personal conversations and I have not been instructed to make any changes in my journaling. This particular message has been recorded as dictated. As with all messages, we urge you to pray to the Holy Spirit for discernment as you read the following. The message began quite differently than other messages as there was not a visual as such, but it was as though I (Pat) was in the midst of a crowd and heard the following:

There is shouting everywhere..... everyone demanding to be heard for all felt they heard the word of God. My mind was a deluge of familiar gospel scriptures..... but the words were so powerful and could not be comprehended as quickly as they were being heard. Finally...... which seemed like an eternity......... a sweet aromatic breeze seemed to push the confusion aside and I heard My Lord speak.

"There is much confusion in the minds and hearts of My children ....for you tend to speak before <u>I have finished speaking</u> .... thus you do not properly hear and understand My words. You become so eager to respond that My words have had no time to filter from your heart to your head. Our conversations are prayers .... intimate moments of reflection from one heart to the other ...... and must be contemplated and allowed to be absorbed into your spirit........ where intuitiveness disseminates the wisdom of My love .... for all of My children.

Too many hearts needlessly suffer as "self-righteousness" becomes a battlefield where truth and reality pry at one another.........truth prevails ....yet reality cannot be denied. A humble heart protects the heart from such contention. Pride only amplifies it. The self of pride not only blinds the eye .... but darkens the soul. Your world has become a darkened mass of decay.......... <u>heartless and cold.</u> My Mother cries tears of holy love which withhold My hand. Pray that the light of My love will shine brightly within your world. All hearts must respond to the warmth of Divine Love.

Love and show mercy as I .... your Jesus of Mercy .... love and am merciful. Then life will become a greater challenge for holiness .... a test of forgiveness and mercy. It is a test of spiritual strength which one acquires through denial of "self".............and acquisition of humility. Be My little children who hear My voice and respond with the confident assurance .... of the whisper of My Divine Love."

May 17, 2002

(Residence in Elburn, Illinois - Our Lord speaks)

This particular message is perhaps only personal in nature, but due to its contents it is being presented as is and each may discern as they feel led by the Holy Spirit. There is no reason not to believe His words may apply to any or all of us; hence, we publish.

Strangely, at the hour of 1:00 p.m., I felt the need to pray the Chaplet of Divine Mercy. I asked the Lord to place my spirit before Him in adoration that my prayers for the sick and dying might receive His special grace of mercy. I found myself in a heavy mist (even smelling the aroma of incense) where nothing was visible except an enormously brilliant Monstrance in which Our Lord's radiance spoke to my heart. His words were like coals of fire which touched every part of my being. It was like a shower of purifying graces was immersing my soul as His Mercy became an audible sound. It seemed to become an echo of great love. Each time I prayed it appeared as though a gentle breeze (probably the Spirit of

251

Mercy) carried the prayers to whomever they were intended and then returned to where I prayed. As each spiritual prayer returned, the brilliance of Our Lord intensified until the Divine Light was too intense to gaze upon.

(Our Lord then said): "Such prayers please the Father who beseeches your loving perseverance for souls. You must continue through the darkness of the soul .... when you feel so far away............. when the dryness of your bones becomes as dust and everything is an effort .... to pray and to trust. The refreshing mist of My Mercy is always there..... awaiting your call!"

(Personal message) (He then began again)....... "You see...........through prayer our relationship becomes personal. You see Me as a loving... . caring Lord who guards you in ways unbeknown to you....... and once again .... you begin to trust. What delight a trusting soul gives Me. Do not allow fear to cause seeds of imaginary anxiety to lead you along the path of disillusionment. Your prayer life must be strong........... as it is you whom I send into the fields planting My seeds of Love. I bless you this night with My reassuring peace. Remember to treat each soul with tenderness as many wounds are painful to the touch.......... easily bruised and clinging only by the thinnest thread of hope!"

May 24, 2002

Residence in Elburn, Illinois - Mary speaks

(Mary) "Come, My children, to find refreshment for your soul. This is a place of Our choosing where each shall learn to discipline himself by not only hearing Our words, but by living them........ for it is by truly living in the Word and Will of God that one becomes a true child of God .... obedient........ loving........ often denying oneself for the greater good of others. Oh, chosen little ones who carry your cross with joyful resignation.......... you radiate as tiny lights sparkling throughout your world. If I were to make a comparison, it would be what you see as you glance at the stars scattered across a vast darkened sky. We see a world of souls with small but visible flames........... illuminating each soul which tries..... even with all its faults.... to cling to Jesus and the promise of His Mercy.

Pray........ pray....... pray the Rosary and the Chaplet of Divine Mercy, which My Son requests. Even the most frightened sinful soul will find compassion and peace..... as he trustingly calls upon the Mercy of God. Bring all the wounded hearts to the Fountain of Divine Mercy........ for the rays of light emanating from My Son are a spiritual laser of healing ..... leaving no scars ..... only complete trust in His unfathomable loving Mercy.

As you place yourselves spiritually before My Son in adoration .... you receive many graces..... for your prayers become endowed with rays of reflective love. As you adore Him, He in turn calls upon your soul to look upon others with a compassionate heart.......... denying self to bring others into the Kingdom of God.

252

One soul, My children ....one precious soul .... would you not do all within your power to help save just one soul? Pray and persevere for the Glory of God........ if not out of duty .... than for love and love alone!"

Long personal message afterwards in which She (Mary) said many things.

"Do not be surprised or disappointed with what shall transpire. God's plans are flawless..... meant only for the good of His children..... accept them as such and you shall lead holy productive lives. My hand shall guide you as you venture forth with great confidence in Our love. A fine tuned instrument you shall become .... . nurtured by the goodness of God."

(Tongues) (She continued there would be many healings ...... many conversion and much hope.)

" Trust in God will increase as lives become centered in prayer. Much work is ahead.....for each of your lives will change .... attitudes towards each other require immediate attention... .pray.........pray ...... pray and forgive so that the healing power of God may flow unrestrained . .... .from His vessels of love."

(A blessing was given)

(Visual): Saw in the Heavens a huge hand from which came a tremendous waterfall......glistening lights falling upon the earth......broken vessels (souls) being mended to hold the graces God is pouring out. Graces to be used ...... not stored as grain (to spoil and lose its nourishment).

May 31, 2002

(Mary speaks)

(Mary) "My dear children,

During these times of My visitations, I have patiently sought to reawaken you to the love of God. The infant as it comes into the world is still strongly bonded to God. But through time....... you My children, become distracted .... losing your way. There is no interest in pursuing God........ you instead, chose to pursue paths leading to destruction. *(our Lady sounded very sad)* It is God who continuously pursues you to bring you back. You are like His prodigal child. He awaits you..... to share in His glory .... the inheritance of eternity in the light of God's love.

The many graces being poured out during these times.........are a sign of the warmth of God's love. Those who choose to absorb these graces ....live without fear in the Will of God. You are children of God.....created in His image. He calls you. Love, for your world cannot heal without love and forgiveness. Relationships are broken .... there is no attempt to seek God's healing. How sad

253

My children .... how sad (said with much expression) that families .... the core of love, struggle to love and forgive. How can peace come about when families cannot heal? Poor children .... do you not understand? ......(*Tongues*)......

I ask you to become a simple sponge .... a sponge that absorbs water and when completely filled is rung out.......... ready to be refilled once again. I ask you to be a sponge of God's love and mercy .... who at His command, you will stand ready .... to be emptied out .... that He may refill you with prayerful graces. Oh, My children, You who hear My words......... remember them.... for the time soon comes........... that your strength will lie in My words. If you have not heeded them.....it will be as the sand upon the seashore.......... that once the water comes ..... you are taken out with the tide.... . lost. But if you listen carefully to My teachings .... your strength is and will be in God. He will always stand beside you............ forming you into the rock which shall never be broken. It will stand in strength and in love .... as God wishes each of His children to stand in strength and love. I bring you peace and a gentle reminder... that time is of the essence. In Their will to love (references the spiritual world)... and the power in willing to love is such...... that in terms of your world..... you would not understand, or to love as Jesus loves. What a weapon you have, My children..... if only you would forget yourselves..... and love unconditionally.....with no expectations .... but complete trust in God. I bless you and encourage you..... My dear, dear children."

(Visual): "I see a rocky coast... the waters splashing against the rocks .....as though a storm is covering them... the waters recede, but the rocks remain. (I hear) We are the rocks rooted in Jesus... the waters are the trials, the temptations that strike at us every day of our lives, and yet we shall remain strong... for Jesus is always with us!"

June 7, 2002

(Our Lady Speaks)

"Children of God

How do you perceive God's purpose for your lives and by what means do you pursue His Holy Will? Lay first the foundation of humility through which the transformation of truth evolves into earnest pursuit of holiness. In seeking holiness, recall the lives of the Saints who sought only to glorify God in simplicity and obedience in their everyday lives.

In these days of deception and temptation, it is imperative to seek the peace of Jesus which enlightens the soul and transforms fear and anxiety into a calm serenity of trust.......... trust in God's love and mercy. Those seeking to avoid suffering .... whether it be physical or mental ...... will find themselves drawn

254

as if by a magnet to the Foot of the Cross where healing begins. For it is the Father Himself who monitors each of His children and with tender love seeks to dwell with His children and they with Him.

It is a great awakening when souls turn from sin realizing they are temples of the Holy Spirit in which God seeks His rightful place upon the throne of their hearts. It is unity, My children, unity with God which shall invigorate each soul to seek the lost and forsaken with unconditional love drawing them from despair to the joyful confidence of God's love and mercy." *(Long prayer in tongues . When She continued there was a slightly different inflection in Her voice)......*

"Those who know so much .... yet so little..... I pity thee..... for there is no room for compassion. Your mind is set as an immovable force. The precious oxygen of love needed to keep the body alive can no longer reach the heart. Thus, the journey from the head to the heart is blocked by a decadent clotting and unless treated... .death shall ensue........ death to the soul....... where true joy has been stolen like by a thief in the night. Realize now... .God's plan is perfect..... accept each trial with joy. The evil one will continuously strike at your most vulnerable point. Strike back with love and forgiveness. The battle is exceptionally intense and shall not become easier. Give everything to God Who shall attend to everyone according to his need."

(Visual): I see a great barrel shaped object (almost like a wind tunnel) brilliantly lit with souls (people) continuously going in and out. It reminds me of a bee hive with so much activity... only there is no buzzing sound... but a beautiful humming...high pitched but peacefully alluring. It would appear to be a sort of sanctuary where the presence of God dwells. It's power is like that of the magnet spoken of earlier where souls diligently work for the Glory of God where we too should be working for the Glory of God.

(Footnote): There was also a very powerful underlinedaudio message from the guardian angel "Samuel" during the evening Rosary at Mary's Knoll. He confirmed their role and assignment from God to protect and guide us through our journey in this world and into the next. Much of the audio is of a very personal nature yet the Angel Samuel broadens and applies the conversation to everyone. After hearing this audio one would find it difficult to deny that angels exist. With our groups discernment we will advise if we are to publish.

June 14, 2002

(Our Lord Speaks)

(Visual) "Everything is dark...... so dark. It's just the sun, it's coming up over the horizon. The ground is so hard......... there is no moisture. There is nothing but places to stumble......places to try and survive. My Jesus I don't know what this means......... but I trust in you .... I know that You will explain ......"

(Jesus) "Child of mine........... You feel the heat as it burns your skin.....You feel your lips parched from lack of moisture .....yet the burning of your heart has nothing to do with the sun and its rays. It is the power of the Omnipotent God who burns deeply within your heart.........that you might feel his presence ....that you might know of His love and of His comfort."

(Pat) "My Jesus, I am nothing and so confused ...... please help me."

(Jesus) "It is the power and the love of God that gathers each of his children through these difficult times....... you struggle through the heat of the desert ...... parched and dry ... stumbling as you go.........look at My Church ..... stumbling........parched and dry. As I predicted many years ago, there would come a great trial for My Church..... But My Church shall stand. You are My Church... . You who love... . You who obey ...... You who follow my word. Is there more to say? Then, God is in control .... trust Him and in His mercy .... all shall be resolved."

(Pat) "There is a dew like presence ...... moisture in the air. It is scented with an aroma of encouragement. It is a bouquet of all Gods flowers (souls) gathered together emitting the most beautiful aroma."

(Jesus) "It is the aroma of the church that will not fail. The gates of Hell will not prevail against My Church. Go busily about your daily tasks.....pray much .... tend to your families..... but above all give God all praise and glory..... for He shall show you the way through this turmoil. Trust Him as you trust Me......... Your Lord. I send My Mother in these difficult times .... all through the world to bring comfort and strength in a gentle motherly way............that there should be, no fear ...... but hold tightly .....hold tightly to the threads of love..... for you are bound as My Children .... and I shall protect you and I send My Angels, and a multitude of Saints that pray continuously........for you and your salvation .... fear not................ fear not. All must come as I have said...... all must come. Through prayer you may lessen the severity, but it shall come My Children. Be awake; do not sleep .... for the time shall come when you shall see how you stand before God. It is a time of great grace .... a time God gives you out of His Holy Love......... to choose..... and choose well you must .... for time runs out. Oh beautiful precious children .... time runs out."

(Pat) "My Lord ... It sounds as though You are preparing us for something so great. Help us that we will not fear, but as You said, we will choose well. Our hearts are yours ..... mould them as you will ... for they belong to none other. You are the Lord Our God".

(Visual) "Oh My Jesus it's a clock .... it's a clock in the sky ...... not a clock ...... an hour glass ...... time sifts so quickly and moves. Our Lord says if you fear you will not accomplish His purpose. We are to place complete trust in Him, whatever message he gives us .... it is complete trust in God that will see all of us through .... eternity with Them."

(Pat) I see Thee, Oh My God * (see commentary below) surrounded in majesty as I kneel in prayerful contemplation of Thy great love for us ...... your children. How great Thou art Oh Lord to humble Thy self disguised as bread and wine to breathe new life into your children.

The World awaits your next move as though life were a game of chess ...... each move contemplated and re-contemplated before our hands dare to move into position ...... not a chess piece but a portion of our lives. Father, it is you who guards us through this mirage of squares upon this board of life. You know I know nothing of chess ... except there is a King, Queen, Knights and other lower class pieces which when moved about the board cause situations of gain or loss.

Is it just my ignorance alone which keeps me from understanding or is it the understanding itself which defies my simple reasoning and this brings me to "check" ... or eventually.... "checkmate" ? It is all a matter of contemplated choices. Life reveals so much when we take the time and carefully gauge our every move. Somehow I am hearing;

(Jesus) "Where do you stand on this board of choices? Have you moved or been moved..... made choices or have they been made for you. You stand to gain eternity or lose everything. Come, My children...do you not see how pieces of this puzzle are fitting into place? Have your eyes been so clouded and your hearts so hardened that you do not recognize the intensity of these times?

I am calling great warriors.... humble servants.....who seek only My Will and the rewards which accompany it. Greatness lies in simplicity... .all must learn and become infinitely small in men's sight yet great in the eyes of the Lord! The more humble one becomes.....the greater He becomes in the eyes of the Lord. Remember, it took only one small pebble in the hands of a child to bring down the giant of pride!

Be prepared to learn, to desire to learn, so that together you will become a mighty force ready to face the armies of spiritual destruction. Pray and fast ..... become strong and unafraid to wage spiritual war against the legions of evil now set loose upon this earth. You are granted only so much time; but, it is more than adequate if you use it well.

My precious children, do not be afraid. You will receive all the assistance necessary to participate in this battle for souls. It is your choice .... you are either a participant or an observer.....which shall it be, My children,...which shall it be! I bless you this night and comfort you with My peace!"

(*Commentary): This particular phrase (I see thee, Oh my God) refers to the 14th

257

Chapter of John (New American Bible - St. Joseph Edition), in which Jesus says "If you know me, then you will also know My Father". He further states, "Whoever has seen me has seen the Father". It is in these particular times when I find myself in prayer in front of our Lord in the Monstrance in which I say "I love thee Oh my God" or in this particular instance, "I see thee Oh my God disguised as bread and wine". I do not see God Himself who is pure Spirit. This is a most important clarification for all who read and discern these messages!

June 28, 2002

Tongues......

(Mary) "My Dear Children,

I am here this night to aid in the healing of many hearts. At this time in your journey you ask yourself.... .what is my purpose? Ask God and patiently await His response. God sent you into this world to learn..... to love..... to forgive, and to obey. You struggle. The dryness of the winds of the evil have hardened the hearts .... have sapped the strength from you My Dear Children, but I tell you ...... that My Son will refresh each soul .... restoring it to the vibrant obedient loving child .... He has called by name."

(Pat) "Am I to speak? (Tongues)............ Yes, Mother."

(Mary) "What good is it, My Children, when you struggle so hard and fail to accomplish your purpose..... for truly you have not relinquished your will ...... to God......... who stands so ready awaiting your call ...... help me, Father .... He waits for you to call........help me, Father.....but you go along your way spending only a few spare moments here and there, acknowledging His presence and those He has sent to protect you. It is a Mother now who speaks who tells you of such love....of a Father Who guards you..................of a Father Who loves you so much, that He created you, to come into this world to be a faithful servant. Oh Children......... persevere. When the drought is there ...... persevere .... for in God's time all will be refreshed".

(Visual): "Yes, I see a beautiful Lady of Lights. She seemingly is standing on parched barren earth. I see nothing about Her but rocks and ground. There is nothing to add beauty......... but what beauty can be compared to the Mother of God. She's calling me and I am so hesitant but I find myself kneeling before Her and I am sobbing and sobbing and the tears won't stop. Why won't the tears stop? I don't know why I am crying. Oh Mother, I cannot see for my eyes are blinded by tears......... and She looks and I hear Her say as only a mother says".

(Mary) "My child, these precious tears are tears of repentance.......... tears of love for God .... tears that shall renew the earth with such heart felt contrition, for as My Son looks upon these tears the gates of the whole of Heaven open and from there comes the showers of graces to renew and refresh your soul and your world. All this takes patience and much trust, but each must deal in their own way with

the crosses that God has given them............. the dryness, the uncertainty .... the anxiety.............. as He shall never leave you unprotected. He shall be there for your every word"................(tongues.)

(Jesus) "I call you to intimacy........ intimacy of love..... where one heart beats so strongly that it cannot contain it's love and must be given to others..........for this is love .... love which must be shared. You, My children, will learn this in time. (Tongues) It is a process in your growth to holiness..... for learning to truly let go of love......... you feel nothing for yourself...... but only for others. As I died upon the Cross, I felt nothing for myself.......... I felt only compassion and love for My children. Can you do the same? Can you follow in My steps... can you follow Me? (long pause)... .follow me... Heaven awaits".

(Pat) Tongues.........."I see the greenness of the trees......flowers are now blooming.........repentance.........thirst for righteousness.........for the tears of contrition.........and watch as God's mighty hand moves.................."

July 5, 2002

(Pat) Tongues. "I can't see exactly what it is. It is a bridge ... a very narrow bridge across. (I can't look down ... it's so far... it's so long). There are people on both sides of the bridge ...lines and lines of people. They are coming to the bridge. The others, a multitude of people. A tremendous burst of light! And thru the light there is a man ... glowing so brilliantly and by His right side is Mary. She is so beautiful. This time She is all in gold But it's not a fabric ...... just glistening fibers. The others ... I don't know who they are. They are dressed in shades of white and other colors as well. I don't understand Mother and I see they are holding something in their hands. It looks like a candle and the flames of the candles are spreading all over this vast area. On the other side of the bridge all these people are just waiting. They are standing and looking but nobody is moving. There are just all these people ... lines of people and I hear a very strong gentle male voice and I know it is Jesus. He is calling out names, but each one has to cross this bridge. It's a little frightening. It's very narrow, it's very long. You have to hold on ... old on tightly. But the voice is so comforting and the lines of people start to move as their names are called. The bridge is filled with people ... once frightened but now smiles ... smiles on their faces. They are becoming like lights ... changing from what we perceive as a body to beautiful lights. They are going to Jesus. Is that right, Mother? "

(Mary) "My Daughter,

This is the bridge of life ..... the trials that all must suffer ......all must endure to reach their final destination with Jesus. Can't you hear by the tone of His voice ....the love He has for each of His children ...... How He beckons you with such confidence as He beckoned Peter to step out of the boat and walk to Him on the water. Do not be afraid. Fear is not of God and will not allow you to cross this bridge to My Son. Allow God to bring comfort into your lives ...... the turmoil your world is in.......... such a state, so many trying so hard to get to where they no not where they are going. It seems a puzzle........does it not?" *(Tongues)*

"My Children,

God does not promise you great joy and prosperity. He sends the trials that you may become wise and humble of heart, and with such wisdom and humility .....your world will finally find its peace. How many My children, are willing to empty themselves out as My Son did upon the Cross? He asks this of you..... empty yourselves that others may find Him ...... that they may hear their name being called across this bridge". *(Tongues)*.
"My Daughter,

I have been with you a very long time. The time of My visitations grows short, but this place shall remain a place of holiness...... a place of healing .... for those that come will have that seed planted within their heart .... a seed that will grow...........a seed that God will nurture and draw them to where He wants them in life. Be not afraid.......for We will never leave you but the visitations will not be as frequent. We love you, dear children. So many lessons We have tried to teach you........ go back ...... go back...... read Our words.... learn and be happy........ be happy for God awaits His children".

(Pat sobbing in tongues) "I love you so much Mother. (inaudible) I love you too".

July 12, 2002

(Mary) "Come, My children, as I gather each of you and draw you into My Immaculate Heart .... to free you from the anxiety and despair which has overtaken many of My children. I am a loving Mother who cares so tenderly for each of Her children. What mother who truly loves her child does heave a deep sigh as that child prepares to leave home ..... to leave without the watchful eye of the mother who directed and protect him. You are this child. No matter what age .....you are this child that must leave and begin your journey ..... the journey to My Son. Do you think My heart was not heavy *(sigh)* when I embraced My Jesus and knew where His journey led? And you my children .... you need not know what lies ahead but only to where you journey............and that is to Jesus. He has provided directions .... signs all along this journey of life. Your directions found in Holy Scripture ...... your signs all about you in this world ....from people you meet ...... to material you read .... all contain signs. It is God Who loves you so intensely and has allowed this journey.

He has sent the Holy Spirit to be your constant companion. My visitations have been a special grace and I love each of you with the heart and the love that only a Mother can express. You, too, must embrace Me and let go...........confident that God is always caring for His children. Draw closer to Him ..... abide in His will.

(tongues) It is My desire that you always be reconciled with The Father ....for around the corner you cannot see... and in God's grace you must stand. <u>It is either Heaven or Hell, My children</u>. I have taught you .... and I have taught you well. You are strong .... believe that you are strong .. let your faith grow by trusting in God's mercy. Oh, little ones, I feel in My Heart... .a slight twinge ....that a Mother feels when She has taught and raised Her children and then sent them on their way....... for She places each and everyone of them into the hands of Her Son. Rest assured you have a place with My Son .....continue in your efforts with joy .....not sorrow .....for I will not leave you .... but it is time .....it is time, My Children.

Embrace Me tonight ..... love Me, as you love Your Mother .....look into My eyes and see the love that will never leave you .... never leave you. I bless you as I have blessed you many times and I shall continue to keep you beneath My Mantle."

(Personal conversation) ... Mother......

(Visual) " It's so bright ..... very different. There is a multitude of people and it looks like they are going their way in life....it seems odd, but they are all taking different forms of transportation. Some are walking ... .others driving and I see what looks like bicycles ....it's more "modern" than I have seen before, and everyone is paying attention because in the middle of this huge multitude there is this great pillar. I want to say a pole..... it's huge ... . it's glowing and it has a light at the top .....one in the center ..... and one at the bottom. The light at the top is on ....everyone stops! The last light has turned and everyone moves and continues their journey. The center light comes on ....it is a golden color and people stop and they reflect ... . some proceed........ some take more time....... they are very cautious and they continue on.........(It looks an awful lot like a stop light ......a traffic signal). Is God directing traffic .... Mother, is that what it is? And I hear a voice that says" ....

(Mary) "It is the yellow light........... the light of caution......... but proceed".

(Pat) "I feel and inner voice ... so powerful. I know that it has to be the Holy Spirit ...sent to lead and direct us ... our conscience......do we proceed ... or do we delay?"

(Mary) "Which ever we choose we must trust completely in the Will of God. For His love will allow no harm to come to us. We are His children .... remain close to Him ..... remain close to Him. I want no more tears oh little children, oh little flowers of My fields. I want great joy for what you have received ..... and yes, I shall return, but I tell you this night that there will be others that will hear My words ..... and they must be courageous and speak My words .... as you, My daughter, have courageously spoken .....even in times of great turmoil you have spoken .....so they too will find the courage to speak. I rejoice with you for My time with you has been a great joy ..... a great blessing."

261

(Note): In preparing to "draft" the message of July 12th, I paused to select a reading from the Diary of Saint Faustina for the Sunday Chaplet of Divine Mercy and Rosary. The book immediately fell open to page 17. I began reading #30 and stopped when I read "I saw an inaccessible light, and in this light what appeared like three sources of light which I could not understand." In my simplistic view of things, the traffic signal I was trying to describe was possibly the Holy Trinity. God the Father in whose presence no one could move, overwhelmed by His Divine Power; (the second light to go on) The Son, in whose peace and love we continue to grow and proclaim His word, <u>without fear</u> ; just busy doing His work in the fields of souls; and, finally the third light to go on – the yellow light of caution; perhaps the Holy Spirit as He guides us, often stirring our conscience to do what is right and pleasing to God. This is truly a message for great discernment!

It apparently was not the order of the lights as they appeared on the pillar, but the significance of the order in which they became illuminated. Father, Son, and Holy Spirit!

July 19, 2002

(Our Lord speaks)

"My children,

You My children who have come to understand the splendor in surrender and abandonment have grown in harmony with My Divine Will. The fragrance of your offerings rises sweetly before Me bringing Me consolation for the <u>many </u>who neglect and ignore <u>My Call of Urgency</u>. Speak to Me of your needs and with a heart seeking union with your Savior tell Me everything as you would your best friend .... <u>for I am your very best friend</u> ..... <u>always there in your time of greatest need</u>. Yes, I know you grow tired and wary; however, you must condition yourself through patience and much prayer ...... for then We communicate one heart to another.

I have known you from the beginning of time ..... a child predestined with a great mission of charity and love. It is in times of self-love you fail to realize the magnitude of such damage to the soul and thus you become preoccupied with unnecessary worldly matters which distract you from the purpose for which you were created.

Love, My children, is in itself holy, but directed in improper ways destroys its true purpose ....that of drawing souls to Me where I will fill and refresh them with holiness. Persevere in times of trial and you, too, will emit the sweet aroma which rises to My Throne and brings joy to your Savior. Never despair for I have great plans for you, My precious children!"

July 19, 2002

(Mary speaks)

(The following message has been transcribed from an audio recording of the message as it was being dictated. It was a most powerful evening as was expressed by many in attendance. Just prior to leaving our residence for the prayer service, Our Lord suddenly began to speak. This was very unusual and as I started writing I was instructed to "go to the computer" (assuming it would be quicker than transcribing the message) and then typing it on the computer for this night's message. The computer decided to make all kinds of unusual changes and my husband finally sent me to the Rosary at Mary's Knoll saying he would straighten it out and follow me there. Because we were not anticipating any further messages, I therefore sat on the floor by my husband as we sang and prayed the Rosary. The next thing I remember was lying on the floor in the bedroom at Mary's Knoll which adjoins the prayer room. It's evident Our Lady also had something to say.)

"My children,

Listen to the words of My Son for He has explained and hopefully joined you closer to your true understanding of your purpose in life. I am here only to bring you comfort this night ....to tell you of Our love .... to tell you, My children, that God's plan is perfect. It is up to each and every one of you to believe that you will become productive instruments in His Holy Will. Oh, children, still children, can you not let go of Me but for a moment? It is time you have learned you know that God has a purpose in your life. I have been sent to remind you that there is a God Who loves you so intensely and wishes only your salvation.

My heart reaches to you and to each of My children that you may feel His love. It is time, My children, to conform your lives into lives of prayer, penance and sacrifice. Time does run short, but be joyful, for knowing that God truly exists is a great gift .....a great miracle that I, your Mother, am allowed to express in this your world .... grown cold and ugly with selfishness and pride ..... but God Forgives ... .for God is pure love. Come to Him ......be reconciled ... .come with your hearts and your hands ready to receive the gifts He gives you .... the gift of humility ...... that you may love...........that you may be filled with great grace. That does not mean that you will not tire and ponder whether it is God's Will ....but I truly tell you .....God loves you and through allowing Me to be with you says everything. Retrieve My children ..... bless them ...... help them back home ... help them to My Son. Children, My precious children, you must learn .....you must believe ...... and you must abide in God's Holy Will."

(Pat) (Tongues) "Mother I know that our weakness is God's strength ...... His love ... His will to be done. Every time that we are weak and often we fail ..... stay by us ... help us and guide us ...for I have known ..... you have allowed me to see the Harvest and the few Harvesters ready to relinquish their lives ... their desires to do God's Will. What a blessing when we are allowed to realize..... for we are children chosen to do His Will ..... I love you."

(Visual): "A coral colored dress with a blue mantel. She holds a rosary within

*her hands ... always praying for us ... teaching us to pray. I have seen you
before ...... Holy Mother of God." ...... (sigh) ... (Pat sang in tongues to all)*

July 26, 2002

(Jesus Speaks)

*(Pat) tongues. "I see ... there is a very rough almost mountainous path. Very
narrow ... barely lit ... quite long. You would almost have to be a mountain
climber or athlete to make such an arduous journey. There are lights. It looks like
a male figure! It is a man and He is very calmly walking this path." ....tongues......*

(Jesus) "Tell My children .... as I walked this path I foresaw each and everyone of
My children who will be following in My footsteps. These are the footsteps of
Love. I ask you to be vessels transformed into those of humility and charity
which equal Love. Love for the forgotten.....the neglected .... the abused... .and yes,
even Love for those insensitive souls who refuse My Love......... My perfect
unconditional Love. They have hardened their hearts and will not allow Me to enter.
It is the uniting of hearts that brings healing .... the uniting of each one of
your hearts with Mine in which healing begins. ..... *tongues ......*
My children, do not reject Me. When you reject Me, you reopen all My wounds
...and the Love which I have for you... still remains.......is still poured forth from the
blood that flows from every opening of My body. I wish of you, beloved children,
to gather each of the precious souls that have lost their way. Be examples of My
Love. Draw them to My heart where they will be refreshed.

(Tongues) It is not the strength of the athlete that gives you the courage to take
this journey through this narrow arduous path. It is the strength of the Holy Spirit
that guides you. Listen to Him..........for He is the Wise Counselor. If you close your
ears to His words, your faith will become weaker and weaker and you will lose
your footing and find yourself on an easily acceptable path ...... more to your liking.
But, My Children, it leads to destruction. Heed the words of the Holy Spirit.
Learn to listen to Him as you listen to Me........ for He truly will guide you safely
along the path that leads to eternity with God."

*(Visual): "Everything is fading. Oh there is a very large flame ...not a fire. Just a
huge flame and something is forming around it ... it's all in lights ... it's a heart
and there is a pen. (Oh, My Jesus, I am so inadequate to explain things. How do I
express the beauty that you give?)... tongues ... The pen is like what I believe we
would call a quill and it is dipped into what appears to be a golden Chalice. As
the pen receives its precious contents, it begins writing names on the heart. It
repeats this and repeats this until every soul that is called by God has its name
written on His heart. The heart is fading ... It is like it is being consumed by this
fiery flame and I hear."* "Yes, My daughter .... it is the flame of Divine
Love." ... *tongues ......*

(Samuel speaks)

(Pat) *"It is thee I see tonight. Yes, it is true ... the weariness has drained many in our efforts to fulfill the will of Our Lord. I knew you were there ... and here you are tonight."*

(Samuel) "Yes, My Charge........ I am here tonight as I am here every night .... every moment of your life. When you grow tired and weary and thoughts do not make sense .... call upon Me and rest your head upon My shoulder. Many of My Lord's children suffer greatly. They suffer physically but more importantly .... spiritually. For they do not believe in what they cannot see .... but you little daughter and others throughout the world like you ....you have been given a great gift. You see the flickers of lights about you in this room ...... those who stand guard .... those who come to sing. .... to bring refreshment ...... yes, refreshment through the voice of the Angels."

(Chimes are heard sounding ...... very soothing)

(Pat) *"Oh, Samuel what is it I am to say tonight?"*

(Samuel) "You must encourage each of God's children to be reflections of His Love........ to persevere in their afflictions and to find joy in the trials and sufferings. As you grow tired ....call upon us. The Holy Spirit will come to refresh you. You will find strength will be unleashed like a river............a dam that has burst ..... will refresh the souls."

(Pat) *"There are so many Samuel ... so many hearts that are so broken ...... so many problems. We witness so much and feel so helpless."*

(Samuel) "You have not relinquished that portions of your will to God .... for He alone is the strength that sustains........ the strength that heals the families ....that heals the broken bodies. We here tonight are here also to guard you ..... to strengthen you .... to allow peace and refreshment once again to come into your soul. I pray thee child, do not become discouraged and all of these children who find despair in life .... that is not of God........ (tongues) ..... It is His peace that He wishes each to have buried deeply within their hearts ....a peace that will be reflected upon each face so that each face will glow with love. You need but a smile to bring refreshment to one in pain. Comfort those you can, as we shall always comfort you. *(long pause)* Yes, tell them."

(Pat) *"I see a man ... He looks like a homeless person. He is just wandering through the crowds ... no one paying attention ... no one caring...... but someone stops and looks into the eyes and brings a cup of water...... and everything changes ...for Jesus walks amongst us disguised ..... and we do not bother to make the effort to see Him in others. Oh, Samuel, how ashamed ...... how many times have I looked at the face of my Lord and looked at my brothers and*

sisters and not seen Him. Help me ...... oh unworthy soul that I am ...... that I
might find such peace in the eyes of my brothers and sisters ... for I know that it is
the peace of my Lord."

Intense personal message followed...............

August 9, 2002

"My Dear Children,

*Those of you in whom My Son dwells must not allow an anxious heart to disturb
your peace. Pray and persevere in all circumstances. Do not let your mind be
cluttered with useless thoughts ..... for you are children of Jesus. My dear ones, if
you but knew the magnitude of that statement you would joyfully accept every trial
and every humiliation and offer it to Him with a heart of love."*

Tongues .... ("Do I speak?") ....

*(Visual) "I see something I have never seen before .... it is a side view of a
very young fragile woman. She appears to be washing clothes in a basin. She
very carefully takes these clothes and places them into a basin adjoining the one
she used for washing. She must be rinsing the clothes. She very gently releases the
water from the clothing and lays each piece in a nearby basket. She takes the basket
.... walks a few steps and everything becomes nothing but lights. She, herself, is
not dressed majestically, but as a humble housewife doing her duties. There is a line
..... (a rope?) ...... a very long line .... but nothing is holding it up ...... it just
goes on forever ...... and she takes each piece of clothing .... lifts it up ......
hangs it on the line and then secures it with little lights; I'd say clothes pins, but
they are not ...... they are beautiful little lights ...... and she takes each piece ......
it's like the multiplication of the fish and the loaves. The basket never empties, but
she never tires, She just diligently lovingly takes each piece and places it
across the line. As I don't see what holds the line, I don't see what she is standing
on .... there is nothing beneath her .... there is no ground, She is just
there. (tongues) .... yes .... I am led to understand that the line itself simply
represents God's love and mercy. It is faith which lifts us up to the line and the
little lights which secure these pieces of cloth to the line are prayers .... and I am
looking as far as I can see down the line and each piece (some only have a few)
.... but most of them have intermingled within their lights ...... the most beautiful
blue (almost shaped like a rose) ...... such a beautiful light. It far out shines the
others and I know that this light represents the times Our Dear Mother has
interceded for us before the Throne of Her Son. If we only could understand the
power of prayer .... we would never cease praying" (Brief personal message
followed regarding Her "sons" (Priests).*

*(Commentary): An individual who witnessed the receiving of this particular
message was gifted with the following interpretation: The first basin represented
Mary washing souls in the Blood of Divine Mercy. They were then rinsed in the*

266

second basin which contained the Water of Divine Mercy. Once they had been washed and rinsed in the two basins, they were placed in the "basket" which represented Purgatory. They (the souls) remained in the basket until there were sufficient prayers. Then they were hung on the line of God's never ending love. The "blue lights" represented Mary's intercessory prayers which were interspersed with the prayers of families and friends were represented by the "white lights".

August 16, 2002

(Mary and Samuel speak)

(Mary) "My Dear Children,

Why waste such precious time which passes so quickly on useless activities, unproductive thoughts .... when God has blessed you and called you, each by name to be His disciples .... His disciples of love and mercy. Yes, My Daughter, here stands Samuel!" *(Pat-Tongues)*

(Samuel) "My Charge,

At the command of My Lord, I stand here with The Most Holy Queen to express Our Lord's command that all should listen and dwell within His Divine Will. When you step beyond these boundaries............. it is I and The Guardian Angel of each of His Children who redirect your footsteps on the path that leads to God. Do not ignore or turn your back upon these directions ...... for you shall shortly require all assistance in your ministry and in your love for Our Lord. <u>For all shall be tested</u> as gold has been tested .... so shall you." *(Pat-Tongues)*

"Little things My Children .... little things .... I speak for all the angels here this night. It is the little things that become so great that distract and destroy. Concentrate, trust ..... without trust you are left to the mercy of evil......... but God has foreseen all and has protected His Children. The words you hear which distract you .... which destroy your peace ...... shall not penetrate your heart............ for your heart has been sealed by the Divine Love of Almighty God."

(Mary) "Listen My Children,

God does not leave you alone. I desire that you continuously make an earnest effort to pray more, to acknowledge the presence of your angels ...... for they have been sent to guard you ..... and to guide you ....and to protect you. From God himself, from His Very Throne He *ordained each and every one of His precious Angels ..... sent them to the precise person .... the precise soul for which they

were intended. Do not fear nor despair........... but believe and trust as I have continuously taught you. Children, My children I wish to hold you so that you would believe .... you would trust for that which you cannot see you must believe that we are always with you"

(Pat Tongues) "Mother ...... may I speak? I have never heard of an *angel being ordained". *(said of God) - reference Webster's 2002 College dictionary.*

(Mary) "My Child, Many things you do not comprehend ...... trust in God and in the being He has sent as your constant companion"*

(Pat) "Oh Samuel, (sigh) I am so ignorant of the depths of theology, and other readings of the Saints. But that does not matter ...... what matters is I thirst for the desire to love souls to look beyond the exterior and sneak secretly within each soul that is hiding from God, and I wish ...... but who am I to wish such a thing. I wish to bring that treasure [soul] before Our Lord and Our God ...... But who am I but a fragile unworthy child that clings to the Mercy of God. Help me ... for no one must be lost. Many hide and God sees them ...... but we must seek them out. For this I thank you Almighty God ... for the hunger for those who do not know you ...... and therefore do not love you".*

A private sequence followed concerning lost souls.

No public message on August 23, 2002

August 30, 2002

(Our Mother Speaks)

(The following message was received prior to the Friday night Canyon Rosary and was transcribed as it was being dictated. During these last few weeks, there have been numerous occasions upon which this writer has found herself amidst large groups of people speaking on "fear" and "anxiety". That in itself is enough to make the hair rise on any timid person's arms and seemingly feeling myself with my back against a wall, I made my way forward and began to speak. This was only accomplished when I realized it was not the wall which supported me, but the Lord Himself. As with all messages, we urge you to pray to the Holy Spirit for discernment as you read the following):

"My Dear Children,

You lose strength when your focus is distracted from Jesus, for He alone is your strength and salvation. In your weariness......... cling to Me. The Mother..... sent by God to encourage and support you as you journey to My Son. In all of life's trials........ that of self-sufficiency poses many problems..... for it is pride in disguise. Your vision becomes clouded and blurred ....thus, in your short sightedness ..... you take your eyes off of Jesus and find yourself lost in worldly ways. The scale (I questioned if I had heard correctly) ...... a harmonious relationship with God ..... begins to tilt .... you lose your footing ...... and so slightly, that it is barely detectable ....a downward spiral takes hold.

Pray, My children. A life centered in prayer is productive and rewarding......... for it is the fruits of prayer which .... one day ..... shall ripen into great delicacies which you shall offer to God."

(Visual): I see what appears to be a cross in the sky. It resembles the letter "T" ...... but from each end of the cross-beam hangs a long chain with a shallow basin. On one side I see the basin being filled with many souls. It becomes out of balance, the other side begins to rise into the air. There is a great noise breaking the silence of the vision. I hear voices filled with anxiety. They realize their lives are out of control. There is another voice, singular in nature ...... which, as it resounds throughout the world, a great sense of peace prevails. It is a strong but gentle and compassionate male voice, which says ... "Pray".

The souls begin to pray ..... praising God, thanking Him for all things ...... their trials, suffering and joys. There is an explosion of great light. A glisteningly bright figure appears on the scale, which resembles a cross with a flaming heart exposed. As the souls pray ... little arrows pierce the Heart and tiny drops of blood and water fall into the other basin ... until the scale is balanced. God's love and mercy have balanced the scale. Prayer brings peace into our hearts as we unite ourselves in love for Almighty God.

September 6, 2002 (Our Lady speaks)

"My dear children

Tonight I wish to extend to each and everyone of you an invitation ... an invitation to holiness. This invitation is now being prepared and it will soon be given to each of My precious children.

What is an invitation to holiness, but to dwell in the Divine Will of Almighty God. This invitation ..... written in blood ....the precious Blood of My Son .... is now being recorded. For all must be prepared for this great festivity ....this great joining of souls ...... to praise, honor and love Almighty God. Are you ready to hold out your hand ..... to receive this invitation? What is written, My children? Are there dress codes and other stipulations..............no, My children. You come as you are with a joyful heart .... a pure heart. *(tongues)* Yes, My daughter........ the date has not been completed.......... nor the hour........ for each shall receive the invitation according to God's plan for their lives.

(Tongues) All those, My children, who bear much sorrow and much suffering .... for trials seem so much greater for some more than others .... do not be deceived ... for many have learned to hide deeply within themselves their sorrows ... that others may see only the joy only the love of Jesus. Is that not all that matters .... that you love My Son and share that love with all your brothers and sisters? My heart goes out to each of you .... for I see what lies deeply within and Your Mother embraces you, holds you so closely that surely you may feel the beating of My heart .... when your trials and sufferings are for those whom you

love. Come, My children, prepare yourselves. It is the inside that must be prepared. Are your garments clean.......... have you sought reconciliation with God? Then be about the business of My Son with a pure heart and a clear conscience that nothing will disturb your peace.

My precious children I have spoken these words so that you will remember as time goes by........... remember the Mother that stood in your midst .... that held you ... . loved you ..... and sang to you. Now you, My precious warriors, sing to My Son with a heart of joy............ a melody of love. You do not need to read music ..... for He reads your heart which is a melodious chiming of love."

(Visual): She stands in a white gown with a white mantle trimmed in golden lights ... all lights ... so beautiful and I see a large heart ... and from this heart their starts to come ...... I want to say an envelope. It is gold ... but the letters are red. She very sweetly and ever so tenderly reaches to receive the envelope. She glances ... smiles and searches for the face of the one who is named on the envelope ... which is the invitation ... the call from God. She passes each one out as She sees them. Not everyone is receiving an envelope. [Mother, I do not understand] Is this not a festivity where all are invited?...... and She says ..."Yes, My child, all are invited, but all are not yet prepared. Pray and be reconciled so that you may receive this precious invitation."

Is it at life's end that we receive this invitation, Mother? It's an invitation to God's Kingdom ... an invitation to the banquet where our Lord stands ready to welcome all of His children. People are so happy ...... look at the smiles ...... the serenity. There must be music. It is so beautiful ...... oh, let us all prepare ...... let us be ready ... for time is so short ...... and there is still so much to do. We do not want to miss our chance. Prepare you hearts and hold up your hands praising God that He may place this invitation within your hands.

September 13, 2002 *(Mary Speaks)*

"My child,

The words you have spoken have been spoken well. For the tongue indeed is an instrument of destruction when left unbridled. Look amongst you and among those throughout the world, that have been cut, wounded and torn apart by words unjustly spoken . By words that cannot be retrieved to mend the wounds. I call all of My children .... all of My faithful ones to a pure heart For a pure heart illuminates the soul and it takes but one venial sin to tarnish the soul.

Dear children,

Must I stay with you to hold your hands ....to guide you always? You know this is not possible. *(tongues and private conversation)* I ask you to be child like in your faith........trusting in God .... totally abandoning yourselves to the ways of this

270

world and clinging tightly to Almighty God and His Divine Will. I repeat and repeat these phrases..... do you listen .... do they mean something to you? For they must ....they must My children if you are to survive ...... if you are to become true children of God. Words now float as do the feathers ....unable to be retrieved. So guard well the tongue and listen well with your heart that the words I speak will take root deeply within you and the words you speak will be well guarded with much consideration............ with much patience. I love you My children and desire only what is best for you. Pray for that purity of heart that your soul will be joined with the Light of Eternal Love."

September 20, 2002 *(Jesus and Mary speak)*

(Mary) "My Dear Children,

I greet thee this night in this holy place as the mother sent to console Her children. To bring them closer to God and to find peace in the Sacred Heart of My Beloved Son. In the times I have come to instruct you. I have observed you as children gathered about me as I taught you. As I loved you and now I have prepared you to go forth as warriors of peace. For tonight you shall be known as my gentle peacemakers, armed as always, with My Rosaries and Scapulars."

[Pat] "There's a large hill, well lit. I can see many walls. Sitting high above, is a man all in lights and beside him a lady. Our Lady of Lights. The man begins to speak. The lady, Our Mother, lowers hers eyes with great love and respect as Her Son says;"

[Jesus] " I send you out as flickering lights into a darkened world as bearers of My Love and My peace. Fear not My Children, for I have gone before you and I will always be with you. But the world now calls for each of MY Children to valiantly pick up their cross and with the gentleness of a dove to go forth as my Disciples."

[Pat] The little lights, little souls flicker and as they were gathered around us .... this mountain, a large hill .... they now begin to descend and the valley below that was so dark is now filled with the lights flickering ..... flickering with hope ...... flickering with the love of God."

[Mary] "My Child,

Soon times will become more difficult and the only true weapon to fight the enemy is prayer. Pray with a heart filled with love and you shall conquer the evil that lingers throughout your world."

Private conversation followed.

September 27, 2002 *(Mary speaks to the prayer group)*

(Pat) "I shall whisper words of love to thee My Lord. For Thou holds my heart."

Tongues

(Mary) "My Child,

I thank you for having responded to My call. Know how pleased we are with your efforts .... with the efforts of those precious children who are endeavoring to do the Will of God.

I speak to you personally... *(pause)* ......listen ... *(pause)*......I shall smile greatly upon this endeavor and know that the Holy Sprit shall be the column which shall support your efforts.

Think of a huge umbrella under which you shall busily go about doing the work of My Son. My warriors of peace .... spread God's love. Proclaim His Mercy and gather the lost into the fold of His mighty love. Take courage and never become discouraged. For you will be given the wisdom ... the discernment to do all that God has planned for you and this beautiful endeavor. Many souls shall be touched by the Holy Sprit. Many will be healed and restored to their faith in God.

Oh how joyful is My Heart .... that you have taken courage and shall go forth. Pray........always be prayerful my little ones ..... and gentle ....kind and loving. For by these things and by the way you live your lives others will see that Christ truly reigns within you. Bear one another .... for all shall be tested and as the weeds seek to come up amongst the wheat. Do not pay heed ....but nurture the wheat that it will grow strong and let God attend to the weeds. Learn to support one another through love .... through patience and understanding. I desire kind hearts ....open hearts .... that My Son may enter and dwell within each and every one of you. Prepare and be busy now doing the Will of God .... for your efforts will not go un-rewarded.

(Pat) tongues .... "I see a huge vibrant tent. I would call it a rainbow but it's shaped like a tent and it's covering these ...... all of these souls .... these people. It truly is an umbrella of God's love and His Mercy. It is The Holy Sprit that shall direct the steps ...... of the Children of God."

(Update - October 2002). Before any new messages (if given) are published they will be approved for publication by Pat's new spiritual advisor. Pat's new spiritual advisor is her confessor and pastor, Fr. Greg at St. Andrew the Apostle Catholic Church in Sierra Vista, Arizona.

On October 4, 2002 a private message, presently not to be published was received during the Friday Rosary.

No public message was received on October 11, 2002

October 18, 2002

"My dear children,

I come as the consoling Mother to bring peace into the anxious hearts and trouble minds. I come to call you to deeper contemplative prayer. For without prayer …. you become vulnerable bait for the traps of despair and temptation.

God loves you, little children, and He wishes you to be united with Him in His love. To become united with God, you must relinquish the self will in your lives … that God will be the only focus. Look into the eyes of Jesus …… the love that He has for you."

"My child, *(Here Our Lady wishes to emphasis that She speaks to each of us individually; therefore, the reference has changed from a general "grouping" of Her children to a more specifically direct approach to each individual "child")*

What price can you put on unconditional love? You are treasures........... priceless treasures to God and in loving God and uniting yourself to Him you own the greatest treasure. For the things of the world shall fade and grow dim .... then your spirit will yearn to soar and be united with God. Trust in His mercy for the perils of this world are great and My heart weeps as My eyes too fill with tears ....for My children are so unprepared. *(tongues)* You, My little children, My little faithful remnant, must go forth …… filled with God's Spirit doing His Will. Into the Harvest you go … and blessed you shall be for the Holy Spirit shall always be with you. For the strength and courage you need to persevere, will always be there. Be bold, my children. Now is not the time to be timid, but with great love … stretch out your arms to embrace your brothers and sisters . For so many are in need.......... so many wounds to be healed. The time is dark, but the light shall shine brightly if you persevere."

(Visual): (Tongues) ..... (Singing is heard in the background from the prayer group) I see a shield ...... is that right Mother?..... a shield ...... a huge shield in the sky. It looks like a shield against a blackboard. It is illuminated so brightly. In the center of the shield there are three letters. P...A...X, all in red. Beside the shield is a very large sword gleaming against the darkened sky. Beautiful to see. The shield is "silence" The sword is "love". We are being armed with the shield of silent love. This is our weapon. Above all else ..."love" will conquer all.

October 25, 2002 *(Mary speaks)*

"Daughter,

We shall go slowly this night, for you bear much. For the soul in need of this ..... your time of trial. This you shall tell my children."

"My Dear Children,

God has bestowed upon each of His children .... treasures ..... graces from heaven which you are to uncover and use for the glory of God. Many are unaware of such graces. For each day new life begins and this is in itself a great treasure ... another gift from God. How well do you use such treasures? You My disciples of Mercy have been trained as merciful servants of My Son .... helping the needy loving the unloved. You have seen the treasure buried deeply within the hearts of those God places upon your path. Help those precious children to discover the treasure within their own lives. Those who carry much pain and suffering ..... dwell only upon the pain and suffering .... and fail to see the beauty and the joy in presenting such suffering, such trials, to Our Lord. *(Inaudible conversation by recipient)* Yes child, you see what my daughter?"

(Visual) "I see a large book. I think it's a book but it looks like a book of maps. I haven't seen this before ...... help me mother. (pause) Each page is a map of sorts. (The only way I can explain it.) It begins with a great burst of light and a journey as the lines progress across the pages. Little signs, little detours denoting significant instances in each life where they have received graces from God and have either used them well or do not realize they have received them. It is as though the gift was in vain, but God used it in His own way to serve His purpose. I'm looking at all the pages. There are all these names, and apparently every one of God's children has a page. You can see the journey their life has taken. How those served Him so well and were so filled with joy even though the map ... (the pages were worn and some appeared torn). But you can see also that they have been mended and it's as though they were never torn. But it's the healing grace of God that restored this life. For it had much to accomplish for the glory of God. (How unusual .... is that mine mother?) As I turn the pages some have but the moment of conception and then there are no lines and there are no detours ...... their life never began, as we know it."

"My child,

Do not be disturbed ... for this is a great gift to see that all life has a purpose. All life is beautiful and all life is truly a gift from God ... that must be treasured at all costs. Treasure each moment ...... for you know not if there shall be another."

"My children,

You who seek to hide ... and not be found intuitively ... know Him whose grace has been buried deeply within your heart. You seek My Son ... that you may love Him and Him alone ....yet in so doing ... you try to suppress the grace and forego the gratitude ... which should be given to God.

True humility quietly acknowledges the grace ... with praise and thanksgiving and continues to serve *(others)* ...oblivious to self-needs or desires. Humility seeks only the Will of God .... and rests contentedly in the Sacred Heart of Jesus.

It is My desire to help you acquire many virtues that you may become pleasing to God. Pray always with your heart ... simply and honestly. This will nurture your love for God. Your love will then become a flame ... inextinguishable by the world ... or the things thereof. For your heart will melt into the Pool of Divine Love. Perfect peace shall be your constant companion.

All praise and glory to the Lamb of God. It is He upon whom you will lean in these times to come. Be at peace, My children."

November 15, 2002

"My Children,

Come and gather beneath my mantle where I shall protect you with my warmth ... from the chilled air of uncertainty. My heart ablaze with love for each of our children .... seeks only to draw you closer to the heart of My Son .... the Heart of Mercy. This world, My Children, seeks only the opposite. To draw you from mercy ... to fill you with despair ..... to torment the poor souls who strive so hard ... but whose direction has been altered from the path of Christ. He is the light which you must follow. There are many false lights and many false prophets. These My Children will lead you only to darkness. But you are Children of the light of Christ. And as such, you are being sent into the darkened world ... with the light of His Love beaming brightly within your souls.

My children, I encourage you to rejoice in adversity .... for all the trials shall surely come your way. But God loves you and His hand protects you. His love purifies and perfumes the ardent soul ... with the aroma love."

(Pat) "A sweet, sweet fragrance permeates the air. But I see fire [tongues]. I see two huge fires with flames that reach as high as skyscrapers in the sky.

275

*Around each fire there are groups of people, probably souls ...... but for now I
see groups of people. The first group is praising ...... singing songs of joy and
gratitude to God and the fire burns even more brightly and grows intensely.
There is no fear ...... this is the fire of love, of joy. The second fire, even
though it seems so large and so overwhelming is beginning to diminish in size
and the people standing around this fire are trying to keep the flames burning.
They've taken all that is important to them. I see homes, boats, cars, fine
clothes .... everything imaginable ...... so costly material wise and instead
of making the flame grow larger it becomes smaller and smaller until there's
nothing, there's nothing but smoldering ashes."*

*(Expressed with sorrow) "I feel such a pain in my heart Mother. The first flame
is so brilliant ...... it's parting in the center and there walking through the
flames is a lamb and the people are rejoicing. It's not being burned ... it's
walking through the parting flames and now the flames are no longer flames.
It's just a brilliant, brilliant light. It's turned into a Monstrance ...... a huge
Monstrance in the sky and Our Lord now in the Eucharist is present in the
Monstrance. He has humbled Himself to come to us, to adore. The flames
cannot destroy such love ...... they only accentuate and excite the souls to
praise and love Him. Oh, Mother, does that tell us that our hearts should be
so on fire for Our Lord when we come each day to receive him ... that we
should burn with such intense love and such gratitude? Oh, Mother, words
fail me. My heart is no longer mine. My heart cries for the souls that stand
beside the smoldering ashes. Oh Lord of Mercy be compassionate to your
suffering children."*

November 29, 2002

"My Dear Child,

Often confusion blurs the vision and clouds the minds of My beloved children.
The joys in life, those trials..... those uncertainties..... pain and suffering
appears to have no understandable meaning in your lives. I assure you my
beloved .... that these are times of great joy......... of great strength and of great
character. For in these times you must rely solely upon Jesus. It is He who has
experienced all things and has allowed these trials in your lives that you may grow
and as you grow and the fruits springs forth in your lives, other seeds will generate
from this fruit and a great orchard of souls for Christ shall stand beautifully in the
valley ministering to all those who come in search of Jesus. Many still do not
know or recognize My Son. Pray particularly for these children that they may
obtain the grace of salvation .... the grace to be washed in the Precious Blood of
Jesus.

You will soon enter into a most holy and beautiful season. This is the time when
great spiritual growth shall spring forth. For the beauty of which I seek is the
beauty of souls returning to God. How unfortunate My children that this is a
season only............not a daily practice of love, devotion and of giving of oneself.

This is where you are called to give ….. but give of yourself that which God has given you. For you are richly blessed with an abundance of love and an abundance of forgiveness to be shared with all in need. I shall be with you during this special time in more evident ways. That many will know the presence of My Son as well as your Mother are here on this holy mountain calling all to conversion. Join hands with me and let us joyfully sing praises to God for the great gift, which is to come.

I bless you, especially those whose struggle and yet maintain desire to persevere through all adversity. Rest in Our peace oh dearly beloved"

December 06, 2002

"My Beloved Children,

You faithfully gather in this holy home bringing with you these nights all that your week has entailed ……. those moments of joy………. great happiness and yet those moments too where anxiety, fear, and uncertainly have crept into your lives. This is a time of great joy and great joy it shall be. For you prepare for the season of hope ….. the season of joy …. the birth of the Savior. Children, and yes, you are still children……….come as you always do ……..carrying your burdens, carrying your joys. For all things are used for the greater glory of God.

For you are here. Does that not tell you …….. you have made the effort, you have heard the voice of God calling you. Come, be refreshed ………. find that moment of peace to sustain you through the days ahead. So many things will be placed upon your path. But you my children are being prepared moment by moment to comprehend …. to discern what is of God and what the evil one wishes to place there ….. to distract you and disrupt your peace. But, My Children, he cannot disrupt peace…… for peace is truth. God is truth. His word is truth and when you claim his word, you claim truth and the falseness of the enemy disappears into the depths of nothingness. For you are claimed as precious ones with a mighty mission …… a mighty mission of love and forgiveness."

"My Children,

I have called each of you to a ministry of love………..a ministry which God has precisely chosen for each of you in preparation for this ministry. For this great calling of God. There is a preparation, a basin so to speak. When one would toil the fields and work in their homes and their offices they come home to refresh their bodies ….. to wipe away all the dust and the grime………..to refresh and so too ………… must you as you prepare these ministries. Wash in the precious blood of Jesus. The door is open. It is filled with refreshment……… with consolation and with peace and forgiveness. All you must do is enter …for Jesus awaits you. Jesus awaits to refresh and purify and cleanse you that you may be worthy vessels prepared for the mission each has been assigned. Do not neglect coming to him in

277

such a way. For here your body, mind and soul is refreshed strengthened and filled with the peace of Almighty God. You leave armed with the love of Jesus. You leave armed with His promise of forgiveness. Now you are ready ... now you are ready to love and forgive. For the task awaits you... .a difficult task. But one for which you will be prepared, molded, reshaped and formed into that perfect specimen which God has called you to be. You are his faithful warriors. Rejoice now .... leave the pain the sufferings and the trials of these past few days .... the weakness ... the temptations... for God calls. You have your choice . Do you say yes .... or do you reject His voice when He peaks your name?"

December 13, 2002

"My Daughter,

Why is it that you come to weep upon my shoulder at a time of such joy? All these moments of visitations when I have explained the joy of suffering. Have you not heard...........or better still have you not comprehended? Life will bring many challenges............ many disappointments? But out of such will come joy. For these are allowed by God and are to be offered by you as precious gifts to Him. Are you still in sorrow? I know ..... I know My child the pain in your heart this night. But we will go hand in hand and I shall show you how joy comes from sorrow."

"Is it cold My daughter?"

(Pat) "No Mother ...... I feel the warmth of your love. It is not cold ...... it is bright ...... the stars shine so brightly" "Look about you." *"I see many people rushing here and there all trying to accomplish something. It seems as they should be so happy and yet ...... they are anxious ... they are impatient. What have I missed ...... what do you wish me to see?"*

(Mary) "This my child is a time of joy and preparation .... for soon My Son shall come and all these people ... these precious souls you see are in a hurry. But they are in a hurry for the wrong reason. They overlook the great gift that is not purchased but is given freely. Joy is in the heart ..... not in the pocket where change and money are kept. Joy comes from one heart to the other and this My child is where the pillars of strength must stand. The pillars of love and forgiveness and understanding. For all who follow My Son and anxiously await His arrival are such pillars. Spread the joy of Christ amongst all of your brothers and sisters and yes, even in your deepest sorrow you will find the joy. For He comes to take the pain .... to take the sorrow .... to mix them into a beautiful fragrance that transforms into a holiness of love .... love for one another. Rest with me now and I will ease the pain that you feel."

(Pat) "I wish to be a pillar but I'm not. I am weak and can support nothing."

(Mary) "Yes you are weak My daughter, but you shall grow strong as each of

278

these ... My precious children shall grow strong, in love, in truth, in faithfulness to almighty God". *(tongues)*

Place the table as you have always done beside my statue with those items you wish for me to bless and I shall come the Friday before Christmas. During the Memorare, I shall extend My blessing upon all those things upon the table and those which surround it. I ask in return that you once again honor My Son and place the basket for his gifts within the chapel in a place of prominence .... for all to offer their gift to Him who shall soon come into this world. Take the gifts to him on Christmas morning .... sing to Him a song of thanksgiving. More shall come and greet Him as He shall smile upon you and bless the hearts of His precious children."

December 21, 2002

(Visual) "There are thousands of angels ... ... like a wind chime. I can hear their wings. They are getting ready. Mother's coming ...... Mother ...... blue lighting!"

I see an older man, very tired. I can't tell what's in one hand. It looks like His left hand is carrying a small satchel. His right hand ... He's holding on to a little burro or donkey. I don't know the difference and there is ...... looks like a child, a beautiful child. But She's so majestically holy ...... silent ...... obviously in prayer. They are going down a narrow street, passing poor areas. It looks like towards the end of this street or road ...... a cave that has an opening and Joseph ...... I'm sure it's Joseph, He stops. He drops the reigns of the donkey and he takes a lantern which he's brought with him, bends down and enters this cave like area. Doesn't look like a grotto ...... doesn't look like a manger scene and it's very damp and it's cold ...... but it's empty ... except for a big cow with horns ... an oxen. No one moves ...... the animal doesn't move ... just looks and continues sleeping.

Joseph helps Mary down from the donkey and leads her into this cave like area ...... very little protection from the weather. It's cold now and the dampness makes it even colder and I can feel it in my bones ... it's cold and unpleasant. But Joseph finds some straw. There's two piles, one higher than the other. He takes the one down and spreads it on the ground for a place to make Mary comfortable. He starts a fire and is so patient. He tries to make it dry and warm ...... for Jesus is soon to be born ... and we see the lines on his forehead and the anxiety of a newborn father who is not prepared. He has very little to work with, but what he has he makes excellent use of. He takes a lantern in (his hand) and places it onto something which looks like a tree. Maybe a tree in the cave area and he hangs it on one of the little knots ... not quite a branch ... to give light.

The fire is now warming the area somewhat and He's asked Mary to please lie down and rest. She is so calm and so beautiful. She has a dark blue dress ... but Joseph has taken (I can't tell if it's white or cream) a mantle which she had about her...... kneels and uses it as a cover to help warm her as she lies down. She

279

*smiles at Joseph and says it will be all right Joseph. God will look after us ......
this is His Son ...... be at peace. She lies down to rest. Joseph goes down to the far
end and he's very cold as you can see him shiver ...... but he wants to be sure
she's warm. She's going to give birth.*

*Everything is becoming very blue ......very, very blue. Mary is now on her knees
and she's praying. Her lips barely move but you know she's praying and the
darkness of her gown or robe becomes lighter and lighter and there's so much
blue ...... the most beautiful blue. Everything is immersed in this blue light. I can't
look anymore ... too bright ...... Oh Mother!."*

"I am here, my children and I thank you for this simple trust. The faith which you
brought with you .... for here before me are those articles which I shall bless. I
asked you to bring those things that you personally wished me to bless. It was for
a two fold reason that I asked you to come. For I too wish to bless each of you
...... to touch your heart. As you recall .... I said this would be a very special
advent. It was your interpretation of "special" which you did not comprehend. I
gave you an opportunity to bear many trials .... many pains ....many
sufferings as well as moments of joy. For you are true disciples and true disciples
find joy in their pain and in their suffering.

Children ...be still and listen ......hear the sound of the angels as they gather
about you as I reach forward to touch each precious heart. Do you not feel My
presence? Beloved ones you bring joy to my heart for you serve My Son with
much love and devotion. I have come as I foretold ...... I have fulfilled my
promise. Now you must fulfill yours...............by bringing the gifts to my Son and
place them in the basket in the Chapel which shall be placed in an area of honor
for My Son. I wish only gifts from the heart for these are treasured so highly by
My Son. We shall take them Christmas morning and sing songs of praise and
glory as we present them to him...........the Savior to be born on Christmas day."

December 27, 2002

*(The following year-end message was received during the Friday night Canyon
Rosary and has been transcribed from the audio recorder used to record the
message. As often happens, many present felt the power of the Holy Spirit and it
was another beautiful evening. Please discern as you read the following.)*

"My dear child,

You have heard these words spoken many times in the silence of your heart. But
now it is time to reveal how God loves and chooses His precious children to be
witnesses of His holy word .... witnesses of truth. Many of you go through the
years carrying such heavy burdens........ carrying memories that you cannot forget
.... memories best left on their own ....that God in His great wisdom will
heal and restore the brokenness of the hearts. This is the time for a new beginning,

a time to reflect back through the years and find that special moment ....that special time of joy .... and praise God that you were allowed such a opportunity .... such a grace filled moment............a treasure to keep forever. For memories of joy are indeed treasures and these you shall store and recall from time to time when moments become more difficult in life. You will remember.......... . and the smile will once again come upon your lips and your eyes will light with the fire of love............for God loves you and sends these treasures your way that you may save them......... .savor them and recall them at the proper moment.

Yes, a time of new beginning........... a new strategy. What do you wish to change in your lives ....to draw you closer to Almighty God? What can you do in a simple humble way to bring joy into the heart of another? That is what God asks of you. Always my children, look beyond the exterior for the interior beauty of each of Gods creatures. Search diligently until you find the treasures .... and then rejoice with one another for what was lost has now been found.

I bless you and I encourage you to persevere as you reflect upon My messages of the past. Read them My children for there is much wisdom .....simple guidance ..... simple facts of love and truth. May your year be filled with joy and courage .... that you shall love My Son beyond all measure .... that you shall see Him everywhere you look and praise and glorify His Holy Name. Praise the Name of Jesus .... My precious, precious children."

✶✶✶✶✶✶✶✶✶✶✶✶✶✶✶✶✶✶

Messages from Jesus and Mary

January 3rd, 2003 - December , 2003

January 3rd, 2003 Published 2-2-03

(The following message was received during the Friday night Canyon Rosary at Mary's Knoll and has been transcribed from the audio recording. We have discerned to share this particular message which appears somewhat childish as it revolves around a flashback vision Pat is given. The time frame was around 1955 describing a beautiful <u>memory</u> of Pat fishing with her father on the Potomac River. This Christmas week 2002 Pat was in great sorrow because of the loss of her father. Note how Our Blessed Mother ties in the elementary scene of Pat fishing with her father to present times and requesting <u>all of us</u> becoming <u>fishers of men.</u>)

(Recipient) "As you place the sorrow with joy ...... with simplistic joy, I no longer grieve for Thou art always with me ....and the beautiful sound of the water beneath the bridge .... not really a bridge. It looks like little logs tossed across the creek. I hear the water as it runs over the stones. What a gentle sound ... soft ...... soothing and the light of the day beginning to come through the trees. How beautiful, how simple. Yes ...... [tongues] I will go with you. I beg to go with you Mother ...... such a smile upon on your face .... a face lit by so many lights. You are like a rainbow of lights, and you hold out your hand. Please slip my hand in yours [sigh] for these days have been so difficult. But now there is joy ...... there is peace at last. We walk across this long bridge listening to the water and to the birds singing into the light as it shines about us. We are in a peaceful setting. Yes..... there is a log, not majestic for a queen ...... but still She sits upon the log and beckons me to come to Her ...... want to hear Her words. I want to hear what Mother says. It becomes quiet now."

"My Precious Child,

What are memories but steps through life? Steps taken slowly at first as you learn ..... as you are taught ..... as you begin to comprehend you reflect back now upon these memories. The steps you took with the one loved .... the steps through the trees .... and what it is My Child that you carry upon your shoulder?" *(Pat)* *"A thin pole".* "And the one beside you?....." *"My Father. (sigh) He carries a pole as well and a metal box ...... a gray box with a handle and we walk together. We are walking through the trees and there is a familiar smell ... an aroma that's hard to describe ......but it's the water. We're going fishing! The tide is coming in and "He" (my father) is finding a place for us to fish ... and he's getting my line ready and the little reel that I have and the hook at the end and a little round plastic thing (a bobber ... up a bit from the hook. He places*

*everything just right for me and then he reaches into this can and takes out a
little worm and places it on the hook! I never could do that, but it was still fun wasn't
it, Mother, it was a step ...... it was a memory. And he got his reel ready and he
helped me put the rod back over my shoulder ......and held on really tightly
and then let go ... holding on the string, along into the water and the little round
ball floated on top ... and ... My dad laughed! And I was so happy and he threw
out his line and we sat quietly. So quietly listening ... to what Mother? <u>Listening
to memories.</u> Memories have sounds. I never knew memories had sounds ......
but I hear the water and I look upon my fathers face as together we sit ......
together we share this precious time. Has it been that many years ago? But today
it is as through it just happened ...... for there is joy in my heart ...... there is no
longer the sorrow. For I know that my father is with my Lord and he has the most
beautiful pole and he is there fishing and waiting ......and waiting for me. Oh,
Mother, how beautiful is life even in sorrow. The beauty that comes
......childlike at first ......baby steps and as we grow older the memories become
more vivid ... more distinct ... for we learn to walk. Help us Mother as we walk
this path of memories ... to walk to your Son. For it is He who awaits us smiling
joyfully at His precious children ...all of us with our steps of memories."*

"My Daughter,

Sit with Me awhile longer <u>for My Son calls all of His children to be fishers of men</u>
.....fishers of souls. What a beautiful memory you have retained ....that of a
fisherman. Only then you did not know .... you would become a fisher of men
...........a fisher of souls of Almighty God! Rest as I bless you and all My children."

January 10th , 2003

(Recipient) *"Help me to see. What is it you wish me to see and see correctly and
describe the details and the beauty? There appears to be a most beautiful
tabernacle suspended in the heavens. All in lights of gold and white and the door
...... a door...... but the door is closed. Help me mother that I might understand.
Multitudes and multitudes of Angels surround the tabernacle that is so brilliant
that I can barely look. Oh my Jesus..."*

"My Dear Children,

You asked for wisdom that you might understand that God would counsel you and
draw you into His heart, where you would learn of the beauty that dwells in each
and every heart. For each of us is indeed a Tabernacle where Christ the Lord
dwells. The Tabernacles of many hearts have been closed ... .for they have lost the
faith .....they have lost the power of spiritual communion with My Son."

"Dear precious children,

These times are so great that you must learn............ you must take advantage of every opportunity God gives you ....the tabernacle of your heart. Receive My Son......... for He may dwell with you forever and as you attend Holy Mass .... that tabernacle of your heart opens to receive Jesus the Savior......... . who wishes to do all in his power to bring peace into the lives of each of His children. When Christ dwells with you and within you there is His peace ....there is His Strength. There is perseverance to continue when life becomes so difficult. For He sees the hearts that fling open the door to receive Him and those that remain closed. Pray My children for your world is in need of much prayer. For God must truly reign in the hearts of each and everyone of His children. For love must flow .... the love of God must become so brilliant in each heart that all will know that Christ lives and dwells within you.

You ask so many questions. (*tongues*) It is not just you My Child who feels the emptiness .... the loneness .....the uncertainties of life. But many throughout the world that struggle to do the will of God and remain at peace in doing just that ....trusting in His mercy. For it is only in trusting in the mercy of God that peace is restored to your soul ....that the light of love burns brightly within you. For there is no longer fear, but only joy. Do you trust your parents.........do you come to them with your problems? Yes many do ....but there are those who are frightened to reveal the simple things of life which have led them astray and therefore they neglect the wise counsel of their parents.

God calls you His children. He calls you out of love and out of this, love and obedience. Come to Him .....share all with Him. Let Him love you, forgive you and embrace you .... for all eternity. Again My children it is your choice. Is the door of the tabernacle of your heart open and ready to welcome My Son?"

Note: Message of January 17th, 2003 will not be published.

January 23, 2003

(The following message was received Thursday evening prior to retiring for the evening. It was verbally dictated thus there is no audio of this particular message. It was initially thought this was a private message; however after viewing a video of Matthew Kelly on Friday afternoon, it was discerned Our Lady intended for this to be Her message to us for the week. It was not totally surprising as ill health continues to try and discourage us from "pursuing souls for God"; however, it only intensifies our efforts as His grace sustains us.)

My dear children,

Open your hearts to receive God's graces of love, strength and perseverance. For you must be bound to the Will of the Father to walk with wisdom and discernment in these times of spiritual disruption and confusion. Here lies the confusion which separates you from "spiritual reality" and "human skepticism".

The Father calls you to Divine Love . The building blocks formed by trust in His mercy and the awareness of His justice as dispersed throughout time. This momentous time of mercy is God's precious gift to mankind, but it is sadly being suppressed by weakened trust .... a virus of uncertainty .... attacking a world driven by selfish ambition and success.

My precious ones, the path ahead is lined with grace filled opportunities of love and suffering ...... simply for love itself. Each new day of life is not only a precious gift of love, but one of glorious sacrifices for souls. Pray, My children, for loving perseverance for souls. Bind each suffering and sacrifice to the Passion of Christ and feel the exaltation of true love for souls for the Kingdom of God."

January 31st , 2003

(VISUAL) "It's getting very bright with millions of tiny colors of lights ..... and within these lights I see a most beautiful lady ... a lady who comes to gather us tonight for a simple journey. For she feels the pain ... the suffering ... the anxieties that are oppressing Her children. She smiles just slightly and Her heart ... Her heart is actually pulsating ever so slightly. She reaches out Her hands and invites us to take a very simple journey with Her this night. The lights are so beautiful and so bright and it's difficult to describe. There appears to be a bench and we're all gathered around this bench and there's a sound of running water trickling ...... but constant ..... and the birds are in the trees singing. And there is an aroma ...and the aroma is so delicate. It's not roses. I am not familiar with it ... the aroma is just ... so calming ... so peaceful. I see as the water has run through the brook the stones have been smoothed in some ways ...... to signify something my Mother, I know."

"My Child,

The water is love .... the stones are the souls of Gods children being prepared through love and the gentleness of His mercy. But we must stand and walk a little further down this brook. What is it My child?"

"It looks like someone has tried to built a dam. There are just a few openings where some water gets through ......where the rocks are smooth. But the other rocks are jagged ... not... not conducive you would think to be smoothed by such a gentle stream. Then the lights change and there is a brilliant blue ...... a sapphire blue and it all sparkles and the water takes on a faster current ... and it washes harshly against these rocks and gradually ...... gradually through the force of the water they begin to crumble and find the place where they will rest and be smoothed by love."

"Often times My children you lose the meaning of love within your busy lives.

285

You become so involved with ever day happenings and circumstances that the gentleness of love does not penetrate the soul ......but God perseveres. He is persistent .....for you are His children and He will in His love knock down the barriers of stone that you have placed around your hearts ..... and He will melt them into that pool of love of which we often speak. For there must be love ..... there must be unity ....and this can only be accomplished through prayer and obedience to the will of God. So simple is it not My child?"

"It's beautiful for all the shining souls ... the smooth souls ... the stones that are so smooth ... they glitter... they glitter for they know what love is They found love ... they found the peace of Our Lord Jesus."

"And what would you say of the others?"

"I'm not certain Mother. But I would say ......with God they don't stand a chance. He loves all of us so intensely that in His pursuit He will win the hearts of all of His children. There's a change in the air now. Mother summons us to draw close to Her......"

"My Children,

If you are to continue in a ministry of Christ Jesus ... you must be transformed into love. You must ask Our Lord to open wide the eyes of your heart that you may see the suffering soul beneath the jagged rock ..... and then My child ..... through His mercy and charitable love you shall pray with greater fervor. For no soul must be lost .... each has the responsibility to love .... to forgive and to journey on. God awaits ....hear, listen to the gentleness of the spring .... as it washes the love upon the souls of God's children."

"Mother, but one or two stones still are remaining. I think I can reach them. I think I can help them down so that the water of love will flow over them ..."

"Daughter .... It is in these times when you try to interfere with Gods plan .... (tongues) .... for you do not think as God thinks .... so rest in knowing that He is always in control. You are but to love .... to love ..... and continue to love."

February 7th, 2003

"My Dear Children,

I come this night to restore your courage and strengthen your trust in Jesus. Look at your world ....how many attempts have been made to touch the hearts ...the open souls .....the laborers in the field of God's harvest? Dear sweet children

286

you need not <u>worry</u> ...you need not fear ....for these are not of God and as you have opened your heart to Jesus you have received His strength and His courage to bear the banner. The banner ....the lamb .....shall go before you into this battle for souls.

Many ask ... where is my peace? Wherever I turn there is nothing but destruction. Nothing but negative thoughts words and deeds. But I tell you ......your peace ..... the peace of Jesus is your protection. For when Christ really reigns in your heart ......when it is not just mere words uttered from your mouth .....but a true conversion .....where the peace of Christ reigns ....then nothing will disturb your peace. God loves you. He has sent Me to tell you of such love through all these years. But many ears have been blocked and hearts have been closed. But now ..... now as My Son too joins me .....hearts will be opened .....ears will hear, for ears will hear the truth and that truth will set you free. You do not escape the trials and tribulations of life .....nor temptations .....but by prayer and trust in the Mercy of God ....you learn gradually to overcome such weakness and to become strong vital soldiers ....in the battle for souls.

My Children .....when you are insulted ....when you are put down......... when you are made to feel so insignificant ...remember God's words to look deeply within the soul that confronts you and find that particle .... that love which is of God and focus on that .....which belongs to God and you will find courage. You will find the peace to love as God loves. Your world stands upon a precipice and it is only through much devout prayer ....will destructive circumstances be avoided. But rest assured My Children .... precious children of God.......... that you are His .....and His love shall overcome all ....for life itself is but temporal. It is the soul .....fill your soul with the love of Christ ....with the love of brothers and sisters. Go beyond the necessary .....far beyond until it literally hurts to love. For then you know you have reached a great, great gift of God. You have truly learned to love ....when love seemed impossible.

(*Tongues*) My words are now heard throughout the world. Reflect upon them. Reflect with joy ....pray for discernment that you will find the true meaning that God intends for each and every soul. You are truly blessed ... . for We are here ....always with you .... always to comfort you and to strengthen you. <u>But you must find time for us</u> ... <u>you must find time for Jesus</u>. He awaits you every moment of every day ....find time and you will find the strength you need to persevere in this journey of life. Rest in peace ...for I place My mantle over each of you. Precious children ..... rest in peace .... rest."

287

(Recipient) *"Sweet Holy Mother ...... what has Thou to say to us this night?"*

"What do you see within My Children ... .what do you see buried deeply within their hearts? Daughter ... the gifts you have been given .... the pain that you carry .....the pain that you carried through joy of loving and embracing each of God's children. Your heart touches the minute pain of each and every soul ...and I come to you this night that we together shall comfort each other."

"Mother I am so unprepared. When I pray, I pray in parables and tongues and nothing seems to make sense and yet everything makes sense. It's the beautiful words that flow and I know they praise Almighty God for everything that He has given us. For the friends ... for the trials ... for the perseverance ... the ability to call His name. To say Jesus ... I need You Jesus. How else am I to survive without Thee?"

"Little daughter.........you have chosen well. For it is Jesus who brings the healings to the many wounds that are gathered here this night. Some things so simple .... others cut deeply with the wounds of sorrow. How My Daughter do we heal these wounds?"

"We pray and ask Jesus ......we're His children ...His family ......we pray together. We love Him ...we search for Him .....and even though at times He hides from us ...and we have to look so ... so diligently to find Him ...and our lives and prayers become so dry that we no longer wish to pray. But we know that He is there and He is only testing us [sigh] always there loving us ...always encouraging us. So we pray ...... is that right Mother?"

"Prayer My Child is the instrument of God.......... used to heal the hurting world. Each of you must encourage one another when times are difficult. For God's love is so great .....and He strengthens each of you with just enough ....just enough love ....just enough tenderness to touch the most hardened heart. Talk to Him ...ask Him what He would have you do. This is a time of intimacy between you and your Father. Do not be afraid to come to Him. Look how much He loves you and awaits your presence ....awaits your conversation. How dearly He loves you .... and how His heart aches when that love is not returned."

"We shall help Mother ... we shall pray more ... we shall become a family connected to the love of God. We shall pray daily for one another. Daily for Our Dear Holy Father as He leads His Church through a time of great turmoil. But yet shall come a great rebirth and a great time of joy. So fear we do not. Persevere we shall. Is there anything else Mother?"

"Love My child ....never forget to do everything out of love. Love heals..... though everything may disappear .....love shall remain. For God is love and you are His Children .....chosen .....named and called into His service. Come with a joyful heart ....and the pain that you carry will slowly dissipate ....and you will find the peace ...the peace you must bring to a world that hurts so deeply. Pray My Daughter."

(Extensive tongues) "We come before thee Lord ...You are precious, Lord. We bow before thee and ask of Jesus ...for that grace to preserve. The grace to be vessels of Your love ...void totally of ourselves ...and filled completely with You and Your love."

"Well done My Child .... well done."

(Visual) "Beautiful butterflies ...... Do you hear their wings? They alight on each one's shoulder. The whole room turns blue. Pale blue with glistening lights. For the Holy Spirit is amongst us. He desires to bring His healing power amongst us. Let us be open to His will. Let us listen carefully to His voice. They [butterflies] flitter around Our Blessed Mother. She watches them and smiles as She sees the others land upon Her precious children. They're so unaware of the grace they have been given this night. A gift ... a gift from Our Lord and Our Blessed Mother."

February 21st, 2003

(The following message was transcribed by a member of the prayer team during the Friday Night Canyon Rosary at Mary's Knoll as the audio recorder failed to function. Therefore, we have eliminated quotation marks indicating the transcription is as accurate as possible concerning recording circumstances of the message. There were many events during this particular message that lends towards its authenticity.)

Visual: The large book ...with dots upon the pages ...and large pens are being taken. Almost as though being placed in invisible hands. Each pen begins to connect the dots ...like a children's book connect and make a picture. There's a multitude of them. It's like a high book (hundreds of feet high) ......in a binder. That each page is carefully removed and the pen connects one dot to another until all the dots are connected and now makes ... (visual pause) ....There are faces! The pen has connected the dots and formed the faces of all the souls. Please help me, Mother, I don't understand the meaning.

My Dear Children. The pen is the hand of God. The ink .....the grace He places upon each precious soul. The dots which have been connected are all the trials and tribulations which each soul has endured .... held together by their faith an trust in God in His love and mercy.

*(Recipient) He signs each page like a golden gossamer (glistening web)......
difficult to describe ......a signature visible...yet lights penetrate each page.
Each soul is gathered and very carefully ... tenderly, placed into the "Book of
Life.*

Blessed are you My children, who have found courage to endure the trials and
obstacles placed in your path. Blessed are you whose faith remains strong ....
allowing God's grace to sustain you with courage and His love. Each little dot,
my children, has been placed by God to allow your souls to be formed into the
blessed child, which He created. Rejoice! ....for God allows you to see that
you are His beloved child.

*(Recipient) The book lies on an altar. No, it's on a stand ... (I'd call it like a
lectern stand at Church) It's placed there next to God and He glances at this,
His creation.*

And as He has created you ... and drawn the dots of grace to form you into His
child, you must be strong and loving.........for God asks of you in this time when
storm clouds gather, to let the lights of the precious dots glimmer ....that others,
too, may find the courage to trust in the hand of Almighty God."

February 28th, 2003

*(Recipient) "What would thou have me say this night. This night has great
expectations ......of great joy..."*

"My Daughter,

These words you shall tell My children. It is My Son ....The Lord Jesus himself
who tonight stands amongst you. He brings with Him those graces that each heart
requires. The graces of strength and perseverance for the trials that lie ahead for
each and every one of His precious children. He has been observing each heart as
have I. ....each heart that wanders, each heart that says I will believe. I will open the
doors of this My Precious Heart and allow My Lord to enter. Beware as you invite
Jesus into your lives ....for they shall never be the same." (*Tongues*) ......

"Yes My Child,

Once committed ...truly committed to following Jesus is a life long journey .....a
journey of disappointments .... but a journey of great joy with unmentionable
rewards awaiting .... awaiting that final moment when each child shall come
before Him. Think carefully what you do with every moment of your lives. Take
each moment ..... make each moment a day ....each day a week and see the
changes in your lives and those that your lives have touched."

"Precious Children,

So much to learn .... yet you have done so well .....for you have surrendered and come before Jesus........receptive to truth ..... to the word of God."

"Mother. Thou know'est these times are most difficult when one would rather run than face the task at hand. I have been so guilty. But I know My Jesus awaits me still with his arms spread wide. To welcome me and all those like me who have failed ... but yet trust ... trust in the mercy of Our Lord. So here I am ...standing before My Lord. I am empty My Jesus. I am empty now. I am ready. I stand with all those who are empty of everything that is of themselves ... and come to that fountain ... to the fountain of your mercy ...and asked to be filled. Filled Lord Jesus with everything that is of You. My Lord ......the air is so different. It is though we stand in clouds of brilliant light ......surrounded by melodious hymns ......chimes. As you gaze around us Our hearts are filled with joy" ... *(tongues)*

"Yes My Daughter,

My Son receives each of His children .... and each of those who come desiring to be filled with His grace shall be filled to overflowing. For His love is great and His mercy is un-ending. Pray.....pray that all souls will find Jesus ......and run into His arms seeking His mercy and forgiveness."

March 7th, 2003

"My Child, what does thou say this night?"

(Recipient)......... *"Mother...... I've had so little time to prepare .....to fully understand what you have been revealing to me. So I submit myself totally to your care."*

"Will you come with me My child?"

"Of course Mother,

There's a beautiful scene of many hills ... little valleys and a town ... a village in the distance and all in lights. It's a figure of a man. He walks very slowly ...... deliberately with great grace. He looks upon the town below but His eyes quickly turn upwards. The sky now filled with stars. Seems to take on a meaning of such depth that I can barely express in words. (yes) As Jesus raises His eyes towards the heavens ... a huge cup ... chalice, as we would call it. It forms and the stars take many colors to distinguish the cup separately from the darkness surrounding it. The cup though huge, now comes down into the raised hand of Jesus. He stands prayerfully holding this cup and looking up, praying. I only hear "Father". He's going to turn. Mother, hold My hand. He's going to turn! The cup ... no hands holding it comes toward me and I'm told to look and to drink. I take the cup ......

291

press it to my lips and what seems sweet is bitter. I want to reject it. I want to reject it . No more ... it's bitter. But now there's much peace. The cup returns to the hand of Jesus and in an instant is back high in the sky ... so large. I need you Mother ...... help explain ..."

"The cup My child is the cup from which each must drink .....it is the cup from which My Son first drank. The bitterness .....the taste of sin. For all are filled with sin. But by My Son drinking this cup the bitterness turns to sweetness ...... a sweetness of absolution for you and all of His children who willingly walk this Lenten journey ......bearing your cross as each trial comes uniting itself to your particular cross. They are but petals from the roses ......graces sent by Jesus to strengthen you and to allow your sufferings to reach and touch suffering souls throughout the world. For this is a journey for souls ......and now is a time of great power .....of great significance. For all your efforts, your sacrifices will be united with those of My Son."

(Tongues) *"Father"* ......

(Mary) "My child,

I shall not be with you this Lenten season as I have been .....but you will receive the strength .... as you will carry many crosses. Do so out of love ......o u t of gratitude and the souls for whom you pray will rejoice one day with you as you come before My Son. Do not despair ......but accept what comes with joy. Jesus will not leave you .....nor will I . But the cup shall pass amongst you and each must choose to drink ......or not. It is your choice. Will you let this opportunity to aid in the salvation of souls pass you by ......or will you gratefully hold out your hand and grasp the cup to drink your portion?"

March 14th, 2003

Again this year as we journey into Lent we are blessed with a renewed graphic journey following The Passion of Jesus Christ.

(Jesus) "My Children,

What are earthly possessions .....but just that. Possessions that shall turn to dust ......leaving the true teeth into which we shall enjoy the meal of truth. Truth and love shall prevail, dust shall scatter ....but love and truth shall remain forever.

I have questions for you this night. Questions that each must discern in their own hearts. As I speak ...... I will listen to the response from your heart. What do you say when you see your Savior . . ..about to be sacrificed for you and for all sinners?

What do you say Little Children of Mine? Are you the seed that will be planted as I too will be planted .....and shall you .... as Children of God bring forth the shoots of new life ....new hope .....new thanksgiving to Almighty God .....or are you the children that have been lulled asleep and missed the opportunity to receive the graces that God has showered upon you ......because you have been obsessed with the love of self and of possessions. Think my children .....think of the souls in need of Harvesting. Think as you grow ....as the seed within your souls grows and matures .....and is filled with the love and the life of God. Think of those souls. Love them, caress them .....bring them to the Table of Plenty where God Himself shall shower them with His Divine Love ....and once showered with Divine Love .....there is no other path ....there is only the path to love and to forgive.

Children you must journey with Me this Lenten season ......for I shall take you places where you have not been. I shall show you things you have not seen. Look into the depths of your heart. See a garden surrounded by small trees .... see the stars in the skies and see Me on My knees asking My Father if this is His will. For Thy will be done Father ... not as I would have it ...... but as You, My Father commanded.

Are you ready .....to hear the whispers of love ......which God gives to each of you ...and are you willing with a joyful heart .....to sprout forth the joy and the compassion for your brothers and sisters? Do you think that it was easy for Me as I came into the garden ......knowing My Disciples would sleep ......and yet there was work to be done................salvation depended upon it. My Father sent Me .....so I was to fulfill His purpose." (*Tongues*)

"When you contemplate My prayerful time with My Father .... when I asked in silent prayer to be spared this cup and yet I knew that My Father's will must be obeyed ..... could you not see the turmoil ..... the meticulous beatings of My body ..... in which flesh was torn ..... and yet there was a purpose. My children, your flesh is not torn as mine ...but your crosses are heavy .....and I ask you to walk with Me .....and we will carry our crosses together to Almighty God. Let us give Him thanks and praise for the love He has for each of us. We are all called ..... it is how we respond that makes the difference. Be filled with the patient understanding joy that God pours forth upon you during this time. Pray My children. Pray for courage ....pray for understanding .....but above all pray for love. For as I said .....all will pass away ...but love. Divine Love will remain forever .....and I bless each and every one of you ....in the name of The Father and The Son and The Holy Spirit."

(Visual by recipient): I was allowed to see Jesus take a piece of His clothing and wipe the blood that had emitted from His body. Jesus then took the cloth and placed it beneath the rock out of sight. He knew what lay before Him and He wished to cause no further consternation to His beloved disciples. Jesus then acknowledged Himself to His pursuers as the One they were seeking.

March 21st, 2003

(Angel greeting) "Children of God,

Rejoice and prepare thyself ....for The Almighty stands in your presence. Hear His words ....open your hearts ..... receive Him."

(Jesus) "My child,

It is what I wish you to see this night ....the journey that you shall take and those that follow. Look deeply within My eyes that you may see My pain and see My joy .... for I come for each of My Children."

(Visual by recipient) I see My Lord as I do not remember seeing Him before ......tall ...regal. Yet He is gray ...almost a mask of pain and suffering ......and He flees into the open arms of His Mother with the embrace and praise where their hearts are united ...beating in unison ...in unison for souls. Each looks at each other ...there are no spoken words   but each one knows that they shall part now. For He has a mission ... a mission to complete. I see the sorrow in the Mothers face that understands the pain of their child ...and yet knows She must let go. For His mission is also Her mission. For no matter where either may be ......their hearts are always joined ...always united. He steps back ... She trembles. He places His hands on Her upper arms ...cups Her lowered head in His hands ......raises Her face to meet His eyes once again. For they know what must come. He begins to walk away ...turns once more with a reassuring glance of love ...of complete understanding and then hurriedly begins His journey down this path away from this house ...away from this heart that clings so tightly to His.

My Lord I know not why you have placed me here ...what is it that I am to do? You ask me to be a mother ...... a mother to many ......and I wish to place my arms around this Holy Mother and dry Her tears and ease Her suffering ...and yet I am so unworthy. But She regains Her composure, sadly but regally.

I hear myself whispering. I must run now Mother... I must run. I must catch up with him because he can't be alone ... we can't leave Him alone. I beg Thy permission to stay with Him ...... to go with Him every step He takes ... to bear His pain ... the sorrow that He feels... and I'm running and I'm running ...... and I reach the garden ... and it's too late. They are gathered around Him (He is already bound with ropes and chains). Ropes and chains around Divine love? I don't understand Mother, for ropes and chains are but straw compared to the strength of Love. Only straw binds Thy mighty love. But You choose to be bound ... to be dragged literally. You can barely walk. They have bound you so tightly and they forced you to go through these bushes ... and the limbs swipe against and

scratch your face. Even little pieces of hair cling ... and they harshly treat you. Their words I cannot repeat. For I am there My Jesus ... little as I am ... the dust that I am. To make reparation for all those sins that have been committed against

Thee ... and for which Thou shall endure much.

There's a stream. I don't know how He is going to cross the stream when He can't even walk . ..... and they drag Him ... they drag Him and His head goes into the water and it strikes a stone and blood comes on the stone. But they don't care ... and they lift Him up. They lift Him up only because they know only more horror is in store for Him. This One who claims to be the Son of God. This meek ... humble ... loving soul that now stands covered with mud ... with filth ... . covered with our sins. I want to run to Him and I want to run. What have I got? I have nothing. I want to wipe Him off and clean Him and make Him beautiful as He is ... and yet I can't ... there is nothing. But I will praise My Lord and I will join my heart with yours and beg Thee never to be separated from Thee. Allow me, Lord, to take the abuse... to take the insults ...... to take the offenses in reparation for all that has been committed against Thee. And He stands there and with the most loving look I see in His eyes ... and He whispers to me" "Love, My child, love them, forgive them and if you love and if you forgive .....we shall complete this journey together. You know what comes. My child, I love you."

March 28th , 2003

(The following message was received during the Friday night Canyon Rosary at Mary's Knoll and has been transcribed from the audio recording. The realistic [by body movement from the recipient] visual given in this message continues to follow the Passion of Christ as indicated by Jesus in the messages of 3-14; and 3-21, 03. We urge you to pray to the Holy Spirit for discernment as you read the following.)

"My Child,

Tonight we again continue our Lenten journey. This is a recognized place for you."

[Recipient visualizes a dungeon] "Yes My Lord. But it is one that brings great wounds to my heart."

"But thou must have courage now child .... for you shall find some meaning as we take this journey."

"It is always so dark and dense ... and so difficult to see. It's so dim ... the lights ...... barely enough to see. I have to feel the wall."

"Then feel the wall .... and what do you feel?"

"The stones ... moist ...damp ... but mostly the darkness. I can't see the steps very well ... so I have to cling to the wall."

"And what is different this time my child?" (*Jesus reference a similar dungeon view given last year*)

"This time I will not run .... I will not leave Thee .... I will come to comfort Thee. And each stone that I will touch ...... will remind me of a temptation that Your grace averted. Then I shall count them as precious jewels for souls. But you're no longer beside me."

"But I have not left you."

"I know. It's getting a little brighter. I think my eyes are becoming a little more accustomed to this ...... the dimness of the lights. I can make out what appears to be cells. Even though I see ... the stench has never left. The stench is still the same and I fear I shall be sick. Oh My Lord ... what have they done ... what have they done?"

"Here My Child........."

"I am looking...."

"Further down........ "

"I will not run .... I will come...."

"You have found Me my loved one.........."

"But there's a door ... I cannot see! Just barely ... Oh ... My God ......"

"Look not at the wounds .... but concentrate on the face of love. Do you see your wounds inflicted upon My Body?"

"There are so many ... but I know mine are amongst them ..."

"And does that mean I love thee less? I called you to comfort Me ... to spend a few moments with Me in My agony where I might hear the sweetness of your love."

"My Jesus ...... My Jesus. If I could but kiss each wound ...... to bring thee relief ... to bring thee healing ...... I would do so. But who am I but this frail creature who loves thee ... but yet is incapable."

"It is enough to know that you bring comfort to Me. Because you bring me your heart .....you bring Me your love ......and that alone will sustain Me. It is time for you to leave. For you must gather your strength. For more difficult times are ahead and I need your prayers. I need the love of My simple creatures .... My children who love Me and repent. For they see the stench is not the surrounding areas of filth ....but it is the stench of sin itself which will be cleansed and purified by every drop of My Blood. Bid Me farewell as we gaze into each others eyes .... for we shall meet again My Child."

"I do as Thy say .... But I would stay with Thee and I would comfort Thee."

"Obedience ...."

"Yes ...... I will do as Thy say. It's so difficult to walk back. It's as though I've had some potion to drink that binds me that I cannot feel ...... that I cannot touch and ...... I find the wall ... just enough light to see the steps ......and I struggle up the stairs and I envision You, My Lord, as you must struggle up these stairs with all the wounds. Even Thy poor feet ... to feel every pain ... to feel all that we have brought upon You. But yet there is a great over powering sense of grace. My Lord, I love Thee and I shall do whatever Thou asks. It is not important now that I understand. For surely my poor mind could not. But I wrap Thee in my love ... and I leave Thee. But only for a short while ... until we are joined together. I seem to touch the top step and it is as though I am standing outside on a clear street. No one ... no vehicles ... no carts ... no horses. I am standing there and I lift my head."

"Father ......you are my Father too. Strengthen your Son for He is our only chance to be with You one day in eternity."

April 4th , 2003

(The following message was received during the Friday night Canyon Rosary at Mary's Knoll. The visual given in this message continues to follow the Passion of Christ as indicated by Jesus in the messages of 3-14; 3-21; and 3-28,03. The text style has been contrasted to clarify the conversations.)

(Jesus) "Did I not say My Child .... there would be more difficult times ahead?"

(Recipient) "Yes My Lord ... ...and I have tried to avoid these times. I have tried because You have taken me there before and I was unable to help. I was unable to do anything but bring Thee comfort. And what little comfort it was with this poor soul. But my heart is yours ...and wherever You lead me this night I shall follow. I shall run if You run ahead of me ......and I shall catch up with Thee ....and together ... together this night, we will remain as one."

"What do you see?"

"I see the scene where You left me before ... at a deep dark stench filled dungeon into a starlit sky, but void of any sign of life."

297

"Listen carefully."

"So many voices ... there's so many voices My Jesus ...... but I can't see them. And now you are bound ... bound once again and in Your pain and sorrow You struggle forth. What would Thou have Me do?"

"I would have thee be My faithful servant who loves and forgives. I would have you hear the words that torment My very soul. I would have you see the marks upon My Body. I would have you see the glaring lights of the eyes of My children as they penetrate with hatred and I would have you turn all of this into love."

"My Jesus ......We are heading to Pilate. (sigh) ... No cross, no cross, My Jesus. I should carry the cross. I am the one ...... I am the one. Not Thee O Loving Savior."

"And where are all of My Faithful Ones who followed Me and stayed with Me all these years? Whom I taught and brought to fulfillment in their mission while my life was still meant to be upon this earth? Look do you see them?"

" I see some familiar faces. Mainly women and the little ones. And I see a very frail young man (John) who peers behind a column to catch a glance of Thee. And I see that your eyes meet, but there are no spoken words. Such love ... My Lord, such love. Would Thou teach me how to love in all this adversity ... in all this turmoil ......when I know what's going to happen! How My God do I ...... to love and feel the pain ... and turn the pain to joy?"

"There's a door. I don't know where I am. I knock on the door and there's no answer. But the door slowly opens ... and I see .... I see You My Mother all dressed in very dark blue. Such strength You must have. And the young one (John) ... who hid behind the pillar and followed You, is with You. (Mother) ...and I hear."

"That He (John) must be strong. That he must be forgiving as The One he loves so intensely forgives."

"I hear a conversation ... like questions". "where is He now ......what have they done? Tell me ... tell me truthfully." "He suffers, ... but He is bearing up."

(Mary to John) "My Son, I desire only the truth .....and the full meaning of the truth. For know I have walked this journey with Him .....and felt the pain .....the sorrow and the shame. We must go now ....but first this table."

"There's a table ... a cloth ... cup ... some utensils. She says".

"Take these .....gather them carefully .... put them away. We will hide them here in the shelf and then we will hurry. We must hurry .....we must be quick."

"Everything is done so quickly. The door opens and He leads Her down this path from this little house."

"Oh God ...... (sigh ... sigh) .... He already carries His Cross. This cross which should be mine, He carries. And I search for His face ... and the blood has blurred His vision .. and His hair is mangled ... and His beard is torn. But His eyes ... His eyes are radiant. It is as though He were saying with just the look of His eyes."

"It is almost over … almost complete now. But though My journey here will soon end ....yours will continue. And you must lean to love as I love ..... to forgive as I forgive .... to embrace those that would turn their back on you. Allow them to feel the beat of Our Hearts that say" "I love You." " Do not concern yourself with what shall follow .....for we have been there before. But each time you take this journey you will learn a new lesson .... a new way of life.... a new way to separate yourself from the ways of this world into a world of spiritual life. It is there where you will dwell with Me .... spiritually My Child .... without fear and complete control. For I dwell within you. I am your strength. Trust Me, but do not leave Me. For these journeys are most important."

"He stumbles ... He stumbles. His knees ... His right knee is torn. The bone barely exposed. And His Cross rubs against the rough stones causing more pain, more affliction. I want to run .... I want to run not away ... I want to run to You. I want to run. I want to kiss that cross. I want to help You My Lord. Let me carry my piece ..... my piece of the cross. For I shall follow You wherever You shall go. Just say the word My Lord. For I am but your child who runs after the one she loves."

(After the conclusion of the Rosary the recipient of the message was directly told by Jesus to speak to the group to clarify certain parts of the visual message. The recorded talk transcribes as follows:)

"I can remember that Our Lord was actually taking us through the Passion and not only allowing us to see the horror of what was happening, but to learn, to learn a lesson somewhere in that particular episode of what He was talking about. Tonight what struck me, when we had come out of the dungeon area and we were on the street, just Jesus and myself and He said" "Listen what do you hear" *"you hear all of these voices and the sad thing is these voices were calling out all kinds of blasphemies, all kinds of terrible things. They weren't singing Hosannas in the Highest, they were calling Him terrible, terrible names. These were people Our Lord loves, healed, embraced and in an instant of time, it seemed as so every evil had been released, to come into the hearts and souls of these people that erased the beauty of God's love for that instant. That He had to as part of His journey feel the rejection, even though He loved and He knew at the time that these people were so grateful and how much they loved Him. I was listening to the voices. I couldn't discern what was being said, but He told me that these were people that He had healed. The blind He gave sight, the lame that walked. All of these precious people, they weren't shouting"* "Save Him, save Him, save Him" . *"It*

was an unleashing of Satan's desire to take us away from Our Lord, to allow us not to see that love is the most powerful thing there is and Jesus who sits upon that wall (references the mural in the prayer room at Mary's Knoll) who holds (in His hands) that cross, Chapel, Madonna, who hangs upon the crucifix, is the same loving God that listened to all of these people, that listens to us today. We're all guilty. We all have a moment that we wish we had not said something that came out wrong. It came out the way we wanted it to, but it hurt somebody and above all it hurt God. So each night if we're just learning a slight lesson, I praise God for that. I praise God that in the hour of insignificance, in the dust that we are, He loves us so much to have gone through such horror for each and every one of us and I pray that we find that love, that we never stop searching for that unconditional love that draws us closer to Him and to each other. I praise you Jesus and God bless each of you."

April 11th, 2003

(The visual given in this message continues to follow the Lenten Passion of Christ as indicated by Jesus in the messages of 3-14; 3-21; 3-28; and 4-7-03.)

(visual by recipient) "Yes, I hear You My Lord. Thou must give me great strength, if I am to repeat what Thou would have me see. It's very hot ......and many, many people line these narrow streets ......and Jesus as He is, struggles to carry His cross. No one sees me. I'm right in the middle. It's though I am walking right besides Him. I have to stay close. No one sees me. [sigh] My Lord.

He walks with great difficulty ......bearing His Cross. He falls with great pain. He struggles to His feet ......more pain...more suffering. But He goes on. Is there no compassion? Why are they so angry? Everyone is angry. They gather closer to Him ...but the soldiers force them back ...and then He falls. At what point this is I cannot tell, but one of the soldiers realizes He is too weak to continue and he summons this man. He has a child and a little burro and he calls him." "come, carry...assist this man". He's very unwilling at first. He obviously doesn't want to do it and he turns to his son, whispers something in his ear and sends the little one down the path with the burro. He helps lift the cross ......for Jesus is now too weak ...too weak to carry it.

I see a frail lady, child like ...she's so small a woman, she defies the guards and rushes to help her Lord. She only briefly takes a cloth. It is pressed to His face to wipe away the blood and all the filth that He now bears. There's no talk, no communication ......only the look, the look acknowledging love for one another. She's forced back ... she's forced back into the crowd.

The pain from His People's reactions is more distressing. It is though it opens the wounds so much wider. When love has been rejected the wounds open...but what comes forth is only compassion and love. They're close now ...they're really close(to Calvary). It is barren and desolate. The hill (mound) not very big is

300

crowded with people. Some (way in the back) are dressed differently …silent though, but their thoughts are gleeful." "this will teach Him they say …this will end it all."

"They are in place now. The hole is ready; the cross has been tossed on the ground and Jesus too has been made to lie down, very gruffly tossed on the ground. He sees His executioners and still there is no bitterness …there is no anger, but only love. They don't understand Father…I know. I can hear them talking …now the stake is picked up. His right arm first…there is already a hole. (sigh) Then you hear metal against metal and once …twice …three times … making sure it is secure. Then they take His left arm …someone is kneeling on His chest. He can't breathe and they have prepared a stake or spike …and the hand doesn't line up with the hole. Just like last time (referencing last years vision)…it doesn't line up. And they pull and they yank His arm out of joint …and then they take the stake with the hammer and again…metal against metal. He says nothing …quietly just sighs …and then this un-kept person gets off His chest and now sits upon His legs. The hole seems too short but they lifts the legs slightly and start again …metal against metal [sigh] and then finally …finally it's over. And the cross is lifted and dropped into this hole and His whole body jerks. The crown that is worn on His head is knotted badly at the back of the neck …and it bleeds as it turns so violently back against the cross and the sharp thorns on the forehead spout more blood. He looks …looking for those He loves …and finally someone, an officer I think, recognizes His Mother and allows Her to come up with John. He doesn't question John. John assists Her and together they stand and kneel and they too are cursed. And time lapses now…for God's work is almost complete. But He suffers so to breathe …His throat burns…it burns …there is no relief. There is the peace in knowing He has served His Father and will be the Savior of the World. It becomes very dark ……almost frightening the way it's gotten so dark ……mid afternoon but it's dark …people are becoming nervous. The crowd is starting to back away. Jesus and Mary's eyes meet. He speaks to Her…to John and finally with what little strength He has left He raises His head so slightly …His eyes toward heaven and says" "Father" …(The scene ends).

(Tongues) "My Child, this you shall say. These cruel but yet unknowingly bitter souls have tried to destroy Truth …..but what is Truth? Pilate asked"…… "Is it true?" " And yet He did not pursue asking" … "what is truth"? "Truth asks only to be known in order that it may teach. I am the Truth …come to me and I will lovingly and with great patience teach you the way that leads to truth. Come My Children there is nothing to fear …for you must grow in your faith ….you must be strong in My Words …and you must always rely on My Truth. I am He who lives and thirsts for souls. Come to Me … come to Me at My table … receive the food to nourish your soul …the food of eternal life".

April 25th, 2003

(The following message was received during the Friday night Canyon Rosary. We were surprised to again personally hear from Our Blessed Mother as there were

301

some indications the messages would be less frequent. We continue to believe that if these messages are heeded and bear fruit more could follow.)

"My Dear Children,

You have emerged from these 40 days of penance and sacrifice scarred by Divine Love. What were My words to you prior to this Lent? Did I not tell you this would be a most difficult Lent? There were the trials, circumstances and devastations upon devastations. You My children awakened to the love of Our Most Merciful God. You wish to make many changes in life. I say change must first begin within each heart. Until you learn to succumb to the fragrance of The Divine Will ....you will be unable to understand that the scars of Divine Love are etchings beautifully engraved in each soul ......allowing that soul to be purified and perfected before the eyes of Almighty God."

"I bless you this night with a Mothers love for your continued perseverance and I shall intercede for each of Our Children before the Throne of God. I shall remain with you through this journey. Be not afraid O Little Children of God .....but confidently walk in the Masters steps and you shall reach your goal of life eternal ..... filled with happiness and joy as you enter the Kingdom of God."

(Visual by recipient) "I see what appears to be ......it looks like where a storm has gone through and there's great destruction. I see just piles and piles of debris. Wood ash ... like a great fire might of gone through It's not pleasant to see. For surely there must have been a loss of life. It brings sorrow to my heart to see such things. The ashes are parting ...there are tiny lights emerging through the debris. Looks like little sprouts of some sort and then a greater light from above shines down and these little seedlings find the strength to push themselves through all of the debris which must be the trials of life . And they are the souls that have loved Our Lord and have fought so valiantly to follow His Will. No struggle has kept them from Him. For love ......all souls search for love...Divine Love."

(The following text is transcribed from the recorded audio oration given by the recipient after her visual. She attempts to explain what was previously given.)

"This was one of the first times that I remember that Our Lady had spoken of the Divine Will in such terminology. When I heard the words scarred by Divine Love, I wondered if I had heard correctly and then She said"

"Unless we learn to succumb to the fragrance of The Divine Will, we cannot understand the <u>scars</u> of Divine Love which are etchings carved beautifully into our souls and these are nothing more than the everyday trials. The disappointments ... all those things that come our way that we have to deal with .....those things allowed by God. We're His masterpiece. He is carving us using our sorrows and our pains. Molding us into the people that He calls His children. All through Lent we walked the suffering of Our Lord and now She is telling us that the journey made us more beautiful because we endured with love. All sacrifices, whatever came our way. Whether we understood it or not we trusted in the Mercy of Our Lord. I praise God for this evening and I thank our Blessed Mother for returning to us. For speaking to us so gently. For teaching us with so much wisdom and promising us that God will never leave us and She will always be our intercessor that tells us that we need to pray. To keep ourselves in a state of grace so that we might prove ourselves worthy servants. Worthy children of Our Lord and Savior Jesus Christ. These evenings are very special. We never quite know what is going to happen but we praise God that He has blessed us so abundantly. That He has placed this Holy Mountain in an area accessible to many people who are able to not only find, but literally feel the peace and the love of Our Lord Jesus Christ. Praise be to Jesus."

Message of May 2nd, 2003

(The following message was received late Friday afternoon in Elburn, Illinois. It was transcribed as dictated as no audio equipment was available at the time.)

"My Child,

To share with others is to expose yourself to the many affections which inflict wounds into your very soul. Thus, you become vulnerable …….. a victim so to speak of skepticism and doubt. Within such perimeters lies the arena of martyrs for Christ. How doest thou defend thyself? The answer ….. thou doest not! Christ is thy defender in all truth and wisdom!

Speak freely ……without hesitation of the great Mercy of God and you will find reassuring confidence in Divine Intervention. God allows difficult situations in order to perfect His chosen souls.

These words I have spoken many times before. Yet, regrettably, they go unnoticed. Should I speak in great theological terms, they would confound the wise. Yet, the humble of heart would absorb such wisdom and great would be their reward. You live in a world of confusion and great diversity of belief. There is only one true and omnipotent God! Though all powerful, He is full of mercy and compassion.

Come and praise His Holy Name! Detach …. I repeat …. detach yourself from worldly possessions. For all you possess is God's. A gift to cultivate for His Kingdom. Toil the field of souls and great will be your reward in Heaven!"

(Recipient's commentary) This message appears so simple and straight forward; yet, it is in these particular messages where Our Lady compels us to look beyond the "words" to the "meaning of the words." To share with others is actually a hunger for souls. The inbred desire in each heart belonging to Christ to evangelize the "Good News of Salvation" and capture that soul with the love of

Christ. In so doing, we become vulnerable to criticism and other negative clouds which would attempt to obscure our vision, the focus of following Our Lord Jesus Christ. Thus, we sometimes struggle in our efforts of conversion. There is, however, great glory in such struggles which, as we cling to Jesus, molds us into the instruments He has chosen each of us to be. Could that be the martyrs of which Our Mother speaks? What joy, Oh Lord, to bear Thy scars of Divine Love.

(No public message on May 9th.)

May 16, 2003

(The following message was received during private meditation today with Our Lady in Elburn, Illinois. One particular thing of interest I wish to share is Our Lady's strong affection for families and our responsibilities to them. While we were in conversation, I was called to a family matter needing my attention. She stopped Her conversation, and told me to respond to the family situation. Once the matter was taken care of we resumed our conversation as though there had been no interruption. Perhaps this alone is in itself a lesson requiring a much deeper understanding of the value Our Lord and Our Blessed Mother place on our response to the needs of others.)

"My Dear Children,

Unto this holy mountain I shall draw many souls thirsting for what many of you, My little ones, are presently cultivating deeply within your hearts ....the joy and peace in loving and serving Almighty God. You are being refined and fine-tuned as instruments of such love.

We know that your days are long and filled with unceasing interruptions ...all aimed at disturbing your peace. Until you are at peace with God, you cannot be at peace with your brothers and sisters. All this comes with a commitment ....an internal "fiat" which exudes the sweet fragrance of loving unconditionally.

One does not reach such goals without the scars of which I spoke earlier. An athlete does not reach his peak of ability without much sacrifice and discipline. The word I desire you to hear is <u>discipline</u>. It is your choice. How much are you prepared to deny yourself ? For to deny oneself for the Glory of God is a true gift of the Spirit. You will hunger for God as your prayer life becomes stronger. Be assured when you truly hunger for God in such a way, He will bless you with an insatiable hunger for souls .....souls which too shall hunger for God.

Let My calm reassurance of Our love reassure you in these times of uncertainty. Be at peace, little ones. The love and mercy of God shall overcome all obstacles.

Trust and believe!"

May 23rd, 2003

(In preparing for the Divine Mercy Chaplet as the prayers were mentally being contemplated, Our Lady came. She said nothing at first only observed and then related as to how the messages would take on a new emphasis. I can only express my personal feelings that She was referring to more commentaries not only by this recipient but also by others as the Holy Spirit moves them. As we have been blessed by Their presence for so long, it is time that we as Spirit filled children begin to express what lies within our own hearts. So many people hurt deeply within their souls but seemingly cannot reach the light of Jesus Christ. We must be such instruments that love Him so much that we cannot help but be those tiny beacons around the world that reflect the Love of Christ to others.)

"My Dear Children,

Today I extend an invitation to Love …..to fall in love with Jesus. So many of Our children say they know Jesus, but they have left no room in their heart for Him. He must dwell totally within in order for you to emit His sweet presence to others. He desires not the obstructions of pride and selfishness, but rather to fill the void left in many lives. As He invites you …. so must you, in turn, invite Him. Life then becomes an artistic work in the stages of completion. All comes about in time. It is most unfortunate to see the <u>hourglass</u> of <u>life</u> which sifts through with so much left undone.

Make a difference, My beloved children, for the Spirit thrives in hearts which know only the way to Jesus. Trials and sacrifices …….yes, but such great joy to know and serve the Lord."

(Our Lady then said to write Her personal words to this recipient given Friday, May 16th. She said during the private conversation.)

"We *(Her children)* abuse the privilege of being responsible by neglecting our responsibilities."

(Recipient): This is really a powerful statement that hits most of us right between the eyes. If Christ really reigns in our lives, we have an awesome responsibility to be Christ like in every way. This particularly means when it is most inconvenient or uncomfortable. It is so easy when we feel good, but difficult when the pressures of everyday life fall heavily upon our shoulders. Our <u>crosses</u> (preciously made for each of us) have somehow gotten confused with someone else or so we would like to think. But God Who with such tenderness laid them upon our shoulders knows what is best for us. We must always believe with an unalterable trust that He who made us will never give us more than we can bear. We have responsibilities, so let us each meet our responsibilities in the eyes of God.

(The following message was dictated in our private residence after 6:pm while in preparation for the Friday night Canyon Rosary. It was clearly stated this was to be made available to the group prior to the praying of the Rosary. As Our Mother is always so compassionate and understanding, She dictated this rather than have the recipient's husband who was in bed sick try to record it. The second conversation that occurred at the Rosary was not recorded. I can only ask that you pray to the Holy Spirit for discernment as you read the following:)

"My Dear Children,

You have journeyed with Me these many but yet, few years. For time is unequivocally a Divine measurement …. incomprehensible and thus miscalculated. You think of time as the hands of a clock, moving second by second. Yet, I tell you time is a place recorded and instituted by God for His Master Plan in each precious soul.

We have walked in the gardens, smelled the aroma of each fragrant flower and seen the beauty which lies beneath the soil of fertility. Do you recognize the meaning of My words. The gardens are the souls …… some sprouting forth nurtured by love …. others awaiting compassion and understanding. Souls such as these you encounter each day. You need only to ask for the grace to recognize these golden opportunities God has made available to you. When you seek such graces for the sake of others, you console My Son, and your heart then becomes a refuge for Divine Love!"

{Recipients commentary}: Often due to the limitedness of our human mind's capabilities to capture the full meaning of Our Lady's words, it becomes an all out faith filled walk of trust and obedience. It is in the silence of our hearts when we are vulnerably aware of God's nurturing love that we begin to slightly realize not only the beauty, but also the importance of Their words. As Our Lady said, "When you seek such graces for the sake of others, you console My Son, and your heart then become a refuge for Divine Love." Perhaps in our simple acts of trying to make reparation for the sins committed against the Sacred Heart of Jesus and the Immaculate Heart of Mary, we become partakers of Love while remaining co-workers in the harvesting of the field of souls. God gives us many opportunities to live a grace filled life. When temptations and distractions arise, we must continuously ask for the graces necessary to perform the task at hand. They never fail us. Sometimes our vision becomes clouded, but eventually God's ways become clearer and we are able to see once again that love, patience, kindness, gentleness of spirit and all the fruits of the Spirit enjoin our hearts to always seek the Lord in all things.

June 13th, 2003

"My Dear Children,

These many times I have spoken with you ……. I have not stood upon the highest peak and with a loud voice called you." " Come to My Son …come back to Him". "For what comes back is but an echo of My own voice. I have chosen instead to work the fertile fields of each heart where I may whisper and draw each of you closer to My Beloved Son. Many of you have experienced such trials ….. such temptations in life and have found yourselves lost without an answer. And this My Dear Ones is where I come to strengthen you. To tell you ….. you must seek your spiritual direction from someone in authority. For great temptations lie around the corners ….and without such guidance you are often misled … become confused and disillusioned. God does not want that My Children. He wants each of you to be His loving healthy forgiving and giving children who seek more for the best of others than for yourselves.
You have begun the process of emptying your lives of so much clutter that God now has room to rule in your lives. Such joy you will find as God takes control. And you find such peace ..…. for worries, temptations, all the trials that come your way, you have given to Him ….. and He refreshes you with the courage and the wisdom to go forward ….. continuously seeking to nourish the souls of this world with the true love, peace and forgiveness of God Almighty.

Praise be to Jesus, Who's love is so great. He has blessed you so abundantly and continues as you ask Him to guide each step you take …. each word you speak. Hold tightly My Children and watch carefully over your words for they are such a powerful instrument. Far greater damage is done by the human tongue than by the many weapons of your world. See how great is your responsibility …. see how much We love you and place such confidence in your continued grace to walk the path Christ has set before you.

Be at peace My Children. Seek forgiveness ….. seek a heart that knows nothing but love and you will become that instrument of pure love. I bless you this special night and especially those who could not be here. Know that My blessing and joy rests upon them as they will have the courage and the strength given by Almighty God to do His will … to be obedient servants. *For they have been chosen, they have been marked by My Son."

(Commentary; *We feel Our Lady was especially referring to the Deaconate candidates who were to be ordained the next day in Tucson by Bishop Gerald.)

June 20th, 2003

"My Dear Children,

Intimate fellowship with God is the beginning of understanding of total abandonment to self where not even a shadow lingers reminding you of time once spent ......wasted and gone forever. It is the springtime of the soul which longs only to do and abide in the Will of God. Such souls are refreshed by reparation, love and mercy, and when mixed together form a most delightful honey. Sweet to the taste of Him who longs for consolation by His chosen ones.

You, little ones ....who wage such wars against the repugnance of sin .....must in your own wretchedness ...raise high the Standard of Righteousness as you continue the battle for souls.

God loves you. Endear yourselves to His heart and find lasting peace."

(Commentary by recipient) In this particular message Our Lord encourages us to recognize the absolute need to re-evaluate our personal relationship with Him. True life with Christ fills the voids left by attachments to a world in which all in it will at some point die. "All are ashes" as the Bible says and will return to same. We are called to a greater life. That of perfection of the soul. It is a state in which we can only strive to attain while on earth. This is what we as Christians are called to do. "Be perfect as I (Jesus) am perfect." How we attain that perfection is through purification ......not a pleasant thought to some, but necessary in the eyes of Our Lord. If we could only see with the eyes of Divine Love, our thoughts of purification would not be ignored, but embraced as a true gift from God. Though brief, this message will require time and discernment as it will speak to many hearts and perhaps reveal different perceptions as each of us journey through life.

June 27th, 2003

(Recipient) "How is it that My Lord should come to me so many times in one day? My Lord, thou know'est my heart can bear only so much for it is filled with love and yet I must do Thy bidding. My Lord. Let Thy words come freely for Your Children listen."

"My child,

You are correct. My Children do listen. My Children know My voice .....and My Children come to Me. On this day I have gathered many throughout the world and drawn them to My Sacred Heart. Is My Heart not ablaze with love for all of My Children?"

"Yes My Lord. For all of Your Children."

"And what My Daughter would you as a child believe to be the fuel which fires My Heart?"

"I would say love My Lord. What fuels love is love. Your Heart that burns so much for us. But I don't understand, My Jesus, how we, we help fuel your heart."

"By love and yes even by failures. There are many of My Chosen Souls who through consciousness see that they are unable to draw souls into perfection. They humble themselves and come before me as dust rolls in the storm ……begging for My Mercy and for forgiveness of their weakness. But I tell you ….when a soul consciously sees its humility …… it's weaknesses and it's failures …… it comes to Me and begs for the souls of others. I take that …..that tiny grain of imperfection and draw it close to My Heart where the flame erupts and thereby purifies the souls.

My Children, you seek a road of holiness with many questions …..many I have answered, many My Mother has answered. There are an abundance that remain unanswered. Do not concern yourselves My beloved ones but only listen closely to the voice of the Shepard who leads His sheep. Who draws them closely to His heart where He may purify and perfect them. You have experienced much this week and yes you have been weakened. But weakened in a sense that strength has come from such weakness. Strength to trust ….strength to pray …..strength to expect that God hears and answers your prayers.

You are My Children who believe and who trust in My Love and the abundance of My Mercy."

(Recipient) "The dark sky reminds me of the mountains. All flickering lights… great distances apart. And now they are all moving together as though they are drawn to form a particular design. It's a huge, huge red cross surrounded by a heart. Lights flicker……the heart grows brighter and brighter and yet they remain as one. The cross united with the heart. We go to the cross and are embraced by the Sacred Heart of Our Lord."

(Commentary by recipient) I believe the last portion of Our Lord's message pertains to the emotional stress caused by the fire up on our mountain which began the Saturday prior to this Friday's rosary. Although there was considerable damage to the vegetation, there were no personal injuries or damage to any structures. It was as though the Hand of God guided the flames as the firefighters gallantly worked to bring the fire under control. The high winds certainly were directed by a power far greater than human hands. When we prayed, we praised God for being in control and thanked Him knowing all would be in accordance to His Will.

July 4th, 2003

(This particular evening has been an early inspiration by Our Blessed Mother to reference the passage in Scripture in Psalm 86. This being the date in which our country celebrates its independence from tyranny must also become a date firmly planted in our hearts and minds that it must represent a date of awakening of our dependence on Almighty God. It is through the direction of the Holy spirit and the urging of the Holy Spirit that the following is meant to be shared by all those

309

whose hearts are open to the urging of the Spirit. As you read the following, please pray to this same Holy Spirit for discernment. Even though these words are for all practical purposes those of the recipient, they are shared without quotation marks. The word "reflection" was clearly placed in my heart and mind and thus the following came into being.)

During Mass today, our Pastor reflected as he often does with direct eloquence on a Nation. Our country, founded strongly by faith-filled men and women who understood, apart from God we are nothing. Our Constitution guarantees us the right to life, liberty, and the pursuit of happiness. It, however, as Father stated does not insure our happiness, only the right to pursue it. What is happiness to one may be total boredom to another. However, a Christ centered life is one of indescribable joy. He fills the voids, renews our courage to believe and centers us deeply in His Mercy, all the while dispelling fear.

His "words" make everything so "clear". Let us always open our hearts to His love. Maybe we will feel only a little trickle at first. But keep believing and trusting until that faith becomes an ocean, cascading down the mountain as a waterfall into the valley below where all will be immersed into this great Miracle of Mercy. May God bless this country as we, His little children, pray for "the open void" in our country to be filled with the true love of Christ!

Later during the 3rd decade of the Rosary an eight minute visual was recorded as experienced by the recipient. It graphically described a multitude of people following the sound of that of an American Revolutionary war drummer. Originating in much earlier times it matured into current times. Visible to more than one was a banner waving with the sign of the lamb. At the head of the multitude was a woman in Blue and finally the shoeless drummer was visible as the Child Jesus. This same symbolic banner and marching multitude was seen and described by a priest two days prior at Mary's Farm in the canyon.

July 11th, 2003

"My Beloved Children,

How appropriate this night such scripture has been read, [Corinthians 12] for tonight I wish to dwell upon the gifts that each and every one of God's Children has been given."

"My Dear Children,

When you were baptized you received the gifts of the Holy Spirit. They were wrapped as a gift …… so beautifully wrapped that many of our children marveled at such an exquisite package. The wrappings of gossamer ….the bows trimmed

310

with gold. And you said." "Surely such a gift must be too valuable to open. I will place it where it will be safe and at some point I will open it ....but it is far to valuable now. I must admire it!"

"Children; are you so enraptured by the outside that you cannot see what lies within? These gifts are gifts from My Son ....these gifts of The Holy Spirit which He gave you to be opened, to be cherished and to be used. When you open them do not place them where they may only be admired but not used. For then what good is the Gift? As you have been baptized in The Holy Spirit ......it is when The Holy Spirit is released in your life that you become aware of the greatness of the gift that God has given you. You become first of all aware of the beauty of the Sacraments and you fall in love with the Sacraments. Secondly you are strengthened in your faith to be bold, courageous warriors now filled with the Spirit to go forth .....bearing your gift to be shared amongst your brothers and sisters. Such gifts often bring miracles .....yes miracles. When you pray filled with the power of The Holy Spirit and someone who is ill is instantly cured ...... a miracle has taken place. When you pray and someone who is sick, slowly, gradually whether through the aid of physicians ......begins a healing process, that person also receives a healing. Healings are faith filled instruments of the Holy Spirit given to each of the children whose hearts are open to receive them. Too many are afraid to open this beautiful gift ....and therefore it remains un-used ....unproductive.

My Children, Do not be afraid. For God does not give you fear. He gives you love. And a gift so beautiful is one meant to be shared. Allow your trust and your faith in God to give you the courage to receive with the heart of gratitude. And yes, you may .....unwrap slowly ....delicately enjoying the beauty of the package. But most importantly, rejoice with the gift God has given you. Believe My Children and you shall receive. For each carries within themselves that special gift. The Holy Spirit holds this tightly within His hands ......and awaits for your faith to burst through .....so that the Power of God, through the instrument of you as simple human vessels .....releases the power that God has entrusted into the hands of those who believe. Have much faith. The world is in need of much faith ...much trust. For My Son will be always with you .....guiding you ....directing your steps and remember My Children, that God is most generous with His Children. Ask of Him .....expect an answer and place your trust totally in Him knowing He has heard you and He will answer your prayers. Bear with much patience ....for much joy will be your reward."

(Visual by recipient) "It's all white. Mother, it looks like snow or ice ...and someone......I can't see a face ......but they are chipping away at the ice. It appears quite thick. I don't understand ...but I don't understand a lot. A line, a fishing line is placed in the water beneath the ice and a moment later there's a fish on the end of the line. (Yes) Now I understand. Sometimes, when we are given gifts we must work very hard, very diligently, not knowing what lies beyond but trusting God through His Grace, as the ice was broken, apparently it would appear, that no life was there. It is through our constant efforts to reach our

311

brothers and sisters that a soul is touched.

We're all fishermen. Fishers of God for all the souls that deny and reject Our Lord. We must continue to persevere even in the bleakest circumstances. For there is life and we as servants of Our Lord Jesus must make that effort to reach each and every soul."

July 18th, 2003

"My Dear Children,

In the patient practice of loving God with sincere hearts, opportunities of great magnitude will present themselves. These opportunities are grace filled moments in which the soul is transfixed upon God and the grandeur of simplicity far over shadows anything of this earth. You develop an insatiable appetite for the salvation of souls. A redemptive instinct surfaces from the depths of your soul. Life becomes more meaningful as those seeds of love long ago planted by God in each heart begin to mature into great delicacies. The sweet aroma of holiness permeates the air as the soul, like a bud of a flower begins to open and emits the fragrance of Divine Love. Do you understand My meaning, Child?"

(Here, when Our Lady says "Child", I believe She was speaking not only to me, but to all of her children.)

The following was the recipient's response to Her question. "Oh, Mother, in such times I am lost for words." "Slowly, My child." "My mind cannot conceive such eloquence nor is my poor dialogue sufficient to even attempt to understand. My poor heart beats so rapidly as though a thousand words would flow from my tongue, but only <u>the pureness of a simple mind uncluttered by worldly distractions comes to my heart</u>. It is in simply loving God beyond all else that His peace brings true peace and understanding to our souls. In our desire to be holy humble children, we become the buds awaiting their moment to open."

(She smiled so beautifully and said;)

"Tell My children, I await their bouquets of love".

Second Message of July 18th, 2003

"My Children,

I have gathered you together as My warriors. My chosen ones to dispel the fear that rages throughout My people. Fear of life .... fear of illness .... fear of death

312

..... fear of disease .... fear ... fear. You My Children are to cast out this fear in My Name. In the name of Jesus cast out this fear ...... that these hearts .... these beautiful hearts that come to Me.... come seeking love ... .come seeking peace .... come seeking relief in their lives .... will find My peace. When My peace is found new life begins .... new growth .....new spiritual life. It is in the life of the spirit. For you will grow and you will prosper and you will find true joy.

My Children,

You have been taught much. You have read, you have observed. See those with whom My Spirit dwells ... see the peace .... see the love. For that is meant for you. That is a gift that must be shared ...... once you to receive this gift, you too must share. It is a beautiful chain .... a chain of love ...one link at a time .... one soul at a time ....all stretching along this journey of life. How pleased you have made Your Lord in all your efforts to evangelize .... to spread My love. For it is My love that brings you the healing. And I tell you this day from this very moment the Power of the Holy Spirit shall ascend ... and shall rest upon each and every one of you. Healing ... renewal of faith and confidence shall fill each soul. Those of you who come with illness ......be restored to health. Those who come with doubt ..... your doubt will be dispelled. Those who come in earnest expectation ..... open wide your heart and receive an abundance of My Grace. And those who come simply to love ...... you are My beloved. You know My words ..... you know My will .....you know what must be done . I have great confidence in you My Children .... My blessed ones .... My faithful ones. Stay close to Me. Allow the Holy Spirit always to guide you and seek the mantle of My Mother ...... where She will gather you and warm your hearts beneath the gentleness of a mother..... the compassion that reaches the eyes of Her Son.

I bless you this night with My peace ......My mercy and the grace to fulfill My will."

July 25th, 2003

(This was a particularly difficult message to transcribe as the recipient received this message while partially in the prayer room, not in the usual private designated area of reception. Initially only minor pieces of the conversation were picked up by the recorder as the singing of the attendees was overwhelmingly heard actually welcoming Our Lady when the message began.)

Tongues...(participants were loudly heard to be singing "Ave Maria").

"Yes, My child. You were taken by surprise".

(Recipient) "Mother, everything was in disarray. Nothing was as I thought it should be"

"And what is it that you learned?"

"That we walk the path of Jesus ......no matter how difficult it may be .....for He is in control. It is His steps that lead us to glory."

"Listen My Children as these words are prayed. Let them be deeply felt within your heart. This is My Son ..... meditate then ... meditate upon His Passion. "I will whisper to you a lesson that all must learn. Do you hear Me My Child?" *"(Yes Mother)"* "So many of My Dear Children seek the gifts that God has given them through The Holy Spirit ..... and with such gifts, they become so enthused ... so overwhelmed with joy that they fail to take the time to understand. You ask so many questions...."

" But mother, they will be asked of me"

"Tell them My Child that God created each of you with your own special gifts. He does not call you to read book after book by one famous author and another. He calls you by your name ...to be yourself ......and He calls you before His Tabernacle that together you may learn. He is the Master ... .the Teacher .....you the student. You learn from the very best ....there is no other."

Be the person God has chosen you to be. Do not waver from this. For you will find yourselves overstressed ....overburdened and totally out of the realm of possibilities that God has planned for you. He knows you ....He knows everything about you. Each gift is finely tuned within each precious soul. But it requires patience and true devotion to Almighty God. Learn from the One who created you .....for He seeks to teach the open and pure heart. The heart that is humble. Quietly comes before Him and say;" "Speak Lord ....your servant is listening". "Let all of Our Children learn this precious gift to listen that we might truly hear the Word of God and do not become intimidated when you see what you perceive as such magnificent gifts of others ....of God's Children. For your gift is just as precious ....just as valuable. All are children ....all will learn .....all will bring others into the Kingdom of God. Cling to Him ....never let go ....for your gifts shall mature.

Yes My Daughter .... do not seek beyond what God has for you. But in all humility rejoice that you are His Child ....chosen in this battle for souls. Praise be Jesus ... as I bless you who are faithful and true to My Son."

August 1st, 2003

(Recipient) "Oh sweet Holy Mother. For She who comes so faithfully to speak with us, to guide us and to help us. Forgive my frailty. Help me sweet mother to hear your words as you speak them this night."

"Tonight I call you ......the lambs of His field. Which one amongst you has not gone searching ....leaving behind those gathered together in safety and

searched out the one who has lost his way? You go through many trials ......
many times of great despair and disappointment. But still you do not give up ...
because you know that it is Jesus Himself who left the flock in search of you at
some point in your lives. You are now given that responsibility ....for Christ
dwells within you. And He sends you into the fields and into the rocky hills and
mountains to find that lost sheep ......that child that has gone astray .....that
person who has caused you so much pain ....whether it be in your daily life, in
your job, in whatever circumstance you may have found yourself. This is a sheep
which now comes into the fold and is called by My Son. Each must do the task
assigned to him or her whether in good health or in poor ....whether in joy or in
sorrow. For through your faith you know that there is hope and in hoping there is
love ....love eternal.

My Children,

Many times I have spoken of trials and difficulties in life. And you have accepted
My words not knowing fully what those words meant or how they would come
about. But a heart that falls in love with Jesus recognizes those obstacles placed
before them and does not flee, does not run ....does not hide. But boldly steps
forward and reaches out the hand .....the hand of Christ to draw that soul ...that
sheep .... back into the fold of Christ. Believe My Children, for I have been here
many times .... spoken many words. But the word I leave you with is love ....and
with love will come the patience to persevere. Always persevere My Children for
such love awaits you ... a love beyond your imagination. Believe .....trust ... but
love in spite of all obstacles. Love and you shall reach the reward that God has
waiting for each of His beloved children. Rest now for many are tired ....many are
fatigued from the journeys of life ....the trials and tribulations. But rest in the
peace of Christ."

*(Recipient) There was an inaudible pause in Our Lady's message which appeared
to have been concluded. However, She then left us with the following sentence to
contemplate as She more frequently now interjects a word or phrase which allows
us to ask ourselves how does this apply in my life?*

"You have to have but the intention to save the soul. God recognizes the effort and
love with which you strive for souls for His kingdom."

August 8th, 2003

"My Dear Children,

It pleases Me greatly to see so many gathered together in ardent prayer. I wish this
night to take you on a further journey of prayer. Prayer in which you will learn to
persevere ... prayer in which you will learn to see the face of Jesus. My Son
walked the beautiful path in Nazareth. His holy feet running in the dust playfully.
His little toes wiggling in the grass. Then His feet journeyed to Gethsemane. His

holy feet …. Yes, My Children … His holy feet that began in the dust walked to Gethsemane …. journeyed to Jerusalem and then these holy feet muddied and bruised were nailed to the cross. But this was not the end for these feet nor the end of their journey, but it was the beginning. For these feet …. the feet of My Son, journey with each and every one of you in your daily lives. Did you notice the smile on the face of the child you passed today? Did you notice the old, the worn faces as they searched through dumpsters and barrels of garbage searching for a meal? Did you look at the eyes of pain the eyes of years of torment and struggle?"

"My Children,

Many times you walk with Jesus … but your eyes have not been opened. For you must learn to see with your heart … to love, as Jesus would have you love. Pray with conviction My Children and when you pray with conviction …. when you say to the mountain ….. be moved ….the mountain will be moved. But who moves the mountain? The one in whom you place your faith.

Recognize the mountains He moves each day of your lives. Each trial …. each moment you hold back an angry word ….an impure thought ….. you turn your back on temptation. Those are mountains, My Children. Do you not recognize them? They are mountains …. and yet through the love of Christ … that they have moved. For you have sought His help … you have believed…you have prayed. For only through prayer and obedience to His words are the mountains of your lives moved. Watch My Children and pray intensely and you will see ever so slightly … each mountain shall move. Beloved ones, I am filled with joy that you have gathered … .but remember, when you gather in prayer your hearts must be one with Jesus … .expect an encounter with love. No more …… for there is no greater encounter than the encounter with love himself."

(Visual by recipient) "Mother, a small child by a pond. He has no features but the back of a little boy. He has a line in his hand, a string, not even a pole, just a string tied to his little finger … and it has been tossed into the water and he is just a little boy waiting with great expectation for something so wonderful to happen. And the string makes a sudden movement …… and that's not a fish! Fishing for souls …… it must be Jesus, string in hand not letting go. Patiently waiting for each of His children as He draws the string closer to His heart. He draws each of our souls as well. The light shines so beautifully on the water, it must be sunset … maybe it's the sunset of our lives. How wonderful to know that He never let's go. I know He never let's go. He tied a string to each of our fingers"

August 15th, 2003

The Feast of the Assumption

It was a beautiful night of prayer. We had an overflow group with an Italian priest and two deacons in attendance. This being the Feast of the Assumption, during the afternoon Mass, Padre Bruno Martinelli Pazzaglia gave a beautiful sermon expressing how after Our Mothers death She was assumed into heaven. In the last paragraph of the evening message we were given the gift of hearing Our Mother confirm events of how She was lifted into heaven.)

(Extensive Tongues) "Sweet Mother of God."

"My Precious Children,

What joy it brings to Your Mother when a soul recognizes the tremendous gift of relinquishing its self will .....and chooses instead to grasp and cling tightly to The Divine Will of My Son. For this is true joy. In abandonment, you have not lost, My Children. On the contrary ......you have gained tremendous wealth. For the things of this world no longer hold importance .....and only those .....those that focus on Jesus see the treasure that lays hidden beyond the realm of glory. Would you My Children give your Fiat this night ..... an abandonment of self ......for the glory of My Son and the salvation of souls? Would you lose yourself so that others might be found? The blind wish to see ....the lame wish their limbs to be restored .... the hungry seek food. But My Children .....has God failed you in His promises? I ask you to persevere with only love .....with love you find the humble heart . The heart that searches for My Son ...searches for the light ..... the true light that illuminates the path to holiness." *(Tongues)*

"Come My Children and see as My Child sees all the angels that lifted me gently through the air ......petals of flowers dropping slowly to the earth. Do you see ....can you smell the aroma of a such a joyous time? All heaven rejoices as I ask you, My Children ..... to rejoice in the love of My Son."

A second intense private sequence followed.

August 22nd, 2003

(Tongues) Our Lady then extensively spoke. Only the following highlights were recorded from notes.

"My Children,

In time of selflessness think of Charity towards others.

So many of our children say we will pick up our cross and follow You [meaning Jesus] . Yet when they pick up their cross .....they carry it only for a short while. My children you must learn to love and embrace the cross. Joy and sorrow are melted together in a large pot continually stirred by the hand of Divine love. Rejoice for there are chosen souls among you."

(Recipient) The pot of which Our Lady speaks is a form of purification. This (the Hand of Divine Love) stirs them with His love and through this loving purification allows the soul to see how much it is loved. We are not to fear to carry the cross, which is given to us!

(Recipient) Upon further prayerful discernment, it was felt Our Lady knew exactly how the evening would progress and how each of us would react without having the actual audio recorder to rely upon. It is interesting how in the midst of what may have seemed at the time to be utter chaos such beautiful participation from the attendees blossomed into a spontaneous opening up of "hearts". The portions of the message, which were written down, seemed to apply to so many and they felt the spirituality of the evening. In reflecting upon Our Lord and the Cross, one realizes that the two are inseparable. Someone mentioned that the melting pot of joy and sorrow in essence seemed a contradiction; however the <u>sorrow</u> of our sins of the Cross carried by Jesus eventually turned into <u>joy</u> (the joy of His Resurrection and the hope for our salvation through His precious blood). Perhaps this will help us to understand to a greater degree the Mercy of Our Lord through the suffering of the Cross. A cross which each of us must carry in one form or another. When you feel your cross is too great to carry, remember the Master and the Cross He bore out of Love for all mankind. God bless you!

August 29th, 2003

(Recipient) " My Dear Mother . I renew my commitment to Your Beloved Son, My Lord Jesus Christ ......that these words penetrate the hearts of all who hear them. Touch my lips sweet Mother that all will be purified."

"My Children,

Speak tenderly to all who seek Gods love and they will see through your nothingness the working of The Holy Spirit. Be humble My Children . Do not seek to avoid humiliation …. but rather rejoice in silent gratitude for the grace the Lord has allowed you to offer Him this gift, which pleases His most merciful heart."

(Tongues) "Yes, these times are most difficult. But My Children, you are not asked to do the impossible …you are asked to do the possible with much love for Jesus. In all things you may find a gift to offer My Son ......to appease the wrath that now rages within His Heart. A wrath inflicted by those who ignore and turn their back on Him. He is your only recourse My Children. This must be expressed and accepted by His Children. Love, pure love, must prevail if your world is to survive. We have spoken ….yes …and spoken often of many things …but only through love and continuous prayer will the results come about which will help mitigate the Chastisement that will come.

Dear ones,

Do not fear when your hope is in the Lord. For He is your protector …..your Savior …your Redeemer. Trust in His mercy ….submit yourselves to His Holy Will and your heart will find joy and peace in service to others."

(Recipient) "Yes Mother, if I could but see what it is that lies ahead perhaps I could be more prepared. But I know not what Thou would truly have me do. It is only by walking with You day by day that I receive your strength ……know of Your love and share that love. But I am nothing … and in being nothing how can I harm anything or anyone? Shall we seek to be nothing … nothing but children hidden behind the mantle of a Mother who loves us so much? A Mother that leads us to Her Son. Keep us close to You Dear Mother that we will not offend. We will not harm ……we will only love.

(Tongues) Each tear we share, or rather shed out of love for Her Son, in remorse for our sins, brings Him much joy, for a contrite heart pleases Him most greatly."

September 5th, 2003 *(First message)*

"My Dear Children,

It is in the joyful solitude of silence where one finds such great opportunities to serve God. Words which would fall from the mouths untamed and unrestrained become venomous weapons free to roam and spread destruction wherever they may go. Well chosen words of comfort and love produce an opposite effect …….. a healing remedy to be absorbed and discerned. The festering wounds of a careless tongue are helpless against the balm of "Love" which whispers only love and forgiveness. It is the breath of new life in the grace of God which allows all hearts to be opened …… so that a truly loving heart barely even notices when someone does it wrong. You feel only a twinge of grace filled enlightenment to say to Me"……….. *(conversation stopped, recipient expresses)"Your child is in need of your direction."*

"When you relinquish that human desire to rush in and take control and place everything in Our hands you have progressed still further in your goal of holiness. It is a lifetime process, My children, but Love …….God's Love will conquer every circumstance in which you may find yourself. Detach yourself from the things of this world … so that by His grace you will see that which draws you closer to His most merciful heart."

Second Message of September 5th, 2003

(Guardian Angel Samuel speaks at Mary's Knoll) This second unexpected message is from Samuel, the recipients guardian angel. This message is especially published for all those who have witnessed or experienced abuse of all kinds.

(Recipient) *"I test the Spirit......in the name of the Father, Son and Holy Spirit. If it not be of Jesus it must be gone by the power of The Name of Jesus. It is unfinished?......Yes I remember......but it has been quite awhile. It pleases me my Samuel, that you should come to me this night."*

"My little charge,

I am here at the bidding of the Queen of all Angels .....the Queen of Heaven and Earth who has sent me to speak with you. During these last few weeks and the trials that you have endured .....during these times you have not sought my direction my consolation and my guidance. But yes little one, you have prayed .... and that is of most importance. For these troubles and trials are of great consequence and must be dealt with in a most heavenly manner. First, you must open your heart and allow God to work through you. To heal not only the wounds that have been inflicted in your heart ....but the wounds of those who are so young that now approach thee for comforting. It is God's will that you lean on me for assistance ......that you do not become anxious and overly concerned. But allow me to guide you ....through prayer .... to receive the consolation that God has for you and for all children like you who experience these difficulties in life.

It has been my joy and also my sorrow to see the struggles which you have endured. The joy to see you struggle and so valiantly become the winner .....and my sorrow to see you suffer defeat. But My child, that does not lessen the love and the comfort that I shall continue to bring you. For little charge you may be .... no matter what your size or what your stature .....you are my little charge entrusted to me and I shall guard and protect you.

If these precious children could only see the angels that stand beside them they would live in less anxiety and fear and stress in their lives. They would talk freely and abundantly and resolve many, many of life's problems. For God has not left you orphans ..... He has left you with your guardian angels and with the Holy Spirit which is to be the light which guards your life.

What did the Blessed Mother say this night? Did She not say there would be an out pouring of the Holy Spirit? For He shall come and He shall immerse each of His children into a bath of revival ... a bath of renewal. A bath that shall re-freshen the soul of not only yourself but of all those who come your way. Do I speak too quickly .... do I speak too harshly? Then I beg your forgiveness little child ..... for there is only love that comes from my heart that must flow to yours. But listen you must ......when you hear the voice of God ....when you hear the whisper of His love .... do not turn but rejoice. And with great trust expound on His words that others may know and be filled with the Spirit ...... as He pours it forth and in abundance. For this a time of great glory ...... of great revival . Rejoice oh little charge and all the children who shall hear these words .....rejoice

......for the Lord Your God is in control. He is in control of all things and all people. What is there to fear when God is in control? Rest now my weakened and tired charge .....for you were not expecting me this night .....but my words are most important."

(Extensive tongues by recipient and Samuel. It was apparent that this was a private conversation)

"Rest....Rest"

September 6th, 2003

(This message was given at the La Purimisa retreat center concluding the Our Lady of the Sierras retreat.)

"My Gracious children,

You have gathered and worked so hard to bring about the beauty of this day. I bless you and hold you deeply within My Heart. For My Heart has room for many but too few wish to enter. My Heart is like the rocky path that some find too steep to climb. Yet others without difficulty found the path in leaps and leaps of joy and then leap into My Heart, which remains open for them and them alone. What glory it brings Me to see so many hearts .... so many different hearts .....yet all joined with one purpose ..... to love and be loved. I tell you this night I have poured forth many graces and granted the request of many hearts. This night you shall see healings .... you shall witness the pouring out of The Holy Spirit .... for the sheep of My field. You My sheep have heard My voice and have gathered the lost lambs from My fold."

(Recipient) "I smell Lilies...... perhaps Jasmine. We have been visited by many Saints."

September 12th, 2003

(recipient – tongues) " How beautiful......Oh Mother, how can I describe someone so beautiful. There are no words adequate. You stand high above, all radiant in blues and whites and a gold sash and something gold is in your hand. You stand in a pool of water". "Yes, the pool of water is the sanctifying grace about which you *(the recipient)* are to speak."

"My Dear Children,

I stand here this night in this pool .... a pool of tears glistening against the darkening sky like diamonds which shine. But they are not diamonds My

Children. They are the tears your Mother has shed for so many of Her children."

"You wish me to describe in detail?

The pond now becomes a cascading waterfall surrounding Her all the way around all four sides ...the whole body. And She says that as Her tears mingle with the tears of Her Children who with contrite hearts pray ...... their tears become mingled with Hers... and many, many graces are passed throughout the world. She says" "One must never to be afraid to cry, to show emotion ...... for tears restore health to the body as well as to the soul." " Tell My Children"... "That all the tears throughout their lives have not gone wasted."

"I have gathered each one and taken it as it drips through My hands to purify it, as a precious gift for My Son. <u>For tears which are offered for Him are pure and holy</u>. <u>Tears we offer for others are also pure and holy</u> .... <u>if offered with that contrite heart of which I speak</u>."

"I see now that as the tears of waters have cascaded down into to which was once a darken area, there's now new growth. It's...it is so beautiful. Oh Mother the souls for whom we prayed have blossomed into Your heavenly court."

(Tongues) "It pleases My Son when you allow yourselves to be opened to His desires. When you welcome ill health, difficult circumstances in life, frailty, misfortune, all are gifts.....gifts purified by hearts which love My Son."

"If I could but touch the water, the tears and mine too, would be mingled with Yours. Oh Mother......take my tears offered for so many souls and with your most loving hand mix them into ripples of love."

September 19th, 2003

(This visual narration was given through the recipient and recorded during the Friday night Rosary. Much group prayer could be heard in the background. The verbal narration was followed by a short unexpected message. Our Lady had previously stated due to the health of the recipient She might not give a public message. Again we ask you to pray to the Holy Spirit and discern as you read the following.)

(Tongues) (Visual - Pat) "The sky is coral ......with hues of purplish blues ...... touches of gold and in the center is a huge cross. Upon the cross is Our Lord ...... but He smiles in His agony. He smiles and watches. I must be to the side of Him. For I am able to see a huge valley with multitudes of crosses. Different colors though. I'm not sure what that represents, but you can see the track where the cross has been carried. Some have dug so deeply into the earth that the soil has left a great crevice. A great crevice has been left from this beautiful soul which endured much to get to the foot of The Cross of Christ. It's all neatly arranged beneath His Cross. It's something of awesome beauty, yet great holiness and as

each cross comes I do not see the soul that carries the cross. But it is as though there is a niche into which each cross precisely fits. And over and over I hear chimes, beautiful chimes. It's a harmony of the angels and the souls that sing together in praise and thanksgiving to Almighty God.

Oh how much He loves us. See the beauty in the depths of His eyes that are endless pools of love. He doesn't speak but with a glance of His eyes He welcomes each of His children who have faithfully borne their cross and exchanged that cross for a crown. There's no longer a figure on the cross. The cross fades ...... there's a huge most glorious throne. My eyes cannot behold what sits upon the throne, for it is too bright ...but beautiful. And each of these souls now carry their precious gifts and lay them before the Throne of God. It's almost as though you can hear the cheers. A heavenly cheering team that says well done and all these names ring out ......the names of each one who has carried their cross ......exchanged it for a crown and now presents it to Our Lord. How beautiful. Thank you My Lord that You allow us to struggle...... to know that glory awaits all Your children. A strong burst of light; nothing is left but sweet fragrances and a sense of serenity which words cannot describe.

"Come to me .....all you who are burdened and I shall give you rest".

(An extensive conversation in tongues followed that was not recorded. A voice was then heard referencing Jerry not recording the given tongues.)

"Why have these tongues not been recorded, My son.....for one day they shall be interpreted and you shall see their meaning?."

September 26th, 2003

(At approximately 8:00P.m. while in meditation in our Hereford home, I (the recipient) heard "wake up My child" and was instructed to write the following message as dictated. Being ill, I was unable to attend the Friday night Canyon Rosary and was somewhat disappointed. For this visit was by a dedicated out of state group had been planned for some time. Physical problems had continuously plagued me for the last three consecutive weeks. However, God works in mysterious ways and His ways are always perfect.)

"My Dear Children,

I hear the whispers in your hearts that She shall not come tonight. But you, My precious children ... with all the spiritual baggage in your hearts for healings, intercession in family and financial matters ....for the strength and courage and commitment to God of your total self ......that in itself shows you walk by faith. A faith well lit by the Holy Word of God and by the traditions of our Holy Church. For though centuries have long passed, we still speak to each and every heart. Some, yes, require much tender molding marked <u>fragile handle with care</u>.

While others receive His word and are drawn to truth. One does not hide from the truth, as truth seeks in every absorbing opportunity to be a way of witnessing to the Life and Love of Jesus Christ.

So this night these are words of peace and joy. You have not come to see the messenger but to hear the message. Mark well my words for each here is precious to God. A Heart that longs for the salvation of others is an infinitely more precious gift. For one eventually learns you are all in the soul serving business. As you leave, may you be blessed with the presence of Our Peace. When you return, the peace you now carry will emit a fragrance of holiness to be shared with many of Our children. My peace I give to you this night".

October 3rd, 2003

(Recipient) The following message was received during a time of private reflection while in the silence of God. This particular evening, I did not attend the Friday night Canyon Rosary, but spent the time away from the group in prayerful contemplation. Many items were discussed which will be revealed in God's time. It was made known I will withdraw into a deeper silence, which will strengthen the intensity of faith and trust in His plan for greater spiritual and physical healings.

"My Dear Children,

At times it becomes necessary for one to step back from the project at hand to see everything in its proper perspective. As one looks too closely your focus becomes limited. Yet, in taking just a few steps back ......you either see a total canvas with multitudes of possibilities ......or a minor imperfection upon which you dwell. Life resembles the canvas. Upon what do you concentrate My children? Your lives are full of imperfections and distractions.

However, the beauty of the canvas upon which you desire to see the beauty of God in all His creatures, remains as a tapestry of perfection. For you do not see as God sees! God sees man's choices .....whether good or bad. And only God knows how the tapestry is repaired ......through repentance and penance.

As God weaves His thread of Mercy through these precious souls ...beauty unbeheld by human eyes, becomes a Masterpiece known only to the eyes of God."

October 10th, 2003

(Tongues) "Yes My Child ......so many wounded souls ......so many souls in despair and so many souls that shall be healed and filled with joy this night."

(Tongues between our Blessed Mother and recipient in which the recipient asked Our Mother if it was now time for Her to verbalize Her message for all to hear.

She replied to recipient.) "I will Speak now My Child."

"My Dear Children,

Once again I stand amongst you, looking into every heart. Gazing at the pain, the sorrow and the joy which this week has brought. And tonight as a mother I ask you, out of love for Me and My Son, to shed your tears of suffering and add them to Ours, as We suffer much for mankind. Now My Children, is a most difficult time ….. a time when all must follow the light of Christ. That there are so many obstacles to distract ….. to blur the vision. You must pray and you must pray frequently, with great intensity. Pray My Children …… pray in the quiet solitude of your heart, where only you and Jesus shall meet and He shall calm your fears, renew the joy in your heart, strengthen you and prepare you, for what lies ahead. I have not come these many years with so many messages, without a purpose. For surely you know that God has a purpose in all He does. You are My prayerful warriors. We place Our trust in you. When We ask for prayers, We know, We receive them and those prayers, though you do not see, are used in so many ways, to save a soul that is in danger of being lost.

Souls My Children are your key position ….your key job in this life …. to love and to serve …… to gather souls for Jesus. The path is difficult I know. My Son walked it. I followed in His footsteps and now you too are called to do the same. Do not reject this mission that God has chosen you to do and when I speak I do not speak only to this group, My beautiful children who gather here so faithfully... I speak to the world …… a world that must change …. a world that must become one of love and one of forgiveness. For time runs quickly. Again the hour glass is sifting so fast My children you do not realize how quickly time passes. You are called to do much in a short period of time ……but you are called because you are faithful …….because you trust. You trust not only in the justice of God, but you trust in His mercy. Believe My Children, trust Him ….love Him ….for He is the light that leads to eternity. He is love ….pure love and as love He opens His arms and then His heart and says;" "Welcome My beloved faithful children."

*** No public message on October 17th ***

October 24th, 2003

(The following messages were received during the Friday night Canyon Rosary. This was another evening of unexpected multiple responses. On the original audio recordings as each being orates, one hears each distinctive voice including what is to be presumed is one from an aborted child spoken with a child's voice.)

(Extensive Tongues) "I Michael, guardian of the Queen of Heaven and Earth greet thee this night. I escort Her with legions of angels. Listen to Her with great reverence … .with much faith. For Her words will penetrate your heart …..will heal the wounds that so many suffer. Listen ….do not be distracted, for there are

those who wish to distract. But My Angels stand ready. They stand amongst you …..to protect you ….to guard you that you may hear Her words and feel the gentleness of Her heart."

"My Precious Children,

I invite you this night to praise Almighty God by loving Him with all your heart …. your mind ….. your body … your soul and your strength. Love Him with your mind that your thoughts will be His thoughts. Love Him with your body that it would do His work. Love him with your heart that it will love others. Love him with your soul. For it belongs to God and longs to be with Him. And love Him with your strength. All your strength My Children for this is required of thee. There is no middle ground. You either love God and serve Him or follow the other path which leads only to destruction.

How precious you are little ones with so many problems. Yet so faithful ….. so loving ….so generous and so kind that you do reach out to love and serve others. And this is what God asks of you. To love others …..to serve them ….to be with them to comfort them. For they like you need the comfort that comes from one another. And from where does such comfort come? Only through the love of Jesus as He takes each heart melting and molding it ……preparing it for each situation.

My children, how blessed you are and yet there are those who do not understand ……who cannot conceive that God can send His Mother to this earth ….. to various places throughout the world …. to say I love you. I am here ! I comfort you. God is real! He awaits you with His arms spread …His heart open. A little knock! Do you hear the little knock as He knocks on the door of your heart? Open your hearts precious Children of God that you may receive every grace He has for you. That you may truly be His Precious Children. Walk with Him ….talk with Him. Pray that you will become stronger in life's long journey with Him …that you will learn the things He wishes you to know and how to use them. For you are His Children ….He is your teacher and has so many gifts for each of you …. if you but open your hearts and welcome Him.

You are to pray for the children. For the children are being misled …… and there are so few who find the true love of God at such a early age and cling to that love and hold tightly through this life on earth. A love that shines so brightly and is shared with so many. Pray ..… pray especially for the children."

(This second message followed. It was heard and recorded in a child's voice and discerned possibly as from an aborted child. Due to the unusual nature of the subject, recipient's spiritual advisor further discerned and has permitted publication.) (This actual audio may be available on Our Lady's website.)

"I am but a little child of God, sent home early because my parents did not want me. But I am safe and I am so filled with joy. I missed my chance to offer my talents whatever they may have been. But my great joy is being with My Lord, with My Father and praying for my family who hurt so deeply for this mistake. But yet, God gives me all these others to pray for. <u>There are so many of us</u>. But please pray that others will still have the chance to make their contribution to your world …. to show God's Love as we cannot have that chance."

October 31, 2003

(Soft tongues; recipient spoke) " Oh Mother, it is so bright. Why is it so bright tonight? The room glitters. It sparkles. Such peace, such beauty" .

"My Dear Children,

The beauty of which My Child speaks is the beauty of the light of love carried upon the shoulders of each of His children …...particularly those who persevere through the most difficult of circumstances. Yet it is the joy that emanates from their very soul which lights the area around them. For it is the light …..the love of Jesus Christ. How beautiful My children if all could see what God has planned, even for this Our Little Holy Mountain …...you would rejoice and you would carry your crosses with greater perseverance. For God has many plans. Some to be revealed very soon …...others must wait. For all must be in order. Our church must speak and follow in obedience as each of you must do. For We guard you and protect you and lead you for that you may not stray but will remain true to the church founded by My Son. That is the beauty of tonight. The lights that glimmer …. although lights glimmer in other places, for unholy reasons. *(Meaning Halloween)* Tonight they glimmer with love ….love for My Son. But most importantly …...the love which He has for each and every one of you, His precious, precious children."

All the struggles, the temptations, all the obstacles placed in your way …..will one day form a path of glory, which shall lead you to heaven. Cling tightly to God's words. Believe My Children, believe …...for He sends many signs. But so many are blinded …...they cannot see for doubt clouds their vision. But pray and pray diligently for all God's Children to see His love buried deeply within the hearts of each one of you. Take a simple look around this holy room …... do you see smiles of great joy of great reverence? Yes My Children, for tonight as we do each Friday night …….the world is blocked from this holy place …..that we may pray … that we may praise Our God.

Blessed you are oh faithful ones. For one day …one day soon for some …...you shall see the glory that God has prepared for you. Walk with great confidence … stand boldly, though heavy the cross may seem and let the smile shine brightly …..for you march to victory with My Son."

(Tongues) "So many are lost. Your job is to seek them out and bring them back …. always to Jesus. Does He not smile at you? What do you see as you look at the mural of God …..of such love who awaits His Children? Be always busy My

327

Children for there is much to do. Yet in the silence of your heart there is much preparation to be made. For God will touch your heart with the strength that each will require …… no matter what your physical condition. God holds your heart. He beckons …..come …..run to Him joyfully …sing praising His Holy Name."

(An extensive gentle conversation in tongues followed) "My blessed Mother, I love you" .

November 14th, 2003

(Recipient) "Oh Dear Mother…….that you should come again…and embrace us this night……and you come to console us……to give us strength……to persevere through all the trials of life. What brings thee this night dear Mother?"

"My Dear Child,

I have come this night that the aroma of My love will spread throughout this room. That all hearts will be open to receive such love where so many are broken ….so many are tired and yet, what is it I see in your heart My Child? I see joy ….. is that not right?"

"Thou know' est sweet Mother……how much I have asked Our Lord for these things He gives me ……these beautiful gifts that I must hide … and my heart bursts with joy."

"As all hearts should burst with joy if they but knew the value of suffering. Suffering is joy. For you suffer for the souls of those who do not know My Son. Yes, Jesus, they do not know Him. But you precious ones shall help them ….. shall help them come to know the one who loves them beyond belief. Who gives all to them ….. every grace to sustain them and with a heart that is open …… open to hear them …... open to hear their cries when that seed in them bursts. The bud on the flower begins to open and they see The Jesus of Mercy. The Jesus of forgiveness who stands arms spread saying" "Come …… come My Children …. gather about Me that I may hold you and that I may love you." "This is the Jesus I want them to see in your eyes. I wish you to be filled with joy, in all ways in all circumstances, with joy of love emanate from every pore of your body. May your soul be enriched with the love of God, the strength of the Holy Spirit, that all will see and rejoice in knowing that they carry the love of God deep within their heart …… it has but to be awakened.

For there are those who sleep … not as you would sleep and rest and recline … but sleep in a way that blinds them from Christ and His love and see only what the world has to offer. It is as though they lived in a dream. Though reality comes and it shall come soon enough. So be bold My Children as I have always asked of thee

328

.... for We shall give the strength to persevere."

(Tongues) "Yes love .... but love often must begin with forgiveness and all too often the forgiveness is the most difficult one ..... when one cannot forgive himself. The door is open ...... see My Child."

(Recipient) "There is a door......a bright light pours forth from the doorway. Light emanates everywhere... sparkling, powerful yet not intimating, it's welcoming. It's so warm and there stands in the doorway, a man who holds within his arms a lamb. (yes Mother, I have seen this before). How Jesus searches for each of His Children. He leaves the ninety nine and searches for the one who is lost. He does not give up until all are resting safely within His pasture. (tongues) Yes I know...my heart does flame with love. Oh if this fire is not quenched Oh Mother, I shall be consumed, consumed by love. Oh My Jesus, set my heart so on fire for souls. Consume me My Lord...for thou has called me. Help me Lord as You help all of us, to be ready when our name is called."

(Angel) " Little Child ..... it is time once again to rest ...... but you are warm and you are at peace."

(Recipient) "I am warm and at peace. For your wings cover me."

No public Message on November 21st 2003

November 28th, 2003

(By recipient) The following message was received after reading scripture in preparation for the Friday night Canyon rosary. It was not totally surprising to receive such a message as Our Mother previously mentioned that She would be guiding us and directing our paths as we continue serving Jesus. It is my personal opinion that there will be less audible messages as I am drawn into more contemplative prayer. It is my prayer that all hearts will become more aware of these intensely corruptive times in which we live and we will all surrender our will to that of our Divine Savior, Jesus Christ.

"My Dear Children,

This night I call you My Servants of Mercy. All who hear the word of God and allow its profound meaning to take root in your hearts are Servants of Mercy.

Are you beginning to understand the significance of this? Our Mountain of Mercy ....where the most hardened of sinners when once exposed to God's unconditional love through the True Presence of Christ will find themselves drawn to remorseful repentance.

This is Holy Ground ......well guarded by God's angels and visited by many Saints whose intercession is invoked. Still, My children, your work has not been completed. For each of you must continue in prayer to become visible examples of mercy. Through much love and patience you are being prepared to love unconditionally as well.

I desire more effort through prayer to help reveal the holiness of this mountain to all who come. A kind word spoken with great love will gently reveal to more pilgrims that reverence is due to Love Himself, Who dwells here amongst you. Continue My children, to persevere as We will continue to pour forth the graces necessary for this your mission. I bless you this night as you praise My Son!"

Second Message of November 28th, 2003

(Visual by recipient) "Mother............You wish to explain? I see a large mountain covered with beautiful flowers, all kinds, all colors. Such fragrance ......so, so beautiful. A huge bouquet on some mountain ......and I hear a noise and hear laughter, running and there are people running through the flowers and stepping on them and they are pushing them down into the ground breaking them off and running and laughing and picking and pulling and ...Oh Mother!"

"Just be at peace My Child, for this is as I have spoken this day. The flowers represent the souls that have been stepped upon .... Ignored. But a folly for those who come to This Holy Place. Yet they do not realize what they have done. This I wish you to know ......that each one who gathers here upon the mountain .... each one whose heart belongs to Jesus is responsible to help these souls. To be filled with reverent awe, knowing they are in the presence of Our Lord. So many distractions in the world draws their attention away from Him who deserves all attention. Yet this is your mission ....something so important you are called to do ... to be gentle guides, to restore that which has been neglected. Reverence, peace and a love which is offered in this holy place."

(Tongues) "Mother, we are so gentle with souls as You ask us to be. Look at these flowers that have been stepped upon ......the souls ......now limp upon the ground no longer standing strong and standing beautiful ...... but limp and wilted ......uprooted, Mother. What shall we do?"

"Gather them My child. Then tenderly with an abundance of love ... replant them in God's love and mercy. Be very gentle especially with those that have been uprooted. For they have been away a long time ...and they are going to find their way back because of your gentle love and concern. Yes My child, your concern for each and every soul. You are My gardeners as well as My Children of Mercy. I have taught you. You know My child what I expect of thee and thee alone. But others too must know that they have a great responsibility to be gentle, yet firm. That these uprooted souls ...are replanted in fresh soil ... where their hearts would be made whole again ...and renewed with the Love of Jesus. See ...... He stands, watching, waiting, inviting. Put your tools in your hands My children ......the tools of love, obedience, gentle forgiveness and gently help nourish these precious souls back to My Son. He loves you so very much. Won't you do what you can …. for time is so very short.

How beautiful to see the mountain undisturbed, in full bloom once again."

(Personal conversation followed) *"When one day my heart shall burst, out of love for You." (Powerful tongues) "Amen"*

December 5th, 2003

"My Dear Children,

During this special time of Advent in which many hearts are busily preparing for the arrival of My Son, I wish to commend you for the manner in which you have undertaken to make this season as it should be ……one of Holy anticipation of the Birth of Our Savior Jesus Christ. Many are making extra efforts to be gifts of themselves to others through deeds of mercy and kindness. How this pleases Our Hearts and aids in the purification of your soul.

As Divine Love approaches, My Heart, which bore True Love, is enraptured by My Son's precious gift of merciful contemplation placed within each heart, which seeks only to please Him and Him alone. My heart, too, bursts into innumerable pieces, which seek a resting place within each heart. Let us rejoice together, My Children, as Divine Love searches each heart for that special place which says"…….. "Welcome Lord Jesus!"

"As My continuous gift to you, I shall come the Friday before Christmas (unless Christmas falls upon that exact Friday, in which case I shall come the week before) and bless all items placed on what shall be known as" "Our Mother's Blessing Table". "As in previous years, this table shall be placed near My Statue. As you pray the Memorare, My special blessing shall rest upon each item and extend to the person for whom the item is intended. It is a two-fold blessing and one I will continuously extend as long as My Son allows.

You in turn shall more importantly, place a beautiful treasure box in the Chapel for My Son. This shall be filled with <u>Spiritual Gifts</u> for My Son and shall be taken to Him Christmas morning with joyful songs of praise. I desire this treasure box to be available at the start of Advent in order for more pilgrims to be able to participate with their special "gifts" for Jesus. This too, shall continue annually. Prepare a special table for this treasury of gifts for all to see for this too shall allow the "giver" to receive many graces. All that I ask of you is to have much faith!

331

Remember these words ......for though My time with you grows short. You shall grow tall as the mighty oaks ......strong and well rooted in your faith. Pray with a sincere heart for with such faith ......mountains shall indeed move!

Rejoice always and in all things be grateful for the hand of God shall rest upon you ... to encourage and strengthen you as you continue your journey home. Peace and joy I leave with you this night."

December 12th, 2003

"My Beloved Children,

I wish to share with you the night of joy ......when My heart was so full. So full of love ......so full of gratitude to Almighty God. For that heart which beat in My womb .....and continuously beats ......one with mine.

Dear children,

This is such a time of joy. If only those children who have strayed could realize the peace and joy that God desires to instill within their hearts. I ask you this night to be so filled with the joy that fills My Heart as it did when I bore My Son. And continuously is filled with joy ....for He has given Me a great gift as well ... .a gift of His Children. I, the Mother of all seek each heart and call each one to the reverent joy of knowing and loving My Son. Peace My Children .... yes peace I desire for each of you. But you find such peace and such joy in the gift of charity .... a gift of love. Those are the gifts most appreciated by My Son. He sees you in your moments of love when you care for others in whatever way God has given the grace for you to do so. Be pleased My Children that you have found great favor with Him. For your hearts beat as one ....with the One. The One True One who's love is truth. It means My Children that your life is a continuous journey of trials also and foremost, a journey of charity and love.

Tell Me My Children on which store shall you purchase charity and love? Is there a sale which so many have rushed to take advantage of ... or is the great sale a gift that God wishes to give you found in peace, in love and in charity? You have chosen well little favored ones. Continue to seek the face of Christ as you await His coming in eager anticipation. It is the faith also in those who come. Rejoice continuously in this season of Advent .... of preparation. Yes, of continuous preparation. For you do not know with whom you speak and of what results your kindness and love shall bring about in that person's life. Souls My Children ... it is about souls. Great is your responsibility but greater still is the love bestowed upon you to accomplish your mission. Rejoice with Me as He eagerly awaits to share His peace ....with His children."

(Visual by recipient) "The angels sing as they gather about Our Mother. Not songs as we know them but beautiful melodies words cannot describe. Bells ring

332

*in preparation for such a beautiful, beautiful time. There are so many (angels)
...... all different sizes, all gathered around Her with such joy and in anticipation.
How beautiful and how humble She remains". (repeated sighs)*

December 19th, 2003

*(This Christmas message was given through the recipient and recorded during the
Friday night Rosary. The dimly lit prayer room had been especially prepared with
decorations, candles and a small nativity scene placed inside the fireplace. This
particular evening was one of special joy in anticipation of the blessing of our
special items.)*

(Recipient) *"How beautiful thou are this night, all in white. A gold sash......the
lights penetrating through Her gown, again like gossamer...(transparent) gold,
white, beautiful lights. The lights of a beautiful holy face of The Mother of
God.................Oh Mother."*

"My Dear Child,

It is with great joy that I see the emotion in the hearts of so many of My faithful
children. For it is by faith that they have come this night bringing their precious
gifts once again for My blessing ..... a blessing I will soon bestow upon them. Do
not be dismayed or lose focus My children when things do not go as you have
planned. For I tell you truly .....that they are done according to God's plan be at
peace. No anxiety of the heart, but only prayer with the heart to ease the pain and
suffering of this world.

Rejoice My Children, for by your faith, many will be blessed. Many will come to
know My Son .... to love Him and to serve Him. My message is brief but My
blessing to each one here this night ....especially the precious little ones, will
extend through their lifetime as well as yours. And the gifts that you have brought
too, carry a special blessing as well, for all who receive them.

I smile as I look about the room and see the candles burning.....the warm fireplace
.....now a beautiful manger scene. All the beautiful items that have been brought,
so many with beautiful memories that touch your hearts, will now touch them
even more deeply. Be at peace My Children as I Your Mother bless you this night.
See My Angels as they gather amongst you, touching each and every one of you.
Oh My Children, should the scales fall from your eyes you would utterly expire
......for the beauty which lies before you.

Peace My Children and My blessing."

(Recipient) *"So beautiful and the lights. She says you have but to look at the stars
above this Holy Place to see that God has well lit His Holy Mountain."*

****

333

Messages from Jesus and Mary

January 2, 2004 – June 1, 2004

January 2nd, 2004

*(The following message was received and audio recorded as given thru the
recipient at the Friday night Canyon Rosary at Mary's Knoll. It was played in
English and then repeated as translated into Spanish. Prior to the Rosary it was
suggested by one of the group we sing "Oh come all Ye faithful" between the
decades of the Rosary. Note the timing of the sequence as Mary spoke.)*

(Recipient – Inaudible) "Oh My Jesus ......Oh Mother how beautiful He is" ......

"My dear children,

Praise be Jesus . . .. whom you have come to love, honor and adore. Praise be His
Holy Name ....the name etched upon each and every heart that loves and
follows His words.

My dear ones,

I have come to join you .... to praise Him. The one who has come to redeem the
world. Sing My children .....how beautiful the song. Sing joyfully that He may
hear each and every voice as it rises to His throne. You sing now before a child
born in Bethlehem .... a child born greeting the world. Sing now for this child
walks amongst you receiving your prayers .....receiving your petitions, receiving
those prayers held deeply within your heart. (*At this time the prayer group was
singing a stanza of Come all ye Faithful)* For this is the time when His children
come forth in more abundance to praise Him, to thank Him, to be filled with His
joy.

Rest my children in the assurance of God's love and in His mercy. Do not fear to
come to Him in complete trust ......complete faith that He can move the mountains
in your lives. Simply love as a child loves. A child who's eyes open wide in
expectation for the gift they have asked for and pray to receive. Let us rejoice
always together. For He who knows all .....sees all ......is with us this night.

I bless you my children but more important ....My Son blesses you.

*(A private message and conversation with the recipient followed. In this sequence
there were confirmed indications the recipient's responsibility to serve the
community would continue for awhile longer. She was told to:)*

334

"Stand firm upon the ground which you have been planted. For there you shall grow and midst the winds and midst the storms, until you are called. Where there is no fear, there is only joy and great expectations. Keep open your heart and We shall continue to fill it with our love. We shall fill it with every grace necessary in your mission to help others."

No message on January 9th, 2004

January 16th, 2004

(Recipient) "Our hearts are yours."

(Visual) "It appears as though it's early afternoon but the sun is high in the sky. But it moves from place to place ... dancing ...... pulsating and Our Lady is there and She holds ...... or what is held for Her is a basket. But it's more like one I cannot describe. It is so beautiful and it is filled with every imaginable flower. But each one is so fragrant. The whole area is inundated by this beautiful aroma. There are many people who see this. Our Lady takes Her precious hands and reaches into this golden light woven basket and gently tosses into the air the petals from these flowers. All the people are so in awe to see the dancing sun ..... to see the petals fall to the earth. They are so eager to capture their treasure. Oh Mother ... please tell me what it is you wish to say."

"My dear child,

The dancing of the sun is a gift from my Son. The petals from this basket represent the sweet graces that each of you have received and have treasured because you have recognized the significance of God's signs and wonders. All these things of which we have spoken during these many years have brought comfort and consolation to you our precious children. It is now time for you to recognize the world in which you live is on the brink of a great abyss.

Without your prayers ....without your constant intercession for others ..... without your willingness to suffer for souls in need, so many will miss the great opportunity that God has planned for them.

Yes, you are workers in the field of my Son .....the field of souls. And each of you ... as each one is unique and possess a special gift. Each is important my child. For together you form the Body of Our Lord. Seek to do your part. Accept what God has given you with a grateful heart and be strong my children. Hold your weapons tightly within your hands. Let your fingers fall upon each bead of the rosary. Each prayer echoes in my heart .... for I my children am not deaf. I hear the prayers .... the multitude of prayers that are said .....especially those that are prayed for the healing and conversion of others.

God has poured forth this great time of mercy .... a time of un-fathomable grace to cover His children who are willing to accept this great gift. It is time now to be bold ... to be bold in love .....and charity and self denial. For these things you shall present to God. Above all love ..... love for God and love for the souls of whom you have prayed.

I bless you this night and cover you with my mantle for protection.

January 23rd, 2004

(Among those in attendance were a Hispanic group of 50 including their supporting priest. <u>During the Rosary</u> and before the audio message was later played one young lady from a local youth group confirmed she visually saw butterflies. Spiritual gifts for others were also confirmed. The visual text by the recipient that follows suggests what took place. The evening concluded by a blessing from the priest and then "laying of hands" by the prayer team.)

(Visual by recipient) "Sweet Mother ... what is it that you hold in your hand? It is so bright ......very unusual. I have never seen this before! Light illuminates the path wherever you go. The room has become darkened and I see a lady of lights. In Her right hand She carries a golden lantern and she passes from one person to the next ..... pausing ...... lovingly glancing as though actually examining the heart of that particular person. She smiles as She passes from one to the next. There are some who appear to require more prayer. Then I see a look of sorrow and She stays with that person a little longer and until at last She smiles. Just a simple smile and goes on until She has touched each and every one that is amongst us. Mother I don't understand the meaning but I know and I trust you will explain."

"My child,

This symbolizes the lantern in which I looked into the heart ..... seeking the just and loving soul committed to My Son. Where I have paused I have prayed much for that particular soul. For I see that they are unwilling to accept Christ's strength in place of their weakness. Pray for these children for it is so difficult for them to accept a world in which you are called for much penance and sacrifice. Yes the strings of the world hold tightly to you ....but what is in my other hand my daughter?"

"A scissors? Mother I think they're scissors ...... and you snip away at the strings which holds these precious souls so closely to the world. They are scissors in a sense they are love. Sweet mother, how you love your children. How you come to protect us and to guide us that we may free ourselves from the ways of the world. But only through our faith and our trust in your Son. Yes, is this correct mother?"

"My daughter,

You have learned to read many hearts. I place the scissors of love within your hand that you too may be an instrument of God's Mercy ....to love with such intensity that no longer will the world bind our children."

(Recipient) "There are a lot of lights now mother. Mother they look like butterflies but they are so brilliant and they're landing on each of your precious children. A special blessing this night for those whose hearts truly belong to Jesus. Help us sweet mother to increase our faith, our trust in the mercy and love of your Son. We praise His Holy Name. He is Our Lord and Our God. I feel something touching my face. It's so beautiful. No longer is the room dark. It is aglow with love ... a love which has surrendered to Jesus ...... so beautiful ......"

January 30th, 2004

(On this particular day prior to the Rosary we had two specific requests for prayer from distressed mothers who were in sorrow because of problems with their grown children. As one reads or hears this message we cannot help feel it will give peace to many. Please pray and discern it's meaning for you.)

(Recipient) "Sweet Mother; I seem to come to you with so many questions lately and you ever so patiently reply to them. Mother, so many have asked for their children ...... for their sorrows and sufferings. How Mother shall I answer them"?

"My dear child,

You shall say to each of these parents whose children are in various forms of difficulties, whether it be health, financial ...but more importantly ...that they are away from God. You shall tell them that the sufferings that they bear for their children are a source of purification for the parent .....the parent that continuously prays for their children. Each has a free will, which God will never deny. How that will is used is up to each individual person. You cannot change their lives ... but through prayer you may strongly influence them that they may see the love of Christ emanating all around them.

Do you not think that Our Heavenly Father does not feel the sorrow of your hearts when He sees His children? Yes, His struggling to maintain a sense out of life ...and you as parents .....your sense of suffering has a purpose. For through the prayers that I have asked for and continually asked for .....many souls will be saved. Do you think I have excluded your children? For all belong to God. They are but on loan to you. To care for .... to pray for .... to introduce them to Our Lord.

337

This is the most difficult time for the youth of the world who are distracted and pulled in so many directions that there is little time left in their lives for God. You must reverse this process, for God shall come first. Then only through your prayers ....your persistent prayers ....will this come to be.

Listen well .... as I am the Mother who knows the pain inflicted upon Her Child. And yet ....the joy that God has placed in My heart. For My Son lives and awaits for all of these other children that He has given to Me. He has placed them in my care. I ask for your prayer. Prayer is not just a word ... prayer is the most powerful of weapons. Believe and trust and see the Mighty Hand of God as He works miracles in your lives."

(Recipient-Visual) Extensive private intercession occurs for two particular souls that have been called this night. One wears a very old cross received by a grandmother. It was perceived this grandmother has continuously prayed for the grandchild as she, the grandmother is praying from heaven.

February 6th, 2004

(Recipient's visual) "Sweetest Mother ... what is it you wish me to say? To bring to light the message of your love ... of prayer ...... of unity in families? What shall I say?......What I see?"

"The room has grown immensely. It is filled with many people sitting upon chairs praying, singing. What they do not see is the soul that stands before them with their guardian angel whose wings wrap around this precious soul. It is a moment of enlightenment ...... a moment of great joy. Shall I tell them? Oh mother how do I tell them to see with your heart, all the pain and suffering and to see this precious soul before you now in radiant joy with his faithful companion and what has brought them here. But my dear brothers and sisters this is by your prayers ... for this is what our mother says. Is that right?"

"My dear child,

The graces that you have received are many and the graces that others will see will multiply. For this is a place of faith and thru faith many miracles come about. I wish you to pray now that all of these beautiful souls will be given the gift to see
with their hearts. The soul that stands before them and says;" "thank you for your prayers ... for it was through your intercession that my life changed.

There are bright lights fluttering ... everything is so bright. Yet so many cannot see. For so many agonize over the trials of this world and have been unable to surrender their hearts to Jesus. Through time and much faith the beauty of trust will bloom within each soul and great graces shall befall them. For they shall see with the eyes of pure love. The heart and soul for which they pray." (*tongues*)

"It takes many years for a precious soul (person) to be perfected. Thus it may take many years for the most precious of all of these gifts .....the soul itself to be perfected. Pray unceasingly and pray with joy and great conviction ..... for God is truly among you working His miracles. Open your eyes as well as your hearts that you may see and believe. I bless you, as you are Our Precious Children with a great love for the souls of many. You have known your mission and you have valiantly picked up your weapons. Your rosaries, your scapulars, your precious medals and you have fought so valiantly for each and every soul. Little ones though you may be ... the power of your prayer is incomprehensible. Trust.... trust your mother ..... but most importantly .... trust My Son who loves you unconditionally."

(Visual) "A very large fishbowl ...... it's clear, although it's a liquid inside and there are various pieces of different obstacles resembling moths and I see the faces of many. Many who swim contained by a world that has drawn them from you. They are in a fishbowl ...... no way out ... the same routines. So little space and yet I know mother, that by the power of The Holy Spirit, through our prayers, this bowl will become empty. For these souls too will find life without God is not life. It is simply existence in time."

(Recipient's talk that followed Rosary)

"When I was listening to the message, especially the part where we know to pray for other souls. I remembered how important it is that one day hopefully these souls will be praying for us. So when she said" "their companions the guardian angels were around them." "That made me reflect that these were souls that are in purgatory because ...... (I am not very knowledgeable) ... Let's just say I believe that once we finally reach our hopefully homeward destination point of heaven that our guardian angels have completed their mission that God assigned to them and that is to watch over our soul. So if the soul is still here with their guardian angel, then I would think that, that soul is in purgatory receiving our prayers for them, because they cannot pray for themselves, but they can pray for us. So I just thought it was a beautiful way of expressing that our prayers are important and we've learned this so much through the study of Saint Faustina and constant prayer ......constant intercessory prayer. I don't know that we will ever reach that level. Well, let's just say that nothing is impossible, but there's some doubts. That as long as we learn, as long as we try ......that's the important thing and to give our heart completely to Our Lord Jesus Christ. And let Him do with it what He is going to do with it and He is going to melt it and He is going to mould it and He is going to form it and do whatever He wishes to save these souls. That fish bowl was empty. Near the end there was nothing but a mass of souls swimming, going nowhere and how many of us have been in a situation in life for years that we have gone absolutely nowhere. However, because of the power of prayer, at the very end the fishbowl was empty.

Someone asked me a very profound question today; never asked me this before. When I became a Catholic and I always said I turned Catholic when my husband and I got married in 1984. But tonight, I said I didn't become a true Catholic until

339

I went to Medjugorge when I knew that something miraculous was happening. When I attended churches back here [then in Illinois] my heart wasn't ready. This was just a monotonous routine that I had been given instructions in but it didn't penetrate. I truly became Catholic, I truly became in love with Our Lord and Blessed Mother when I went to Medjugorge and I saw the people there that loved so much. The churches were packed. The confessional lines were so long and I felt like I didn't belong but yet I wanted a taste of whatever they had and I wanted to keep it ......but at the same time I wanted to share it. I didn't know how all of this was going to come about, but I praise God. For people who do not like to travel, He allowed us that one pilgrimage that opened our hearts, our minds, our bodies and souls, to Our Lord and His Blessed Mother. We became more and more in love with the sacraments. We were just like sponges that wanted to sap up everything they had for us and I praise them for that and I praise them for all these tremendous blessings and for you precious souls. You precious prayer warriors that come and pray and I know it is not just here on Friday nights that you pray, you pray every day. You all have loved ones that you pray for. We all have needs, that yes we pray for and God hears them and yes in God's time He's going to answer all of these prayers, in a way that we probably would have not expected. But we will be overjoyed and rejoicing in His presence and we thank Him for allowing us to see how He worked so many miracles in each and every one of our humble lives. So I thank you and I bless you for being here tonight.

No message on February 13th

February 20th , 2004

(Recipient-Tongues) "Oh Mother ...why is it so dark? It's moving in and out, in and out. Dearest Mother, have you come as a sorrowful mother? It is your sorrowful heart in which there is so much darkness. It is crowded with so many souls for whom you weep. For the souls for which you intercede that remain indifferent toward your son and yet you hold them and you pray for them as a mother holds a child that has suffered an injury. A child who is confused ...... a child who cries upon a mothers shoulder. All these are tucked in your heart. Oh mother what shall I say?"

"My daughter,

It is indeed my most sorrowful heart into which you look and see the souls of so many of my children. Souls who have turned their back or have not encountered My Son at all. And yet I, as a mother, hold them deeply within this heart ... this heart that has been pierced and will soon be pierced again. For only love, prayer and sacrifice shall restore these hearts ... these precious souls, that I may release them as a precious gift to My Son.

I will not appear with you this Lent, as previously has been my custom. For you must learn to walk in the steps of Jesus, experiencing all that life gives you at each moment that you live. For one moment brings happiness and joy. The other, great disappointment and tremendous difficulty. But notice my dear children, that each and every foot though different, still fits within the footprints of My Son. There you will find comfort in knowing you walk in the footsteps of the master. He has shown you how to live your lives with great faith, through all difficulties and he has shown you how to experience the joy that only knowing and living His will can bring.

Make this Lent a special time in your life in which you seek not only a cleansing of your soul but of many souls that God will send your way. Let them see your struggles .... but let them also see the joy with which you struggle. For it is the love of Christ that enables each and every one of you to persevere through this life. I shall be with you my children, to watch your steps ... to reach down as you stumble ..... for yes you shall stumble. But I shall not be with you *[meaning no Lenten messages]* in this particular sense. Is it not far greater to know, that your mother holds tightly to your hand and remains with you through this journey of life?" (*tongues*)

"Mother there are so many who do not want to see. They do not want to hear that the love that you have for them is real. It's the strength, a beautiful strength that you have given us to keep on going. But this world ... this world. Oh mother ...... what shall I say about this world? What shall I say that pleases thee and brings thee comfort when my heart is so dark and so sorrowful for the many souls contained there?

Let us all do penance and sacrifice greatly for the many souls which our mother yearns ... to be gifted to her Son. (extensive tongues) I accept the lance. I accept all that you wish me to bear and do all your children who love you. But most importantly as always, to love Jesus. Help us mother ...... for where He has walked ......where He has walked, has been most difficult."

"Be assured, I shall be with you, as shall the Angels to help guide you and protect you through this journey. You will see, though it be most difficult, in time, the rewards will be joyfully overwhelming."

(Note) On Wednesday, March 3rd, Pat the recipient of the messages broke her left hip on a fall. As a result, a full hip replacement was required and it appears the preceding message was prophetic. The healing process took several weeks. After six weeks absence the messages resumed on April 16th, 2004

April 16, 2004

(Rosary at Mary's Knoll.) Because Pat was still healing from her first hip transplant it would have been a physical risk for her to go into one of the previous intense modes of message reception. First received in private, this message was quietly given visually only to her. It was given in a manner that after the message

had originally ended the recipient was allowed <u>to repeat un-interrupted </u>what she experienced and it was then recorded. Of interest, the week before, on Good Friday and prior to starting the evening Rosary of the 16th, both prayer leaders emphasized slow and personal intensity of ones prayers to God and Our Lady. Please pray to the Holy Spirit and discern it's meaning to you.

(Recipient) Tonight as we were praying the rosary, the Blessed Mother presented me with a glass of wine. She asked me to smell the wine and I said it had a strong aroma. She corrected me and said that it was the bouquet and then the taste of the wine was very strong and she said, this was the body of the wine. Then She showed me a large table and around the table were numerous glasses to be filled with wine. I had but one glass, the glass She showed me. I took the glass and I poured a drop or two into each of the glasses that were on the table and She said that the Master of the House requires that the glasses be filled. The only thing there on the table was water. I took the water and I poured it into each glass, filling the glass as She had asked.

She told me that now the wine had become diluted. There was no bouquet. It had lost its body. She said this in reference to prayer. When we do not pray with the heart, when we have become side tracked by the anxieties of the world and all the temptations which it holds, our prayer life suffers because we take time to pray only when it is convenient and only in the manner which we choose, not that which is most pleasing to God. When we pray with the heart, a true sincere prayer, we have the body of the wine as well as the fragrant bouquet and this all rises to the Throne of God and becomes a pleasing offering to Him. An offering in which He hears the cries of our hearts and the intensity of our prayers, which are so pleasing that He hears with the heart of a Father, that melts as He answers the prayers of His children.

We must remember that at all times when we speak to God, we must speak with the heart and not just words but a heart that rings true and clear. A heart that is filled with an aroma, a bouquet and a full body of taste that pleases our Lord. All these things we can accomplish when we stay focused on God and we relinquish the ways of the world. Temptation is always there, but remember the glass. The glass must be filled as the Master has said. It must be filled with our true contrition ... our true desire to please by serving the Will of the Father. When we relinquish our will and seek only the Will of the Father, the glass becomes filled. The glass is prayer ... a powerful prayer...an aromatic prayer ...... a prayer of the body (heart) with a taste most pleasing to God.

April 23rd, 2004

(Note) Attending this particular Friday Rosary were many Hispanics and it became truly bi-lingual. It seems when our Blessed Mother is with us, She expresses Her message in an appropriate way that applies to most everyone's hearts, minds and ears. The immediate translation of the evening's message into

Spanish was a tearful gift.

"My dear children,

Tonight as I gaze upon the many faces .....the many precious souls gathered in prayer My heart rejoices. For throughout the world there are so many more who do not gather.............do not pray and therefore my heart weeps for those precious souls. Here tonight as you pray, pray for those who have lost their faith ... who have strayed so far from my Son. As my Son looks upon Me, His Mother, ... your mother He sees the sorrow in my heart. He sent me into the world to bring.... back His children ......and so many of His children have not only rejected Him but have rejected me as well.

How can I help you if you do not trust ..... if you do not believe? For mercy is being poured out in great abundance. Now is the time to stretch forth your hearts and your hands to receive what God has planed for you. Do you think that I am only present at certain moments of your lives? No my children ..... I hear and I see all the wounds. All the trials that you endure and so faithfully struggle out of love for God, to offer Him all things in thanksgiving. There are many I know, who speak of my messages and say they are incapable of following those messages. They are too difficult ..... or so they say.

My children,

If only you would become childlike in your faith, you would find that my messages are not difficult but in reality are quite simple. How long must I ask you to pray and to pray with your heart? You see the children who come in awe ..... their eyes wide open ....their hearts beating so rapidly .....filled with joy. When they recognize who stands before them they are not intimated. They are filled with such love ..... no fear .....and they come and their little hearts pray simple prayers; yet God is so moved by their prayers. That is how He asks that you pray ..... simply but from your heart and as you do this, you will become accustomed to becoming more and more childlike in your faith. Peace will reign supreme in your life .....for Christ will truly dwell with you. All things will be done with Him and through Him. My dearly beloved children trust in His mercy. Trust the mother who comes to lead you back to the Son."

(Pat) "I hear the sound of trumpets intermingled with the sound of chimes (believed to be the voices of angels in prayer). This is a most critical time. A time that we must concentrate on our prayers, not out of fear, but as a child who trusts and out of such trust it becomes a natural instinct to love, to obey and to do God's will."

This recorded message is from the recipients guardian angel, Samual. It was given strong and clear.

"My little charge,

It has been some time since we have spoken and the words I wish to reveal to you tonight you may share, for they are meant for all to hear. It is my duty as well as the duty of each and every guardian angel to bring comfort and courage to each of their charges .... and yes I say charges, for God has placed us in a position of charge ..... a position of caring .... a position of protection.

You must rely on these great gifts of God. For He has placed within each mouth, upon each tongue and yes tonight, touched your lips that they may reveal the words I wish spoken. You are not to fear, for God himself will reveal what you are to say and to whom you are to say it. You must have courage my children. Courage .....all of you .... to speak truth ..... to speak the word of God to all who will listen. For there are so many who do not know of God and time <u>is of the essence.</u> You must speak of God and you must humble yourself and in the gentleness of your voice reveal the love that God has for all of His children. Bring them back . Bring them back, for God awaits them. He calls you to be instruments .... instruments that He will use to bring back His children.

You say you cannot speak because you are too fearful ....you are not to fearful. You have only to trust in God. He will place those words upon your lips and sweet

they shall be, as the ears of those who need to hear them shall opened and all will be revealed to them. Listen as the prayers are being said. As almighty God is praised and loved ..... so you too must be instruments of this praise and of this love. Go forth renewed in your spirit ....renewed with the courage that God is with you and He has sent us to always be with you ..... to be beside you .... to strengthen you."

"What do you see?" *(recipient)* "*I see this dry land...brownish earth color ...nothing seems to be growing ...just barren. What does this mean?*" "My little charge .....how many times has your soul been so barren as the barren earth you see? When you have been so dry that you felt that you could not utter a prayer. A prayer to thank God for all things. For thanking Him for the bareness that He will renew it with the freshness of the rain of His graces that He will rain upon you." "*Sometimes it seems so difficult as though nothing will ever be the same*" . "Little one ....all things change but the love of God remains constant. His love for you ....for all of His children remains constant."

(Tongues) "Oh sweet Lord. You who love us so much and all of us struggle. But yet You bring comfort to us in such ways that how can we express our gratitude. How can we say to You ...Lord God my heart is so on fire for love ...for the

love that you have placed within me ...for all the gifts that you have given us? Where shall I find the words? Where do each of us find the words? Perhaps we only need to say ... I love You ...and that is sufficient. For truly if we love You, we love all our brothers and sisters as well."

May 7th, 2004

(Note) The recorded message was extremely touching as Our Lady confirms the upcoming conclusion of our seven years of continuous messages soon to be published.

"My dear children,

You who have been so faithful to the Sacred Heart of Jesus and to My Immaculate Heart. I receive you with great joy. And the message I have for you tonight, I wish you to understand with a heart that has been touched by God and not by human hands ...... a heart that has been prepared for many years to do the will of God. It is now time My children .... yes time has at last come when I will take my leave from you. I will remain with you in spirit only. I will reveal to you in times of great need what My Lord and God wish you to know. Many times I have expressed to you, this fine gold thread which binds all hearts to ours. It has not been cut away .... it has been made stronger ....it is now the strongest rope that nothing will ever cut away. You belong to us and now you must do as you have been taught. You have been asked thru these last few messages to prepare yourself for another step in this journey. You began as toddlers, barely able to stand. And now My children you are ready to go out into this world .....to proclaim the word of God with your love ...with your gentle hearts and with the peace that only The Body of Christ can give you? Do you understand?"

"The Eucharist.........do you refer to the Eucharist?"

"Yes, My daughter. It is in frequent confession .....frequent reception of the Body and Blood of my Son that you will be strengthened and encouraged to do the task that is ahead. And this you shall do, for we will always be with you. For as we said, your lips have been touched, your hearts are ready and the ears of those who need to hear ... will hear. This is not a time of sorrow but it is a time of great joy. Think of your children when they go through school and come to this great moment of their life called" "graduation". This is your "graduation" to the next step of this journey.

I will come from time to time but not as frequently as I have before." *(Our Lady indicates this above when She relates to Her revealing information to us in times of great need.)* "There is no need my children, for you hear our voices within your hearts. You know all that we have given you through these years in the messages. Refresh your mind, your heart and your soul once again. Re-read and prepare yourself for there is such a greatness ahead when you see the conversion of so many souls that come to God. What glory awaits them and how glorious the reception in Heaven. All the angels and saints pray and receive these great gifts *(souls)* with such gratitude to God. And look at you, oh little ones, the part that you shall play in restoring a life .....restoring a soul back to God.

There is no sorrow. For there is but a smile upon your lips as you see the fruits of your labor coming together when this life has become a story. And at what point *(of the story)* are you in my children? You have begun to walk and now to speak and speak boldly, gently, lovingly and convincingly of the Truth of Our Lord Jesus Christ. Be strong for we will always be here. You need never fear. I have repeated these words and repeat them again." " I will never fear for God is always with you." " Go now, my beloved and do as you have been instructed."

(2nd message) "These words are only for my daughter." (*A private message followed concerning an upcoming event. For all practical purposes, the recipient believes <u>the upcoming event </u>to be a form of closure after seven years of messages.)*

(3rd message) – *This audio message is from *St. Gemma – She had appeared before to the recipient but had never spoken.*

"My little sister,

I shall be with you and teach you as the Lord has taught me .... to offer such suffering for all the souls who will be lost unless you willingly offer your suffering for them. You have been prepared but in a much less degree than you

will see in the future. I will be with you and I will teach you. Speak to me when you are troubled and always speak to your Spiritual Director that he will know that I have finally come as it was foretold to him. I am your Gemma"

*St Gemma Galgani is a Italian Saint 1878 - 1903 who was canonized in 1940. The book [The life of St. Gemma Galgani] was republished by Tan Books in the year 2000. ISBN 0-89555-669-3

(This visual of Mary then came to the recipient) " *I see a Lady of Lights dressed in white – a gold sash about her waist – radiant and joyful because her children will come. They will believe. They will be healed in body and in soul. There are so many angels on that mountain – legions of angels constantly protecting their children. Oh what great joy – how we have been so blessed – so much to do – so much to do!"*

There were no public messages between May 7th and June 1st.

In the unpublished portion of the message given on May 7th 2004 Our Lady previously confirmed she would give a final message at 7pm on the 7th anniversary and in the same place as the original first message. This location is at the original small shrine above and behind the large cross. At 6pm Our Lady, two priests, two deacons and our close group gathered for a beautiful mass in the small chapel. Then at the conclusion of the mass we all journeyed up the holy hill while praying the Rosary to await her message. In view of all, the recipient went into ecstasy and Our Lady clearly spoke the following recorded message.

(Recipient) "Oh Maria ....sweet mother .....my heart is in pieces. Oh most sweet Jesus... through the power of your most precious blood ......cover each and every one of us that only your words and your words alone shall be spoken."

"My dear children,

Praise be Jesus who has allowed me to be with you these seven years. My heart is filled with joy. Yet as a mother there is a little sorrow as I take my leave from you. Remember as I first came and most importantly, I always asked that you pray with your hearts. When you pray with your heart you grow closer to sanctity and purification.

Your world is in a state of turmoil ....a state so degrading my children, that only the most sincere prayers ....those prayers from the heart will withhold the hand of my son. He loves you my children as I love you and as I have come to teach you the way to follow in His steps. Do you recall the many times I have told you to stay focused on My Son? And when you stay focused on Him you are not distracted by the ways of the world.

I call you to a passage of the ancient prophet Jeremiah. A passage in which he speaks of false prophets. It is a time My children <u>as so many claim to hear my voice</u> that you discern greatly ....that you have direction in your life ... to know the sound of my voice as it penetrates your heart and releases peace. For only peace comes from God and so many have been drawn away. Drawn from His love into a world which loves only comfort and satisfaction. No greater satisfaction comes than through the love of God and knowing His will. His commandments are simple my children ....simple guidelines through life that each of you are called to contemplate and to follow.

Remember His words. His words He spoke of love for each of his children. As He hung upon the cross did you not see the love that remained in His eyes? Though His body was torn and tortured ....there was nothing but love and compassion within His heart .....which reflected into His eyes as He gazed about the world .... not only then ....but through the centuries to come.

I call you as I have always called you to be children of peace. But to use great discernment in these times. For my love for you is so great and yet I cry for the many children who will not hear my words .... who will not practice what I have taught. And after all these years I have called you ..... practice what you have been taught. Pray .... Fast .... do penance .....make sacrifices in your lives and be reconciled to God and to your neighbors.. For the greatest of all things I call you to .... is to love. It is easy to love the child ..... to love the spouse. But can you love the one who has wronged you and caused you great pain? When you can do these things ..... you have progressed my children .... to be true children of God. Love above all must prevail.

Do not forget what I have shared with you .....the moments ....the visions I allowed you to see .... and the hope that has been planted into each heart. Listen well ...receive the graces that God wishes you to receive."

(Recipient – Tongues) " Our Blessed Mother holds a glass ... a crystal glass. Not a chalice, but a glass in one hand and in the other it looks like an umbrella. She's asking (me) to look at the glass. It's half full mother ...it's half full. It looks like water but it glistening. It's so beautiful and the glass itself I can't describe, for the colors are like rays of lights ....but I don't understand the umbrella."

"My dear child,

God pours forth multitudes of graces upon each of His children. The glass symbolizes those graces that have been received. The umbrella symbolizes those who have rejected the graces that God has sent and therefore have protected themselves .....protected themselves from God ....poor souls. How many times has there been a slight mist .... a refreshment in the air sent by God? You can smell the aroma ....you can feel the moisture on your cheeks and yet you run .... to cover yourself .... to place an umbrella above your head that you will not be dampened. It is similar My children .....allow the graces of God to fill your lives. Do not hide from Him .... do not reject Him. For the glass which you see ....you say is half full. To many say it is half empty ...because they did not allow the graces to enter their lives. I bless you my dear faithful children ....sent into this world to be ambassadors of love and mercy. I will always be your loving interceding Mother and I will always draw you closely to My Son. But tonight .... a special blessing for you .....for your loved ones. For you believe and you come. Hear your name as My Son calls you.

Blessed be my children."

This Christmas message was given through the recipient and recorded during the Friday night Rosary. In attendance was an overflow group of many nationalities. The dimly lit prayer room had been especially prepared with decorations, candles and a small nativity scene placed inside the fireplace. Again the evening was one of special joy in anticipation of the blessing of our special items. In this night's message, Our Blessed Mother confirms the mortality of our lives upon this earth and asks us to start preparing to pass on to our successors, the future keys to the Shrine of Our Lady of the Sierras. We ask you to pray to the Holy Spirit and discern as you read the following.

(Tongues) "My most beloved children,

How My heart is filled with such joy this night as so many gather to honor My Son. Oh sweet children ..... I see the hearts of so many opening up to Jesus. The Holy Spirit is pouring forth such love ... such tenderness ...such understanding.

Listen My Children .....for there is one other thing I wish you to know. This shall become a custom ... a tradition. Long after you have been called from this earth I shall continue to bless those gifts that are left for me. I shall continue to come the Friday before Christmas. But you must pass down to your children and the youth that follows that this is indeed a special night. Not because of My blessing dear children ....but because of the pending birth of The Redeemer of the World.

Do not forget your spiritual gifts ....for they must be presented to Him on Christmas morning. I have repeated these words to you ..... so that you will know when you are called home .....there will be those still here to continue this tradition. This is what My Son wishes you to know this night. His Heart too is filled with joy.

My dear children if you could only see the multitude of angels that surround you. For I blessed you .....each and every one of you with the love of a mother.

Rejoice now.............for Christ soon comes to dwell amongst you."

(Note) Our Mother followed with a confirmation. There will be two healings tonight, one spiritual and one physical.

***** Finish *****

Addendum

Messages 2005 -2006

Message of December 23rd, 2005

The following messages were audio recorded as received thru the recipient at the Friday night Rosary at Mary's Knoll. As confirmed on the Message of December 24th, 2004 Our Lady expressed she would come and bless items placed in Mary's Knoll on the Friday before Christmas. The second message was given in "unique" manner, as it was then un-recorded and given directly to the group thru the recipient for all to hear "live".

7:35 pm. [Recipient - tongues] *"She said to remember to tell them about the flickers of light as many angels will be here this night, but they are not to be distracted, only to be comforted, to know that so many [angels] are here with them receiving Our Lady".*

8:45 pm. [Our Lady speaks directly to the group, that is, it was not a re-played earlier recording]

"It is a heart filled with gratitude when I look amongst you and see so many with pain and in anticipation of my visitation. There are many who came who say" "I do not see her, I do not see anything ....but a statue ......but a mural on the wall"......"but I tell you that faith fills the void where you are unable to see. With human eyes you must trust the eyes of your heart. For the eyes of your heart reveal many mysteries. My womb is filled with great expectation for the coming of the Savior of the World.

My joy is inexpressible in human terms. But I tell you my children, Emmanuel comes. The Savior comes and He is filled with such joy to come to His children who accept him ....who believe in Him and who love and serve Him.

Dear little ones .....you expect such great miracles and yet the greatest miracle goes un-noticed. As you shop ...as you prepare for a great festive occasion ....the greatest miracle, un-noticed .....un-wanted awaits that special moment in each heart and at last the spirit fills them and they cry out".....".Emmanuel ......My Lord and My Savior."

"I ask each of you now as I bless each heart ....to place your hand upon your heart and if you can feel such the joy of each instant beat ......the warmth of the Mother of God ...... you will know how much He loves you. It is a brief moment and yet such power .....such love. I ask the parents and those who have small children to place their hands on the heart of their little ones ......that they too may experience the love of God. A brief flicker of love that will grow and grow as they grow.

I bless you .....each of you this night as I bless each and every gift that has been presented to me for my special blessing. Know that there is a three-fold blessing. I bless first the gifts as you have brought them. Secondly, I bless the recipients of the gifts and thirdly, I bless those that are the givers of the gifts. Our Lord loves a cheerful giver.

So this evening let you hearts be filled with joy and with peace. For you have the blessing of the Father and the Son and the Holy Spirit …..and the blessing of your Mother within. I take my leave but shall return as I am called.

Bless you my children ……..as I wave good-bye to you tonight."

Insights & Reflections

August 2nd, 2006

Dear Brothers and Sisters in Christ,

During these particularly difficult times in our lives, it is felt that our Lord desires to offer words of encouragement to His children. These are not simply words that we read, but special words which will help lessen the severity and anxiety which many people are experiencing during these tumultuous moments in our lives.

Above all, our Lord is calling us to Charity in thought, word and deed. With Charity (Love) we are able to move about this world with a peaceful countenance which reflects the love of Jesus Christ. This does not mean we will not face countless onslaughts of diabolical dishevel in our lives. It means through acts of humility and charity we allow ourselves to be molded into the image that Christ originally intended and through our relinquishing of human will in compliance to the will of Christ we become instruments of Divine Love. Peace through humility changes not only our own personal attitudes, but allows spiritual growth which is nurtured by the indwelling of the Holy Spirit

Jesus always calls us to spiritual cleansing. We take showers of water to cleanse our bodies; however, Jesus showers us with graces to cleanse our soul. It is sad, to say the least, when the cleansing graces of our Lord slip through our fingers and we find ourselves left spiritually void and empty of the nourishing food for our souls which Our Lord in His mercy pours forth upon us. Oh, how grateful we should be for the Sacraments which our Lord has provided for each and everyone of us so that we may come to His table" cleansed through reconciliation and partake of the "bread of life". We are then abundantly filled with new life which invigorates our spirits to proclaim the "Good News" to all those whom we daily encounter.

As parents, how many times have we "encouraged" our children to do something or not to do something for their own well being? If you are like most of us, the times have been too numerous to count. It is our responsibility to assist our children in order to allow them to be able to receive the multitude of graces that God has designated for them. We cannot perform our duties to God, our children, and to one another unless we ourselves are spiritually prepared.

Thus said, let us endeavor to become more in tune with the Word of God (scripture), embrace the Sacraments, and listen with full attention to the promptings of the Holy Spirit!

May God bless each and every one of you..........

A servant of Jesus and Mary (Pat)

****

Message of September 29th, 2006

In prayer, let us hear and discern the following message that was received after the Friday night Rosary. Please note quotation marks are used as direct verbiage from Our Blessed Mother. Other remarks, which further clarify the intention or understanding of Her remarks, will be indicated in another manner.

(Pat's introduction.) In the silent whisper of Almighty God, may our ears and hearts become attentive to every word, which vibrates the inner most particles of our being allowing us to become immersed into His Holy Will. May His words saturate us with Divine infusion of incomprehensible love, which arouses the soul to respond with complete submission. It thus becomes empty of self and filled entirely with this indescribable humility that says nothing but absorbs God's truth and love and disperses it where God directs.

(Mary) "As I spoke to you this evening my child ...... of unity and peace ...... infusion of the spirit .....you rested upon the field of Armageddon along with the other soldiers, the weapons of Christ. But your breastplate was The Precious Blood and breastplate of my scapular and in your hand the rosary. As you have walked with Christ these years, tell me what you saw ...."

(Pat) "There are many bodies ... multitudes of bodies ... all appear dead and yet ... all are not dead. Those with the breastplates and the weapons of the rosary rise to their feet as though lifted by angels ... the warriors for Jesus that you spoke of. The faithful never die for we are protected, always with weapons ... with your words of love ... the scapular and the rosary.

We are ready. We are ready Jesus to go on again. We will march to the next battlefield and though it looks as if we have been defeated ...... we know we will rise again ...for we are your warriors." (Tongues) ... "Yes Mother...

You say that unity is so important ...... it's an infusion of love ... love for God ... love for the souls that He gives us to care for. You will have to teach us ... for to be infused with such love ...... I know not how to express myself ...... but you Mother will show us. You always teach us Jesus' ways ......Your Son, Our Lord."

Over all the fields of battle there has flown the same banner. It is white with gold fringe. In the center, there is the Lamb ... only the lamb is not white ...... the Lamb is red. The Lamb has shed His blood that we might rise again ... refreshed and renewed warriors of Christ ...... sprinkled with the blood of the Lamb."

Christmas Message of December 22nd, 2006
Our Lady speaks

Again this year Our Lady returned to Mary's Knoll and at 8:37 pm responded with a verbal Christmas message as previously indicated in her Christmas message of December 24, 2004. This home, as She called "My Holy House" here in Southern Arizona was filled to capacity with over 150 pilgrims. The Joyful Mysteries of the Rosary were shared in a bi-lingual manner and were supported by singing and ethnic fellowship. For the first time it was discerned that Her message could be shared in an un-questionable manner "live as given" by usage of a second microphone.

In a previous message, Mary indicated she wanted a simpler manger built to indicate how primitive and humble was the first surroundings experienced by Our Lord. In response one of our prayer team members hand built without any modern hardware, a crib built out of small dried sections of our local Yucca plants. In this crib the personal written prayer gifts of our visiting pilgrims were placed. This overflowing crib was brought up Christmas morning to the mountain grotto just above the shrine and placed in the outdoor manger. The message follows;

[The message recipient spoke in extensive tongues to Maria]

(Maria) "My dear Children,

I invite each of you to join in prayer in the accompaniment of My legion of angels gathered here tonight. As you entered the door of this "My holy house" you were greeted by an angel. Did you not feel the presence my children, of love as you came to my home? Tonight I call you not only to prayer but to fast. Thru prayer and fasting the shackles that hold you bound upon this earth will be broken and you will be set free.

Faith My children, have great faith for the seed that is planted in your heart will be nurtured. It will sprout, grow and bring forth good fruit. Now, more than ever before, you must bear good fruit. You must be my warriors, my instruments of peace. Allow yourselves to be pliable that you may be molded as God desires you to be .... that His word will be ever fruitful and living within your lives. As you

353

have come this night in great expectation for the birth of Divine Love, know that the savior comes to heal and restore His children.

I bless with My maternal love each and everyone of you this night as I bless too those items brought with faith. Faith My children ....never let the light of faith grow dim. Peace ....enjoy the peace of My Son who wishes to come to you as a child ....for you to love ....and to worship. He is Christ the King. Let every knee bow before the name of Jesus. Thank you for this manger ....for all the names that have been placed in it ......for I shall take them to My Son who is Mercy and He will touch each and every one of them for they are His precious children. I love you My Children. Be strong for these times are grave, but rejoice because My Son soon comes."

****

All web messages that are given for the public can be PDF computer downloaded as published on our website. [www.ourladyofthesierras.org]

If unsuccessful use your computer search. [our lady of the sierras]

For additional books email [ourladysierras@theriver.com]

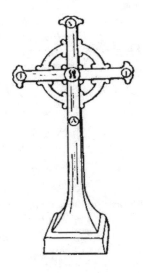

Rosary Prayers

The sign of the Cross.

In the name of the Father and the Son and the Holy Spirit. Amen.

Apostles Creed.

I believe in God, the Father Almighty, Creator of heaven and earth; and in Jesus Christ, His only Son Our Lord; who was conceived by the Holy Spirit, born of the Virgin Mary, suffered under Pontious Pilate, was crucified, died and was buried. He descended into the dead; the third day He arose from the dead; He ascended into Heaven; sitteth at the right hand of God, the Father Almighty; from thence He shall come to judge the living and the dead. I believe in the Holy Spirit, the Holy Catholic Church, the communion of Saints, the forgiveness of sins, the resurrection of the body and life everlasting. Amen

Our Father.

Our Father who art in Heaven, hallowed be thy name; Thy Kingdom come .Thy will be done on earth as it is in heaven. Give us this day our daily bread and forgive us our trespasses as we forgive those who trespass against us and lead us not into temptation but deliver us from evil. Amen.

Hail Mary.

Hail Mary, full of grace, the Lord is with Thee; blessed art Thou among women and blessed is the fruit of Thy Womb, Jesus. Holy Mary, Mother of God, pray for us sinners, now and at the hour of our death. Amen.

Glory Be.

Glory be to the Father and to the Son and to the Holy Spirit; as it was in the beginning, is now and ever shall be world without end. Amen.

Hail Holy Queen.

Hail Holy Queen, Mother of Mercy, our life, our sweetness and our hope! To Thee do we cry, poor banished children of Eve. To Thee do we send up our sighs, mourning and weeping in this valley of tears. Turn then, most gracious Advocate Thine eyes of Mercy towards us; and after this our exile show unto us the blessed fruit of thy womb, Jesus. O clement, O loving, O sweet Virgin Mary.

V. *Pray for us O Holy Mother of God.-*
R. That we may be made worthy of the promises of Christ.

Let us pray:

O God, whose only begotten Son, by His life, death, and resurrection has purchased for us the rewards of eternal life, grant us we beseech Thee, that meditating upon these mysteries in the most Holy Rosary of the Blessed Virgin Mary, we may imitate what they contain and obtain what they promise, through the same Christ Our Lord. Amen.

SHRINE AREA MAP

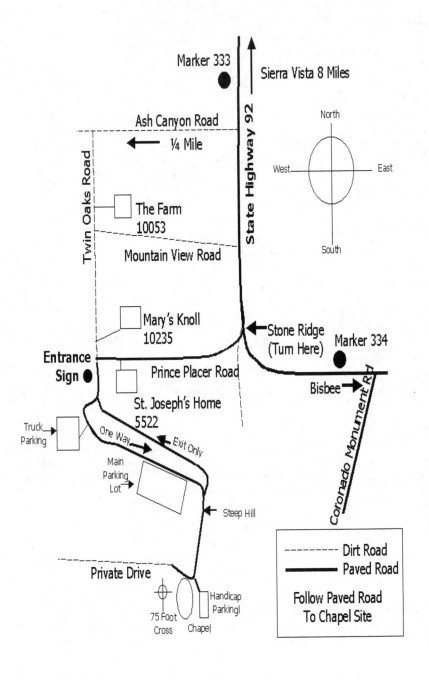

Marker 333

Sierra Vista 8 Miles

North

Ash Canyon Road

¼ Mile

West — East

State Highway 92

Twin Oaks Road

The Farm
10053

Mountain View Road

South

Mary's Knoll
10235

Stone Ridge
(Turn Here)

Marker 334

Entrance
Sign

Prince Placer Road

Bisbee

St. Joseph's Home
5522

Coronado Monument Rd

Truck
Parking

One Way

Exit Only

Main
Parking
Lot

Steep Hill

--------- Dirt Road
———— Paved Road

Private Drive

Follow Paved Road
To Chapel Site

75 Foot
Cross

Handicap
Parkingl

Chapel